800 KETO DIET RECIPES

by Johanna Green

Copyright 2020.

All Rights Reserved.

All rights reserved. No part of this book may be reproduced or copied in any form or by any means, electronic or mechanical, including photocopying, recording or by any information storage and retrieval system, without written permission from the publisher, except for the inclusion of brief quotations in a review.

Warning-Disclaimer.

The aim of the information in this book is to be as accurate as possible. However this is not a medical book, so it is for informational purposes only and comes with no guarantees. The author and publisher shall have neither liability or responsibility to anyone with respect to any loss or damage caused, or alleged to be caused, directly or indirectly by the information provided in this book.

All product and company names used in this book are Trademarks™ or Registered® Trademarks of their respective holders. Their use in this book does not imply any affiliation with or endorsement by them. All trademarks and brand names used in this book are for clarifying purposes only.

Contents

VEGETABLES & SIDE DISHES 16
1. Mediterranean Asparagus with Halloumi Cheese 16
2. Italian Cheesy Roasted Tomatoes 16
3. Cauliflower Coconut Soup 16
4. Italian-Style Broccoli Pilau........................ 16
5. Classic Chicory with Butter and Pine Nuts 16
6. Cream of Cauliflower Soup with Almond Milk 17
7. Creamed Cabbage Coleslaw 17
8. Sichuan Cabbage Stir Fry 17
9. Fathead Vegetarian Pizza 17
10. Classic Rich Rutabaga Chowder 17
11. Spanish Champinones Al Ajillo 18
12. Spicy Eggplant Stew 18
13. Spinach and Cheese Muffins 18
14. Italian Mixed Greens 18
15. Zucchini and Cheese Fritters 18
16. Kohlrabi with Mushroom Sauce 18
17. Celery with Cream-Rum Sauce 19
18. Skinny Salad with Macadamia Nuts 19
19. Mediterranean-Style Broccoli Quiche 19
20. Louisiana-Style Spinach 19
21. Cabbage and Sour Cream Soup 20
22. Bok Choy with Prawns and Garlic 20
23. Cabbage Stir-Fry with Bacon 20
24. Greek Wine-Braised Vegetables 20
25. Mixed Green Salad with Blueberries................ 20
26. Zoodles with Mediterranean Mushroom Sauce 21
27. Traditional Polish Kapusta 21
28. Chinese Spicy Cabbage 21
29. Classic Cheese Ball with Pine Nuts 21
30. Stuffed Peppers with Cremini Mushrooms........... 21
31. Stuffed Tomatoes with Chicken and Parmesan 22
32. Veggie Noodles with Beef Sauce 22
33. Vegetarian Pasta Alfredo 22
34. Spicy Mushroom Stew with Wine 22
35. Traditional Provençal Ratatouille 23
36. Pepper and Cheese Bake 23
37. Zucchini with Greek Yogurt Sauce 23
38. Roasted Vegetables with Herbs 23
39. Pancetta Cheese Stuffed Mushrooms 24
40. Saucy Japanese Mushrooms 24
41. Pancetta and Cream Cheese Stuffed Avocado 24
42. Broccoli Florets in Cheese Sauce 24
43. Green Beans with Provençal Tapenade.............. 24
44. Cheese and Spinach Mini Frittatas 25
45. Chanterelle Mushrooms with Enchilada Sauce 25
46. Dijon Mushroom and Cauliflower Bake 25
47. Italian Cauliflower and Mushroom Stew 25
48. Creamed Greek Salad 25
49. Roasted Asparagus with Pancetta 26
50. Garden Vegetable Salad 26
51. Artichoke, Olives and Mozzarella Bowl 26
52. Colorful Vegetable Fritters........................ 26
53. Baby Bella Mushrooms with Broccoli............... 27
54. Spicy Vegetable Risotto 27

POULTRY.. 28
55. Chicken Soup with Harvest Vegetables 28
56. Cheesy Chicken Wings and Broccoli 28
57. Turkey Meatballs with Cheese 28
58. Cheese Pate with Turkey Ham 28
59. Chicken with Olives and Herbs 29
60. Chorizo Sausage in Tomato Sauce 29
61. Dijon Chicken and Egg Salad 29
62. Ground Duck Casserole 29
63. Easy Chicken Parmigiana 29
64. Chicken Roulade with Prosciutto.................. 30
65. Prosciutto and Cheese-Wrapped Chicken 30
66. Turkey Wings with Herbs and Marinara Sauce 30
67. Chicken Legs with Sherry Sauce 30
68. Chicken Sausage with Cream and Spaghetti Squash... 31
69. Chicken with Tomato Sauce 31
70. Cheesy Ground Chicken Skillet 31
71. Mediterranean-Style Chicken with Halloumi Cheese... 31
72. Chicken Meatballs with Parmesan and Tomato Sauce ... 32
73. Grilled Ranch Kabobs 32
74. Chorizo and Bok Choy Casserole 32
75. Rutabaga, Taro and Chicken Soup 32
76. Chicken and Avocado Salad 33
77. Turkey Bacon and Cheese Fat Bombs 33
78. Chicken, Cauliflower and Cheese Bowl 33
79. Romano-Turkey Meatballs with Basil Chutney...... 33
80. Dijon Turkey with Gravy 33
81. Turkey Soup with Cauliflower and Sour Cream 34
82. Chicken Sausage with Spanish Peppers 34
83. Tangy Turkey Drumsticks with Herbs 34
84. Turkey Drumsticks with Cottage Cheese Sauce 34
85. Chinese Cabbage with Turkey and Bacon 34
86. Chicken Drumettes with Herb Tomato Sauce 35
87. Spicy and Hearty Chicken Stew 35
88. Rich Grandma's Turkey Chowder 35
89. Smoked Paprika Chicken Stew 35
90. Sauvignon Chicken Breasts with Brussels Sprouts ... 36
91. Turkey Rouladen with Wine and Herbs 36
92. Chicken Wigs with Avocado-Mayo Sauce........... 36
93. Turkey and Baby Bok Choy Soup 36
94. Duck Cutlets with Brandy and Cream 37
95. Winter Vegetable Chicken Chowder 37
96. Paprika and Garlic Chicken Fillets 37
97. Holiday Chicken Aspic 37
98. Mediterranean Rum-Glazed Chicken 38
99. Greek Chicken with Wine 38
100. Romano Cheese Crusted Chicken 38
101. Chicken Breasts with Italian Sauce............... 38
102. Champagne Turkey Meatballs 38
103. Tomato, Chicken and Yogurt Chowder............ 39
104. Creamed Chicken and Cauliflower Soup 39
105. Chicken Drumsticks with Salsa 39
106. Three-Cheese Turkey Dip 39
107. Chicken Liver Pâté 40
108. Chicken Salad with Dijon Mustard and Cheese ... 40

109. Duck Breasts with Creamed Vodka Sauce 40
110. Chicken with Cashew-Basil Pesto 40
111. Chicken with Marsala-Mustard Sauce 40
112. Chicken Drumsticks with Herbs 41
113. Chicken with Broccoli and Cheddar Cheese............... 41
114. Duck and Eggplant Bake 41
115. Oven-Roasted Chicken Legs with Herbs 41
116. Chicken Tacos with Bacon 41
117. Chicken Fajitas with Cotija Cheese 42
118. Spicy Chicken with Brussels Sprouts 42
119. Greek-Style Zucchini Soup 42
120. Chicken with Romano Cashew Pesto 42
121. Chicken with Herbs and Olives 42
122. Sticky Rum-Glazed Chicken 43
123. Thanksgiving Turkey Breasts 43
124. Aromatic Garlicky Chicken Drumettes 43

PORK.. 44
125. Mediterranean Pork Rouladen 44
126. Milk-Braised Pork Sirloin Roast 44
127. Italian Pork Muffins 44
128. Italian Pork and Pepper Casserole 44
129. Cheesy Pork Meatloaf with Marinara Sauce 45
130. Easiest Baby Back Ribs Ever 45
131. Country-Style Pork Jambalaya 45
132. Fall-Off-The-Bone Ribs 45
133. Spicy Italian Ribs 45
134. Pork Sausage and Cheese Fat Bombs 46
135. Herb Pork Medallions 46
136. Country-Style Pork Goulash 46
137. Pork Loin with Spicy Cheese Sauce 46
138. Pork with Kale and Bell Peppers 47
139. Classic Pork Au Jus 47
140. Butter Pork Chops with Vegetables 47
141. Pork Blade Steak with Red Wine 47
142. Chunky Pork and Pepper Bake 48
143. Traditional Greek Souvlaki 48
144. Pork Shoulder and Broccoli Medley 48
145. Mexican Spicy Pork 48
146. Parmesan Meatballs with Marinara Sauce 49
147. Pork Sausage and Pepper Frittata 49
148. Pork, Wine and Mushroom Stew 49
149. Classic Glazed Pork Meatloaf 49
150. Old-Fashioned Hungarian Gulyás................................ 50
151. Braised Boston Butt with Spring Onions 50
152. Herb Butter Pork Chops 50
153. Tangy Spare Ribs with Lime 50
154. Ground Pork Mini Frittatas 50
155. Country-Style Stuffed Peppers 51
156. Curried Pork Loin with Romano Cheese 51
157. Vietnamese Pork Lettuce Wraps 51
158. Avocado Pork Soup.. 51
159. Chinese Pork with Cauliflower 52
160. Polish Zasmażana Kapusta 52
161. Greek Warm Pork Salad 52
162. Smoked Ham with Cabbage 52
163. Pork, Sausage and Bacon Meatloaf 52
164. Bacon and Cheese Keto Balls 53
165. Zucchini Boats with Pork and Mushrooms 53
166. Spare Ribs with Italian Peppers 53
167. Grilled Pork Skewers 53
168. Grandma's Pork Goulash 54
169. Old-Fashioned Meatballs with Brie Cheese 54
170. Country-Style Sticky Ribs 54
171. Creole Smoked Pork 54
172. Pork with Classic Barbecue Sauce.............................. 54
173. Chinese Pork Shoulder with Gouda Cheese 55
174. Pork and Kale Bowl 55
175. Wine-Braised Pork Butt Steak 55
176. Spicy Ground Pork with Swiss Chard 55
177. Tangy Pork Stew with Avocado 56
178. Pork Medallions with Scallions and Herbs 56
179. Mexican Pork Spare Rib Soup 56
180. Roasted Pork with Marinara Sauce 56
181. Meatballs with Double Cream Sauce 57
182. New Orleans Pork Gumbo 57
183. Pork Stew with Serrano Pepper and Cheese 57
184. Carrot and Meat Loaf Muffins 57
185. Roasted Pork Shoulder with Asiago Cheese 58
186. Pork and Pepperoncini Soup.. 58
187. Pork and Romano Cheese Muffins.............................. 58
188. Mustard Pork Cutlets with Veggies............................. 58
189. Roasted Sherry Ribs with Peppers 59
190. Classic Wine-Braised Pork Chops 59
191. Spicy Pork Soup with Roma Tomatoes 59
192. Crock Pot Ribs with Wine 59
193. Pork in Chilorio Sauce.. 60
194. Pork and Bacon Meatloaf... 60
195. Milk Braised Pork Loin with Sage 60

BEEF 61
196. Beef Meatloaf with Halloumi Cheese......................... 61
197. Thai-Style Porterhouse Steak 61
198. Bacon Meatballs with Parsley Sauce 61
199. Beef and Ale Stew... 61
200. Hungarian Marha Pörkölt 62
201. Lasagna with Beef and Cheddar Cheese 62
202. Beef Sausage Vegetable Stir-Fry 62
203. Spanish-Style Beef Tenderloin 62
204. French Ventrèche and Beef Soup 63
205. Montreal Meatballs with Thyme-Butter Sauce 63
206. Sloppy Joes with Mustard and Paprika 63
207. Easy Spicy Sloppy Joes 63
208. Rib Eye Steak with Herbs and Wine 64
209. Cheesy and Marsala Beef Brisket 64
210. Guinness Beef Stew with Mint 64
211. Ground Beef and Cheese-Stuffed Tomatoes 64
212. Beef, Tomato and Wine Mélange 65
213. Beef and Vegetable Soup with Lemon-Chili Drizzle............... 65
214. Pot Roast with Scallion Sauce 65
215. Authentic Hungarian Pörkölt 65
216. Marsala Steak with Brussels Sprouts.......................... 66
217. Chuck Roast with Horseradish Mayo 66
218. Cheesy Saucy Corned Beef Brisket 66
219. Tender Filet Mignon Steaks 66
220. Ground Beef and Sauerkraut 67
221. Hamburger, Cabbage and Cream Soup 67
222. Strip Steak Omelet 67
223. Keto Tortilla with Spicy Ground Beef 67
224. Mediterranean Barbecued Flank Steak 68
225. San Diego-Style Beef Tacos 68
226. Beef and Mexican Cheese-Stuffed Tomatoes 68

#	Recipe	Page
227.	Classic Chunky Cheeseburger Soup	68
228.	Beef Sausage and Tomato-Mayo Sauce	69
229.	Keto Z'paghetti Bolognese	69
230.	Chuck Roast with Provolone Cheese	69
231.	Country-Style Beef Stew	69
232.	Tangy Rib-Eye Steak	70
233.	Cheese and Beef Sausage Dip	70
234.	Greek-Style Beef Sausage Souffle	70
235.	Flank Steak with Port Wine	70
236.	Ground Beef and Broccoli Bowl	71
237.	Cheeseburger Soup with A Twist	71
238.	Dijon Garlicky Beef Brisket	71
239.	Spicy Sausage and Vegetable Bake	71
240.	Mexican Tacos with Bacon and Beef	72
241.	Meatballs with Cheese and Peppers	72
242.	Summer Steak Medallions	72
243.	Grandma's Beef Brisket and Vegetables	72
244.	Ground Chuck, Cabbage and Cheese Bake	73
245.	Roasted Short Ribs with Tomato and Wine	73
246.	Chuck Roast with Serrano Pepper	73
247.	Spiced Beef Sauerkraut Goulash	73
248.	Ancho Marinated Steak	74
249.	Cheesy Blead Roast with Vinegar	74
250.	Curried Ground Beef with Broccoli	74
251.	Wine-Marinated Skirt Steak	74
252.	Roasted Skirt Steak with Wine	74
253.	Marinated Beef Shoulder with Mustard and Wine	75
254.	Homemade Beef Soup	75
255.	Beef, Cheese and Mustard Sauce	75
256.	Mini Mushroom Meatloaves	75
257.	Filet Mignon with Marsala Wine	75
258.	Roast Beef with Horseradish-Cheese Sauce	76
259.	Cheese and Beef Stuffed Avocado Boats	76
260.	Thai-Style Spicy Steak Salad	76
261.	Colby Cheese, Beef and Tomato Quiche	76
262.	Beef and Mushroom Stew with Egg	77
263.	Shish Kebab with Garlic-Mustard Relish	77
264.	Greek-Style Sausage with Aioli	77
265.	Mediterranean Steak Salad	77
266.	Italian-Style Peppery Tenderloin	78
267.	Italian Wine-Braised Sausage and Vegetables	78
268.	Sea Scallop Salad and Olives	78
269.	Marsala Fish Stew	78
270.	Ground Beef, Cabbage and Pepper Soup	79
271.	Rum-Mustard Marinated Tilapia	79
272.	Steak and Brussels Sprout Skillet	79
273.	Creamy Herby Meatloaf	79

FISH & SEAFOOD 80

#	Recipe	Page
274.	Cottage Cheese and Tuna Pâté	80
275.	Sherry Prawns with Garlic	80
276.	Stuffed Tomatoes with Salmon and Cheese	80
277.	Greek Halibut Salad	80
278.	Traditional Louisiana-Style Gumbo	81
279.	Creamed Mint and Mackerel Chowder	81
280.	Tuna Salad with Bocconcini and Olives	81
281.	Easy Fish Kabobs	81
282.	Fisherman's Stew with Sauvignon Blanc	82
283.	Lemon Tuna with Brussels Sprouts	82
284.	Mackerel with Mushroom Coulis	82
285.	Baked Cod with Cilantro and Mustard	82
286.	Shrimp with Classic Mignonette	83
287.	Creamed Prawn Salad with Mayonnaise	83
288.	Swordfish Cutlets with Greek Cauliflower Puree	83
289.	Italian Seafood Stew with Wine	83
290.	Old Bay Pollock Soup	84
291.	Shrimp Salad with Avocado and Aioli	84
292.	Cod Fritters with Romano Cheese	84
293.	Creamed Shrimp Pate	84
294.	Cod with Broccoli and Tomato Chutney	84
295.	Italian Zuppa Di Pesce	85
296.	Classic Fish Cakes	85
297.	Salmon with Herbs and Wine	85
298.	Rich Salmon Dipping Sauce	85
299.	Thai-Style Fish Curry	85
300.	Keto "Breaded" Cod Fillets	86
301.	Grilled Clams in Tangy Sauce	86
302.	Keto Fish Pie	86
303.	Spanish-Style Salad with Crab Mayonnaise	86
304.	Indonesian Pollock Curry	86
305.	Lime Herb Halibut Steaks	87
306.	Seafood Chowder with Cream and Wine	87
307.	Dijon Tuna Steaks with Spinach and Lemon	87
308.	Amberjack with Romano Cheese Sauce	87
309.	Creamed Sardine and Mayo Salad	88
310.	Curried Trout with Basil Chimichurri Sauce	88
311.	Dijon Salad with Snapper and Cheese	88
312.	Cod Fish with Green Salad	88
313.	Old Bay Mackerel Steak	89
314.	Salmon Stuffed Peppers	89
315.	Crab Legs with Bacon and Vegetables	89
316.	Clams with Sherry-Tomato Sauce	89
317.	Creole Seafood Jambalaya	90
318.	Mackerel and Vegetable Bake	90
319.	Cheese Tuna Mousse	90
320.	Halibut Fillets with Mushrooms and Sour Cream	90
321.	Sea Bass and Port Wine Chowder	91
322.	Lemony Tuna Fillets	91
323.	Za'atar Salmon with Cheese	91
324.	Halibut Fillets with Cheesy Cauliflower	91
325.	Seafood Pickled Pepper Boats	91
326.	Marsala, Red Snapper and Herb Soup	92
327.	Halibut with Italian Sauce	92
328.	Creamed Tuna and Avocado Salad	92
329.	Herring Keto Fat Bombs	92
330.	Sole Fillets with Mustard and Parsley	93
331.	Creamed Spiced Prawn Salad	93

VEGETARIAN 94

#	Recipe	Page
332.	Spicy Turnips with Peppers	94
333.	Blackberry, Hemp and Coconut Pudding	94
334.	Stuffed Mushrooms with Vegan Parmesan	94
335.	Spicy Braised Cabbage	94
336.	Creamed Eggplant Soup	94
337.	Squash and Cocoa Smoothie Bowl	95
338.	Broccoli and Monterey Jack Bake	95
339.	Eggplant Parmigiana Casserole	95
340.	Vegetarian Chinese Wok	95
341.	Berry Smoothie Bowl	95
342.	Vegan Mushroom Stroganoff	96

343. Greek Vegetables with Halloumi Cheese 96
344. Chinese-Style Brussels Sprouts 96
345. Stuffed Avocado Boats 96
346. Cream of Cauliflower Soup with Paprika 96
347. Asparagus with Parsley and Feta Cheese 97
348. Traditional Mexican Guacamole 97
349. Tofu and Pecan Zucchini Boats 97
350. Cremini Mushrooms with Enchilada Sauce 97
351. Appenzeller and Pepper Quiche 97
352. Zoodles with Classic Cashew Parmesan 98
353. Spanish Vegetables with Herbs 98
354. Easy Cheesy Spinach 98
355. Mediterranean Fennel in Cherry Tomato Sauce 98
356. Ultimate Fathead Cauliflower Pizza 98
357. Garlicky Broccoli Masala 99
358. Creamed Broccoli and Spinach Soup 99
359. Creamed Kohlrabi with Mushrooms 99
360. Movie Night Swiss Chard Chips 99
361. Mediterranean Crunchy Salad with Seeds 100
362. Vegan Stuffed Mushrooms 100
363. Chocolate, Chia and Almond Smoothie 100
364. Romano Tomato Chips 100
365. Celery and Carrot Salad with Sriracha Vinaigrette .. 100
366. Asparagus with Traditional Baba Ghanoush 101
367. Easy Cauliflower Slaw with Olives 101
368. Easy Breakfast Smoothie 101
369. Asian-Style Curried Cauliflower and Peppers 101
370. Baked Zucchini Boats 102
371. Raspberry and Peanut Shake 102
372. Keto "Cereal" with Almond Milk 102
373. Peanut and Coconut Candy 102
374. Hazelnut Chocolate Bark 102
375. Butternut Squash Smoothie with Chocolate 102
376. Colorful Roasted Vegetables 103
377. German Savoy Cabbage 103
378. Stuffed Berbere Cauli Rice Peppers 103
379. Asian-Style Brussels Sprouts 103
380. Roasted Asparagus with Eggplant Dip 104
381. "No Oats" Oatmeal with Hemp and Berries 104
382. Tofu with Garlic, Sesame and Pine Nuts 104
383. Masala Broccoli with Sesame Paste 104
384. Almond Milk and Berry Shake 105
385. Crunchy Granola with A Twist 105
386. Oven-Roasted Cabbage with Sesame Seeds 105
387. Berbere Cauliflower
Rice-Stuffed Peppers 105
388. Tempeh with Savoy Cabbage 105
389. Tofu and Brussels Sprout Bowl 106
390. Easy Traditional Guacamole 106
391. Fennel with Aromatic Tomato Sauce 106
392. Peanut Butter Blackberry Delight 106
393. Fried Sticky Oyster Mushrooms 106
394. Eggs with Parmesan-Kale Pesto 107
395. Cheese and Tomato Omelet 107
396. Spinach and Cheddar Cheese Mini Frittatas 107
397. The Best Keto Donuts Ever 107
398. Creamed Cauliflower Soup with Coriander and Nuts ... 108
399. Spicy and Fluffy Eggs with Sour Cream 108
400. Jaffa Chia Pudding 108
401. Adobo Celery Chips 108
402. Keto Crunch Cereal 108
403. Brown Mushrooms with Cauliflower and Tomato 109
404. Flambéed Sweet Strawberry Omelet 109
405. Chocolate, Spinach and Coconut Smoothie 109
406. Marinated Spicy Tofu with Peppers 109
407. Ricotta Keto Bites 109
408. Keto Paprika Chips 109
409. Voodles with Avocado Sauce 110
410. Swiss Cheese Cauliflower Cakes 110
411. Squash Stew with Tomatoes and Wine 110
412. Avocado Boats with Mushrooms 110
413. Spicy Crispy Fried Tofu 111
414. Peanut Butter Shake with Mixed Berries 111
415. Tangy Peppery Cabbage Chowder 111
416. Stuffed Peppers with Caciocavallo Cheese 111
417. Italian Zuppa di Zucchini 111
418. Oyster Mushroom Paprikash 112
419. Punjabi Cauliflower Masala 112
420. Swiss Chard, Tomato and Zucchini Chowder 112
421. Mushrooms with Walnuts and Parsley 112
422. Chanterelle Mushroom and Wine Goulash 113
423. Spanish-Style Artichoke with Tofu 113
424. Mediterranean Chard Dip 113
425. Greek Broccoli Dipping Sauce 113
426. Oven-Roasted Vegetables with Vegan Parmesan ... 114
427. Fried Tofu with Cabbage and Celery 114
428. Spicy Hot Tofu with Vegan Tzatziki 114

EGGS & DAIRY 115
429. Avocado Boats with Asiago Cheese and Sardines 115
430. Italian Eggs with Genoa Salami and Carrot 115
431. Winter Pancetta and Cheese Bites 115
432. Breakfast Pancetta Muffins 115
433. Egg Salad with Celery and Hot Sauce 116
434. Scrambled Eggs with Swiss Chard Pesto 116
435. Classic Keto Pan Pizza 116
436. Greek-Style Egg Muffins 116
437. Classic Scotch Eggs 116
438. Sausage and Egg Stuffed Zucchini 117
439. Double Cheese Omelet 117
440. Baked Egg Zucchini Boats 117
441. Sage Pork Sausage Frittata 117
442. Spicy Frittata with Asparagus and Cheese 118
443. Muffin in a Mug 118
444. American-Style Frittata 118
445. Crabmeat Scramble with Cheese-Garlic Sauce 118
446. Stuffed Avocado with Queso Fresco 118
447. Pickled Eggs with Onions 119
448. Pepperoni and Pepper Quiche 119
449. Keto Burritos with Mushrooms 119
450. Curried Asparagus Frittata 119
451. Dijon Mustard and Bacon Deviled Eggs 119
452. Genoa Salami Mug Muffin 120
453. Mediterranean-Style Cheese Balls 120
454. Gorgonzola Mini Frittatas 120
455. Greek Egg and Anchovy Salad 120
456. Grandma's Breakfast Waffles 120
457. Chinese Dan Hua Tang with Tofu 121
458. Italian Breakfast Roll-Ups 121
459. Omelet with Cherry Tomatoes and Cheese 121

460. One-Pan Eggs with Chorizo Sausage 121
461. Egg Salad with Bacon and Scallions 121
462. Italian-Style Fat Bombs 121
463. Greek Yogurt and Apple Muffins 122
464. Greek-Style Stuffed Tomatoes 122
465. Italian Mini Frittatas with Spinach and Bacon 122
466. Old-Fashioned Scotch Eggs 122
467. Mediterranean Cheese Logs 122
468. Omelet with Asiago and Boursin Cheese 123
469. Mediterranean Salad with Almond-Cheese Balls 123
470. Loaded Guacamole Tacos 123
471. Keto Sausage Muffins 123
472. Mediterranean Eggs with Sausage and Herbs 123
473. Provençal Eggs with Bayonne Ham 124
474. Frittata a La Mexicana 124
475. Amish Pickled Eggs 124
476. Italian-Style Cheeseburger Casserole 124
477. Egg, Mortadella and Mayo Fat Bombs 124
478. Romano Cheese and Sausage Muffins 125
479. Baked Cheesy Avocado Boats 125
480. Folded Omelet with Prosciutto di Parma 125
481. Deviled Eggs with Peppers and Cheese 125
482. Gorgonzola Cheese and Onion Soup 125

FAST SNACKS & APPETIZERS 126
483. Glazed Portobello Mushrooms 126
484. Country-Style Meatballs 126
485. Rustic Almond and Gorgonzola Balls 126
486. Cauliflower Florets with Greek Yogurt Dip 126
487. Camembert and Bacon Fat Bombs 126
488. Loaded Cheesy Meatballs 127
489. Italian Pizza Dip 127
490. Tuna Deviled Eggs 127
491. Keto Chips with Guacamole 127
492. Barbecued Cocktail Wieners 127
493. Balkan-Style Roll-Ups 128
494. Cheddar Cheese, Artichoke and Chive Dip 128
495. Double Cheese, Mayo and Pepper Dip 128
496. Bacon and Cheese-Stuffed Mushrooms 128
497. Crispy Zucchini Bites 128
498. Roasted Vegetable with Spicy Dip 128
499. Cheesy Chouriço Bites 129
500. Cheese Sticks with Red Pepper Dip 129
501. 15-Minute Taco Cheese Chips 129
502. Paprika Bacon Crisps 129
503. Cottage Cheese Balls 129
504. Old Bay Mushrooms with Neufchâtel Cheese 130
505. Classic Rutabaga Chips 130
506. Oven-Baked Chicken Skin Cracklings 130
507. Parmesan Cauliflower Balls with Greek Sauce 130
508. Avocado and Cotija Cheese Balls 130
509. Chicken Bites with Spicy Tomatillo Dip 131
510. Caramel Cheesecake Fat Bombs 131
511. Paprika Bacon Fries 131
512. Greek-Style Ground Meat and Feta Dip 131
513. Double Spicy Cheese Crisps 131
514. Greek Colorful Skewers 132
515. Greek-Style Fat Bombs 132
516. The Best Lil Smokies Ever 132
517. Mediterranean-Style Celery Sticks 132
518. 15-Minute Bacon Chips 132
519. Spicy Cucumber Rounds with Goat Cheese 132
520. Mexican-Style Pork Fat Chips 133
521. Zingy Cheesecake Balls 133
522. Cheese, Kale and Prosciutto Mini Frittatas 133
523. Salami, Feta, and Mayo Balls 133
524. Mexican Wings with Habanero Dip 133
525. Rich and Easy Cheeseburger Sauce 134
526. Chorizo and Cream Cheese-Stuffed Peppers 134
527. Butter Dill Zucchini Chips 134
528. Cheesy and Parsley Chicken Wings 134
529. Fat Bombs with Salami 134
530. Mini Frittatas with Spanish-Style Sauce 135
531. Italian Cheesy Baby Carrots 135
532. Tomato Cheeseburger Pie 135
533. Spicy Shrimp Scampi 135
534. Sriracha Bacon Bites 135
535. Cheese, Salami and Olive Muffins 136
536. Spicy Cheese Chips 136
537. Shrimp with Sesame and Wine 136
538. Greek-Style Cheese and Ham Bites 136
539. Sticky Carrot Bites 136
540. Sardine and Aioli Egg Bites 136
541. Turkey Tenders with Sriracha Sauce 137
542. 10-Minute Party Cheese Ball 137
543. Chicken Wings with Greek Dip 137
544. Crispy Parmesan Chicken Wings 137
545. Dill Pickle and Cheese Fried Balls 138
546. Party Creamy Meatballs with Cheddar Cheese 138
547. Easy Chicharrones with Chili Cheese Sauce 138
548. Swiss Chard and Cheese Dip 138
549. Boozy Fat Bombs 139
550. Paprika Crackers with Seeds 139
551. Pimentón Cheese Crisps 139
552. Italian Shrimp and Vegetable Skewers 139
553. Spicy Pancetta Egg Bites 139
554. Salmon and Avocado Balls with Seeds 140
555. Double Cheese Meatballs 140
556. Romano Cheese Sticks 140
557. Cajun Celery Fries 140
558. Spicy Tomatoes with Chive Sauce 140
559. Cheesy Paprika Meatballs 141
560. Chicken Wingettes with Greek Cheese Dip 141
561. Tangy Chicken Wings 141
562. Parmesan Cauliflower Bites 141
563. Pancetta Meatballs with Parsley Sauce 142
564. Pepperoni Keto Bombs 142
565. Ciauscolo Salami and Mozzarella Bites 142
566. Soppressata Keto Bombs 142
567. Swiss Cheese and Beef-Stuffed Avocado 142
568. Provençal Muffins with Salami 143
569. Dijon Chorizo Fat Bombs 143
570. Meatballs with Pecorino Cheese 143
571. Cheese and Prosciutto Crisps 143
572. Herbed Mini Muffins with Hunter Salami 143

573. German-Style Sausage Fat Bombs 144
574. Mascarpone and Bacon Balls 144
575. Herring-Stuffed Pickled Peppers 144
576. Baked Stuffed Avocado Boats 144

DESSERTS 145
577. Easy Buckeye Candy 145
578. Greek-Style Chia Pudding 145
579. Easy Chocolate Panache 145
580. Classic Jaffa Dessert 145
581. Nana's Ice Cream 145
582. Blueberry Protein Smoothie 146
583. Almond Brownie Cupcakes 146
584. Rum Chocolate Cheesecake 146
585. Classic Pistachio Candy 146
586. Iced Cappuccino Toffee 146
587. Rustic Walnut Dessert 146
588. Peanut Butter Custard 147
589. Chocolate and Peanut Butter Chewy Cake 147
590. Coconut Raspberry Shake 147
591. Mediterranean-Style Chocolate Pudding 147
592. Rum and Walnut Truffles 147
593. Chia Pudding with Coconut 148
594. Chocolate and Almond Squares 148
595. British Strawberry Dessert 148
596. Berry Cheesecake Squares 148
597. Vanilla Rum Cheesecake Cupcakes 148
598. Caramel Chocolate Candy 149
599. Light Peanut Butter Mousse 149
600. Avocado Coffee Popsicles 149
601. Buttered Whiskey Cupcakes 149
602. Nutty Fat Bombs 149
603. Rum Coconut Candy 150
604. Rustic Almond Cheesecake 150
605. Dad's Rum Caramels 150
606. Fluffy Coconut Cheesecake 150
607. Flourless Chocolate Cake 150
608. Fluffy Brownies with Pecans 151
609. Rum Cake with Cream Cheese Frosting 151
610. Light Walnut Pudding 151
611. Creamy Lemon Jell-O 151
612. Old-Fashioned Greek Cheesecake 151
613. Almond Bar Cookie 152
614. Traditional Brigadeiro with Berries 152
615. Boozy Walnut Candy 152
616. Greek-Style Walnut Cheesecake 152
617. Home-Style Coconut Pastry 152
618. Fluffy Chocolate Cupcakes 153
619. Macchiato Chocolate Bark 153
620. Espresso Vanilla Shots 153
621. Rich Chocolate and Walnut Dessert 153
622. Walnut Butter Penuche 153
623. Greek-Style Ice Cream 154
624. Chocolate Walnut Teacakes 154
625. White Chocolate and Almond Penuche 154
626. Berry Lemony Macaroons 154
627. Birthday Chocolate Cake 154
628. Favorite Fat Bombs 155
629. Zingy Peanut Buttercream 155
630. Classic Apple Crumble 155
631. Coconut Cheesecake Pudding 155
632. Classic Coconut Cheesecake 155
633. Coconut Cognac Bon Bons 156
634. Almond Fudge Cake 156
635. Peanut Butter Candy 156
636. Old-Fashioned Scones with Berries 156
637. Old-Fashioned Bourbon Walnut Cheesecake 156
638. Mint and Hazelnut Clusters 157
639. Classic Chocolate Cake 157
640. 10-Minute Creamy Cupcakes 157
641. Easy Crème Brûlée 157
642. Aromatic Chia Pudding 157
643. Vanilla Avocado Pudding 158
644. Homemade Hazelnut Brittle 158
645. 10-Minute Homemade Ice Cream 158
646. Harvest Pear Crisp 158
647. Chocolate and Walnut Toffee 158
648. Traditional Greek Frappé 158
649. Iced Cocoa Candy 159
650. Vanilla Pecan Pralines 159
651. Grandma's Homemade Chocolate Bars 159
652. Orange Butterscotch Popsicles 159
653. Italian Panna Cotta 159
654. Skinny Curd Pudding 160
655. Homemade Coconut Ice Cream 160

KETO FAVORITES 161
656. Easy Bacon Chips 161
657. Swiss Cheese Balls and Celery Fries 161
658. Creamy Almond Porridge 161
659. Easy Homemade Cheeseburgers 161
660. French Rum Crêpes 161
661. Keto Breakfast in a Jar 162
662. Baked Eggs, Cheese and Pancetta in Ramekins 162
663. Decadent Rum and Cheese Pancakes 162
664. Herbed Keto Bread 162
665. Country-Style Porridge with Pecans 162
666. Gorgonzola Cheese and Bacon Gofres 162
667. Comte Cheese and Chanterelle Mousse 163
668. Old-School Meatballs 163
669. Italian Salami Pizza Muffins 163
670. Gofres Belgas Caseros 163
671. Sour Cream and Crab Meat Frittata 164
672. Cauliflower Mash with Goat Cheese 164
673. Greek-Style Cheesecake Apple Muffins 164
674. Fluffy Russian-Style Cheese Pancakes 164
675. Decadent Sopressata Wafers 164
676. Jaffa Chia Pudding 165
677. Greek Mezze Board 165
678. Italian-Style Ribs 165
679. Classic Salmon Spread 165
680. Famous Keto Coffee with MCT Oil 165
681. Savory Panna Cotta with Mushrooms and Herbs 165
682. Taco Vegetables with Sausage 166
683. Mascarpone Keto Balls 166
684. Rich and Easy Spanish Tortilla 166
685. Prosciutto Baked Rolls 166
686. Omelet with Cheese and Blueberries 166

687. Spring Omelet with Greek-Style Yogurt 166
688. Cheese Custard with Anchovies and Scallions 167
689. Mascarpone Cheese-Stuffed Avocado 167
690. Traditional Homemade Aioli 167
691. Chicken Tenders with Cheese and Garlic 167
692. Creamy Almond Bars 167
693. Grandma's Mini Meatloaves 168
694. Hemp Heart Porridge 168
695. Seed and Egg Bread 168
696. Rustic Pumpkin Mousse 168
697. Tomato and Cheese Fondue 168
698. Pancetta and Goat Cheese Cups 169
699. German-Style Turkey Rinderrouladen 169
700. Chocolate-Glazed Donuts 169
701. Dilled Double Cheese Sauce 169
702. Rustic Pecan Pie 169
703. Nut and Seed Crunch 170
704. 15-Minute Keto Pizza 170
705. Flatbread with Kulen and Romano Cheese 170
706. Traditional Keto Quesadilla 170

MORE KETO RECIPES 171
707. Homemade Coconut Ice Cream 171
708. Mustard Greens with Cheese 171
709. Loaded Hamburger Muffins 171
710. Cream of Cabbage Soup 171
711. Italian Pizzelle with Prosciutto 171
712. Chunky Cheesy Beef Chowder 172
713. Peanut Butter Penuche 172
714. Old-Fashioned Beef Stew with Egg 172
715. Rustic Tuna and Walnut Pâté 172
716. Creamed Green Cabbage Coleslaw 172
717. Traditional Creole Jambalaya 173
718. Omelet with Brown Mushrooms, Avocado and Salsa 173
719. Skirt Steak in Wine 173
720. Pasta with Green Beans 173
721. Crispy Roasted Chicken 173
722. Cheesy Roast Beef 174
723. Classic Keto Taco Shells 174
724. Pork and Avocado Soup 174
725. Blueberry Mocha Cappuccino 174
726. Vegetables with Sour Cream Dip 174
727. Roasted Mexican-Style Vegetable Medley 175
728. Italian Wine-Braised Steaks 175
729. Panna Cotta with Chive Cream Cheese 175
730. Pork Meatloaf with Tangy Sauce 175
731. Creamed Greek Salad 176
732. Creamiest Chicken Salad Ever 176
733. Classic Asparagus Spears with Pancetta 176
734. Rainbow Steak Salad 176
735. Classic Blueberry Crumb Cake 176
736. Easy Jaffa Popsicles 177
737. Sausage with Spicy Tomato Sauce 177
738. Turkey Sausage in Spicy Sauce 177
739. Mediterranean Pork with Gorgonzola Cheese Sauce 177
740. Tilapia Fillets with Spicy Tomatillo Chutney 178
741. Coffee with Coconut Cream 178
742. Za'atar Pork Tenderloin and Brussels Sprouts 178
743. Fish Salad with Grilled Halloumi Cheese 178
744. Belgian Gofres with Limburger Cheese 179
745. Easy Seafood Bowl 179
746. Provençal-Style Vegetables with Cheese 179
747. Nutty and Spicy Keto Salad 179
748. Colby Cheese Broccoli Casserole 179
749. Vegetarian Cremini Mushroom Burger 180
750. Greek Pork Souvlaki 180
751. Chicken Breasts with Deli Mustard Sauce 180
752. Mexican-Style Roast Beef 180
753. Homemade Rum Pralines 181
754. Easy Bavarian Sauerkraut with Beef 181
755. Thai Beef Sausage Bowl 181
756. Vanilla Chocolate Candy 181
757. Cheesy Cauliflower Cakes 181
758. Meatloaf Muffins with Vegetables 182
759. Thai Cod Fish Chowder 182
760. Mediterranean Eggplant Casserole with Romano Cheese 182
761. Baked Eggs with Steak and Spanish Peppers 182
762. Easy Bok Choy with Bacon 182
763. Mediterranean Eggs with Herring and Capers 183
764. Colorful Vegetable Croquettes 183
765. Stuffed Tomatoes in Marinara Sauce 183
766. Fish Cakes with Mustard and Cheese 183
767. Double Cheese and Cauliflower Fritters 184
768. Porterhouse Steaks in Red Wine 184
769. Salmon with Cauliflower and Cheddar Cheese 184
770. Mexican Sausage with Cabbage 184
771. Curried Greens with Ricotta Cheese 184
772. Cheesy Mushrooms with Salami 185
773. Meatloaf Cups with Swiss Cheese 185
774. Spicy Vegetable and Mushroom Stew 185
775. Creamed Egg Salad with Cheese and Anchovies 185
776. Chicken Drumettes with Mediterranean Herbs 186
777. Sea Bass with Mustard and Paprika 186
778. Cabbage and Ground Beef Soup 186
779. Keto Mac and Cheese 186
780. Chunky Pork and Vegetable Soup 186
781. Steak a La Moutarde 187
782. Turkey and Mediterranean Vegetable Skewers 187
783. Creole Tilapia Soup 187
784. Marinated Spare Ribs with Veggies 187
785. Pork with Chevre Goat Cheese 188
786. Baked Spicy Chicken in Marinara Sauce 188
787. Swiss Cheese and Tomato-Glazed Meatloaf 188
788. Garlicky Portobello Mushrooms 188
789. Greek Beef and Cheese Casserole 189
790. Easy Cheesy Meatloaf Cups 189
791. Taco Turkey Wings 189
792. Stuffed Tomatoes with Tuna 189
793. Nona's Stuffed Peppers 189
794. Pizzelle della Nonna 190
795. Mediterranean Stuffed Peppers with Salmon 190
796. Traditional Hungarian Pörkölt 190
797. Rustic Slow Cooker Pork Shoulder 190
798. Rum Chocolate Truffles 191
799. Roasted Asparagus with Goat Cheese 191
800. Paprikás with Beef and Wine 191

INTRODUCTION

I've spent a good portion of my life trying to lose weight. I tried almost all popular weight loss diets, from my first year of college until my mid-thirties. Diet trends come and go, from paleo to vegan diet, so I was full of hope, trying to fit into my skinny jeans. It seemed a simple problem to solve – I have to eat less, cut back on the takeaways and move more. And yes, the number on the scales went down for some time but I gained that weight back. In the 12 to 13 years that followed, I fought with yo-yo dieting. I've spent over 18 years of my life being miserable, struggling to maintain my healthy weight. I was disappointed and I have eaten nothing for days, drinking only water and natural juices. Eventually, I'd get stomach problems and gastritis. I was told so many times that if I couldn't lose my weight, I'd have trouble finding a good job and getting married. I thought that I can't stand the pressure anymore, I couldn't listen to all those information, suggestions, tips, and tricks. I am sick and tired of dieting. I felt like a hamster on a wheel! Enough is enough! I gave up dieting and felt like a stone was lifted off my shoulders. Shortly afterwards, I discovered a ketogenic lifestyle, a healthy dietary regime that has changed millions of lives all over the world!

Losing weight and reducing appetite, while enjoying big portions of high-fat foods sounds good to me! I thought it could be worth considering! I don't have to follow any strict rules; I just have to change my eating habits. A keto diet is a low carb diet. In fact, if you eat food with low to zero carbs, your body makes ketones and use them as the main source of energy. Otherwise, if you eat high-carb foods your body uses glucose, which causes excess fat to be stored in your body and you are gaining weight. It means that your body produces less glucose on a keto diet so you will be able to lose weight naturally. In other words, your body experiences ketosis, a natural state that occurs as a result of a calorie restriction. The human body can easily adapt to this process because it is natural and can significantly improve our mental performances. After I have been on the ketogenic diet for about a week, my body simply got used to it.

A keto diet is easy to follow since you don't need to make radical changes in your diet. However, there are certain rules and suggestions you should know. You should consume a low-carb, adequate-protein, and high-fat foods. In practical terms, I can eat high-quality protein from food sources such as seafood, poultry, and eggs, whole foods such as vegetables, nuts, and seeds and foods with a large amount of vitamins and minerals such as avocado, mushrooms, greens, algae, unsweetened dark chocolate, broccoli, and so forth. The foods that get the big thumbs down include rice, legumes, grains, and rice.

Besides being highly efficient in improving weight loss, cutting out carbs can prevent common diseases such as hyperglycemia, metabolic syndrome, type 2 bipolar disorder, and certain cancers. I experienced increased awareness, cognitive functions and energy levels during daily activities. For me, the most exciting part of my new dietary program is stepping on the scale after 3 weeks. I was shocked by the number. I lost 6 pounds but I saw the first results after 4 days of dieting.

I realized – it is absolutely possible to enjoy my favorite foods such as burgers, fries, desserts, and even snacks! Most ketoers cook their own meals to avoid there-is-nothing-to-eat situation on a diet. I started cooking at home regularly so my family is much healthier now and we do not eat fast food anymore. Plus, my favorite foods are back on the menu! Here's what I learned after all these years: I'm done with dieting! I just stopped being obsessed with the numbers on the scales and thinking about food. I've made peace with my body. People who cook at home are more likely to have healthy eating habits than those who eat out, which brings us to the next point –What to eat, what to avoid? So, here goes!

Basic Keto Diet Rules

You can eat:

Fish & Seafood – especially fatty fish such as tuna and salmon, as well as shellfish such as lobster, shrimp, sea scallops, or crab meat.

Meat – beef, veal, pork, and goat.

Poultry – chicken, turkey, and duck. You can eat deli meats on the ketogenic diet, but you should check the carb content first.

Dairy products – full-fat sour cream, Greek-style yogurt, cheese, and heavy whipping cream.

Eggs – whatever you like (hard-boiled, deviled, scrambled, frittata or omelet). Eggs are highly recommended for people trying to gain healthy weight and build muscle.

Vegetables – you can eat above-ground veggies, including broccoli, tomatoes, garlic, greens, cauliflower, Brussels sprouts, zucchini, cucumber, peppers, asparagus, onion, and cabbage. You can include pickled vegetables into your keto dietary regimen but check the labels first. This includes pickles, sauerkraut, and olives.

Nuts – you can choose from any type of nuts - walnuts, almonds, coconut, macadamia nuts, hazelnuts, pecans, Brazil nuts, pine nuts, and peanuts or you can mix them all up! You can eat unsweetened, homemade nut butter too. Nuts contain high-quality protein, fiber, mono and polyunsaturated fats, Vitamin E, iron, potassium, zinc, magnesium.

Seeds – you can add chia seeds, sesame seeds, flax seeds, pumpkin and sunflower seeds to your meals. Scatter them over your keto salad to stay fool longer and include healthy fats in your diet. You can consume all types of seed butter as well. Incorporating seeds into your keto diet will not only keep you healthy but will also strengthen your heart and improve digestion.

Fats – you can choose from any type of healthy fats - butter, ghee, olive oil, coconut oil, seeds, nuts, and avocado. Avoid manufactured trans fats such as margarine and other hydrogenated oils.

Fruits – opt for nature's candy such as avocado, berries, lemon, and lime, and consume them in moderation.

Vegetarian protein sources – tofu, tempeh, coconut yogurt, nut milk, Shirataki noodles, and seaweed.

Herbs, spices, condiments – adding aromatics and condiments is highly recommended on the ketogenic diet since they contain zero carbs in their natural state. Make sure they do not have added sugar or preservatives. You can experiment with vinegar, hot sauce, mustard, tomato sauce, and mayonnaise but check the labels first.

Baking ingredients: you can re-create your favorite baked goods using coconut flour, almond flour, flaxseed meal, psyllium husk flour, ground chia seeds, ground sunflower seeds, cricket flour, oat fiber, baking powder, baking soda, sugar-free chocolate, and unsweetened cocoa powder.

Beverages: you can enjoy coffee and tea without sugar, zero carb drinks, and sparkling water. As for alcoholic beverages, you can consume brandy, rum, vodka, whiskey, and tequila.

Keto sweeteners: you can use stevia, monk fruit, erythritol, xylitol, and Splenda.

You can't eat:

Common types of flours – whole-wheat flour, all-purpose flour, cake flour, and cornmeal.

Grains – oats, millet, corn, quinoa, and barley.

All types of rice – white, brown, jasmine, basmati, and wild rice.

Sugars – all types of sugar, sugary drinks, flavored water, and juice are pretty much off limits. Packaged foods, instant foods, sauces and coffee creamers are full of hidden sugars too.

Legumes – beans, chickpea, lentils, and peas.

Starchy vegetables – basically, you should avoid underground plants such as potatoes, beets, yams, and other root veggies.

Fruits – they are the big no-no on a keto diet since they contain lots of sugar. You should avoid both dried and canned fruits.

Trans fats – you shouldn't cook with margarine, corn oil, cottonseed oil, and soybean oil and eat products that contain them.

The Best Tips to Get into Ketosis

Include protein-rich foods
On the ketogenic diet, twenty percent of your daily calorie intake should come from protein. Eat chicken, fish, seafood, and eggs to prevent muscle loss and reduce appetite. Protein-rich foods can kickstart and maintain ketosis faster and longer.

Increase healthy fat intake
On the ketogenic diet, you should cook with extra-virgin olive oil, consume fatty fish at least once a week, snack on seeds and nuts, add avocado slices to your salads.

Make sure to get all important nutrients

It is extremely important to include a variety of foods in your diet. I tried to cover all the food groups in this collection so you can enjoy eating a variety of foods. A keto diet promotes whole foods that are full of good protein, omega-3 and omega-6 fatty acids, vitamins, and minerals. Do not let processed food that is loaded in hidden carbs sabotage your weight loss.

Do not underestimate the importance of physical activity

You should avoid high-intensity workouts and practice low-intensity cardio workouts (jogging, cycling or swimming) as well as weight lifting (fewer reps with lighter weights).

Throughout this recipe collection, you'll find eight hundred foolproof keto recipes that are easy to make in your kitchen. From old-fashioned breakfast and snacks to trendy appetizers and cakes, you'll learn how to prepare the best ketogenic recipes the whole family will love!

3-Week Meal Plan

DAY 1

Breakfast – 15. Zucchini and Cheese Fritters
Snack – 483. Glazed Portobello Mushrooms
Lunch – 133. Spicy Italian Ribs; 1 handful of iceberg lettuce
Dinner – 61. Dijon Chicken and Egg Salad

DAY 2

Breakfast – 1 slice of bacon; 1 hard-boiled egg; 1 shake with 1/2 cup of coconut milk and protein powder
Lunch – 232. Tangy Rib-Eye Steak; 1 serving of cauliflower rice
Dinner – 281. Easy Fish Kabobs; 1 medium tomato
Dessert – 73. Grilled Ranch Kabobs

DAY 3

Breakfast – 432. Breakfast Pancetta Muffins
Lunch – 56. Cheesy Chicken Wings and Broccoli
Snack – 503. Cottage Cheese Balls
Dinner – 366. Asparagus with Traditional Baba Ghanoush

DAY 4

Breakfast – 370. Baked Zucchini Boats; 1 slice of bacon
Lunch – 248. Ancho Marinated Steak; 1 serving of coleslaw
Dinner – 274. Cottage Cheese and Tuna Pâté; 1 keto roll; 1/2 tomato
Dessert – 641. Easy Crème Brûlée

DAY 5

Breakfast – 658. Creamy Almond Porridge; 1/2 cup Greek yogurt
Snack – 656. Easy Bacon Chips
Lunch – 266. Italian-Style Peppery Tenderloin; 1 serving of cauliflower rice
Dinner – 314. Salmon Stuffed Peppers

DAY 6

Breakfast – 341. Berry Smoothie Bowl; 1 hard-boiled egg
Lunch – 188. Mustard Pork Cutlets with Veggies; 1 serving of cabbage salad
Dinner – 108. Chicken Salad with Dijon Mustard and Cheese
Dessert – 579. Easy Chocolate Panache

DAY 7

Breakfast – 576. Baked Stuffed Avocado Boats
Lunch – 64. Chicken Roulade with Prosciutto; 1 large tomato
Dinner – 8. Sichuan Cabbage Stir Fry

DAY 8

Breakfast – Scrambled eggs; 1 tomato; 1 keto roll
Lunch – 59. Chicken with Olives and Herbs; 1 serving of cauliflower rice
Dinner – 299. Thai-Style Fish Curry
Dessert – 585. Classic Pistachio Candy

DAY 9

Breakfast – 477. Egg, Mortadella and Mayo Fat Bombs; 1/2 cup of unsweetened almond milk
Lunch – 296. Classic Fish Cakes; 447. Pickled Eggs with Onions
Snack – 517. Mediterranean-Style Celery Sticks
Dinner – 23. Cabbage Stir-Fry with Bacon

DAY 10

Breakfast – 44. Cheese and Spinach Mini Frittatas
Snack – 602. Nutty Fat Bombs
Lunch – 406. Marinated Spicy Tofu with Peppers
Dinner – 273. Creamy Herby Meatloaf

DAY 11

Breakfast – 695. Seed and Egg Bread; 1 tablespoon of peanut butter;
Lunch – 724. Pork and Avocado Soup; 322. Lemony Tuna Fillets
Snack – 493. Balkan-Style Roll-Ups
Dinner – 250. Curried Ground Beef with Broccoli

DAY 12

Breakfast – 661. Keto Breakfast in a Jar
Snack – 561. Tangy Chicken Wings
Lunch – 262. Beef and Mushroom Stew with Egg
Dinner – 468. Omelet with Asiago and Boursin Cheese

DAY 13

Breakfast – 463. Greek Yogurt and Apple Muffins
Lunch – 167. Grilled Pork Skewers; 25. Mixed Green Salad with Blueberries
Dinner – 323. Za'atar Salmon with Cheese

DAY 14

Breakfast – 36. Pepper and Cheese Bake
Lunch – 75. Rutabaga, Taro and Chicken Soup; 1 handful of baby spinach with 1 teaspoon of mustard and 1 teaspoon of olive oil
Dinner – 127. Italian Pork Muffins
Dessert – 591. Mediterranean-Style Chocolate Pudding

DAY 15

Breakfast – 450. Curried Asparagus Frittata; 1 tomato
Lunch – 246. Chuck Roast with Serrano Pepper
Snack – 462. Italian-Style Fat Bombs
Dinner – 435. Classic Keto Pan Pizza

DAY 16

Breakfast – 37. Zucchini with Greek Yogurt Sauce; 2 hard-boiled eggs
Lunch – 207. Easy Spicy Sloppy Joes; 290. Old Bay Pollock Soup
Dinner – 60. Chorizo Sausage in Tomato Sauce
Dessert – 587. Rustic Walnut Dessert

DAY 17

Breakfast – 535. Cheese, Salami and Olive Muffins
Lunch – 196. Beef Meatloaf with Halloumi Cheese
Dinner – 428. Oyster Mushroom Paprikash

DAY 18

Breakfast – 372. Keto "Cereal" with Almond Milk
Lunch – 199. Beef and Ale Stew
Snack – 527. Butter Dill Zucchini Chips
Dinner – 195. Milk Braised Pork Loin with Sage

DAY 19

Breakfast – 385. Crunchy Granola with A Twist
Lunch – 411. Squash Stew with Tomatoes and Wine
Dinner – 260. Thai-Style Spicy Steak Salad
Dessert – 580. Classic Jaffa Dessert

DAY 20

Breakfast – 684. Rich and Easy Spanish Tortilla
Lunch – 49. Roasted Asparagus with Pancetta; 55. Chicken Soup with Harvest Vegetables
Snack – 519. Spicy Cucumber Rounds with Goat Cheese
Dinner – 79. Romano-Turkey Meatballs with Basil Chutney

DAY 21

Breakfast – 368. Easy Breakfast Smoothie
Lunch – 3. Cauliflower Coconut Soup; 63. Easy Chicken Parmigiana
Snack – 521. Zingy Cheesecake Balls
Dinner – 315. Crab Legs with Bacon and Vegetables

VEGETABLES & SIDE DISHES

1. Mediterranean Asparagus with Halloumi Cheese

(Ready in about 15 minutes | Servings 6)

Ingredients

1 ½ pounds asparagus spears
2 tablespoons extra-virgin olive oil
2 garlic cloves, minced
1 red onion, chopped
1 cup Halloumi cheese, crumbled
Salt and black pepper, to the taste

Directions

Brush your asparagus with extra-virgin olive oil. Toss with the onion, garlic, salt, and black pepper.

Roast in the preheated oven at 395 degrees F for about 15 minutes.

Top the roasted asparagus with the cheese and place under the preheated broiler for 5 to 6 minutes or until the cheese melts. Enjoy!

Per serving: 128 Calories; 9.4g Fat; 2.9g Carbs; 6.4g Protein; 2.9g Fiber

2. Italian Cheesy Roasted Tomatoes

(Ready in about 25 minutes | Servings 4)

Ingredients

1 cup Caciocavallo cheese, shredded
1 teaspoon Mediterranean spice mix
1/4 cup extra-virgin olive oil
Sea salt and pepper, to taste
1 tablespoon balsamic vinegar
2 garlic cloves, pressed
1 ½ pounds tomatoes, sliced

Directions

Start by preheating your oven to 390 degrees F.

Toss your tomatoes with olive oil, vinegar, garlic, salt, pepper, and Mediterranean spice mix. Place tomatoes on a lightly oiled baking sheet.

Roast in the preheated oven for about 20 minutes until your tomatoes begin to caramelize.

Top with Caciocavallo cheese and place under the preheated broiler until the cheese is hot and bubbly. Enjoy!

Per serving: 247 Calories; 19.8g Fat; 5.3g Carbs; 11g Protein; 1.8g Fiber

3. Cauliflower Coconut Soup

(Ready in about 20 minutes | Servings 4)

Ingredients

1 cup coconut milk, unsweetened
1 thyme sprig
3 cups cauliflower, cut into florets
3 cups roasted vegetable broth
1 cup avocado, pitted and chopped
Salt and pepper, to taste

Directions

In a heavy-bottomed pot, simmer the vegetable broth over medium-high heat. Add in the cauliflower and continue to simmer for 10 to 15 minutes more.

Add in the coconut milk, avocado, salt, pepper, and thyme. Partially cover and continue to cook for a further 5 minutes.

Puree the mixture in your blender.

Per serving: 260 Calories; 22.5g Fat; 4.1g Carbs; 7.2g Protein; 4.2g Fiber

4. Italian-Style Broccoli Pilau

(Ready in about 20 minutes | Servings 4)

Ingredients

1 celery rib, chopped
1/2 teaspoon garlic, smashed
1/2 shallots, chopped
1/2 stick butter
1 head broccoli, broken into a rice-like chunks
Salt and pepper, to your liking
1 Italian pepper, chopped
1 habanero pepper, minced

Directions

In a saucepan, melt the butter over a moderately-high heat. Saute the shallot, garlic, and peppers for about 3 minutes.

Stir in the broccoli and celery; continue to cook for 4 to 5 minutes or until tender and aromatic. Season with salt and pepper to taste.

Continue to cook for 5 to 6 minutes or until everything is cooked through.

Per serving: 126 Calories; 11.6g Fat; 5.4g Carbs; 1.3g Protein; 2.7g Fiber

5. Classic Chicory with Butter and Pine Nuts

(Ready in about 10 minutes | Servings 4)

Ingredients

2 heads chicory, cut into chunks
3 teaspoons butter
Salt and pepper, to taste
2 garlic cloves, crushed
1 shallot, chopped
1/4 cup pine nuts

Directions

Parboil the chicory in a pot of lightly salted water for 5 to 6 minutes; drain.

Melt the butter over moderately-high heat and sauté the chicory with garlic and shallots.

Season with salt and pepper. Top with pine nuts.

Per serving: 65 Calories; 4.7g Fat; 5.7g Carbs; 2.1g Protein; 1.5g Fiber

6. Cream of Cauliflower Soup with Almond Milk

(Ready in about 20 minutes | Servings 4)

Ingredients

- 1 cup almond milk, unsweetened
- 1 cup avocado, pitted and chopped
- 3 cups cauliflower, cut into florets
- 1/4 teaspoon freshly cracked mixed peppercorns
- 1 bay leaf
- 1/4 teaspoon Himalayan rock salt
- 3 cups chicken broth

Directions

Simmer the chicken broth over a moderate flame. Add the cauliflower and cook for 10 minutes.

Turn the heat to low. Add the remaining ingredients and cook for a further 5 minutes.

Puree the mixture using an immersion blender. Bon appétit!

Per serving: 260 Calories; 22.5g Fat; 5.1g Carbs; 7.2g Protein; 4.1g Fiber

7. Creamed Cabbage Coleslaw

(Ready in about 10 minutes + chilling time | Servings 4)

Ingredients

- 2 tablespoons sesame seeds, lightly toasted
- 1 cup mayonnaise
- Salt and pepper, to taste
- 3/4 pound cabbage, cored and shredded
- 1/4 cup fresh chives, chopped
- 1 teaspoon fennel seeds
- 1 large-sized celery, shredded
- 1 teaspoon deli mustard
- 1/4 cup fresh cilantro, chopped

Directions

Toss the cabbage, celery, mayonnaise, mustard, cilantro, chives, fennel seeds, salt, and pepper in a bowl.

Sprinkle toasted sesame seeds over your salad.

Per serving: 242 Calories; 20.5g Fat; 6.2g Carbs; 1g Protein; 3.1g Fiber

8. Sichuan Cabbage Stir Fry

(Ready in about 15 minutes | Servings 4)

Ingredients

- 1/2 teaspoon Sichuan pepper
- 1 pound Chinese cabbage, outer leaves discarded, cored and shredded
- 1 celery rib, thinly sliced
- 1/4 cup vegetable stock
- 1/2 cup onion, chopped
- 1/4 teaspoon fresh ginger root, grated
- 1 teaspoon garlic, pressed
- 1 tablespoon rice wine
- 4 tablespoons sesame oil
- 1/2 teaspoon sea salt

Directions

In a wok, heat the sesame oil over a medium-high flame. Stir fry the onion, and garlic for 1 minute or until just tender and fragrant.

Add in the cabbage, celery, and ginger and continue to cook for 7 to 8 minutes more, stirring frequently to ensure even cooking.

Stir in the remaining ingredients and continue to cook for a further 3 minutes.

Per serving: 142 Calories; 11.6g Fat; 5.7g Carbs; 2g Protein; 1.8g Fiber

9. Fathead Vegetarian Pizza

(Ready in about 25 minutes | Servings 4)

Ingredients

For the Crust:
- 1/2 cup Colby cheese
- 4 medium-sized eggs
- 1 tablespoon olive oil
- Salt and pepper, to taste
- 1/4 cup double cream
- 1 pound cauliflower florets

For the Topping:
- 1 cup mozzarella cheese
- 1/2 cup romaine lettuce
- 1 cup lollo rosso
- 1 tomato, pureed
- 1/2 cup green mustard
- 1/4 cup black olives, pitted and sliced
- 1 tablespoon fresh basil

Directions

Parboil the cauliflower florets in a large pot of salted water until it is crisp-tender; add in the cheese, eggs, cream, olive oil, salt, and pepper.

Press the crust mixture into the bottom of a lightly oiled baking pan. Bake in the middle of the oven at 385 degrees F. Bake for 13 to 15 minutes or until the crust is firm.

Top with the other ingredients, ending with the mozzarella cheese; bake until the cheese is bubbly and hot. Bon appétit!

Per serving: 234 Calories; 16.1g Fat; 6.3g Carbs; 13.6g Protein; 3.6g Fiber

10. Classic Rich Rutabaga Chowder

(Ready in about 45 minutes | Servings 4)

Ingredients

- 1/2 cup rutabaga, cubed
- 1 teaspoon cayenne pepper
- 1 cup chicken consommé, canned
- 1/2 cup leek, chopped
- 1 tablespoon fresh parsley, chopped
- 1/4 teaspoon garlic, granulated
- 1/2 cup taro leaves, roughly chopped
- Salt and black pepper, to taste
- 1/4 teaspoon ground cloves
- 2 carrots, peeled
- 2 celery stalks
- 3 cups water
- 1 pound chicken thighs

Directions

Add all of the above ingredients, except for the cayenne pepper, to a large-sized stock pot. Bring to a rapid boil over high heat.

Now, turn the heat to medium-low. Let it simmer, partially covered, an additional 35 minutes or until the chicken is pinkish-brown.

Next, discard the chicken and vegetables. Add the cayenne pepper to the broth; allow it to simmer an additional 8 minutes.

When the chicken thighs are cool enough to handle, cut off the meat from bones. Afterwards, add the meat back to the soup.

Bon appétit!

Per serving: 256 Calories; 8.9g Fat; 6.2g Carbs; 35.1g Protein; 2.1g Fiber

VEGETABLES & SIDE DISHES

11. Spanish Champinones Al Ajillo

(Ready in about 20 minutes | Servings 6)

Ingredients

1 teaspoon garlic, minced
1/2 cup almond flour
1/2 teaspoon baking powder
1/4 teaspoon flaky sea salt
1 egg plus 1 egg yolk, beaten
1/4 cup coconut flour
2 tablespoons psyllium powder
1 teaspoon Spanish paprika
1 tablespoon butter
1 pound button mushrooms, thinly sliced
8 tablespoons coconut oil, melted

Directions

Mix the flour with the baking powder, psyllium and salt until well combined.

Add in 6 tablespoons of coconut oil, egg and egg yolk; pour in the water and stir to form a dough; let it stand for about 15 minutes.

Divide the dough into 6 pieces and roll them out to form a disc. Use the remaining 2 tablespoons of coconut oil to bake the naan bread.

In a sauté pan, cook the mushrooms and garlic in hot butter until the mushrooms release liquid; season with Spanish paprika. Taste and adjust seasonings.

Per serving: 281 Calories; 21.4g Fat; 6.1g Carbs; 6.4g Protein; 1.4g Fiber

12. Spicy Eggplant Stew

(Ready in about 35 minutes | Servings 6)

Ingredients

3 ounces eggplant, peeled and chopped
2 tablespoons port wine
2 tomatoes, pureed
Sea salt and pepper, to taste
3 ounces acorn squash, chopped
1 large onion, chopped
1 celery, chopped
2 tablespoons fresh parsley, roughly chopped
1/2 teaspoon ancho chili powder
2 tablespoons olive
2 garlic cloves, finely chopped

Directions

In a heavy-bottomed pot, heat the olive oil over a moderately-high heat. Sauté the onion and garlic about 5 minutes.

Add in the acorn squash, eggplant, celery and parsley; continue to cook for 5 to 6 minutes.

Add in the other ingredients; turn the heat to a simmer. Continue to cook for about 25 minutes.

Per serving: 113 Calories; 7.9g Fat; 3.7g Carbs; 2.8g Protein; 2.2g Fiber

13. Spinach and Cheese Muffins

(Ready in about 25 minutes | Servings 6)

Ingredients

5 eggs
1/2 cup milk
1/2 pound smoked ham, chopped
1 teaspoon Mediterranean seasoning mix
Salt and pepper, to taste
10 ounces baby spinach, cooked and drained
1 ½ cups goat cheese, crumbled

Directions

Thoroughly combine all ingredients in a mixing bowl. Spoon the batter into a lightly oiled muffin tin.

Bake in the preheated oven at 350 degrees F for about 25 minutes.

Per serving: 275 Calories; 15.8g Fat; 2.2g Carbs; 21.6g Protein; 1.2g Fiber

14. Italian Mixed Greens

(Ready in about 25 minutes | Servings 5)

Ingredients

1 teaspoon garlic, chopped
1/2 cup shallot
1 tablespoon olive oil
1/4 cup cream of celery soup
Sea salt and pepper, to taste
1 cup Caciocavallo cheese, shredded
2 pounds mixed greens, fresh or frozen, torn into pieces
1 tablespoon balsamic vinegar

Directions

Het the olive oil in a Dutch oven over a moderately-high heat. Cook the garlic and shallot for 2 to 3 minutes or until tender and fragrant.

Add in the mixed greens and cream of celery soup; continue to cook, partially covered, for about 15 minutes until greens are wilted.

Add in the vinegar, salt, and pepper; heat off.

Top with cheese and cook until the cheese melts completely. Enjoy!

Per serving: 160 Calories; 10g Fat; 5.1g Carbs; 11g Protein; 4.6g Fiber

15. Zucchini and Cheese Fritters

(Ready in about 15 minutes | Servings 6)

Ingredients

1 cup Halloumi cheese, shredded
2 tablespoons cilantro, chopped
Sea salt and pepper, to taste
1/2 cup onion, finely chopped
1 egg, whisked
2 celery stalks, shredded
1 pound zucchinis, shredded
1 teaspoon garlic, finely minced
2 tablespoons butter

Directions

Thoroughly combine all ingredients in a mixing bowl.

Form the mixture into 12 patties and arrange them on a parchment-lined baking sheet.

Bake in the preheated oven at 365 degrees F for 12 minutes, rotating the pan once or twice.

Per serving: 153 Calories; 11.8g Fat; 6.6g Carbs; 6.4g Protein; 1.1g Fiber

16. Kohlrabi with Mushroom Sauce

(Ready in about 15 minutes | Servings 4)

Ingredients

1/2 cup white onions, chopped
1/2 teaspoon garlic, chopped
Kosher salt and ground black pepper, to taste
3/4 pound kohlrabi, trimmed and thinly sliced
3 tablespoons olive oil
1/2 pound button mushrooms, sliced
1 ½ cups sour cream

Directions

In a large pot of salted water, place the kohlrabi and parboil over medium-high heat for about 8 minutes. Drain.

In a saucepan, heat the oil over medium-high heat. Sauté the onions, mushrooms, and garlic until they've softened.

Season with salt and pepper to taste. Add in the sour cream and stir to combine well.

Per serving: 220 Calories; 20g Fat; 5.3g Carbs; 4g Protein; 3.8g Fiber

17. Celery with Cream-Rum Sauce

(Ready in about 40 minutes | Servings 6)

Ingredients

1 teaspoon garlic, smashed
2 tablespoons balsamic vinegar
2 tablespoons ghee, room temperature
Kosher salt and white pepper, to taste
1 ½ pounds celery, trimmed and halved lengthwise

For the Sauce:
1 cup double cream
2 tablespoons ghee
1/2 cup onions, minced
1 ½ cups cream of celery soup
3 tablespoons rum

Directions

Start by preheating your oven to 410 degrees F.

Toss your celery with 2 tablespoons of ghee, salt, white pepper, balsamic vinegar, and garlic.

Roast the celery in the preheated oven for about 30 minutes.

In the meantime, melt the 2 tablespoons of ghee in a cast-iron skillet over a moderately-high heat. Once hot, cook the onions for 2 to 3 minutes until tender and translucent.

Add the rum and cream of celery soup; bring it to a boil. Continue to cook for 4 to 5 minutes. Turn the heat to a simmer.

Add in the double cream and continue to simmer until the sauce has thickened and reduced.

Per serving: 183 Calories; 14.2g Fat; 6.5g Carbs; 2.6g Protein; 2.2g Fiber

18. Skinny Salad with Macadamia Nuts

(Ready in about 5 minutes | Servings 4)

Ingredients

1/2 teaspoon Sriracha sauce
1 tablespoon sunflower seeds
1/2 lemon, freshly squeezed
1 Lebanese cucumber, sliced
1 bell pepper, sliced
Sea salt, to season
3 tablespoons olive oil

1 cup radishes, thinly sliced
2 cups butterhead lettuce, torn into bite-sized pieces
1 white onion, sliced
1 ounce macadamia nuts, chopped

Directions

In a mixing bowl, toss all ingredients until well combined.

Taste and adjust seasonings.

Per serving: 184 Calories; 16.8g Fat; 4g Carbs; 2.1g Protein; 1.4g Fiber

19. Mediterranean-Style Broccoli Quiche

(Ready in about 25 minutes | Servings 3)

Ingredients

1 teaspoon Mediterranean spice mix
3 eggs, well-beaten
1/2 cup double cream
3 tablespoons sesame oil
1 red onion, minced

2 garlic cloves, minced
2 ounces Colby cheese, shredded
3/4 pound broccoli, cut into small florets

Directions

Begin by preheating your oven to 320 degrees F. Brush the sides and bottom of a casserole dish with a non-stick cooking spray.

In a frying pan, heat the sesame oil over a moderately-high heat. Sauté the onion and garlic until just tender and fragrant.

Add in the broccoli and continue to cook until crisp-tender for about 4 minutes. Spoon the mixture into the preparade casserole dish.

Whisk the eggs with double cream and Mediterranean spice mix. Spoon this mixture over the broccoli layer.

Bake in the preheated oven for 18 to 20 minutes.

Top with the shredded cheese and broil for 5 to 6 minutes or until hot and bubbly on the top. Bon appétit!

Per serving: 195 Calories; 12.7g Fat; 6.7g Carbs; 11.6g Protein; 3.2g Fiber

20. Louisiana-Style Spinach

(Ready in about 10 minutes | Servings 4)

Ingredients

1 cup Creole cream cheese
1/2 stick butter
1/4 teaspoon caraway seeds
1 teaspoon garlic, pressed

2 pounds spinach, torn into pieces
Sea salt and pepper, to taste

Directions

Melt the butter in a saucepan over medium-high heat; now, sauté the garlic until tender and fragrant.

Add the spinach, salt, pepper, and caraway seeds; continue to cook for about 6 minutes until warmed through.

Top with the cheese and cook until cheese melts completely. Enjoy!

Per serving: 208 Calories; 13.5g Fat; 6g Carbs; 14.5g Protein; 5.1g Fiber

VEGETABLES & SIDE DISHES

21. Cabbage and Sour Cream Soup

(Ready in about 25 minutes | Servings 4)

Ingredients

1 yellow onion, chopped
1 bell pepper, chopped
4 cups roasted vegetable broth
2 garlic cloves, minced
1 cup sour cream
1 celery, chopped
2 cups cabbage, shredded
1 ½ tablespoons olive oil

Directions

In a heavy-bottomed pot, heat the olive oil over a moderate flame. Sauté the onion and garlic until just tender and aromatic.

Add in the celery, cabbage, and pepper and continue to cook for about 6 minutes, stirring occasionally to ensure even cooking.

Pour in the roasted vegetable broth and cook, partially covered, for 10 to 12 minutes longer.

Puree the mixture with an immersion blender. Stir in the sour cream; and remove from heat; stir to combine well.

Per serving: 185 Calories; 16.6g Fat; 2.4g Carbs; 2.9g Protein; 1.9g Fiber

22. Bok Choy with Prawns and Garlic

(Ready in about 15 minutes | Servings 4)

Ingredients

1 ½ pounds Bok choy, trimmed and thinly sliced
10 ounces prawns, peeled and deveined
1 teaspoon garlic, minced
Salt and pepper, to taste
1 tablespoon fish sauce
2 tablespoons peanut oil
1 (1/2-inch) piece ginger, freshly grated

Directions

Heat 1 tablespoon of the peanut oil in a frying pan over a moderately-high heat. Sauté the garlic until tender and aromatic.

Stir in the Bok choy, ginger, fish sauce, salt, and pepper; cook for 5 to 6 minutes, stirring periodically to ensure even cooking.

In the same pan, heat the remaining tablespoon of oil and cook the prawns until opaque, about 4 minutes.

Serve your prawns with the reserved Bok choy.

Per serving: 171 Calories; 8.4g Fat; 5.8g Carbs; 18.9g Protein; 1.9g Fiber

23. Cabbage Stir-Fry with Bacon

(Ready in about 15 minutes | Servings 4)

Ingredients

2 teaspoons red wine
Kosher salt and black pepper, to taste
4 eggs
1 teaspoon garlic, smashed
1 bay laurel
1 thyme sprig
4 rashers of bacon, chopped
1 cup red onions, minced
1 rosemary sprig
2 cups cabbage, shredded

Directions

Cook the bacon in a non-stick skillet over medium-high heat; reserve. Sauté the red onions and garlic in 1 tablespoon of bacon grease.

Add in the cabbage and continue to cook, stirring frequently, until it has softened or about 4 minutes.

Add a splash of wine to deglaze the pan. Add in the spices and continue to cook for a further 2 minutes.

Fry the eggs in 1 tablespoon of bacon grease. Add in the reserved bacon and top with the fried eggs.

Per serving: 173 Calories; 10.6g Fat; 5.6g Carbs; 14.2g Protein; 1.6g Fiber

24. Greek Wine-Braised Vegetables

(Ready in about 15 minutes | Servings 4)

Ingredients

1 teaspoon Greek seasoning mix
1 teaspoon garlic, minced
1/4 cup white wine
1/2 pound brown mushrooms, chopped
1 medium-sized zucchini, chopped
8 ounces feta cheese, cubed
1 vine-ripened tomato, pureed
1 cup broccoli, cut into small florets
2 tablespoons olive oil
1 onion, chopped

Directions

In a medium pot, heat the oil over a moderately-high heat. Sauté the onion and garlic for about 5 minutes, adding a splash of water if needed, until tender and aromatic.

Add in the mushrooms, broccoli, zucchini, Greek seasoning mix, tomato puree, and white wine. Continue to cook for 4 to 5 minutes or until they've softened.

Serve with feta cheese. Enjoy!

Per serving: 318 Calories; 24.3g Fat; 5.1g Carbs; 15.4g Protein; 1.7g Fiber

25. Mixed Green Salad with Blueberries

(Ready in about 10 minutes | Servings 4)

Ingredients

1 cup lollo rosso
1 cup avocado, pitted, peeled and sliced
Sea salt and white pepper, to taste
1/2 cup blueberries
2 tablespoons fresh parsley, chopped
1/2 lime, freshly squeezed
2 cups baby spinach
1/3 cup goat cheese, crumbled
1 cup romaine lettuce
2 tablespoons extra-virgin olive oil

Directions

Toss all ingredients in a mixing bowl. Taste and adjust seasonings.

Place in your refrigerator until ready to use. Bon appétit!

Per serving: 190 Calories; 17.6g Fat; 7.6g Carbs; 4.3g Protein; 3.9g Fiber

VEGETABLES & SIDE DISHES

26. Zoodles with Mediterranean Mushroom Sauce

(Ready in about 15 minutes | Servings 4)

Ingredients

1 cup vegetable broth
1 teaspoon Mediterranean sauce
1 yellow onion, minced
1 cup pureed tomatoes
2 tablespoons olive oil
2 garlic cloves, minced
1 pound oyster mushrooms, chopped
2 zucchinis, cut into thin strips

Directions

Parboil the zucchini noodles for one minute or so. Reserve.

Then, heat the oil in a saucepan over a moderately-high heat. Sauté the onion and garlic for 2 to 3 minutes.

Add in the mushrooms and continue to cook for 2 to 3 minutes until they release liquid.

Add in the remaining ingredients and cover the pan; let it simmer for 10 minutes longer until everything is cooked through.

Top your zoodles with the prepared mushroom sauce and serve.

Per serving: 85 Calories; 3.5g Fat; 6.4g Carbs; 5.8g Protein; 3.3g Fiber

27. Traditional Polish Kapusta

(Ready in about 20 minutes | Servings 6)

Ingredients

3 strips bacon, diced
1/2 teaspoon red pepper flakes, crushed
1 bell pepper, finely chopped
1/2 cup vegetable broth
1 pound cabbage, shredded

Directions

In a Dutch oven, fry the bacon for 5 to 6 minutes. Add in the cabbage and pepper and continue to cook until they've softened.

Add in the broth and red pepper flakes and cover the pan. Turn the heat to medium-low and let it simmer for 10 to 13 minutes or until cooked through.

Taste and adjust the seasonings. Bon appétit!

Per serving: 259 Calories; 18.1g Fat; 3.6g Carbs; 15.5g Protein; 1.8g Fiber

28. Chinese Spicy Cabbage

(Ready in about 15 minutes | Servings 4)

Ingredients

1 teaspoon Chinese Five-spice powder
1 tablespoon sesame oil
1 shallot, sliced
1 tablespoon soy sauce
2 tablespoons rice wine
3/4 pound Chinese cabbage, cored and cut into chunks
Salt and Sichuan pepper, to taste
1/2 teaspoon chili sauce, sugar-free

Directions

Heat the sesame oil in a wok a moderately-high heat. Sauté the shallot until tender and translucent. Add in the Chinese cabbage and continue to cook for about 3 minutes.

Partially cover and add in the remaining ingredients; continue to cook for 5 minutes more.

Per serving: 53 Calories; 3.7g Fat; 3.2g Carbs; 1.7g Protein; 2.1g Fiber

29. Classic Cheese Ball with Pine Nuts

(Ready in about 25 minutes | Servings 2)

Ingredients

1 ounce Neufchatel
1 ounce Feta cheese
2 tablespoons pine nuts, chopped
1 teaspoon salt
1 tablespoon fresh basil, chopped
1 Lebanese cucumber, chopped

Directions

Salt the chopped cucumber and place it in a colander. Let it stand for 30 minutes; press the cucumber to drain away the excess liquid and transfer to a mixing bowl.

Mix in the cheese and basil. Shape the mixture into a ball and top with chopped nuts. Enjoy!

Per serving: 133 Calories; 9.9g Fat; 6.8g Carbs; 6g Protein; 0.7g Fiber

30. Stuffed Peppers with Cremini Mushrooms

(Ready in about 30 minutes | Servings 6)

Ingredients

3/4 pound Cremini mushrooms, chopped
1 teaspoon garlic, minced
2 tablespoons olive oil
1 onion, chopped
1 teaspoon mustard seeds
1/2 cup Cheddar cheese, grated
1/2 cup tomato puree
Salt to taste
6 bell peppers, seeds and tops removed
2 tablespoons fresh cilantro, chopped

Directions

In a frying pan, heat the olive oil over a moderately-high flame. Sauté the onion and garlic until they are tender and aromatic.

Add in the Cremini mushrooms and continue to cook for a further 5 minutes or until the mushrooms release the liquid.

Add in the cilantro, mustard seeds, and salt; stir to combine. Divide this filling between bell peppers. Place the peppers in a lightly greased casserole dish.

Pour the tomato sauce around stuffed peppers. Bake at 385 degrees F for about 22 minutes or until heated through.

Top with Cheddar cheese. Bake the thawed stuffed peppers at 300 degrees F until the cheese melts. Serve warm.

Per serving: 319 Calories; 18.8g Fat; 5.6g Carbs; 10.3g Protein; 1.9g Fiber

VEGETABLES & SIDE DISHES

31. Stuffed Tomatoes with Chicken and Parmesan

(Ready in about 25 minutes | Servings 4)

Ingredients

1/2 pound ground chicken
1 ½ cups Parmesan cheese, grated
1/2 cup onions, chopped
1 teaspoon oregano, chopped
4 tomatoes, scoop out the pulp
1 garlic clove, smashed
1 tablespoon canola oil
Seasoned salt and pepper, to taste
1/2 cup cream of celery soup
1 tablespoon fresh coriander, chopped

Directions

In a frying pan, heat the oil over a moderately-high heat. Cook ground chicken, onion, and garlic for about 4 minutes, stirring periodically to ensure even cooking; set aside.

Add in the tomato pulp, coriander, oregano, salt, and pepper. Divide this filling between tomatoes.

Place the stuffed tomatoes in a lightly oiled casserole dish.

Pour the cream of celery soup around stuffed tomatoes; bake in the preheated oven at 365 degrees F for about 20 until heated through.

Top with Parmesan cheese and place under preheated broiled for 5 minutes until hot and bubbly. Enjoy!

Per serving: 366 Calories; 23.2g Fat; 6.8g Carbs; 23.2g Protein; 2.1g Fiber

32. Veggie Noodles with Beef Sauce

(Ready in about 20 minutes | Servings 4)

Ingredients

3/4 pound ground chuck
1/2 cup onion, thinly sliced
1 pound green cabbage, spiralized
2 bay leaves
Sea salt and black pepper, to taste
1/2 teaspoon garlic, chopped
1/2 teaspoon chili pepper, minced
2 slices pancetta, chopped

Directions

Parboil the cabbage in a pot of lightly salted water for 3 to 4 minutes; drain.

Cook the pancetta over a moderately-high heat for about 4 minutes, breaking apart with a fork and reserve.

Cook the onion and garlic in the bacon grease until they've softened. Add in the ground chuck, chili pepper, salt and black pepper; continue to cook until ground beef is no longer pink.

Add the pancetta back to the pan. Top with the cabbage noodles. Bon appétit!

Per serving: 236 Calories; 8.3g Fat; 5.1g Carbs; 29.9g Protein; 2.9g Fiber

33. Vegetarian Pasta Alfredo

(Ready in about 30 minutes | Servings 4)

Ingredients

1 teaspoon Italian spice mix
2 ounces Ricotta cheese, room temperature
2 cups Romano cheese, grated
3 eggs, room temperature
1 cup double cream
1 garlic clove, minced
1/2 teaspoon wheat gluten
1 stick butter

Directions

Mix the Ricotta cheese, eggs, and gluten until creamy. Press this mixture into a parchment-lined baking sheet.

Bake at 310 degrees F for about 6 minutes. Let it cool for about 10 minutes and cut into strips using a sharp knife.

Cook this the pasta in a lightly salted water for 3 to 4 minutes.

In a saucepan, melt the butter over low heat. Cook the garlic and cream until warmed; stir in Romano cheese and Italian spice mix; heat off.

Fold in the reserved pasta. Gently stir to combine.

Per serving: 614 Calories; 55.9g Fat; 3.6g Carbs; 25.6g Protein; 0g Fiber

34. Spicy Mushroom Stew with Wine

(Ready in about 30 minutes | Servings 4)

Ingredients

1 tablespoon butter, room temperature
1/4 cup dry white wine
1 bell pepper, deveined and chopped
1/4 cup fresh parsley, chopped
1 celery, chopped
Salt and ground black pepper, to taste
2 ½ cups vegetable broth
1 cup tomato puree
2 garlic cloves, pressed
1 teaspoon jalapeno pepper, deveined and minced
1 cup onions, chopped
1 bay laurel
1/2 pound brown mushrooms, chopped
1/4 teaspoon ground allspice

Directions

In Dutch oven, melt the butter over a moderate heat. Cook the onion, peppers, garlic, and celery for about 7 minutes.

Add in the mushrooms and cook an additional 2 to 3 minutes. Add in the vegetable broth, wine, tomato puree, and seasonings; bring to a boil.

Turn the heat to a simmer; let it simmer for about 20 minutes or until cooked through.

Per serving: 133 Calories; 3.7g Fat; 5.7g Carbs; 14g Protein; 3.1g Fiber

35. Traditional Provençal Ratatouille

(Ready in about 1 hour | Servings 4)

Ingredients

- 1/3 cup Parmesan cheese, shredded
- 1 tablespoon fresh basil leaves, snipped
- 1 cup grape tomatoes, halved
- 1 eggplant, cut into thick slices
- 1/2 garlic head, minced
- 1 celery, peeled and diced
- 1 poblano pepper, minced
- 2 tablespoons extra-virgin olive oil
- 1 large onion, sliced

Directions

Sprinkle the eggplant with 1 teaspoon of salt and let it stand for about 30 minutes; drain and rinse under running water.

Place the eggplant slices in the bottom of a lightly-oiled casserole dish. Add in the remaining vegetable. Add in the olive oil and basil leaves.

Bake in the preheated oven at 350 degrees F for about 30 minute or until thoroughly cooked. Bon appétit!

Per serving: 159 Calories; 10.4g Fat; 5.7g Carbs; 6.4g Protein; 5g Fiber

36. Pepper and Cheese Bake

(Ready in about 1 hour | Servings 4)

Ingredients

- 3/4 pound Asiago cheese, shredded
- 1 leek, thinly sliced
- 1/2 teaspoon garlic, crushed
- Sea salt and ground black pepper, to taste
- 1/2 cup Greek-style yogurt
- 1 teaspoon oregano
- 6 whole eggs
- 8 Italian sweet peppers, deveined and cut into fourths lengthwise

Directions

Arrange the peppers in a lightly greased baking dish.

Top with half of the shredded cheese; add a layer of sliced leeks and garlic. Repeat the layers.

After that, beat the eggs with the yogurt, salt, pepper, and oregano. Pour the egg/yogurt mixture over the peppers. Cover with a piece of foil and bake for about 30 minutes.

Remove the foil and bake for a further 10 to 15 minutes.

Per serving: 408 Calories; 28.9g Fat; 4.6g Carbs; 24.9g Protein; 3.5g Fiber

37. Zucchini with Greek Yogurt Sauce

(Ready in about 15 minutes | Servings 4)

Ingredients

- 1 teaspoon garlic, minced
- 1/4 cup extra-virgin olive oil
- 1/2 teaspoon red pepper flakes, crushed
- Salt, to season
- 1 pound zucchini, cut lengthwise into quarters
- For the Sauce:
- 3/4 cup Greek-style yogurt
- 1 tablespoon fresh basil, chopped
- 1 teaspoon fresh rosemary, finely chopped
- 1 tablespoon fresh scallions, minced

Directions

Begin by preheating your grill to a medium-low heat.

Toss the zucchini slices with the olive oil, garlic, red pepper, and salt. Grill your zucchini on a lightly-oiled grill for about 10 minutes until tender and slightly charred.

Make the sauce by whisking all of the sauce ingredients. Serve the zucchini with the sauce on the side. Enjoy!

Per serving: 132 Calories; 11.1g Fat; 4.1g Carbs; 3.1g Protein; 1.3g Fiber

38. Roasted Vegetables with Herbs

(Ready in about 35 minutes | Servings 6)

Ingredients

- 1 garlic clove, minced
- 1 fresh chili pepper, minced
- 1/2 pound turnips, cut into wedges
- 1/2 pound celery, quartered
- Sea salt and ground black pepper, to taste
- 1/2 pound bell peppers, sliced
- 1 teaspoon dried thyme
- 1 onion, cut into wedges
- 1 teaspoon dried basil
- 3 tablespoons olive oil

Directions

Toss all ingredients in a roasting pan. Roast in the preheated oven at 410 degrees F for 30 minutes.

Taste and adjust the seasoning.

Per serving: 137 Calories; 11.1g Fat; 3.1g Carbs; 1.2g Protein; 2.3g Fiber

39. Pancetta Cheese Stuffed Mushrooms

(Ready in about 25 minutes | Servings 6)

Ingredients

- 3 slices of pancetta, chopped
- 2 ounces goat cheese, crumbled
- 1 teaspoon fresh rosemary, minced
- 1 tablespoon oyster sauce
- 1 teaspoon basil
- 2 tablespoons butter, melted
- 12 medium-sized button mushrooms, stems removed
- Sea salt and black pepper, to taste

Directions

Brush your mushrooms with melted butter and oyster sauce. Season them with salt and pepper to taste.

Mix the pancetta, basil, rosemary, and goat cheese. Spoon the mixture into the mushroom caps and arrange them on a parchment-lined baking sheet.

Bake in the preheated oven at 360 degrees F for about 20 minutes or until tender.

Per serving: 98 Calories; 5.8g Fat; 3.9g Carbs; 8.4g Protein; 0.6g Fiber

40. Saucy Japanese Mushrooms

(Ready in about 15 minutes | Servings 3)

Ingredients

- 1 ½ tablespoons butter, melted
- 2 cloves garlic, minced
- Salt and Sansho pepper, to season
- 1 tablespoon lightly toasted sesame seeds
- 1 cup onions, finely chopped
- 2 tablespoons mirin
- 1/2 cup dashi stock
- 8 ounces Eringi mushrooms, trim away about 1-inch of the root section

Directions

Melt the butter in a large pan over a moderately-high flame. Cook the onions and garlic for about 4 minutes, stirring continuously to ensure even cooking.

Add in the Eringi mushrooms and continue to cook an additional 3 minutes until they are slightly shriveled.

Season to taste and add in the mirin and dashi stock; continue to cook an additional 3 minutes.

Garnish with sesame seeds. Enjoy!

Per serving: 103 Calories; 6.7g Fat; 5.9g Carbs; 2.7g Protein; 3.3g Fiber

41. Pancetta and Cream Cheese Stuffed Avocado

(Ready in about 25 minutes | Servings 6)

Ingredients

- 3 ounce Pancetta, chopped
- 3 ounces chive cream cheese
- 2 eggs, beaten
- Salt and pepper, to taste
- 3 medium-sized ripe avocados, halved and pitted

Directions

Begin by preheating an oven to 380 degrees F. Place the avocado halves in a baking pan.

Thoroughly combine the eggs, cheese, Pancetta, salt, and pepper. Spoon the mixture into avocado halves.

Bake in the preheated oven for 18 to 20 minutes.

Per serving: 255 Calories; 21g Fat; 3.3g Carbs; 10.8g Protein; 4.8g Fiber

42. Broccoli Florets in Cheese Sauce

(Ready in about 30 minutes | Servings 6)

Ingredients

- 2 tablespoons green garlic, minced
- 1 ½ tablespoons olive oil
- 1/4 teaspoon turmeric powder
- Sea salt and black pepper, to taste
- 1/4 cup scallions, chopped
- 2 pounds broccoli, cut into small florets
- For the Sauce:
- 1/2 cup Gruyère cheese, shredded
- 1/3 cup sour cream
- 1 ½ tablespoons butter

Directions

Parboil the broccoli florets in a large pot of boiling water for about 3 minutes until crisp-tender. Drain.

Heat the oil in a frying pan over a moderately-high heat. Once hot, cook the scallions and green garlic for about 2 minutes or until tender and aromatic.

Add in the curry turmeric powder, salt, pepper and continue to sauté for 3 minutes more or until aromatic.

Add a splash of vegetable broth, partially cover, and continue to cook for 6 to 7 minutes. Add the reserved broccoli back to the pan.

In another pan, melt the butter over a moderately-high heat. Add in the sour cream and cheese and stir over low heat for 2 to 3 minutes.

Per serving: 159 Calories; 12.3g Fat; 7.2g Carbs; 5.7g Protein; 5.5g Fiber

43. Green Beans with Provençal Tapenade

(Ready in about 15 minutes | Servings 4)

Ingredients

- 1 tablespoon butter, melted
- 1/2 teaspoon fresh garlic, minced
- Salt and pepper, to taste
- 1 celery stalk, shredded
- 1 pound green beans
- 1/2 teaspoon red pepper flakes
- For Tapenade:
- 3 tablespoons extra-virgin olive oil
- 1/2 cup black olives
- 2 anchovy fillets
- 1 tablespoon fresh lime juice
- 1 ½ tablespoons capers

Directions

Steam the green beans approximately 4 minutes or until crisp-tender.

In a saucepan, melt the butter over a moderately-high heat. Sauté the celery and garlic for 4 to 5 minutes or until they are tender and fragrant. Add in the green beans and stir to combine.

Season with red pepper, salt, and black pepper.

To make the tapenade, pulse all ingredients until well combined.

Per serving: 183 Calories; 16.1g Fat; 4.4g Carbs; 3.2g Protein; 4g Fiber

VEGETABLES & SIDE DISHES

44. Cheese and Spinach Mini Frittatas

(Ready in about 30 minutes | Servings 6)

Ingredients

1 ½ cups Caciocavallo cheese, shredded
8 eggs
1 cup full-fat milk
2 tablespoons butter, melted
Sea salt and black pepper, to taste
1 cup spinach, chopped

Directions

Start by preheating your oven to 360 degrees F. Brush muffin cups with a non-stick spray.

Whisk the eggs and milk until pale and frothy; add in the butter, salt, pepper, and spinach. Fold in the cheese.

Bake in the preheated oven for 20 to 22 minutes or until a tester comes out dry and clean. Bon appétit!

Per serving: 252 Calories; 19.7g Fat; 3g Carbs; 16.1g Protein; 0.2g Fiber

45. Chanterelle Mushrooms with Enchilada Sauce

(Ready in about 15 minutes | Servings 4)

Ingredients

1 medium-sized avocado, pitted and mashed
1/4 cup enchilada sauce
2 tomatillos, chopped
2 tablespoons butter, room temperature
4 eggs
1/2 teaspoon ginger-garlic paste
Kosher salt and black pepper, to taste
1 yellow onion, chopped
1 pound Chanterelle mushroom, sliced

Directions

Melt the butter in a saucepan over a moderately-high flame. Cook the onion until tender and translucent.

Add in the ginger-garlic paste, mushrooms, salt, black pepper, and chopped tomatillos. Add in the eggs and scramble them well.

Serve with enchilada sauce and avocado. Enjoy!

Per serving: 290 Calories; 21.7g Fat; 6.5g Carbs; 10.6g Protein; 5.5g Fiber

46. Dijon Mushroom and Cauliflower Bake

(Ready in about 35 minutes | Servings 4)

Ingredients

1 teaspoon Dijon mustard
1 cup cream of mushroom soup
1/2 pound brown mushrooms, thinly sliced
4 eggs, lightly beaten
1 1/2 cup cream cheese
1 teaspoon Italian herb mix
2 tablespoons butter
1 pound cauliflower florets
1 cup Gruyère cheese

Directions

Melt the butter in a saucepan over medium-high heat. Now, cook the mushrooms until they release the liquid. Add in the cream of mushrooms soup, Italian herb mix, and cauliflower.

Continue to sauté until the cauliflower has softened. Spoon the cauliflower mixture into a buttered casserole dish.

In a mixing bowl, whisk the eggs, cheese, and Dijon mustard. Spoon the sauce over the top of your casserole.

Bake in the preheated oven at 365 degrees F for about 30 minutes or until the top is hot and bubbly. Bon appétit!

Per serving: 275 Calories; 21.3g Fat; 5.3g Carbs; 14g Protein; 3g Fiber

47. Italian Cauliflower and Mushroom Stew

(Ready in about 20 minutes | Servings 4)

Ingredients

1/3 cup cream of celery soup
1/3 cup double cream
10 ounces Oyster mushrooms, sliced
2 tablespoons Romano cheese, grated
2 garlic cloves, minced
1/2 stick butter, room temperature
1/4 cup mayonnaise, preferably homemade
1/2 head cauliflower, cut into small florets
Salt and pepper, to taste

Directions

In a saucepan, melt the butter over a moderate heat. Once hot, sauté the cauliflower and mushrooms until softened.

Add in the garlic and continue to sauté for a minute or so or until aromatic.

Stir in the cream of celery soup, double cream, salt, and pepper. Continue to cook, covered, for 10 to 12 minutes, until most of the liquid has evaporated.

Fold in the Romano cheese and stir to combine well. Serve with mayonnaise and enjoy!

Per serving: 300 Calories; 27.9g Fat; 8.6g Carbs; 5.2g Protein; 2.6g Fiber

48. Creamed Greek Salad

(Ready in about 15 minutes + chilling time | Servings 4)

Ingredients

1 cup Greek-style yogurt
8 green oak lettuce leaves, torn into pieces
1 tablespoon fresh lemon juice
1/2 teaspoon oregano
1/4 cup fresh scallions, thinly sliced
2 tablespoons green garlic, minced
6 radishes, sliced
1 teaspoon basil
Sea salt and ground black pepper, to taste
1 cucumber, sliced

Directions

Whisk the yogurt with the green garlic, lemon juice, basil, and oregano.

Toss the remaining ingredients in a mixing bowl. Dress the salad and toss to combine well. Serve well chilled.

Per serving: 318 Calories; 24.3g Fat; 4.1g Carbs; 15.4g Protein; 0.9g Fiber

VEGETABLES & SIDE DISHES

49. Roasted Asparagus with Pancetta

(Ready in about 20 minutes | Servings 4)

Ingredients

4 tablespoons pancetta, chopped
1 teaspoon shallot powder
1/4 teaspoon caraway seeds
Salt and freshly ground black pepper, to your liking
1/2 teaspoon dried rosemary
1 pound asparagus spears

Directions

Toss the asparagus spears with spices.

Bake in the preheated oven at 450 degrees F for about 15 minutes.

Top with the pancetta and continue to bake an additional 5 to 6 minutes. Enjoy!

Per serving: 48 Calories; 1.6g Fat; 4.4g Carbs; 5.5g Protein; 2.5g Fiber

50. Garden Vegetable Salad

(Ready in about 45 minutes | Servings 4)

Ingredients

1 red onion, sliced into wedges
1/4 cup olive oil
2 celery stalks, cut into sticks
2 bell peppers, deveined and sliced
1/2 teaspoon garlic, sliced
1/2 pound broccoli, cut into sticks
For the Spicy Yogurt Sauce:
2 tablespoons mayonnaise
Salt and pepper, to taste
1 poblano pepper, finely minced
1 tablespoon lemon juice
1 ½ cups Greek-Style yogurt

Directions

Toss the vegetables with olive oil and garlic. Arrange your vegetables on a parchment-lined baking sheet.

Roast in the preheated oven at 380 degrees F for about 35 minutes, rotating the pan once or twice.

Thoroughly combine all ingredients for the sauce. Bon appétit!

Per serving: 357 Calories; 35.8g Fat; 5.2g Carbs; 3.4g Protein; 2.5g Fiber

51. Artichoke, Olives and Mozzarella Bowl

(Ready in about 25 minutes | Servings 6)

Ingredients

2 ounces Kalamata olives, pitted and sliced
3 tablespoons capers, drained
1 chili pepper, sliced thin
4 ounces Mozzarella cheese, crumbled
2 tablespoons balsamic vinegar
3 artichoke hearts, defrosted
1 ½ teaspoons deli mustard
3/4 cup scallions, peeled and finely chopped
12/3 cup arugula
1/3 cup mustard greens
1/3 cup green cabbage
3 teaspoon fresh lemon juice
Sea salt and black pepper, to taste
2 tomatoes, sliced
2 tablespoons olive oil

Directions

Start by preheating your oven to 350 degrees F. Line a baking sheet with parchment paper or a silicone mat.

Brush the artickohe hearts with olive oil. Roast the artichoke hearts in the preheated oven at 360 degrees F for about 20 minutes. Season with salt and pepper to taste.

Meanwhile, toss the vegetables with capers, lemon juice, mustard and balsamic vinegar until well combined.

Serve the roasted artichokes on the top of your salad and garnish with olives and Mozzarella cheese.

Per serving: 146 Calories; 9.4g Fat; 6.1g Carbs; 5.8g Protein; 6g Fiber

52. Colorful Vegetable Fritters

(Ready in about 15 minutes | Servings 6)

Ingredients

1 small-sized celery stalk, shredded
2 tablespoons parsley, chopped
2 medium-sized zucchinis, shredded
Salt and black pepper, to taste
2 tablespoons olive oil
1 egg yolk
1 garlic clove, finely minced
Lemon wedges, to serve
2 carrots, shredded
1 white onion, finely chopped
1 cup cheddar cheese, grated

Directions

Start by preheating your oven to 360 degrees F. Line a baking sheet with parchment paper.

Now, press the shredded vegetables firmly to drain away the excess liquid. Then, thoroughly combine all ingredients, except for the lemon wedges, in a mixing bowl.

Shape the mixture into 12 patties and bake for 5 minutes per side.

Bon appétit!

Per serving: 153 Calories; 11.8g Fat; 6.6g Carbs; 6.4g Protein; 1.2g Fiber

53. Baby Bella Mushrooms with Broccoli

(Ready in about 20 minutes | Servings 4)

Ingredients

1/2 head broccoli, cut into small florets
1/3 cup whipping cream
10 ounces baby Bella mushrooms
2 tablespoons Parmesan cheese
1 teaspoon tarragon
1/2 teaspoon kosher salt, or more to taste
1 teaspoon garlic, minced
1/3 cup chicken broth
1/4 teaspoon crushed red pepper flakes
1/2 stick butter, room temperature
1/4 cup mayonnaise, preferably homemade

Directions

Melt the butter in a skillet that is preheated over a moderate flame. Now, add the broccoli and mushrooms and cook until the mushrooms are slightly shriveled.

Add the garlic and continue cooking until fragrant, stirring constantly.

Add the broth, whipping cream and seasonings; cover with the lid and reduce the heat to medium-low. Cook an additional 10 minutes, stirring occasionally, until most of the liquid has evaporated.

Stir the Parmesan cheese into the mushroom mixture until everything comes together.

Bon appétit!

Per serving: 235 Calories; 20.9g Fat; 5.5g Carbs; 4.8g Protein; 2.2g Fiber

54. Spicy Vegetable Risotto

(Ready in about 20 minutes | Servings 4)

Ingredients

1 red bell pepper, chopped
1 Aji Fantasy chili pepper, minced
1/2 stick butter
1/2 celery stalk, chopped
1/2 yellow onion, chopped
1 garlic clove, minced
Salt and ground black pepper, to taste
1 head broccoli, broken into florets

Directions

Blitz the broccoli in your food processor until it has reached a rice-like texture.

Now, melt the butter in a sauté pan over a moderate heat. Sweat yellow onion for 2 to 3 minutes; stir in the garlic and cook until slightly browned and fragrant.

After that, add the peppers and celery; cook an additional 4 minutes or until they're just tender. Add the broccoli "rice" and season with salt and pepper.

Cook for a further 5 minutes, stirring periodically.

Bon appétit!

Per serving: 126 Calories; 11.6g Fat; 5.4g Carbs; 1.3g Protein; 4g Fiber

POULTRY

55. Chicken Soup with Harvest Vegetables

(Ready in about 25 minutes | Servings 4)

Ingredients

2 chicken drumsticks, boneless and cut into small pieces
1 whole egg
1/2 cup turnip, chopped
1 carrot, chopped
Salt and pepper, to taste
1 tablespoon butter
1 teaspoon garlic, finely minced
1/2 parsnip, chopped
1 cup double cream
1/2 celery
4 cups chicken broth
1 cup full-fat milk

Directions

Melt the butter in a heavy-bottomed pot over medium-high heat; sauté the garlic until aromatic or about 1 minute. Add in the vegetables and continue to cook until they've softened.

Add in the chicken and cook until it is no longer pink for about 4 minutes. Season with salt and pepper.

Pour in the chicken broth, milk, and heavy cream and bring it to a boil.

Reduce the heat to. Partially cover and continue to simmer for 20 to 25 minutes longer. Afterwards, fold the beaten egg and stir until it is well incorporated.

Per serving: 342 Calories; 22.4g Fat; 6.3g Carbs; 25.2g Protein; 1.3g Fiber

56. Cheesy Chicken Wings and Broccoli

(Ready in about 50 minutes | Servings 4)

Ingredients

2 cups Colby cheese, shredded
1 pound broccoli, broken into florets
1 teaspoon Italian seasoning mix (such as Old Sub Sailor)
1 teaspoon garlic paste
1 carrot, sliced
1 cup scallions, chopped
3 tablespoons olive oil
1 pound chicken wings

Directions

Preheat your oven to 390 degrees F. Lightly grease a rimmed baking sheet.

Roast the wings until cooked through and skin is crispy, about 35 minutes. Add the broccoli, carrots, scallions, and garlic paste.

Season the chicken and broccoli with the Italian seasoning mix; drizzle them with olive oil.

Roast an additional 13 to 15 minutes. Scatter shredded cheese over the top.

Bon appétit!

Per serving: 450 Calories; 35.5g Fat; 6.6g Carbs; 25.1g Protein; 3.7g Fiber

57. Turkey Meatballs with Cheese

(Ready in about 20 minutes | Servings 4)

Ingredients

For the Meatballs:
1 egg
1/3 teaspoon black pepper
1/3 teaspoon Five-spice powder
1/3 cup cheddar cheese, freshly grated
3/4 pound ground turkey
For the Sauce:
3/4 cup erythritol
2 tablespoons Worcestershire sauce
1/2 cup tomato puree, sugar-free
1/2 teaspoon cayenne pepper
1/3 teaspoon guar gum
1 1/3 cups water
1/3 cup red wine vinegar

Directions

Thoroughly combine the ground turkey, the egg, cheese, black pepper and Five-spice powder in a mixing bowl. Now, form the mixture into balls (about 28 meatballs).

Preheat a non-stick skillet over a medium heat. Brown your meatballs on all sides for 3 to 4 minutes; set them aside.

Next, add the water, vinegar, Worcestershire sauce, tomato puree, cayenne pepper and erythritol to the skillet. Whisk until well mixed.

After that, gradually add the guar gum. Whisk until the sauce has thickened. Decrease the temperature and bring the sauce to a simmer; make sure to stir periodically.

Add the meatballs to the sauce; continue to simmer for 8 to 12 minutes on low or until your meatballs are thoroughly cooked.

Bon appétit!

Per serving: 244 Calories; 13.7g Fat; 5g Carbs; 27.6g Protein; 0.7g Fiber

58. Cheese Pate with Turkey Ham

(Ready in about 10 minutes | Servings 6)

Ingredients

2 tablespoons sunflower seeds
4 ounces turkey ham, chopped
4 ounces mozzarella cheese, crumbled
2 tablespoons fresh parsley, roughly chopped
2 tablespoons flaxseed meal

Directions

Thoroughly combine the ingredients, except for the sunflower seeds, in your food processor.

Spoon the mixture into a serving bowl and scatter the sunflower seeds over the top.

Per serving: 212 Calories; 18.8g Fat; 2g Carbs; 10.6g Protein; 1.6g Fiber

59. Chicken with Olives and Herbs

(Ready in about 40 minutes | Servings 8)

Ingredients

1 Italian pepper, deveined and thinly sliced
1 tablespoon Old Sub Sailor
1 ½ cups vegetable broth
2 tablespoons olive oil
2 garlic cloves, pressed
10 black olives, pitted
Salt, to taste
4 chicken breasts, skinless and boneless

Directions

Rub the chicken with the garlic and Old Sub Sailor; salt to taste. Heat the oil in a frying pan over a moderately high heat.

Sear the chicken until it is browned on all sides, about 5 minutes.

Add in the pepper, olives, and vegetable broth and bring it to boil. Reduce the heat simmer and continue to cook, partially covered, for 30 to 35 minutes.

Per serving: 306 Calories; 17.8g Fat; 3.1g Carbs; 31.7g Protein; 0.2g Fiber

60. Chorizo Sausage in Tomato Sauce

(Ready in about 20 minutes | Servings 4)

Ingredients

1 ½ cups Asiago cheese, grated
2 tablespoons fresh coriander, roughly chopped
1 teaspoon garlic paste
1 teaspoon oregano
4 scallion stalks, chopped
1 teaspoon basil
1 cup tomato puree
1 tablespoon dry sherry
16 ounces smoked turkey chorizo
1 tablespoon extra-virgin olive oil
Sea salt and ground black pepper, to taste

Directions

Heat the oil in a frying pan over moderately high heat. Now, brown the turkey chorizo, crumbling with a fork for about 5 minutes.

Add in the other ingredients, except for cheese; continue to cook for 10 minutes more or until cooked through.

Top with the Asiago cheese and continue to cook until the cheese has melted. Enjoy!

Per serving: 330 Calories; 17.2g Fat; 4.5g Carbs; 34.4g Protein; 1.6g Fiber

61. Dijon Chicken and Egg Salad

(Ready in about 20 minutes | Servings 4)

Ingredients

2 cups boneless rotisserie chicken, shredded
3 hard-boiled eggs, cut into quarters
2 avocados, pitted, peeled and diced
1 tablespoon fresh oregano, chopped
1/2 cup mayonnaise
Salt and black pepper, to taste
1 medium shallot, thinly sliced
1 tablespoon Dijon mustard

Directions

Toss the chicken with the avocado, shallots, and oregano.

Add in the mayonnaise, mustard, salt and black pepper; stir to combine.

Serve garnished with the hard-boiled eggs and enjoy!

Per serving: 353 Calories; 23.5g Fat; 5.8g Carbs; 27.8g Protein; 2.7g Fiber

62. Ground Duck Casserole

(Ready in about 45 minutes | Servings 4)

Ingredients

1 pound ground duck meat
1/2 teaspoon basil, dried
1/3 cup whipping cream
1/4 teaspoon ground black pepper
1/2 teaspoon celery seeds
1/2 teaspoon kosher salt
8 eggs
1/2 pound eggplant, peeled and sliced
1 ½ tablespoons butter, melted
1 ½ cups almond flour

Directions

Preheat your oven to 350 degrees F

Mix the almond flour with kosher salt. Fold in one egg and the melted butter; mix to combine well.

Now, press the crust into the bottom of a lightly-greased baking dish.

Then, heat up a skillet and brown ground duck meat for 2 to 3 minutes, stirring continuously.

In a mixing bowl, combine the remaining eggs with black pepper, celery seeds, basil, and whipping cream.

Stir in the browned meat; stir until everything is thoroughly combined. Pour the mixture into the prepared crust. Add the eggplant slices.

Bake your quiche for 37 to 42 minutes. Transfer to a wire rack to cool before slicing. Bon appétit!

Per serving: 562 Calories; 49.5g Fat; 6.7g Carbs; 22.5g Protein; 1.8g Fiber

63. Easy Chicken Parmigiana

(Ready in about 30 minutes | Servings 4)

Ingredients

1/3 cup Parmigiano-Reggiano, freshly grated
2 teaspoons vegetable oil
1 teaspoon fresh or dried dill, chopped
3 bell peppers, quartered lengthwise
1/3 cup crushed pork rinds
1 garlic clove, minced
1 teaspoon salt
1/4 teaspoon ground black pepper, or more to taste
1 pound chicken breasts, butterflied

Directions

Begin by preheating your oven to 420 degrees F. Cover the sides and bottom of a baking pan with a sheet of foil.

Place the butterflied chicken breast on the baking pan. Season with salt and pepper.

Now, combine the dill, pork rinds, Parmigiano-Reggiano, vegetable oil and garlic clove. Dip each chicken breast into this mixture.

Arrange the bell peppers around the prepared chicken breasts. Bake for 20 minutes or until thr juices run clear. Enjoy!

Per serving: 367 Calories; 16.9g Fat; 6g Carbs; 43g Protein; 0.7g Fiber

64. Chicken Roulade with Prosciutto

(Ready in about 35 minutes | Servings 2)

Ingredients

1 teaspoon cayenne pepper
1 tablespoon fresh coriander, chopped
Salt and ground black pepper, to taste pepper
4 slices of prosciutto
1 pound chicken fillet
1/2 cup Ricotta cheese

Directions

Season the chicken fillet with salt and pepper. Spread the Ricotta cheese over the chicken fillet; sprinkle with the fresh coriander.

Roll up and cut into 4 pieces. Wrap each piece with one slice of prosciutto; secure with a kitchen twine.

Place the wrapped chicken in a parchment-lined baking pan. Now, bake in the preheated oven at 385 degrees F for about 30 minutes. Enjoy!

Per serving: 499 Calories; 18.9g Fat; 5.7g Carbs; 41.6g Protein; 0.6g Fiber

65. Prosciutto and Cheese-Wrapped Chicken

(Ready in about 35 minutes | Servings 2)

Ingredients

4 slices of prosciutto
1/2 cup Cottage cheese
Salt and ground black pepper, to taste pepper
1 teaspoon smoked paprika
1 tablespoon fresh cilantro, chopped
1 chicken breasts, boneless, skinless and flattened

Directions

Start by preheating your oven to 390 degrees F. Line a baking pan with parchment paper.

Season the chicken breasts with smoked paprika, salt and pepper. Spread the Cottage cheese over the chicken breasts; scatter fresh cilantro over the top.

Roll up and cut into 4 pieces. Now, wrap each piece with one slice of prosciutto; secure with a toothpick.

Place the wrapped chicken in the baking pan; bake for 25 to 35 minutes.

Enjoy!

Per serving: 499 Calories; 18.9g Fat; 5.7g Carbs; 41.6g Protein; 1.6g Fiber

66. Turkey Wings with Herbs and Marinara Sauce

(Ready in about 1 hour | Servings 2)

Ingredients

1 pound turkey wings
1 tablespoon Italian herb mix
2 tablespoons balsamic vinegar
1 teaspoon garlic, minced
1/2 cup marinara sauce
2 tablespoons sesame oil
Salt and black pepper, to taste

Directions

Place the turkey wings, Italian herb mix, balsamic vinegar, and garlic in a ceramic dish. Cover and let it marinate for 2 to 3 hours in your refrigerator. Rub the sesame oil over turkey wings.

Grill the turkey wings on the preheated grill for about 1 hour, basting with the reserved marinade. Sprinkle with salt and black pepper to taste.

Serve with marinara sauce. Bon appétit!

Per serving: 488 Calories; 24.5g Fat; 2.1g Carbs; 33.6g Protein; 0.9g Fiber

67. Chicken Legs with Sherry Sauce

(Ready in about 50 minutes | Servings 6)

Ingredients

1 ½ pounds chicken legs, skinless
1/2 teaspoon salt
1/2 cup dry sherry
1 cup heavy cream
1 tablespoon fresh basil, chopped
1 rosemary sprig, chopped
2 thyme sprigs, chopped
1 tablespoon fresh oregano, chopped
1/2 teaspoon mixed peppercorns, freshly crushed
1/2 cup scallions, chopped
2 garlic cloves, minced
2 tablespoons ghee

Directions

Preheat your oven to 400 degrees F.

Melt the ghee in a pan that is preheated over a moderate flame; now, brown the chicken legs for 6 to 8 minutes.

After that, stir in the scallions, garlic, sherry, and herbs. Transfer to a lightly greased casserole dish and cover it.

Bake for 35 minutes or until a meat thermometer registers 165 degrees F; reserve.

Mix the cooking juices with the heavy cream, salt and crushed peppercorns; simmer for a couple of minutes or until it is thickened and cooked through.

Bon appétit!

Per serving: 333 Calories; 20.2g Fat; 2g Carbs; 33.5g Protein; 0.6g Fiber

68. Chicken Sausage with Cream and Spaghetti Squash

(Ready in about 20 minutes | Servings 4)

Ingredients

- 8 ounces spaghetti squash
- 2/3 cup double cream
- Sea salt and ground black pepper, to taste
- 2 teaspoons butter, room temperature
- 1 ¼ cups cream of onion soup
- 1 Spanish pepper, deveined and finely minced
- 1 garlic clove, pressed
- 1/2 cup green onions, finely chopped
- 1 ½ pounds cheese & bacon chicken sausages, sliced

Directions

Melt the butter in a saucepan over a moderate flame. Then, sear the sausages until no longer pink about 9 minutes. Reserve.

In the same saucepan, cook the green onions, pepper and garlic until they've softened.

Add in the spaghetti squash, salt, black pepper and cream of onion soup; bring to a boil.

Reduce the heat to medium-low and fold in the cream; let it simmer until the sauce has reduced slightly or about 7 minutes. Add in the reserved sausage and gently stir to combine. Bon appétit!

Per serving: 591 Calories; 32g Fat; 4.8g Carbs; 32g Protein; 1.5g Fiber

69. Chicken with Tomato Sauce

(Ready in about 30 minutes | Servings 6)

Ingredients

- 1 tomato, pureed
- 1/4 cup coconut aminos
- Sea salt and ground black pepper, to taste
- 1 leek, chopped
- 2 tablespoons coriander
- 2 garlic cloves, minced
- 1 teaspoon cayenne pepper
- 1 bell pepper, deveined and chopped
- 1 teaspoon dry thyme
- 1 ½ pounds chicken breasts

Directions

Rub each chicken breasts with the garlic, cayenne pepper, thyme, salt and black pepper. Cook the chicken in a saucepan over medium-high heat.

Sear for about 5 minutes until golden brown on all sides.

Fold in the tomato puree and coconut aminos and bring it to a boil. Add in the pepper, leek, and coriander.

Reduce the heat to simmer. Continue to cook, partially covered, for about 20 minutes. Enjoy!

Per serving: 239 Calories; 8.6g Fat; 5.5g Carbs; 34.3g Protein; 1g Fiber

70. Cheesy Ground Chicken Skillet

(Ready in about 15 minutes | Servings 4)

Ingredients

- 1/2 cup Asiago cheese, shredded
- 1 pound chicken, ground
- 1 teaspoon garlic, minced
- 1 teaspoon Italian seasonings
- 4 bell peppers, deveined and chopped
- 1/3 cup dry sherry
- 1 cup shallots, chopped
- 1 chili pepper, deveined and chopped
- Salt and black pepper, to taste
- 1 tablespoon olive oil

Directions

Heat the oil in a pan that is preheated over a moderate flame. Now, sauté the garlic and shallots until they are aromatic.

Now, stir in the peppers and ground chicken; cook until the chicken is no longer pink.

Add the sherry, Italian seasonings, salt and pepper. Cook an additional 5 minutes or until everything is thoroughly heated.

Scatter the Asiago cheese over the top and remove from the heat. Bon appétit!

Per serving: 301 Calories; 11.4g Fat; 5.2g Carbs; 37.9g Protein; 1.3g Fiber

71. Mediterranean-Style Chicken with Halloumi Cheese

(Ready in about 35 minutes | Servings 4)

Ingredients

- 1 cup Halloumi cheese, cubed
- 1/4 teaspoon flaky sea salt
- 1 ½ tablespoons butter
- 1 hard-boiled egg yolk
- 1/2 cup extra-virgin olive oil
- 6 black olives, pitted and halved
- 1 tablespoon fresh coriander, chopped
- 1 tablespoon balsamic vinegar
- 1 tablespoon garlic, finely minced
- Sea salt and pepper, to season
- 1 tablespoon fresh lime juice
- 4 chicken wings

Directions

In a saucepan, melt the butter until sizzling. Sear the chicken wings for 5 minutes per side. Season with salt and pepper to taste.

Place the chicken wings on a parchment-lined baking pan

Mix the egg yolk, garlic, lime juice, balsamic vinegar, olive oil, and salt in your blender until creamy, uniform and smooth.

Spread the Aioli over the fried chicken. Now, scatter the coriander and black olives on top of the chicken wings.

Bake in the preheated oven at 380 degrees F for 20 to 25 minutes. Top with the cheese and bake an additional 5 minutes until hot and bubbly. Enjoy!

Per serving: 562 Calories; 43.8g Fat; 2.1g Carbs; 40.8g Protein; 0.4g Fiber

72. Chicken Meatballs with Parmesan and Tomato Sauce

(Ready in about 20 minutes | Servings 6)

Ingredients

For the Meatballs:
3/4 cup Parmesan cheese, grated
1 tablespoon sage leaves, chopped
1/2 teaspoon cayenne pepper
1 teaspoon porcini powder
2 garlic cloves, finely minced
1/3 teaspoon dried basil
1 teaspoon shallot powder
2 eggs, lightly beaten
Salt and ground black pepper, to your liking
1 ¼ pounds chicken, ground
For the sauce:
1 onion, peeled and finely chopped
1 cup chicken consommé
2 ½ tablespoons lard, room temperature
2 tomatoes, pureed

Directions

In a mixing bowl, combine all ingredients for the meatballs. Roll the mixture into bite-sized balls.

Melt 1 tablespoon of lard in a skillet over a moderately high heat. Sear the meatballs for about 3 minutes or until they are thoroughly cooked; reserve.

Melt the remaining lard and cook the onions until tender and translucent. Add in pureed tomatoes and chicken consommé and continue to cook for 4 minutes longer.

Add in the reserved meatballs, turn the heat to simmer and continue to cook for 6 to 7 minutes. Enjoy!

Per serving: 252 Calories; 9.7g Fat; 5.3g Carbs; 34.2g Protein; 1.4g Fiber

73. Grilled Ranch Kabobs

(Ready in about 30 minutes | Servings 6)

Ingredients

2 tablespoons olive oil, room temperature
3 Spanish peppers, sliced
1 onion, cut into wedges
1 tablespoon dry ranch seasoning
1 ½ pounds turkey breast, cubed
2 zucchinis, cut into thick slices

Directions

Thread the turkey pieces and vegetables onto bamboo skewers. Sprinkle the skewers with the dry ranch seasoning and olive oil.

Grill your kebabs for about 10 minutes, turning them periodically to ensure even cooking. Serve warm.

Per serving: 263 Calories; 13.8g Fat; 6.7g Carbs; 25.8g Protein; 1.2g Fiber

74. Chorizo and Bok Choy Casserole

(Ready in about 50 minutes | Servings 4)

Ingredients

1 pound Bok choy, tough stem ends trimmed
6 ounces Gruyère cheese, preferably freshly grated
1 yellow onion, chopped
1 tablespoon lard, room temperature
1 cup cream of mushroom soup
4 mild turkey Chorizo, sliced
1/2 cup full-fat milk
Coarse salt and ground black pepper, to taste

Directions

Melt the lard in a non-stick skillet over a moderate flame; cook the Chorizo sausage for about 5 minutes, stirring occasionally to ensure even cooking; reserve.

Add in the onion, salt, pepper, Bok choy, and cream of mushroom soup. Continue to cook for 4 minutes longer or until the vegetables have softened.

Spoon the mixture into a lightly oiled casserole dish. Top with the reserved Chorizo.

In a mixing bowl, thoroughly combine the milk and cheese. Pour the cheese mixture over the sausage.

Cover with foil and bake at 365 degrees F for about 35 minutes. Bon appétit!

Per serving: 189 Calories; 12g Fat; 2.6g Carbs; 9.4g Protein; 1g Fiber

75. Rutabaga, Taro and Chicken Soup

(Ready in about 45 minutes | Servings 4)

Ingredients

1/2 cup rutabaga, cubed
1/2 cup taro leaves, roughly chopped
2 celery stalks
1/2 teaspoon ginger-garlic paste
Salt and black pepper, to taste
1 cup chicken bone broth
1 tablespoon fresh coriander, chopped
2 carrots, peeled
3 cups water
1 teaspoon paprika
1/2 cup onions, chopped
1 pound whole chicken, boneless and chopped into small chunks

Directions

Place all ingredients in a heavy-bottomed pot. Bring to a boil over the highest heat.

Turn the heat to simmer. Continue to cook, partially covered, an additional 40 minutes. Enjoy!

Per serving: 256 Calories; 12.9g Fat; 3.2g Carbs; 35.1g Protein; 2.2g Fiber

76. Chicken and Avocado Salad

(Ready in about 20 minutes | Servings 4)

Ingredients

1 large-sized avocado, pitted and sliced
1 tablespoon fresh lemon juice
2 chicken breasts
1/2 teaspoon celery seeds
2 egg yolks
1 tablespoon coconut aminos
1/3 cup olive oil
Sea salt and crushed red pepper flakes

Directions

Grill the chicken breasts for about 4 minutes per side. Season with salt and pepper, to taste.

Slice the grilled chicken into bite-sized strips.

To make the dressing, whisk the egg yolks, lemon juice, celery seeds, olive oil and coconut aminos in a measuring cup.

Dress the salad and garnish with fresh avocado. Bon appétit!

Per serving: 408 Calories; 34.2g Fat; 4.8g Carbs; 22.7g Protein; 3.1g Fiber

77. Turkey Bacon and Cheese Fat Bombs

(Ready in about 5 minutes | Servings 4)

Ingredients

4 ounces Neufchatel cheese
1 tablespoon butter, cold
2 tablespoons scallions, finely chopped
1 teaspoon Mexican oregano
1 jalapeno pepper, deveined and minced
4 ounces turkey bacon, chopped

Directions

Thoroughly combine all ingredients in a mixing bowl.

Roll the mixture into 8 balls. Serve well chilled.

Per serving: 195 Calories; 16.7g Fat; 2.2g Carbs; 8.8g Protein; 0.3g Fiber

78. Chicken, Cauliflower and Cheese Bowl

(Ready in about 20 minutes | Servings 2)

Ingredients

2 chicken wings
1/2 head of cauliflower
1/2 cup cheddar cheese, shredded
2 teaspoons butter
2 tablespoons dry sherry
1/2 cup mayonnaise
1 shallot, finely minced
1 teaspoon hot paprika
2 tablespoons fresh basil, snipped
1 teaspoon mustard
Sea salt and ground black pepper, to taste

Directions

Boil the cauliflower in a pot of salted water until it has softened; cut into small florets and place in a salad bowl.

Melt the butter in a saucepan over medium-high heat. Cook the chicken for about 8 minutes or until the skin is crisp and browned. Season with hot paprika salt, and black pepper.

Whisk the mayonnaise, mustard, dry sherry, and shallot and dress your salad. Top with cheddar cheese and fresh basil. Enjoy!

Per serving: 444 Calories; 36g Fat; 5.7g Carbs; 20.6g Protein; 4.3g Fiber

79. Romano-Turkey Meatballs with Basil Chutney

(Ready in about 30 minutes | Servings 6)

Ingredients

2 tablespoons sesame oil
For the Meatballs:
1 ½ pounds ground turkey
1 teaspoon garlic, minced
1/2 teaspoon shallot powder
3 tablespoons almond meal
2 small-sized eggs, lightly beaten
1/2 cup Romano cheese, grated
1/2 teaspoon sea salt
1/4 teaspoon ground black pepper, or more to taste
1/4 teaspoon dried thyme
1/2 teaspoon mustard seeds
For the Basil Chutney:
1/4 cup fresh parsley
2 tablespoons olive oil
1/2 cup cilantro leaves
1 tablespoon habanero chili pepper, deveined and minced
1 teaspoon fresh ginger root, grated
2 tablespoons water
2 tablespoons fresh lime juice
1/4 cup fresh basil leaves

Directions

In a mixing bowl, combine all ingredients for the meatballs. Roll the mixture into meatballs and reserve.

Heat the sesame oil in a frying pan over a moderate flame. Sear the meatballs for about 8 minutes until browned on all sides.

Make the chutney by mixing all the ingredients in your blender or food processor. Serve the warm meatballs with the basil chutney on the side.

Per serving: 390 Calories; 27.2g Fat; 1.8g Carbs; 37.4g Protein; 0.3g Fiber

80. Dijon Turkey with Gravy

(Ready in about 6 hours | Servings 6)

Ingredients

1 tablespoon Dijon mustard
4 garlic cloves, sliced
Salt and pepper, to taste
1 teaspoon dried marjoram
1 tablespoon butter, room temperature
1 large onion, chopped
1/2 teaspoon cayenne pepper
2 pounds turkey wings
For the Gravy:
1/2 stick butter
3/4 teaspoon guar gum
1 cup double cream
Salt and black pepper, to taste

Directions

Rub the turkey wings with the Dijon mustard and 1 tablespoon of butter. Preheat a grill pan over medium-high heat.

Sear the turkey wings for 10 minutes on all sides.

Transfer the turkey to your Crock pot; add in the garlic, onion, salt, pepper, marjoram, and cayenne pepper. Cover and cook on low setting for 6 hours.

Melt 1/2 stick of the butter in a frying pan. Add in the cream and whisk until cooked through.

Next, stir in the guar gum, salt, and black pepper along with cooking juices. Let it cook until the sauce has reduced by half. Enjoy!

Per serving: 280 Calories; 22.2g Fat; 4.3g Carbs; 15.8g Protein; 0.8g Fiber

81. Turkey Soup with Cauliflower and Sour Cream

(Ready in about 35 minutes | Servings 4)

Ingredients

1/2 head cauliflower, broken into florets
4 dollops of sour cream
1 parsnip, chopped
4 ½ cups vegetable broth
Salt and ground black pepper, to your liking
1/2 teaspoon hot paprika
1 rosemary sprig
1 large onion, chopped
2 garlic cloves, chopped
1 celery, chopped
2 bay leaves
2 tablespoons olive oil
1 pound turkey drumettes

Directions

Heat the oil in a heavy-bottomed pot over a moderate flame. Then, sauté the onion, garlic, celery and parsnip until they've softened.

Pour in the broth and bring to a rolling boil.

Add in the cauliflower, turkey drumettes, rosemary, bay leaves, salt, black pepper and hot paprika.

Partially cover and let it simmer approximately 30 minutes. Fold in the sour cream and stir to combine well. Serve hot.

Per serving: 274 Calories; 14.4g Fat; 5.6g Carbs; 26.7g Protein; 3g Fiber

82. Chicken Sausage with Spanish Peppers

(Ready in about 15 minutes | Servings 4)

Ingredients

2 Spanish peppers, deveined and chopped
1 cup pureed tomatoes
2 teaspoons balsamic vinegar
2 tablespoons fresh coriander, minced
1 chili pepper, minced
1 cup shallots, diced
2 teaspoons lard, room temperature
1/4 cup dry white wine
1 teaspoon garlic, minced
4 chicken sausages, sliced

Directions

In a frying pan, warm the lard over moderately high flame.

Then, sear the sausage until well browned on all sides; add in the remaining ingredients and stir to combine.

Allow it to simmer over low heat for 10 minutes or until thickened slightly. Enjoy!

Per serving: 156 Calories; 4.2g Fat; 4.1g Carbs; 16.2g Protein; 2.1g Fiber

83. Tangy Turkey Drumsticks with Herbs

(Ready in about 1 hour | Servings 2)

Ingredients

2 turkey drumsticks
1 teaspoon granulated garlic
1 teaspoon dried marjoram
1 teaspoon dried basil
2 thyme sprigs, chopped
2 rosemary sprigs, chopped
2 tablespoons olive oil
2 tablespoons apple cider vinegar
Salt and black pepper, to taste

Directions

To make the marinade, thoroughly combine the apple cider vinegar, thyme, rosemary, marjoram, basil, granulated garlic, and olive oil in a mixing bowl.

Now, marinate the turkey at least 3 hours in the refrigerator.

Cook the turkey drumsticks on a preheated grill for 45 minutes to 1 hour or until a meat thermometer has reached the temperature of 180 degrees F. Season with salt and pepper to taste.

Bon appétit!

Per serving: 488 Calories; 24.5g Fat; 2.1g Carbs; 33.6g Protein; 0.3g Fiber

84. Turkey Drumsticks with Cottage Cheese Sauce

(Ready in about 1 hour 40 minutes | Servings 4)

Ingredients

1 ½ tablespoons sesame oil
1 tablespoon poultry seasoning
2 turkey drumsticks
For the Sauce:
1 teaspoon fresh lemon juice
1/3 teaspoon sea salt
1 ounce full-fat sour cream
1 small-sized avocado, pitted and mashed
2 tablespoons fresh parsley, finely chopped
1 ounce Cottage cheese

Directions

Pat the turkey drumsticks dry and sprinkle them with the poultry seasoning. Brush a baking pan with the sesame oil.

Place the turkey drumsticks on the baking pan.

Roast in the preheated oven at 350 degrees F for about 1 hour 30 minutes, rotating the pan halfway through the cooking time.

In the meantime, make the sauce by whisking all the sauce ingredients. Serve the turkey drumstick with the sauce and enjoy!

Per serving: 362 Calories; 22.3g Fat; 5.6g Carbs; 34.9g Protein; 3.3g Fiber

85. Chinese Cabbage with Turkey and Bacon

(Ready in about 45 minutes | Servings 4)

Ingredients

1 pound Chinese cabbage, finely chopped
2 ripe tomatoes, chopped
1 teaspoon Five-spice powder
Coarse salt and ground black pepper, to taste
1 tablespoon sesame oil
1/2 cup onions, chopped
1 teaspoon ginger-garlic paste
1 pound turkey, ground
2 slices smoked bacon, chopped

Directions

Heat the oil in a wok over a moderate flame. Cook the onions until tender and translucent.

Now, add in the remaining ingredients and bring to a boil. Reduce the temperature to medium-low and partially cover.

Reduce the heat to medium-low and cook an additional 30 minutes, crumbling the turkey and bacon with a fork. Enjoy!

Per serving: 293 Calories; 17.5g Fat; 9.1g Carbs; 26.2g Protein; 2.6g Fiber

86. Chicken Drumettes with Herb Tomato Sauce

(Ready in about 30 minutes | Servings 4)

Ingredients

- 1 cup chicken bone broth
- 2 cloves garlic, minced
- 1/2 teaspoon fennel seeds
- 1 tablespoon coconut aminos
- 1 teaspoon dried marjoram
- 2 thyme sprigs
- Salt and pepper, to taste
- 2 tablespoons lard, room temperature
- 1/2 cup leeks, chopped
- 1 celery rib, sliced
- 2 tomatoes, crushed
- 4 chicken drumettes

Directions

Melt the lard in a frying pan over a moderate heat. Sprinkle the chicken with salt and pepper to taste.

Then, fry the chicken until no longer pink or about 8 minutes; set aside.

In the same frying pan, cook the leeks, celery rib, and garlic for about 5 minutes, stirring continuously.

Reduce the heat to medium-low; add the remaining ingredients along with the reserved chicken drumettes. Let it simmer for about 20 minutes. Serve warm.

Per serving: 165 Calories; 9.8g Fat; 4.7g Carbs; 12.4g Protein; 1.3g Fiber

87. Spicy and Hearty Chicken Stew

(Ready in about 1 hour | Servings 6)

Ingredients

- 2 tablespoons butter, room temperature
- 1 bell pepper, chopped
- 4 cups vegetable broth
- 1 teaspoon garlic, sliced
- 1 teaspoon dried basil
- 1 celery, chopped
- 1/2 teaspoon smoked paprika
- 1 onion, finely chopped
- 1 chile pepper, deveined and minced
- 1 cup tomato puree
- 1/2 pound carrots, chopped
- 1 pound chicken thighs
- Kosher salt and ground black pepper, to taste

Directions

Melt the butter in a stockpot over medium-high flame. Sweat the onion and garlic until just tender and fragrant.

Reduce the heat to medium-low. Stir in the broth, chicken thighs, and basil; bring to a rolling boil.

Add in the remaining ingredients. Partially cover and let it simmer for 45 to 50 minutes. Shred the meat, discarding the bones; add the chicken back to the pot. Serve hot and enjoy!

Per serving: 280 Calories; 14.7g Fat; 2.5g Carbs; 25.6g Protein; 2.5g Fiber

88. Rich Grandma's Turkey Chowder

(Ready in about 35 minutes | Servings 4)

Ingredients

- 1/2 pound leftover roast turkey, shredded and skin removed
- 1 teaspoon Mediterranean spice mix
- 1/2 cup double cream
- 1 egg, lightly beaten
- 2 cloves garlic, roughly chopped
- 2 tablespoons dry sherry
- 3 cups chicken bone broth
- 1 ½ cups milk
- 2 tablespoons yellow onions, chopped
- 2 tablespoons olive oil

Directions

Heat the olive oil in a heavy-bottomed pot over a moderate flame. Sauté the onion and garlic until they've softened.

Stir in the leftover roast turkey, Mediterranean spice mix, and chicken bone broth; bring to a rapid boil. Partially cover and continue to cook for 20 to 25 minutes.

Turn the heat to simmer. Pour in the milk and double cream and continue to cook until it has reduced slightly.

Fold in the egg and dry sherry; continue to simmer, stirring frequently, for a further 2 minutes. Bon appétit!

Per serving: 350 Calories; 25.8g Fat; 5.5g Carbs; 20g Protein; 0.1g Fiber

89. Smoked Paprika Chicken Stew

(Ready in about 1 hour | Servings 6)

Ingredients

- 1 pound chicken drumsticks
- 1/2 teaspoon ground black pepper
- 1/2 teaspoon smoked paprika
- 2 ripe tomatoes, chopped
- 1/2 pound carrots, chopped
- 1 bell pepper, chopped
- 1 poblano pepper, chopped
- 1 sprig rosemary
- 1 teaspoon dried marjoram
- 1 teaspoon salt
- 2 medium-sized shallots, finely chopped
- 2 garlic cloves, sliced
- 1 quart chicken broth
- 1 celery, chopped
- 2 tablespoons tallow, room temperature

Directions

Melt the tallow in a large heavy pot that is preheated over a moderate flame. Sweat the shallots and garlic until aromatic and just tender.

Now, turn the heat to medium-high. Stir in the chicken broth, rosemary, marjoram, and chicken drumsticks; bring to a boil.

Add the remaining ingredients and reduce the heat to medium-low. Simmer, covered, for 50 minutes.

Discard the bones and chop the chicken into small chunks. Bon appétit!

Per serving: 239 Calories; 9.7g Fat; 6.5g Carbs; 25.6g Protein; 2.3g Fiber

90. Sauvignon Chicken Breasts with Brussels Sprouts

(Ready in about 20 minutes | Servings 4)

Ingredients

- 3/4 pound chicken breasts, chopped into bite-sized pieces
- 2 tablespoons Sauvignon wine
- 1 ½ pounds Brussels sprouts, trimmed and cut into halves
- 2 tablespoons fresh chives, chopped
- 1/2 cup white onions, chopped
- 1/2 teaspoon chipotle chile powder
- 1 cup bone broth, low-sodium
- 1/2 teaspoon whole black peppercorns
- 1/4 teaspoon seasoned salt
- 2 cloves garlic, minced
- 2 tablespoons sesame oil

Directions

Heat 1 tablespoon of the oil in a pan over a moderate heat. Now, sauté the Brussels sprouts for 2 to 4 minutes or until golden brown. Season with salt; reserve.

Heat the remaining 1 tablespoon of oil in the same pan that is preheated over moderately high heat. Add the garlic and chicken; cook about 3 minutes.

Add the onions, broth, wine, chipotle chile powder, and black peppercorns. Bring to a boil and reduce the heat to a simmer. Simmer for 4 minutes more.

Add the reserved Brussels sprouts to the pan and garnish with fresh chopped chives. Enjoy!

Per serving: 273 Calories; 15.4g Fat; 5.2g Carbs; 23g Protein; 6g Fiber

91. Turkey Rouladen with Wine and Herbs

(Ready in about 30 minutes | Servings 5)

Ingredients

- 10 strips prosciutto
- 1 teaspoon garlic, finely minced
- 1 tablespoon Dijon mustard
- 1 sprig rosemary, finely chopped
- 2 tablespoons dry white wine
- 1 ½ tablespoons butter, room temperature
- 1/2 teaspoon chili powder
- 1 teaspoon marjoram
- 2 pounds turkey fillet, marinated and cut into 10 pieces
- Sea salt and freshly ground black pepper, to your liking

Directions

Start by preheating your oven to 430 degrees F.

Pat the turkey dry and cook in hot butter for about 3 minutes per side. Add in the mustard, chili powder, marjoram, rosemary, wine, and garlic.

Continue to cook for 2 minutes more. Wrap each turkey piece into one prosciutto strip and secure with toothpicks.

Roast in the preheated oven for about 30 minutes. Bon appétit!

Per serving: 286 Calories; 9.7g Fat; 6.9g Carbs; 39.9g Protein; 0.3g Fiber

92. Chicken Wigs with Avocado-Mayo Sauce

(Ready in about 20 minutes | Servings 4)

Ingredients

- 1/3 cup almond meal
- 2 tablespoons olive oil
- 1 teaspoon onion powder
- 1/3 teaspoon mustard seeds
- 1 teaspoon hot paprika
- 2 eggs
- Sea salt and pepper, to your liking
- 8 chicken wings, boneless, cut into bite-size chunks
- For the Sauce:
- 1/2 medium avocado
- 1/2 cup mayonnaise
- 1 teaspoon green garlic, minced
- 1/2 teaspoon sea salt

Directions

Pat dry the chicken wings with a paper towel.

Thoroughly combine the almond meal, salt, pepper, onion powder, paprika, and mustard seeds.

Whisk the eggs in a separate dish. Dredge the chicken chunks into the whisked eggs, then in the almond meal mixture.

In a frying pan, heat the oil over a moderate heat; once hot, fry the chicken for about 10 minutes, stirring continuously to ensure even cooking.

Make the sauce by whisking all of the sauce ingredients. Serve the warm chicken with the sauce on the side.

Per serving: 370 Calories; 25g Fat; 4.1g Carbs; 31.4g Protein; 2.6g Fiber

93. Turkey and Baby Bok Choy Soup

(Ready in about 40 minutes | Servings 8)

Ingredients

- 2 pounds turkey carcass
- 1 celery rib, chopped
- 6 cups turkey stock
- 2 carrots, sliced
- 1 tablespoon olive oil
- 1/2 cup leeks, chopped
- 1/2 pound baby Bok choy, sliced into quarters lengthwise
- Himalayan salt and black pepper, to taste

Directions

In a heavy-bottomed pot, heat the olive oil until sizzling. Once hot, sauté the celery, carrots, leek and Bok choy for about 6 minutes.

Add the salt, pepper, turkey, and stock; bring to a boil.

Turn the heat to simmer. Continue to cook, partially covered, for about 35 minutes. Bon appétit!

Per serving: 211 Calories; 11.8g Fat; 3.1g Carbs; 23.7g Protein; 0.9g Fiber

94. Duck Cutlets with Brandy and Cream

(Ready in about 20 minutes | Servings 4)

Ingredients
4 duck cutlets
2 ounces brandy
1/2 cup sour cream
4 green onions, white and green parts, chopped
1/2 teaspoon ground bay leaf
1 ½ cups turkey stock
1 teaspoon mixed peppercorns
3 tablespoons Worcestershire sauce
1 tablespoon lard, room temperature
Salt and cayenne pepper, to taste

Directions
Melt the lard in a skillet that is preheated over medium-high heat. Sear the duck fillets, turning once, for 4 to 6 minutes.

Now, add the remaining ingredients, except for the sour cream, to the skillet. Cook, partially covered, for a further 7 minutes.

Garnish with sour cream.

Bon appétit!

Per serving: 351 Calories; 24.7g Fat; 6.6g Carbs; 22.1g Protein; 1.5g Fiber

95. Winter Vegetable Chicken Chowder

(Ready in about 25 minutes | Servings 4)

Ingredients
2 chicken breasts, boneless and cut into chunks
1 carrot, chopped
1 tablespoon olive oil
1 cup heavy cream
2 bouillon cubes
4 tablespoons fresh chives, roughly chopped
4 cups water
1 cup full-fat milk
1 teaspoon garlic, finely minced
1 parsnip, chopped
1/2 cup turnip, chopped
1 whole egg
Salt and pepper, to taste

Directions
Heat the oil in a heavy pot over a moderate heat; now, cook the garlic until aromatic. Add the parsnip, turnip and carrot. Cook until your vegetables are softened.

Stir in the chicken; cook until it is no longer pink, for 3 to 4 minutes, stirring periodically. Season with salt and pepper.

Pour in the water, milk, and heavy cream. Add the bouillon cubes and bring it to a boil.

Reduce the heat to medium-low; let it simmer for 20 minutes longer. Add the beaten egg and stir an additional minute.

Remove from the heat; garnish with chopped chives.

Bon appétit!

Per serving: 342 Calories; 22.4g Fat; 5.3g Carbs; 25.2g Protein; 1.5g Fiber

96. Paprika and Garlic Chicken Fillets

(Ready in about 30 minutes | Servings 6)

Ingredients
1 teaspoon Hungarian paprika
1 teaspoon garlic paste
1/2 cup tomato sauce, preferably homemade
1/4 cup low-sodium soy sauce
2 tablespoons curly parsley, for garnish
1 teaspoon coarse salt
1/2 teaspoon freshly ground black pepper
1 bell pepper, deveined and chopped
1 large-sized red onion, chopped
1 teaspoon dry thyme
1/2 teaspoon marjoram
1 ½ pounds chicken fillets

Directions
Rub each chicken fillet with the garlic paste and seasonings. Place in a heavy pot that is preheated over medium flame.

Cook for 4 to 5 minutes on each side.

Pour in the tomato sauce and soy sauce; bring it to a boil. Add bell pepper and onion.

Reduce the heat to medium-low. Cook, partially covered, for 25 minutes more; garnish with fresh parsley. Bon appétit!

Per serving: 239 Calories; 8.6g Fat; 5.5g Carbs; 34.3g Protein; 1.8g Fiber

97. Holiday Chicken Aspic

(Ready in about 20 minutes + chilling time | Servings 4)

Ingredients
1 cup Bleu d' Auvergne, crumbled
1 tablespoon avocado oil
Salt and cayenne pepper, to your liking
3 tablespoons water
2 gelatin sheets
3/4 cup double cream
2 teaspoons granular erythritol
2 chicken legs, boneless and skinless

Directions
Heat the oil in a frying pan over medium-high heat; fry the chicken for about 10 minutes.

Soak the gelatin sheets in cold water. Cook with the cream, erythritol, water, and Bleu d' Auvergne.

Season with salt and pepper and let it simmer over the low heat, stirring for about 3 minutes. Spoon the mixture into four ramekins. Enjoy!

Per serving: 306 Calories; 18.3g Fat; 4.7g Carbs; 29.5g Protein; 0g Fiber

98. Mediterranean Rum-Glazed Chicken

(Ready in about 1 hour + marinating time | Servings 4)

Ingredients

1 teaspoon Mediterranean seasoning mix
3/4 cup rum
3 tablespoons coconut aminos
1 tablespoon minced fresh ginger
A few drops of liquid Stevia
1 teaspoon chile peppers, minced
1 teaspoon ground cardamom
2 tablespoons ghee, at room temperature
2 vine-ripened tomatoes, pureed
Sea salt and ground black pepper, to taste
2 tablespoons fresh lemon juice, plus wedges for serving
2 pounds chicken drumettes

Directions

Toss the chicken with the melted ghee, salt, black pepper, and Mediterranean seasoning mix until well coated on all sides.

In another bowl, thoroughly combine the pureed tomato puree, rum, coconut aminos, Stevia, chile peppers, ginger, cardamom, and lemon juice.

Pour the tomato mixture over the chicken drumettes; let it marinate for 2 hours. Bake in the preheated oven at 410 degrees F for about 45 minutes.

Add in the reserved marinade and place under the preheated broiler for 10 minutes. Bon appétit!

Per serving: 307 Calories; 12.1g Fat; 2.7g Carbs; 33.6g Protein; 1.5g Fiber

99. Greek Chicken with Wine

(Ready in about 50 minutes | Servings 6)

Ingredients

1/2 cup port wine
1 teaspoon tzatziki spice mix
1 cup double cream
2 garlic cloves, minced
2 tablespoons butter
1/2 cup onions, chopped
Sea salt and crushed mixed peppercorns, to season
1 ½ pounds chicken drumettes

Directions

Melt the butter in an oven-proof skillet over a moderate heat; then, cook the chicken for about 8 minutes.

Add in the onions, garlic, wine, tzatziki spice mix, double cream, salt, and pepper.

Bake in the preheated oven at 390 degrees F for 35 to 40 minutes (a meat thermometer should register 165 degrees F). Enjoy!

Per serving: 333 Calories; 20.2g Fat; 2g Carbs; 33.5g Protein; 0.2g Fiber

100. Romano Cheese Crusted Chicken

(Ready in about 30 minutes | Servings 4)

Ingredients

1/3 cup crushed pork rinds
1/3 cup Romano cheese
3 bell peppers, quartered lengthwise
1 garlic clove, minced
2 teaspoons olive oil
Kosher salt and ground black pepper, to taste
1 pound chicken fillets

Directions

Start by preheating your oven to 410 degrees F.

Mix the crushed pork rinds, Romano cheese, olive oil and minced garlic. Dredge the chicken into this mixture.

Place the chicken in a lightly greased baking dish. Season with salt and black pepper to taste.

Scatter the peppers around the chicken and bake in the preheated oven for 20 to 25 minutes or until thoroughly cooked. Enjoy!

Per serving: 367 Calories; 16.9g Fat; 6g Carbs; 43g Protein; 0.7g Fiber

101. Chicken Breasts with Italian Sauce

(Ready in about 15 minutes | Servings 6)

Ingredients

1 ½ pounds chicken breasts
Flaky sea salt and ground black pepper, to taste
2 tablespoon green garlic, finely minced
1/3 cup fresh Italian parsley, chopped
2 tablespoons red onions, finely minced
2 teaspoons red wine vinegar
1 ½ tablespoons olive oil
1 stick butter

Directions

In a cast-iron skillet, heat the oil over a moderate flame. Sear the chicken for 10 to 12 minutes or until no longer pink. Season with salt and black pepper.

Add in the melted butter and continue to cook until heated through. Stir in the green garlic, onion, and Italian parsley; let it cook for 3 to 4 minutes more.

Stir in the red wine vinegar and remove from the heat. Enjoy!

Per serving: 357 Calories; 26.2g Fat; 0.6g Carbs; 29.2g Protein; 0.2g Fiber

102. Champagne Turkey Meatballs

(Ready in 20 minutes | Servings 4)

Ingredients

For the Meatballs:
3/4 pound ground turkey
1/3 teaspoon Five-spice powder
1/3 cup Colby cheese, freshly grated
1 egg

For the Sauce:
1 1/3 cups water
1/2 teaspoon paprika
1/3 teaspoon guar gum
1/3 cup champagne vinegar
1/2 cup Swerve
1/2 cup tomato sauce, no sugar added
2 tablespoons soy sauce

Directions

Thoroughly combine all ingredients for the meatballs. Roll the mixture into balls and sear them until browned on all sides.

In a saucepan, mix all of the sauce ingredients and cook until the sauce has thickened, whisking continuously.

Fold the meatballs into the sauce and continue to cook, partially covered, for about 10 minutes.

Bon appétit!

Per serving: 244 Calories; 13.7g Fat; 5g Carbs; 27.6g Protein; 2.2g Fiber

103. Tomato, Chicken and Yogurt Chowder

(Ready in about 35 minutes | Servings 6)

Ingredients

3 chicken legs, boneless and chopped
1 tablespoon flax seed meal
1 onion, chopped
1/2 cup Greek-style yogurt
2 tablespoons olive oil
Sea salt and ground black pepper, to taste
1/2 cup celery, thinly sliced
1 chili pepper, deveined and minced
2 cups tomato bisque
2 cups water
1 teaspoon ginger-garlic paste

Directions

Heat the olive oil in a stockpot over a moderately high flame. Sear the chicken legs for about 8 minutes. Season with salt and black pepper and reserve.

In the same stockpot, cook the onion, celery, and chili pepper until they've softened.

Add in the ginger-garlic paste, tomato bisque, and water. Turn the heat to simmer and continue to cook for 30 minutes more until thoroughly cooked.

Fold in the flax seed meal and yogurt and continue to cook, stirring frequently, for 4 to 5 minutes more. Serve hot!

Per serving: 238 Calories; 15.5g Fat; 6.1g Carbs; 36g Protein; 1.3g Fiber

104. Creamed Chicken and Cauliflower Soup

(Ready in about 30 minutes | Servings 6)

Ingredients

3 cups chicken consommé
1 head cauliflower, broken into small-sized florets
1 celery, chopped
1 ¼ cups sour cream
1/2 stick butter
Sea salt and ground white pepper, to taste
2 ½ cups water
1/2 cup white onion, finely chopped
1 teaspoon fresh garlic, finely minced
1 cup leftover roast chicken breasts

Directions

In a heavy bottomed pot, melt the butter over a moderate heat. Cook the onion, garlic and celery for about 5 minutes or until they've softened.

Add in the salt, white pepper, water, chicken consommé, chicken, and cauliflower florets; bring to a boil. Reduce the temperature to simmer and continue to cook for 30 minutes.

Puree the soup with an immersion blender. Fold in the sour cream and stir to combine well. Bon appétit!

Per serving: 231 Calories; 18.2g Fat; 5.9g Carbs; 11.9g Protein; 1.4g Fiber

105. Chicken Drumsticks with Salsa

(Ready in about 55 minutes | Servings 6)

Ingredients

1/2 stick butter
Salt and cayenne pepper, to taste
2 tablespoons coconut aminos
2 cloves garlic, minced
2 eggs
1/4 cup hemp seeds, ground
3 teaspoons red wine vinegar
2 tablespoons salsa
3 chicken drumsticks, cut into chunks

Directions

Rub the chicken with the butter, salt, and cayenne pepper.

Drizzle the chicken with the coconut aminos, vinegar, salsa, and garlic. Allow it to stand for 30 minutes in your refrigerator.

Whisk the eggs with the hemp seeds. Dip each chicken strip in the egg mixture. Place the chicken chunks in a parchment-lined baking pan.

Roast in the preheated oven at 390 degrees F for 25 minutes. Enjoy!

Per serving: 420 Calories; 28.2g Fat; 5g Carbs; 35.3g Protein; 0.8g Fiber

106. Three-Cheese Turkey Dip

(Ready in about 25 minutes | Servings 4)

Ingredients

1 ½ cups Gruyère cheese, shredded
1 ½ cups Ricotta cheese, creamed, 4% fat, softened
1/2 cup goat cheese, shredded
Salt and black pepper, to taste
1/4 cup sour cream
1 shallot, chopped
1 teaspoon garlic, pressed
1 pound ground turkey
1 tablespoon butter, room temperature
1 Fresno chili pepper, deveined and minced

Directions

Melt the butter in a frying pan over a moderately high flame. Now, sauté the onion and garlic until they have softened.

Stir in the ground turkey and continue to cook until it is no longer pink.

Transfer the sautéed mixture to a lightly greased baking dish. Add in Ricotta, sour cream, goat cheese, salt, pepper, and chili pepper.

Top with the shredded Gruyère cheese. Bake in the preheated oven at 350 degrees F for about 20 minutes or until hot and bubbly in top. Enjoy!

Per serving: 284 Calories; 19g Fat; 3.2g Carbs; 26.7g Protein; 1.6g Fiber

107. Chicken Liver Pâté

(Ready in about 2 hours 15 minutes | Servings 4)

Ingredients

4 tablespoons olive oil
1 garlic clove, minced
10 ounces chicken livers
1/2 teaspoon Mediterranean seasoning blend
1 yellow onion, finely chopped
For Flatbread:
1 ¼ cups almond flour
1/2 cup flax meal
1 ½ tablespoons psyllium husks
1 cup lukewarm water
1/2 stick butter

Directions

Pulse the chicken livers along with the seasoning blend, olive oil, onion and garlic in your food processor; reserve.

Mix the dry ingredients for the flatbread. Mix in all the wet ingredients. Whisk to combine well.

Let it stand at room temperature for 2 hours. Divide the dough into 8 balls and roll them out on a flat surface.

In a lightly greased pan, cook your flatbread for 1 minute on each side or until golden. Bon appétit!

Per serving: 395 Calories; 30.2g Fat; 3.6g Carbs; 17.9g Protein; 0.5g Fiber

108. Chicken Salad with Dijon Mustard and Cheese

(Ready in about 20 minutes | Servings 6)

Ingredients

2 Lebanese cucumbers, sliced
Flaky sea salt and ground black pepper, to taste
1/4 cup Parmesan, finely grated
2 chicken breasts
1/4 teaspoon chili pepper flakes
1 teaspoon dried basil
2 romaine hearts, leaves separated
For the dressing:
1 teaspoon Dijon mustard
2 garlic cloves, minced
1/4 cup olive oil
1 tablespoon fresh lemon juice
2 large egg yolks

Directions

In a grilling pan, cook the chicken breast until no longer pink or until a meat thermometer registers 165 degrees F. Slice the chicken into strips.

Toss the chicken with the other ingredients. Prepare the dressing by whisking all the ingredients.

Dress the salad and enjoy!

Per serving: 183 Calories; 12.5g Fat; 1.7g Carbs; 16.3g Protein; 0.9g Fiber

109. Duck Breasts with Creamed Vodka Sauce

(Ready in about 20 minutes | Servings 4)

Ingredients

1 tablespoon tallow, room temperature
1 ½ cups chicken consommé
2 ounces vodka
4 scallion stalks, chopped
Salt and pepper, to taste
3 tablespoons soy sauce
1/2 cup sour cream
1 ½ pounds duck breasts, butterflied

Directions

Melt the tallow in a frying pan over medium-high flame. Sear the duck breasts for about 5 minutes, flipping them over occasionally to ensure even cooking.

Add in the scallions, salt, pepper, chicken consommé, and soy sauce. Partially cover and continue to cook for a further 8 minutes.

Add in the vodka and sour cream; remove from the heat and stir to combine well. Bon appétit!

Per serving: 351 Calories; 24.7g Fat; 6.6g Carbs; 22.1g Protein; 0.6g Fiber

110. Chicken with Cashew-Basil Pesto

(Ready in about 35 minutes | Servings 4)

Ingredients

1 pound chicken legs, skinless
1/2 teaspoon red pepper flakes
1 cup leeks, chopped
Salt and ground black pepper, to taste
For the Cashew-Basil Pesto:
1/2 cup cashews
1/2 cup Parmigiano-Reggiano cheese, preferably freshly grated
1/2 cup fresh basil leaves
1/2 cup olive oil
2 garlic cloves, minced

Directions

Place the chicken legs in a parchnemt-lined bakign pan. Season with salt and pepper, Then, scatter the leeks around the chicken legs.

Roast in the preheated oven at 390 degrees F for 30 to 35 minutes, rotating the pan occasionally.

Pulse the cashews, basil, garlic, and cheese in your blender until pieces are small. Continue blending while adding olive oil to the mixture. Mix until the desired consistency is reached. Bon appétit!

Per serving: 580 Calories; 44.8g Fat; 5g Carbs; 38.7g Protein; 1g Fiber

111. Chicken with Marsala-Mustard Sauce

(Ready in about 25 minutes | Servings 4)

Ingredients

1 pound chicken breasts, butterflied
2 garlic cloves, minced
1/2 cup fresh parsley, roughly chopped
1/4 cup Marsala wine
2 tablespoons brown mustard
1 tablespoon olive oil
Salt and pepper, to taste
1/2 cup heavy whipped cream
1/2 cup onions, chopped
1/4 cup vegetable broth

Directions

Heat the oil in a frying pan over a moderate flame. Cook the chicken breasts until no longer pink or about 6 minutes; season with salt and pepper to taste and reserve.

Cook the onion and garlic until it is fragrant or about 5 minutes. Add in the wine to scrape the bits that may be stuck to the bottom of your frying pan.

Pour in the broth and bring to boil. Fold in the double cream, mustard, and parsley. Bon appétit!

Per serving: 415 Calories; 33.2g Fat; 4.5g Carbs; 24.6g Protein; 1.1g Fiber

112. Chicken Drumsticks with Herbs

(Ready in about 50 minutes | Servings 4)

Ingredients

1 teaspoon dried basil
1 teaspoon dried oregano
1/4 teaspoon ground black pepper, or more to the taste
1 teaspoon paprika
1 tablespoon olive oil
Salt, to your liking
4 chicken drumsticks

Directions

Pat dry the chicken drumsticks and rub them with the olive oil, salt, black pepper, paprika, basil, and oregano.

Preheat your oven to 410 degrees F. Coat a baking pan with a piece of parchment paper.

Bake the chicken drumsticks until they are browned on all sides for 40 to 45 minutes. Enjoy!

Per serving: 345 Calories; 14.1g Fat; 0.4g Carbs; 50.8g Protein; 0.2g Fiber

113. Chicken with Broccoli and Cheddar Cheese

(Ready in about 1 hour 15 minutes | Servings 4)

Ingredients

2 cups cheddar cheese, shredded
1 pound broccoli, broken into florets
1 cup green onions, chopped
1 teaspoon minced green garlic
3 tablespoons olive oil
1/2 teaspoon dried oregano
1/2 teaspoon dried basil
1 celery, sliced
1 pound chicken drumsticks

Directions

Roast the chicken drumsticks in the preheated oven at 380 degrees F for 30 to 35 minutes. Add in the broccoli, celery, green onions, and green garlic.

Add in the oregano, basil and olive oil; roast an additional 15 minutes.

Top with the shredded cheese and bake an additional 5 minutes until hot and bubbly. Bon appétit!

Per serving: 533 Calories; 40.2g Fat; 5.4g Carbs; 35.1g Protein; 3.5g Fiber

114. Duck and Eggplant Bake

(Ready in about 45 minutes | Servings 4)

Ingredients

8 eggs
1/2 teaspoon fennel seeds
1 ½ tablespoons ghee, melted
1 ½ cups almond flour
Salt and black pepper, to taste
1/2 teaspoon oregano, dried
1/3 cup double cream
1/2 pound eggplant, peeled and sliced
1 pound ground duck meat

Directions

Mix the almond flour with salt, black, fennel seeds, and oregano. Fold in one egg and the melted ghee and whisk to combine well.

Press the crust into the bottom of a lightly-oiled pie pan. Cook the ground duck until no longer pink for about 3 minutes, stirring continuously.

Whisk the remaining eggs and double cream. Fold in the browned meat and stir until everything is well incorporated. Pour the mixture into the prepared crust. Top with the eggplant slices.

Bake for about 40 minutes. Cut into four pieces. Bon appétit!

Per serving: 562 Calories; 49.5g Fat; 6.7g Carbs; 22.5g Protein; 2.1g Fiber

115. Oven-Roasted Chicken Legs with Herbs

(Ready in about 50 minutes | Servings 4)

Ingredients

1 teaspoon dried basil
1 teaspoon dried rosemary
1 teaspoon bouillon powder
1/4 teaspoon ground black pepper, or more to the taste
Salt, to your liking
1 teaspoon paprika
4 chicken legs
1 tablespoon butter

Directions

Start by preheating an oven to 420 degrees F. Line a rimmed baking sheet with a piece of parchment paper.

Next, air-dry the chicken legs and rub them with the butter. Then, sprinkle the chicken with all the remaining ingredients.

Arrange the chicken legs out in a single layer on the prepared baking sheet.

Bake the chicken legs until the skin is crispy, about 45 minutes. Enjoy!

Per serving: 345 Calories; 14.1g Fat; 0.4g Carbs; 50.8g Protein; 0.8g Fiber

116. Chicken Tacos with Bacon

(Ready in about 20 minutes | Servings 4)

Ingredients

1 ½ cups Mexican cheese blend
1 tablespoon Mexican seasoning blend
1 pound ground chicken
1/2 cup salsa
2 slices bacon, chopped
1 cup tomato puree
2 teaspoons butter, room temperature
1 clove garlic, minced
2 small-sized shallots, peeled and finely chopped

Directions

Melt the butter in a saucepan over moderately high flame. Now, cook the shallots until tender and fragrant.

Then, sauté the garlic, chicken, and bacon for about 5 minutes, stirring continuously and crumbling with a fork. Add the in the Mexican seasoning blend.

Fold in the tomato puree and salsa; continue to simmer for 5 to 7 minutes over medium-low heat; reserve.

Line a baking pan with wax paper. Place 4 piles of the shredded cheese on the baking pan and gently press them down with a wide spatula to make the "taco shells".

Bake in the preheated oven at 365 degrees F for 6 to 7 minutes or until melted. Allow these taco shells to cool for about 10 minutes. Bon appétit!

Per serving: 535 Calories; 33.3g Fat; 4.8g Carbs; 47.9g Protein; 1.9g Fiber

117. Chicken Fajitas with Cotija Cheese

(Ready in about 15 minutes | Servings 4)

Ingredients

1/2 cup Cotija cheese, shredded
1 pound chicken, ground
4 banana peppers, deveined and chopped
1 cup onions, chopped
2 garlic cloves, minced
1/3 cup dry sherry
Salt and black pepper, to taste
1 teaspoon Mexican seasoning blend
1 tablespoon avocado oil
1 Habanero pepper, deveined and chopped

Directions

In a skillet, heat the avocado oil over a moderate flame. Sauté the garlic, onions, and peppers until they are tender and aromatic or about 5 minutes.

Fold in the ground chicken and continue to cook until the juices run clear.

Add in the dry sherry, Mexican seasonings, salt and pepper. Continue to cook for 5 to 6 minutes more or until cooked through.

Top with cheese and let it sit in the residual heat until the cheese has melted slightly. Enjoy!

Per serving: 301 Calories; 11.4g Fat; 5.2g Carbs; 37.9g Protein; 2.2g Fiber

118. Spicy Chicken with Brussels Sprouts

(Ready in about 20 minutes | Servings 4)

Ingredients

1 ½ pounds Brussels sprouts, trimmed and cut into halves
1/2 teaspoon ancho chile powder
3/4 pound chicken breasts, chopped into bite-sized pieces
2 tablespoons port wine
1/4 teaspoon garlic salt
1 cup vegetable broth
2 tablespoons olive oil
1 clove garlic, minced
1/2 teaspoon whole black peppercorns
1/2 cup onions, chopped

Directions

Heat 1 tablespoon of the oil in a frying pan over medium-high heat. Sauté the Brussels sprouts for about 3 minutes or until golden on all sides. Salt to taste and reserve.

Heat the remaining tablespoon of olive oil. Cook the garlic and chicken for about 3 minutes.

Add in the onions, vegetable broth, wine, ancho chile powder, and black peppercorns; bring to a boil. Then, reduce the temperature to simmer and continue to cook for 4 to 5 minutes longer.

Add the reserved Brussels sprouts back to the frying pan. Bon appétit!

Per serving: 273 Calories; 15.4g Fat; 4.2g Carbs; 23g Protein; 6g Fiber

119. Greek-Style Zucchini Soup

(Ready in about 30 minutes | Servings 4)

Ingredients

1/2 cup Greek-style yogurt
1 ½ cups leftover turkey, shredded
1/2 cup zucchini, diced
2 garlic cloves, minced
Sea salt and ground black pepper, to season
4 ½ cups roasted vegetable broth
1/3 cup double cream
1/2 stick butter

Directions

In a heavy-bottomed pot, melt the butter over medium-high heat. Once hot, cook the zucchini and garlic for 2 minutes until they are fragrant.

Add in the broth, salt, black pepper, and leftover turkey. Cover and cook for 25 minutes, stirring periodically.

Then, fold in the cream and yogurt. Continue to cook for 5 minutes more or until thoroughly warmed. Enjoy!

Per serving: 256 Calories; 18.8g Fat; 5.4g Carbs; 15.8g Protein; 0.2g Fiber

120. Chicken with Romano Cashew Pesto

(Ready in about 35 minutes | Servings 4)

Ingredients

1 cup scallions
Salt and ground black pepper, to taste
1 teaspoon cayenne pepper
1 pound chicken wings, skinless
For the Cashew-Basil Pesto:
1/2 cup Romano cheese
1/2 cup olive oil
2 garlic cloves, minced
1/2 cup cashews
1/2 cup fresh basil leaves

Directions

Begin by preheating your oven to 392 degrees F. Rub the chicken wings with the salt, black pepper, and cayenne pepper.

Arrange the chicken wings in a lightly greased baking dish; scatter the scallions around the chicken.

Roast for 30 minutes, turning the baking dish once.

In a food processor, pulse the basil, garlic, cashews and Romano cheese. Add the oil in a constant tiny stream. Season with sea salt to taste. Garnish with roasted scallions. Bon appétit!

Per serving: 580 Calories; 44.8g Fat; 8g Carbs; 38.7g Protein; 1.4g Fiber

121. Chicken with Herbs and Olives

(Ready in about 40 minutes | Servings 8)

Ingredients

10 Kalamata olives, pitted
2 tablespoons peanut oil
1 ½ cups chicken stock
2 garlic cloves, pressed
2 sprigs thyme
1 sprig rosemary
Salt and ground black pepper, to taste
1 teaspoon dried oregano
1/2 teaspoon dried basil
1 bell pepper, deveined and thinly sliced
4 chicken breasts, skinless and boneless

Directions

Rub the chicken breast with the garlic and seasonings. Heat the peanut oil in a pan that is preheated over a moderately high heat.

Now, fry the chicken until it is browned on all sides, for 4 to 6 minutes.

Add the remaining ingredients; bring it to boil. Reduce the heat to medium-low. Continue cooking, partially covered, for 30 minutes.

Enjoy!

Per serving: 306 Calories; 17.8g Fat; 3.1g Carbs; 31.7g Protein; 0.4g Fiber

122. Sticky Rum-Glazed Chicken

(Ready in about 1 hour + marinating time | Servings 4)

Ingredients

3/4 cup dark rum
3 tablespoons soy sauce
2 tablespoons olive oil
2 tablespoons Swerve
1 teaspoon paprika
2 ripe tomatoes, pureed
1 teaspoon dried oregano
1 tablespoon minced fresh ginger
1 teaspoon ground allspice
1 teaspoon dried marjoram
2 habanero chile peppers, minced
2 tablespoons fresh lime juice, plus wedges for serving
2 pounds chicken thighs
Sea salt and ground black pepper, to taste

Directions

Start by preheating your oven to 420 degrees F.

Now, toss the chicken thighs with the olive oil, salt, black pepper, paprika, oregano, and marjoram.

In a separate mixing bowl, thoroughly combine the pureed tomato puree, rum, soy sauce, Swerve, habanero peppers, ginger, allspice and fresh lime juice.

Pour the rum/tomato mixture over the chicken thighs and refrigerate, covered, for 2 hours.

Discard the marinade and arrange the chicken thighs on a rimmed baking pan. Bake for 50 minutes or until thoroughly cooked.

In the meantime, cook the reserved marinade in a pan over a moderate heat; continue to cook until the liquid has reduced by half.

Pour the sauce over the chicken thighs and place under the broiler for 4 minutes on high.

Enjoy!

Per serving: 307 Calories; 12.1g Fat; 2.7g Carbs; 33.6g Protein; 1.6g Fiber

123. Thanksgiving Turkey Breasts

(Ready in about 30 minutes | Servings 5)

Ingredients

10 strips prosciutto
1 teaspoon garlic, finely minced
1/2 teaspoon chili powder
1 sprig rosemary, finely chopped
1 teaspoon sea salt
1/2 teaspoon freshly ground black pepper
1 teaspoon cayenne pepper
2 sprigs fresh thyme, finely chopped
1 ½ tablespoons coconut butter, room temperature
2 tablespoons Cabernet Sauvignon
2 pounds turkey breasts, marinated

Directions

Cut the turkey breasts into 10 even slices.

Melt the coconut butter in a non-stick skillet over a moderate heat. Sear the turkey breasts for 2 to 3 minutes on each side.

Sprinkle the turkey breasts with all the seasonings and minced garlic; drizzle with the wine. Now, wrap each turkey piece into one prosciutto strip.

Preheat your oven to 450 degrees F. Lay the wrapped turkey in a roasting pan; roast about 25 minutes.

Bon appétit!

Per serving: 286 Calories; 9.7g Fat; 5.9g Carbs; 39.9g Protein; 0.2g Fiber

124. Aromatic Garlicky Chicken Drumettes

(Ready in about 30 minutes | Servings 4)

Ingredients

4 chicken drumettes
2 cloves garlic, minced
1 thyme sprig
1/2 teaspoon mustard seeds
1 teaspoon mixed peppercorns
1 rosemary sprig
1/2 cup leeks, chopped
1 teaspoon cayenne pepper
1 cup turkey stock
1 carrot, sliced
1 teaspoon dried marjoram
2 tomatoes, crushed
1 tablespoon Worcestershire sauce
2 tablespoons tallow
Salt, to taste

Directions

Melt the tallow in a saucepan over medium-high heat. Sprinkle the chicken drumettes with the salt.

Then, fry the chicken drumettes until they are no longer pink and lightly browned on all sides; reserve.

Now, cook the leeks, carrots and garlic in the pan drippings over medium heat for 4 to 6 minutes.

Reduce the heat to simmer, and add the remaining ingredients along with the reserved chicken. Simmer, partially covered, for 15 to 20 minutes.

Enjoy!

Per serving: 165 Calories; 9.8g Fat; 5.7g Carbs; 12.4g Protein; 1.2g Fiber

PORK

125. Mediterranean Pork Rouladen

(Ready in about 1 hour + marinating time | Servings 6)

Ingredients

2 garlic cloves, pressed
1/2 cup Burgundy wine
1 tablespoon Mediterranean herb mix
1 teaspoon mustard seeds
1 cup roasted vegetable broth
1 large-sized onion, thinly sliced
1/2 teaspoon cumin seeds
1 tablespoon ghee, room temperature
1 ½ pounds boneless pork loin, butterflied
Salt and black peppercorns, to taste

Directions

Boil the pork loin for about 5 minutes; pat it dry.

Now, combine the Mediterranean herb mix, mustard seeds, cumin seeds, garlic and ghee.

Unfold the pork loin and spread the rub all over the cut side. Roll the pork and secure with kitchen string. Allow it to sit at least 2 hours in your refrigerator.

Place the pork loin in a lightly greased baking pan. Add in the wine, broth, onion, salt, and black peppercorns.

Roast in the preheated oven at 390 degrees F approximately 1 hour. Bon appétit!

Per serving: 220 Calories; 6g Fat; 2.8g Carbs; 33.3g Protein; 0.4g Fiber

126. Milk-Braised Pork Sirloin Roast

(Ready in about 1 hour 35 minutes | Servings 8)

Ingredients

3 teaspoons butter, room temperature
2 bell peppers, deveined and thinly sliced
2 cup full-fat milk
1/2 cup onion, sliced
1 teaspoon dried marjoram
2 pounds pork sirloin roast
Salt and pepper, to taste

Directions

Melt the butter in a saucepan over medium-high flame. Sear the pork for about 7 minutes until just browned.

Lower the pork sirloin roast into a baking dish. Season with salt, pepper, and marjoram. Scatter the onion and peppers around the pork.

Pour in the milk and cover the dish with a piece of aluminum foil. Roast in the preheated oven at 330 degrees F for 1 hour 20 minutes, turning the pork halfway through the cooking time.

Let it sit for 10 minutes before slicing. Bon appétit!

Per serving: 293 Calories; 15.4g Fat; 5.4g Carbs; 31.4g Protein; 0.4g Fiber

127. Italian Pork Muffins

(Ready in about 10 minutes | Servings 2)

Ingredients

1/2 pound ground pork
1/2 teaspoon shallot powder
1 teaspoon garlic paste
1/2 cup cheddar cheese, shredded
1/2 cup marinara sauce
Salt and ground black pepper, to taste
1/2 teaspoon paprika

Directions

In a mixing bowl, combine all ingredients until everything is well incorporated.

Spoon the mixture into two microwave-safe mugs.

Microwave for 5 minutes until set but still moist. Bon appétit!

Per serving: 327 Calories; 16.6g Fat; 5.8g Carbs; 40g Protein; 1.2g Fiber

128. Italian Pork and Pepper Casserole

(Ready in about 50 minutes | Servings 6)

Ingredients

1 stick butter, melted
1 Italian peppers, thinly sliced
1 cup double cream
6 eggs, lightly beaten
2 tablespoons fresh Italian parsley
2 ½ cups almond meal
1/2 teaspoon celery seeds
1 ¼ pounds ground pork
Salt and pepper, to the taste

Directions

Start by preheating your oven to 350 degrees F

Thoroughly combine the eggs, almond meal, and melted until well combined. Press the mixture into a lightly oiled baking dish.

In a non-stick skillet, cook the ground pork for about 4 minutes, breaking apart with a wide spatula; season with salt and pepper to taste.

Add in the remaining ingredients and stir to combine well.

Spread this mixture over the crust, using a wide spatula. Bake in the preheated oven at 350 degrees F for about 40 minutes. Let it stand for 10 minutes before slicing. Bon appétit!

Per serving: 478 Calories; 36g Fat; 4.9g Carbs; 33.5g Protein; 0.3g Fiber

129. Cheesy Pork Meatloaf with Marinara Sauce

(Ready in about 1 hour 10 minutes | Servings 8)

Ingredients

1/2 cup marinara sauce, bottled
1/2 cup tomato puree
1 tablespoon Erythritol
1 teaspoon granulated garlic
1 teaspoon lime zest
8 ounces Colby cheese, shredded
1 teaspoon mustard seeds
2 eggs, beaten
1/2 cup onions, chopped
2 pounds ground pork
Sea salt and freshly ground black pepper, to taste

Directions

Mix the ground pork with the eggs, onions, marinara salsa, cheese, granulated garlic, salt, pepper, lime zest, and mustard seeds; mix to combine.

Press the mixture into a lightly-greased loaf pan. Mix the tomato paste with the Erythritol and spread the mixture over the top of your meatloaf.

Bake in the preheated oven at 365 degrees F for about 1 hour 10 minutes, rotating the pan halfway through the cook time. Bon appétit!

Per serving: 318 Calories; 14.7g Fat; 6.2g Carbs; 39.3g Protein; 0.3g Fiber

130. Easiest Baby Back Ribs Ever

(Ready in about 1 hour 40 minutes + marinating time | Servings 6)

Ingredients

1 ½ pounds baby back ribs
1 lime, halved
1 garlic clove, minced
1 teaspoon dried marjoram
Salt and ground black pepper, to taste

Directions

Season the baby back ribs with the salt, pepper and marjoram. Now, rub your ribs with the cut sides of lime.

Cover and transfer to your refrigerator for 6 hours. Place the minced garlic on top of the ribs.

Grill for about 1 hour 30 minutes, turning twice to ensure even cooking.

Bon appétit!

Per serving: 255 Calories; 13.9g Fat; 0.8g Carbs; 29.9g Protein; 0.2g Fiber

131. Country-Style Pork Jambalaya

(Ready in about 35 minutes | Servings 6)

Ingredients

1 tablespoon Cajun spice
8 ounces pork sausage, sliced
1 pound pork shoulder, cubed
3/4 pound okra
1 cup water
2 bell peppers, deveined and thinly sliced
2 shallots, toughly chopped
1 teaspoon gumbo file
1 teaspoon beef bouillon granules
1 teaspoon crushed red pepper
4 cups bone broth
2 celery stalks, chopped
1/4 cup flaxseed meal
2 tablespoons olive oil
Sea salt and freshly cracked black pepper

Directions

Heat the oil in a heavy-bottomed pot that is preheated over a moderately high flame. Now, cook the pork until it is just browned; reserve.

Add the sausage and cook in the pan drippings approximately 5 minutes; reserve.

Stir in the shallots and cook until they are softened. Add the beef bouillon granules, salt, pepper, gumbo file, red pepper, Cajun spice and bone broth. Bring it to a boil.

Add the water, bell pepper and celery, and reduce the heat to medium-low. Cook an additional 15 to 23 minutes.

Afterwards, stir in the flax seed meal and okra; cook for a further 5 minutes or until heated through. Enjoy!

Per serving: 427 Calories; 26.2g Fat; 6.6g Carbs; 35.2g Protein; 4.6g Fiber

132. Fall-Off-The-Bone Ribs

(Ready in about 4 hours 30 minutes | Servings 4)

Ingredients

1 ½ pounds spare ribs
2 teaspoons Swerve
1 Serrano pepper, chopped
2 cloves garlic, chopped
A bunch of scallions, chopped
1/2 teaspoon ground cumin
3/4 cup vegetable stock, preferably homemade
1 teaspoon whole black peppercorns
1 tablespoon lard, at room temperature
2 bay leaves
Salt, to taste

Directions

Melt the lard in a pan over a moderately high heat. Cook the spare ribs for 8 minutes, turning occasionally.

In the meantime, whisk the stock, Swerve, garlic, Serrano pepper, scallions, salt and cumin in a mixing dish.

Transfer the browned spare ribs to your crock pot; pour in the stock mixture. Add the black peppercorns and bay leaves.

Cook for 4 hours 30 minutes on Low heat setting. Bon appétit!

Per serving: 412 Calories; 22g Fat; 3g Carbs; 46.3g Protein; 0.2g Fiber

133. Spicy Italian Ribs

(Ready in about 8 hours | Servings 4)

Ingredients

1 pound baby back ribs
1 teaspoon Italian herb mix
1 teaspoon Serrano pepper, minced
1 tablespoon butter
1/2 teaspoon cayenne pepper
1 teaspoon grated lemon zest
1 garlic clove, crushed
1 Italian pepper, thinly sliced
4 tablespoons coconut aminos
1/4 cup dry red wine

Directions

Butter the sides and bottom of your Crock pot. Place the pork and peppers on the bottom.

Add in the remaining ingredients.

Slow cook for 9 hours on Low heat setting. Enjoy!

Per serving: 192 Calories; 6.9g Fat; 0.9g Carbs; 29.8g Protein; 0.5g Fiber

134. Pork Sausage and Cheese Fat Bombs

(Ready in about 15 minutes + chilling time | Servings 6)

Ingredients

- 8 ounces cream cheese, room temperature
- 2 tablespoons scallions, minced
- 4 ounces mozzarella cheese, crumbled
- 2 tablespoons flaxseed meal
- 1 teaspoon ginger-garlic paste
- 1 tablespoon butter, room temperature
- 1 tomato, pureed
- Sea salt and ground black pepper, to taste
- 3/4 pound smoked pork sausage, ground

Directions

Melt the butter in a frying pan over medium-high heat. Cook the sausage for about 4 minutes, crumbling with a spatula.

Add in the ginger-garlic paste, scallions, and tomato; continue to cook over medium-low heat for a further 6 minutes. Stir in the remaining ingredients.

Place the mixture in your refrigerator for 1 to 2 hours until firm. Roll the mixture into bite-sized balls. Enjoy!

Per serving: 383 Calories; 32.7g Fat; 5.1g Carbs; 16.7g Protein; 1.7g Fiber

135. Herb Pork Medallions

(Ready in about 30 minutes | Servings 4)

Ingredients

- 1 teaspoon dried marjoram
- 1/2 teaspoon fresh ginger root, grated
- 2 tablespoons coconut aminos
- 1 red onion, thinly sliced
- 2 cloves garlic, minced
- 4 pork medallions
- 1/4 cup dry white wine
- 2 tablespoons olive oil

Directions

In a saucepan, heat the olive oil over a moderate heat. Once hot, sauté the onions and garlic until browned.

Cook the pork for about 20 minutes. Add the dry white wine to scrape up any browned bits from the bottom of your pot; add in the coconut aminos, marjoram, and ginger root.

Continue to cook for 8 to 10 minutes or until cooked through. Bon appétit!

Per serving: 335 Calories; 26.3g Fat; 1.5g Carbs; 18.3g Protein; 0.2g Fiber

136. Country-Style Pork Goulash

(Ready in about 25 minutes | Servings 6)

Ingredients

- 1 ¼ pounds pork stew meat, cubed
- 1 cup onions, chopped
- 2 garlic cloves, minced
- 1/2 cup loosely packed fresh parsley, roughly chopped
- 1/2 teaspoon celery seeds
- 2 teaspoons paprika
- 2 cups beef bone broth
- 2 bay laurels
- 2 slices bacon, chopped
- Salt and red pepper, to taste
- 1 cup tomato sauce, no sugar added
- 1 tablespoon olive oil, room temperature

Directions

Heat the olive oil in a stockpot over a moderately high flame. Sauté the onions and garlic until they've softened.

Add in the pork and continue to cook for 7 to 8 minutes. Add in the bacon, salt, red pepper, and continue to cook for about 3 minutes.

Add in the tomato sauce, beef bone broth, celery seeds, paprika, bay laurels, and parsley. Turn the heat to simmer. Continue to simmer for about 12 minutes until cooked through. Enjoy!

Per serving: 228 Calories; 11.7g Fat; 6g Carbs; 23.1g Protein; 1.7g Fiber

137. Pork Loin with Spicy Cheese Sauce

(Ready in about 30 minutes | Servings 6)

Ingredients

- 1 tablespoon lard
- 1 teaspoon dried hot chile flakes
- 1 shallot, chopped
- 1/3 cup port wine
- 1 teaspoon dried rosemary
- 1/3 cup heavy cream
- 2 garlic cloves, chopped
- 1 tablespoon coconut aminos
- 6 ounces blue cheese
- Salt and freshly cracked black peppercorns, to taste
- 2 pounds pork center cut loin roast, boneless and cut into 6 pieces
- 1/3 cup roasted vegetable broth, preferably homemade

Directions

Rub each piece of the pork with salt, black peppercorns, and rosemary.

Melt the lard in a saucepan over a moderately high flame. Sear the pork on all sides about 15 minutes; set aside.

Cook the shallot and garlic until they've softened. Add in port wine to scrape up any brown bits from the bottom.

Reduce the heat to medium-low and add in the remaining ingredients; continue to simmer until the sauce has thickened and reduced. Bon appétit!

Per serving: 348 Calories; 18.9g Fat; 1.9g Carbs; 40.3g Protein; 0.3g Fiber

138. Pork with Kale and Bell Peppers

(Ready in about 25 minutes + marinating time | Servings 6)

Ingredients

2 teaspoons olive oil
1 medium leek, sliced
2 bell peppers, chopped
1 ½ pounds pork cutlets
2 tablespoons fresh lime juice
2 tablespoons oyster sauce
1/4 cup port wine
2 garlic cloves, smashed
2 cups kale
Sea salt and ground black pepper, to taste

Directions

Sprinkle the pork with salt and black pepper. Then, make the marinade by whisking 1 teaspoon of olive oil, wine, garlic, oyster sauce, and lime juice.

Let the pork marinate for about 2 hours in your refrigerator

Heat the remaining teaspoon of olive oil in a frying pan. Fry the leek and bell peppers for 4 to 5 minutes, stirring continuously, until they have softened slightly; set aside.

In the same pan, sear the pork along with the marinade until browned on all sides.

Stir the reserved vegetables into the frying pan along with the kale. Continue to cook for 5 to 6 minutes more. Bon appétit!

Per serving: 234 Calories; 11g Fat; 2g Carbs; 29.8g Protein; 0.9g Fiber

139. Classic Pork Au Jus

(Ready in about 6 hours + marinating time | Servings 4)

Ingredients

Au Jus gravy seasoning packet
2 onions, cut into wedges
1 tablespoon liquid smoke sauce
1 teaspoon chipotle powder
Kosher salt and freshly ground black pepper, taste
1 ½ pounds pork shoulder

Directions

Mix the liquid smoke sauce, chipotle powder, Au Jus gravy seasoning packet, salt and pepper. Rub the spice mixture into the pork on all sides.

Wrap in plastic wrap and let it marinate in your refrigerator for 3 hours.

Prepare your grill for indirect heat. Place the pork butt roast on the grate over a drip pan and top with the onions; cover the grill and cook for about 6 hours.

Transfer the pork to a cutting board. Now, shred the meat into bite-sized pieces using two forks. Bon appétit!

Per serving: 350 Calories; 11g Fat; 5g Carbs; 53.6g Protein; 2.2g Fiber

140. Butter Pork Chops with Vegetables

(Ready in about 30 minutes + marinating time | Servings 4)

Ingredients

2 carrots, sliced
1 celery stalk, diced
2 tablespoons butter, room temperature
1/2 teaspoon celery salt
1 garlic clove
1 teaspoon mustard seeds
2 tablespoons fresh lime juice
1 cup leeks, sliced
4 (2- 1 1/2"-thick) pork bone-in pork rib chops
1/2 teaspoon freshly ground black pepper

Directions

Place the pork, mustard seeds, fresh lime juice, celery salt, salt, pepper, and garlic in a ceramic dish. Cover and let them marinate in your refrigerator for about 3 hours.

In an oven-safe skillet, melt the butter over medium-high heat. Sear the pork cutlets until bottom side is golden brown, about 2 minutes. Flip them over and cook on other side about 2 minutes.

Repeat the process, turning about every 1 to 2 minutes, until an instant-read thermometer inserted into the thickest part registers 150 degrees F.

Add in the leeks, carrots, and celery and continue to cook, partially covered, for 5 minutes more.

Transfer the skillet to the oven and roast the pork with the vegetables for about 10 minutes. Bon appétit!

Per serving: 452 Calories; 34.8g Fat; 4.7g Carbs; 26.3g Protein; 0.6g Fiber

141. Pork Blade Steak with Red Wine

(Ready in about 30 minutes | Servings 4)

Ingredients

1 ½ pounds pork blade steak
2 tablespoons olive oil
1/4 cup dry red wine
1/2 teaspoon salt
1 red onion, peeled and chopped
1 teaspoon mustard seeds
1 garlic clove, minced
1/2 teaspoon freshly ground black pepper
1/2 teaspoon cayenne pepper

Directions

In a frying pan, heat 1 tablespoon of the olive oil over a moderate heat. Now, sear the pork steaks for 8 to 9 minutes per side.

Pour in a splash of wine to deglaze the pot. Sprinkle with spices and continue to cook for 10 minutes more, adding additional water if necessary; reserve.

In the same frying pan, heat the remaining tablespoon of olive oil and cook the onions and garlic until they have softened. Serve with the pork. Bon appétit!

Per serving: 305 Calories; 20.6g Fat; 3.7g Carbs; 22.5g Protein; 0.6g Fiber

142. Chunky Pork and Pepper Bake

(Ready in about 50 minutes | Servings 6)

Ingredients

1 ¼ pounds ground pork
1 red bell pepper, thinly sliced
1 cup heavy cream
1 green bell pepper, thinly sliced
1/2 teaspoon mustard seeds
2 ½ cups almond flour
1 stick butter, melted
1/2 teaspoon dried dill weed
6 eggs, lightly beaten
Salt and pepper, to the taste

Directions

Start by preheating your oven to 350 degrees F

Add the flour, butter and one egg to a mixing dish; mix to combine well.

Press the batter dough in a baking pan that is previously greased with a non-stick cooking spray.

Next, brown the ground pork for 3 to 5 minutes, crumbling with a wide spatula; season with salt and pepper.

In another mixing bowl, thoroughly combine the remaining ingredients; add the browned pork.

Spread this mixture over the crust and bake for 35 to 43 minutes in the preheated oven. Transfer to a wire rack to cool before slicing.

Bon appétit!

Per serving: 478 Calories; 36g Fat; 4.9g Carbs; 33.5g Protein; 0.3g Fiber

143. Traditional Greek Souvlaki

(Ready in about 20 minutes + marinating time | Servings 6)

Ingredients

2 pounds pork butt, cubed
2 cloves garlic, crushed
2 bell peppers, cut into thick slices
1 pound brown mushrooms
1 red bell pepper, cut into thick slices
3 tablespoons coconut aminos
3 tablespoons olive oil
1 zucchini, cubed
1 shallot, cut into wedges
1 tablespoon stone-ground mustard
2 tablespoons fresh lemon juice
1 tablespoon Greek spice mix
Bamboo skewers, soaked in cold water for 30 minutes

Directions

Mix the Greek spice mix, garlic, coconut aminos, olive oil, mustard, and lemon juice in a ceramic dish; add in the pork cubes and let it marinate for 2 hours.

Thread the pork cubes and vegetables onto the soaked skewers. Salt to taste.

Grill for about 15 minutes, basting with the reserved marinade. Bon appétit!

Per serving: 267 Calories; 10.6g Fat; 5.3g Carbs; 34.9g Protein; 1.3g Fiber

144. Pork Shoulder and Broccoli Medley

(Ready in about 2 hours | Servings 6)

Ingredients

1 ½ pounds pork shoulder, cubed
1 cup broccoli, broken into florets
2 bell peppers, chopped
1 chili pepper, chopped
1 tablespoon beef bouillon granules
1 tablespoon flax seed meal
1 brown onion, chopped
1 stalk celery, chopped
1/4 cup dry red wine
2 bay leaves
3 cups water
1/2 teaspoon celery seeds
1 teaspoon garlic, finely minced
2 tablespoons lard, at room temperature
1 teaspoon smoked paprika
Sea salt and ground black pepper to taste

Directions

Melt the lard in a heavy-bottomed pot over a moderate flame. Now, cook the pork for 5 to 6 minutes or until browned on all sides. Season with paprika, salt, and black pepper; reserve.

In the same pot, sauté the onion, celery and garlic until they've softened. Add a splash of dry red wine to scrape up any browned bits from the bottom of your pot.

Add in the water, bay leaves, celery seeds, bell peppers, and chili pepper. Reduce the temperature to simmer and add in the reserved pork.

Continue to simmer for 1 hour 20 minutes. Add in the broccoli and beef bouillon granules and cook an additional 15 minutes.

Add in the flax seed meal to thicken the cooking liquid. Taste and adjust the seasonings. Bon appétit!

Per serving: 326 Calories; 13.9g Fat; 6g Carbs; 23.5g Protein; 1.2g Fiber

145. Mexican Spicy Pork

(Ready in about 30 minutes | Servings 6)

Ingredients

6 pork chops
1 teaspoon dried Mexican oregano
2 garlic cloves, minced
2 tablespoons vegetable oil
1/2 teaspoon red pepper flakes, crushed
Salt and ground black pepper, to taste
1/2 cup chicken stock
2 Mexican chilies, chopped

Directions

Heat 1 tablespoon of the olive oil in a frying pan over a moderately high heat. Brow the pork chops for 5 to 6 minutes per side.

Then, bring the Mexican chilies and chicken stock to a boil; remove from the heat and let it sit for about 20 minutes.

Puree the chilies along with the liquid and the remaining ingredients in your food processor. Add in the remaining tablespoon of the oil. Bon appétit!

Per serving: 356 Calories; 20.3g Fat; 0.3g Carbs; 45.2g Protein; 0g Fiber

146. Parmesan Meatballs with Marinara Sauce

(Ready in about 50 minutes | Servings 6)

Ingredients

For the Meatballs:
1 teaspoon garlic paste
2 tablespoons fresh parsley, chopped
2 ounces full-fat milk
1 pound beef, ground
1 teaspoon onion flakes
1 egg, beaten
Salt and ground black pepper, to taste
1/4 cup almond flour
3/4 cup grated parmesan cheese
1 white onion, finely chopped
1/2 tablespoon chili powder
For the Sauce:
1 tablespoon Mediterranean herb mix
1 cup marinara sauce
Salt and ground black pepper, to taste
2 tablespoons olive oil

Directions

Mix all ingredients for the meatballs. Then, roll the mixture into bite-sized balls and arrange them in a single layer on a lightly greased baking sheet.

Mix all ingredients for the sauce. Pour the sauce over the meatballs.

Bake in the preheated oven at 365 degrees F for 40 to 45 minutes or until they are golden brown on the top. Bon appétit!

Per serving: 237 Calories; 12g Fat; 5.6g Carbs; 26.4g Protein; 1.6g Fiber

147. Pork Sausage and Pepper Frittata

(Ready in about 35 minutes | Servings 4)

Ingredients

8 eggs, whisked
1 teaspoon dried thyme, crushed
1/2 teaspoon ground black pepper
1/4 teaspoon cayenne pepper
1 teaspoon Serrano pepper, finely minced
1 teaspoon salt
3 tablespoons olive oil
2 garlic cloves, minced
1 cup onion, chopped
1/2 pound pork sausages, thinly sliced

Directions

Start by preheating your oven to 410 degrees F.

In a frying pan, heat the oil over a medium-high flame. Sauté the onions, Serrano pepper and garlic for about 5 minutes until they have softened.

Sprinkle with salt, black pepper, and cayenne pepper. Then, cook the sausage until no longer pink, crumbling with a fork.

Transfer the sautéed mixture to a lightly greased baking pan. Pour the whisked eggs over the top and sprinkle with dried thyme.

Bake in the preheated oven for 22 to 25 minutes. Serve warm.

Per serving: 423 Calories; 35.4g Fat; 4.1g Carbs; 22.6g Protein; 0.8g Fiber

148. Pork, Wine and Mushroom Stew

(Ready in about 45 minutes | Servings 8)

Ingredients

2 pounds Boston butt, cut into 3/4-inch cubes
2 tablespoons dry red wine
1/2 teaspoon dried oregano
1/2 cup fresh cilantro, chopped
2 ripe tomatoes, chopped
1 teaspoon sea salt
1/2 teaspoon black pepper
1 teaspoon garlic, pressed
1 celery stalk, chopped
2 carrots, peeled and chopped
2 tablespoons lard, at room temperature
1 medium leek, chopped
1 habanero pepper, minced
3 cups beef bone broth, no sugar added
1 teaspoon dried marjoram
1 cup fresh brown mushrooms, sliced

Directions

In a heavy-bottomed pot, melt the lard until sizzling. Once hot, brown the pork for 4 to 5 minutes; season with salt and pepper and reserve.

Then, cook the leeks, habanero pepper, garlic, carrots and celery until they have softened. Pour in the wine to deglaze the bottom of your pot.

Add in the broth, tomatoes, oregano, marjoram, and mushrooms. Partially cover and continue to cook for 35 to 40 minutes.

Serve with fresh cilantro. Bon appétit!

Per serving: 390 Calories; 27.8g Fat; 4.7g Carbs; 28.3g Protein; 5g Fiber

149. Classic Glazed Pork Meatloaf

(Ready in about 45 minutes | Servings 6)

Ingredients

1/4 cup pork rinds, crushed
1 ½ tablespoons Swerve
1 ½ pounds ground pork
Sea salt and ground black pepper
1 teaspoon celery seeds
1 large onion, chopped
2 cloves garlic, finely minced
1 tablespoon champagne vinegar
1/3 cup almond meal
1 large egg
1 cup tomato puree, no sugar added
1/2 teaspoon dried rosemary
1 teaspoon fresh coriander

Directions

In a mixing dish, thoroughly combine the almond meal, egg, salt, black pepper, celery seeds, ground pork, pork rinds, onion, and garlic.

Press the meatloaf mixture into a lightly greased loaf pan.

In a saucepan, cook the remaining ingredients until the sauce has thickened and reduced slightly. Spread the sauce evenly over the top of your meatloaf.

Roast in the preheated oven at 365 degrees F for 35 minutes. Place under the preheated broiler for 5 to 6 minutes. Bon appétit!

Per serving: 251 Calories; 7.9g Fat; 4.5g Carbs; 34.6g Protein; 1.4g Fiber

150. Old-Fashioned Hungarian Gulyás

(Ready in about 10 hours | Servings 4)

Ingredients

1 pound pork shoulder off the bone, chopped
1 teaspoon sweet Hungarian paprika
2 chili peppers, deveined and finely chopped
1 teaspoon caraway seeds, ground
2 teaspoons cayenne pepper
4 cups chicken stock
1 cup onion, chopped
3 green garlic stalks, chopped
2 ½ cups tomato puree
1 ½ tablespoons butter
For the Sour Cream Sauce:
1 bunch parsley, chopped
1 teaspoon lemon zest
1 cup sour cream

Directions

Melt the butter in a sauté pan that is preheated over a moderate heat. Now, cook the pork until just browned; reserve.

Add the onions and garlic and continue to sauté until they are just tender and fragrant.

Transfer the reserved pork along with the onions and garlic to your crock pot. Add the cayenne pepper, paprika, caraway seeds, stock, tomato puree and chili peppers.

Cover and cook for 8 to 10 hours on low heat setting.

In the meantime, make the sour cream sauce by whisking all the sauce ingredients. Bon appétit!

Per serving: 517 Calories; 35.7g Fat; 6.7g Carbs; 38.2g Protein; 4.3g Fiber

151. Braised Boston Butt with Spring Onions

(Ready in about 1 hour 20 minutes | Servings 8)

Ingredients

2 pounds Boston butt, cubed
A bunch of spring onions, chopped
1/2 cup unsweetened coconut milk
2 cups chicken bone broth
1/2 teaspoon mustard powder
2 tomatoes, pureed
1 jalapeno pepper, deveined and finely chopped
1/2 tablespoon ground cardamom
2 garlic cloves, minced
1 bell pepper, deveined and chopped
1 tablespoon lard, room temperature
Salt and freshly ground pepper

Directions

In a wok, melt the lard over moderate heat. Season the pork belly with salt, pepper and mustard powder.

Sear the pork for 8 to 10 minutes, stirring periodically to ensure even cooking; set aside, keeping it warm.

In the same wok, sauté the spring onions, garlic, and cardamom. Spoon the sautéed vegetables along with the reserved pork into the slow cooker.

Add in the remaining ingredients, cover with the lid and cook for 1 hour 10 minutes over low heat. Bon appétit!

Per serving: 369 Calories; 20.2g Fat; 2.9g Carbs; 41.3g Protein; 0.7g Fiber

152. Herb Butter Pork Chops

(Ready in about 20 minutes | Servings 4)

Ingredients

1 pound pork chops
1/2 teaspoon granulated garlic
1 teaspoon dried parsley
1 thyme sprig, minced
2 rosemary sprigs, minced
1 teaspoon dried marjoram
1/2 teaspoon paprika, crushed
Coarse salt and ground black pepper, to taste
A bunch of spring onions, roughly chopped
1 tablespoon butter

Directions

Season the pork chops with the granulated garlic, paprika, salt, and black pepper.

Melt the butter in a frying pan over a moderate flame. Cook the pork chops for 6 to 8 minutes, turning them occasionally to ensure even cooking.

Add in the remaining ingredients and cook an additional 4 minutes. Bon appétit!

Per serving: 192 Calories; 6.9g Fat; 0.9g Carbs; 29.8g Protein; 0.4g Fiber

153. Tangy Spare Ribs with Lime

(Ready in about 3 hour 40 minutes + marinating time | Servings 6)

Ingredients

1 lime, halved
2 pounds spare ribs
1 teaspoon dried marjoram
Salt and ground black pepper, to taste
1 garlic clove, minced

Directions

Toss all ingredients in a ceramic dish.

Cover and let it refrigerate for 5 to 6 hours.

Roast the foil-wrapped ribs in the preheated oven at 275 degrees F degrees for about 3 hours 30 minutes. Bon appétit!

Per serving: 385 Calories; 29g Fat; 1.8g Carbs; 28.3g Protein; 0.1g Fiber

154. Ground Pork Mini Frittatas

(Ready in about 25 minutes | Servings 6)

Ingredients

3 large eggs, lightly beaten
2 cups ground pork
3 ½ cups almond flour
1/2 teaspoon dried basil
2 tablespoons flaxseed meal
1 teaspoon baking powder
Salt and pepper, to your liking
2 tablespoons full-fat milk
1/2 teaspoon ground cardamom
1 stick butter

Directions

In the preheated frying pan, cook the ground pork until the juices run clear, approximately 5 minutes.

Add in the remaining ingredients and stir until well combined.

Spoon the mixture into lightly greased muffin cups. Bake in the preheated oven at 365 degrees F for about 17 minutes.

Allow your muffins to cool down before unmolding and storing. Bon appétit!

Per serving: 330 Calories; 30.3g Fat; 2.3g Carbs; 19g Protein; 1.2g Fiber

155. Country-Style Stuffed Peppers

(Ready in about 40 minutes | Servings 4)

Ingredients

1/2 pound ground pork
1/3 pound ground veal
1 shallot, chopped
1/2 teaspoon mustard seeds
1 garlic clove, minced
1 ripe tomato, chopped
1 tablespoon vegetable oil
Sea salt and ground black pepper, to taste
6 bell peppers, deveined

Directions

Parboil the peppers for 5 minutes.

Heat the vegetable oil in a frying pan that is preheated over a moderate heat. Cook the shallot and garlic for 3 to 4 minutes until they've softened.

Stir in the ground meat and cook, breaking apart with a fork, for about 6 minutes. Add the chopped tomatoes, mustard seeds, salt, and pepper.

Continue to cook for 5 minutes or until heated through. Divide the filling between the peppers and transfer them to a baking pan.

Bake in the preheated oven at 365 degrees F approximately 25 minutes. Bon appétit!

Per serving: 290 Calories; 20.5g Fat; 8.2g Carbs; 18.2g Protein; 1.5g Fiber

156. Curried Pork Loin with Romano Cheese

(Ready in about 25 minutes | Servings 4)

Ingredients

1 teaspoon Mediterranean seasoning mix
1 tablespoon curry paste
1/2 cup Romano cheese, grated
1 cup roasted vegetable broth
1 tablespoon oyster sauce
1 teaspoon fresh garlic, smashed
2 tablespoons butter, room temperature
Salt and pepper, to taste
1 onion, sliced
2 tablespoons black olives, pitted and sliced
2 tablespoons balsamic vinegar
1 pound pork loin, cut into 1-inch-thick pieces

Directions

In a frying pan, melt the butter over a moderately high heat. Once hot, cook the pork until browned on all sides; season with salt and black pepper and set aside.

In the pan drippings, cook the onion and garlic for 4 to 5 minutes or until they've softened.

Add in the Mediterranean seasoning mix, curry paste, and vegetable broth. Continue to cook until the sauce has thickened and reduced slightly or about 10 minutes. Add in the remaining ingredients along with the reserved pork.

Top with cheese and cook for 10 minutes longer or until cooked through. Enjoy!

Per serving: 476 Calories; 35.3g Fat; 6.2g Carbs; 31.1g Protein; 1.4g Fiber

157. Vietnamese Pork Lettuce Wraps

(Ready in about 15 minutes | Servings 4)

Ingredients

1 head lettuce
2 tablespoons champagne vinegar
1 tablespoon coconut aminos
1 tablespoon sunflower seeds
1 teaspoon mustard powder
2 garlic cloves, finely minced
1 chili pepper, deveined and finely minced
2 scallion stalks, sliced
1 pound ground pork
Celery salt and ground black pepper, to taste

Directions

Sear the ground pork in the preheated pan for about 8 minutes. Stir in the garlic, chili pepper, mustard seeds, and sunflower seeds; continue to sauté for 1 minute longer or until aromatic.

Add in the vinegar, coconut aminos, salt, black pepper, and scallions. Stir to combine well.

Add spoonfuls of the pork mixture to the lettuce leaves, wrap them and serve.

Per serving: 281 Calories; 19.4g Fat; 5.1g Carbs; 22.1g Protein; 1.3g Fiber

158. Avocado Pork Soup

(Ready in about 25 minutes | Servings 4)

Ingredients

2 tablespoons butter, melted
1 white onion, chopped
2 tomatoes, pureed
Seasoned salt and freshly cracked black pepper, to taste
1/2 teaspoon red pepper flakes
1 tablespoon chicken bouillon granules
4 cups water
1 celery stalk, chopped
1 cup double cream
1/2 teaspoon Tabasco sauce
1 carrot, chopped
1/2 cup avocado, pitted, peeled and diced
3/4 pound pork chops, cubed

Directions

In a soup pot, melt the butter over medium-high heat. Cook the onion, celery, and carrot until tender and fragrant or about 6 minutes.

Heat the remaining tablespoon of butter and sear the pork for 4 to 5 minutes, stirring periodically to ensure even cooking.

Add in the water, pureed tomatoes, chicken bouillon granules, salt, black pepper, and red paper flakes, salt, and pepper. Partially cover and continue to simmer for 10 to 12 minutes.

Fold in the double cream and Tabasco sauce. Let it simmer for 5 minutes until cooked through.

Serve with avocado. Bon appétit!

Per serving: 490 Calories; 44g Fat; 6.1g Carbs; 24.3g Protein; 2.2g Fiber

159. Chinese Pork with Cauliflower

(Ready in about 20 minutes | Servings 6)

Ingredients

1 (8-ounce) can bamboo shoots
1 head cauliflower, broken into florets
1/2 teaspoon granulated garlic
Kosher salt and ground black pepper, to taste
1/2 teaspoon dried rosemary
1/4 teaspoon dried thyme
1 ½ tablespoons olive oil
1 shallot, chopped
1/4 cup vodka
1 ½ pounds pork tenderloin, boneless
2 tablespoons fish sauce

Directions

Place the pork, salt, black pepper, thyme, rosemary, granulated garlic, fish sauce, vodka and 1/2 tablespoon of olive oil in Ziploc bag; shake to coat on all sides.

Now, heat the remaining tablespoon of the olive oil in a frying pan over medium-high flame; sauté the onions until translucent.

Add the shallot and cauliflower for about 6 minutes or until they have softened; reserve.

In the same frying pan, brown the pork for 3 to 4 minutes per side. Add in the reserved marinade along with the shallot/cauliflower mixture and bamboo shoots.

Continue to cook for a further 5 minutes or until cooked through. Bon appétit!

Per serving: 356 Calories; 19.5g Fat; 6.4g Carbs; 33.1g Protein; 1.8g Fiber

160. Polish Zasmażana Kapusta

(Ready in about 35 minutes | Servings 6)

Ingredients

1 ½ pounds prepared sauerkraut, drained
1 cup vegetable broth
1/2 teaspoon fennel seeds, ground
1/2 teaspoon mustard seeds
1/3 cup dry white wine
1 Serano pepper, finely minced
1 teaspoon garlic, finely minced
2 pork sausages, sliced
1 onion, chopped
4 slices Polish bacon, chopped

Directions

In a saucepan, fry the bacon over medium-high heat for 7 to 8 minutes; reserve.

In the same pan, cook the sausage until no longer pink for 4 to 5 minutes; reserve. Then, cook the onions until tender and translucent for 5 to 6 minutes.

Add a splash of wine to deglaze the pan.

Add in the remaining ingredients and bring to a boil; turn the heat to simmer and continue to cook for 15 to 18 minutes or until everything is cooked through. Bon appétit!

Per serving: 309 Calories; 20.6g Fat; 4.2g Carbs; 19.3g Protein; 3.8g Fiber

161. Greek Warm Pork Salad

(Ready in about 20 minutes | Servings 2)

Ingredients

1/2 cup Greek yogurt
1/2 cup blue cheese, crumbled
1/2 cup radicchio, trimmed and sliced
1 bell pepper, deveined and chopped
Kosher salt and black pepper, to your liking
1 small head of Iceberg lettuce, leaves separated
1/4 cup beef bone broth
1 tablespoon lard
1/4 teaspoon thyme
2 teaspoons fresh lemon juice
1/2 pound ground pork

Directions

In a frying pan, melt the lard over medium flame; cook the ground pork until browned, crumbling with a fork.

Add the peppers and cook until they have softened. Pour in the bone broth to deglaze the pan; season with salt, pepper, and thyme; cook for a further 5 minutes and set aside.

Garnish with the Iceberg lettuce, radicchio, Greek yogurt and blue cheese. Drizzle fresh lemon juice over everything and serve.

Per serving: 431 Calories; 22.9g Fat; 5.2g Carbs; 42.2g Protein; 5.2g Fiber

162. Smoked Ham with Cabbage

(Ready in about 45 minutes | Servings 4)

Ingredients

6 ounces smoked ham, chopped
1 pound red cabbage, shredded
1/4 teaspoon paprika
2 cups vegetable stock
1 bay leaf
2 cloves garlic, pressed
1 yellow onion, diced
Sea salt and ground black pepper, to taste

Directions

In a heavy-bottomed pot, cook the ham over medium-high heat for 7 to 8 minutes.

Then, sauté the onion and garlic for about 6 minutes or until tender and aromatic. Add in the cabbage and continue cooking for 10 minutes more.

Add in the other ingredients and reduce the heat to simmer. Cover and continue to simmer for 20 to 25 minutes or until cooked through. Bon appétit!

Per serving: 123 Calories; 4.4g Fat; 6.8g Carbs; 9.8g Protein; 2.8g Fiber

163. Pork, Sausage and Bacon Meatloaf

(Ready in about 1 hour 10 minutes | Servings 6)

Ingredients

1 teaspoon lard
1/2 pound pork sausage, broken up
2 garlic cloves, finely minced
1 teaspoon celery seeds
1 egg, beaten
2 ounces half-and-half
6 strips bacon
1 medium-sized leek, chopped
1 ¼ pounds ground pork
Salt and cayenne pepper, to taste
1 bunch coriander, roughly chopped

Directions

Melt the lard in a frying pan over medium-high heat. Cook the leek and garlic until they have softened or about 3 minutes.

Add in the ground pork and sausage; cook until it is no longer pink, about 3 minutes. Add in the half-and-half, celery seeds, salt, cayenne pepper, coriander, and egg.

Press the mixture into a loaf pan.

Place the bacon strips on top of your meatloaf and bake at 390 degrees F about 55 minutes. Bon appétit!

Per serving: 396 Calories; 24.1g Fat; 5.1g Carbs; 38.1g Protein; 0.5g Fiber

164. Bacon and Cheese Keto Balls

(Ready in about 5 minutes | Servings 4)

Ingredients

1/2 cup bacon, chopped
3 ounces cream cheese
3 ounces blue cheese, crumbled
2 teaspoons tomato puree
2 tablespoons chives, chopped
1 ½ tablespoons mayonnaise

Directions

Mix all ingredients until everything is well combined.

Shape the mixture into 8 equal fat bombs.

Serve well chilled!

Per serving: 232 Calories; 17.6g Fat; 2.9g Carbs; 14.2g Protein; 0.6g Fiber

165. Zucchini Boats with Pork and Mushrooms

(Ready in about 50 minutes | Servings 8)

Ingredients

4 medium-sized zucchinis, cut into halves
1/2 cup chicken broth
1 garlic clove, pressed
1 cup cheddar cheese, freshly grated
2 tablespoons olive oil
1 cup tomato puree
1 cup Cremini mushrooms, chopped
1 pound ground pork
1 yellow onion, chopped
Salt and ground black pepper, to taste

Directions

Start by preheating your oven to 365 degrees F. Use a spoon to carefully scoop the flesh out of the zucchinis to create indentations.

In a sauté pan, heat the oil in over medium-high flame. Cook the onion for about 3 minutes until tender and translucent.

Stir in the garlic, pork and mushrooms; continue to sauté for 4 to 5 minutes more. Add in the salt, pepper, tomato puree and chicken broth.

Continue simmer for 10 to 12 minutes or until thoroughly cooked.

Spoon the filling into the zucchini boats and bake in the preheated oven approximately 20 minutes.

Top with the grated cheese and place under the preheated broiler for 5 minutes more until hot and bubbly. Bon appétit!

Per serving: 302 Calories; 21.2g Fat; 5.2g Carbs; 18.2g Protein; 1.1g Fiber

166. Spare Ribs with Italian Peppers

(Ready in about 2 hours | Servings 4)

Ingredients

1 pound pork spare ribs
2 Italian peppers, deveined and chopped
1 cup beef broth
1/2 cup dry sherry
1 red onion, chopped
1 garlic clove, minced
1 thyme sprig
1/2 cup coconut aminos
1 tablespoon tamarind paste
1 rosemary sprig
1 tablespoon lard, melted
1 tablespoon crushed sage
Salt and pepper, to your liking

Directions

Melt the lard in an oven-proof skillet over medium-high heat. Cook the meat on all sides until just browned; sprinkle with seasonings.

Add in the remaining ingredients. Roast in the preheated oven at 330 degrees F for 1 hour 40 minutes. Bon appétit!

Per serving: 370 Calories; 21.3g Fat; 4.3g Carbs; 33.7g Protein; 1.6g Fiber

167. Grilled Pork Skewers

(Ready in about 20 minutes + marinating time | Servings 6)

Ingredients

3 cloves garlic, smashed
1 teaspoon Greek oregano
2 tablespoons coriander, chopped
2 tablespoons fresh lime juice
Sea salt and ground black pepper, to taste
1/3 cup wine vinegar
2 ½ pounds pork tenderloin, trimmed of silver skin and excess fat, cut into 1-inch cubes

Directions

Thoroughly combine all ingredients in a ceramic dish. Cover tightly and let it marinate in your refrigerator for 2 to 3 hours. Thread the pork cubes onto the skewers.

Prepare the outdoor grill and brush the grates with a non-stick cooking spray.

Grill your skewers until well browned and internal temperature registers 160 degrees F on an instant read thermometer.

Bon appétit!

Per serving: 216 Calories; 4.1g Fat; 1.7g Carbs; 30g Protein; 0.2g Fiber

168. Grandma's Pork Goulash

(Ready in about 9 hours 10 minutes | Servings 4)

Ingredients

1 ½ tablespoons lard
2 cups tomato sauce with herbs
1 teaspoon sweet Hungarian paprika
1 teaspoon caraway seeds, ground
4 cups vegetable broth
2 Hungarian hot peppers, deveined and minced
1 cup leeks, chopped
2 garlic cloves, crushed
1 teaspoons cayenne pepper
1 ½ pounds pork butt, chopped

Directions

Melt the lard in a heavy-bottomed pot over medium-high heat. Sear the pork for 5 to 6 minutes until just browned on all sides; set aside.

Add in the leeks and garlic; continue to cook until they have softened.

Place the reserved pork along with the sautéed mixture in your crock pot. Add in the other ingredients and stir to combine.

Cover with the lid and slow cook for 9 hours on the lowest setting. Enjoy!

Per serving: 456 Calories; 28.7g Fat; 6.7g Carbs; 32g Protein; 3.4g Fiber

169. Old-Fashioned Meatballs with Brie Cheese

(Ready in about 25 minutes | Servings 5)

Ingredients

1 pound ground pork
10 (1-inch) cubes of brie cheese
2 tablespoons scallions, minced
2 cloves garlic, minced
1 teaspoon dried rosemary
1 tablespoon fresh parsley
2 eggs, beaten
Kosher salt and ground black pepper
1/3 cup double cream

Directions

Mix all ingredients, except for the brie cheese, until everything is well incorporated.

Roll the mixture into 10 patties; place a piece of cheese in the center of each patty and roll into a ball.

Roast in the preheated oven at 380 degrees F for about 20 minutes. Bon appétit!

Per serving: 302 Calories; 17.3g Fat; 1.9g Carbs; 33.4g Protein; 0.3g Fiber

170. Country-Style Sticky Ribs

(Ready in about 4 hours 30 minutes | Servings 4)

Ingredients

1 tablespoon olive oil, at room temperature
3/4 cup beef bone broth, preferably homemade
2 teaspoons erythritol
1/2 teaspoon ground cumin
2 cloves garlic, chopped
1 Italian pepper, chopped
2 bay leaves
A bunch of green onions, chopped
1 ½ pounds spare ribs
Salt and black peppercorns, to taste

Directions

Heat the olive oil in a saucepan over medium-high heat. Sear the ribs for 6 to 7 minutes on each side.

Whisk the broth, erythritol, garlic, Italian pepper, green onions, salt, pepper, and cumin until well combined.

Place the spare ribs in your crock pot; pour in the pepper/broth mixture. Add in the bay leaves. Cook for about 4 hours on Low setting.

Bon appétit!

Per serving: 412 Calories; 14g Fat; 4.3g Carbs; 43.3g Protein; 0.7g Fiber

171. Creole Smoked Pork

(Ready in about 30 minutes + marinating time | Servings 6)

Ingredients

1 tablespoon Creole seasoning
Salt and cayenne pepper, to taste
2 clove garlic, minced
1 ½ tablespoons coconut aminos
3 teaspoons vegetable oil
A few drops of liquid smoke
1 ½ pounds pork shank, cut into 6 serving portions

Directions

Blend the salt, cayenne pepper, vegetable oil, garlic, liquid smoke, Creole seasoning, and coconut aminos until you get a uniform and creamy mixture.

Massage the pork shanks on all sides with the prepared rub mixture. Let it marinate for about 2 hours in your refrigerator.

Grill for about 20 minutes until cooked through. Enjoy!

Per serving: 335 Calories; 24.3g Fat; 0.8g Carbs; 26.4g Protein; 0.4g Fiber

172. Pork with Classic Barbecue Sauce

(Ready in about 2 hours | Servings 8)

Ingredients

2 tablespoons vegetable oil
1 teaspoon salt
1/2 teaspoon freshly ground black pepper
2 garlic cloves, halved
2 pounds pork belly
For the Barbecue Sauce:
1/3 teaspoon ground cumin
1/3 teaspoon smoked paprika
1 teaspoon hot sauce
1/2 cup tomato puree
A few drops of liquid smoke
1 teaspoon Dijon mustard

Directions

Preheat your oven to 420 degrees F.

Now, rub the pork belly with the vegetable oil and garlic. Sprinkle with salt and pepper.

Roast the pork for 18 to 22 minutes. Now, decrease the heat to 330 degrees F. Roast for a further 1 hour 30 minutes.

Meanwhile, whisk all ingredients for the barbecue sauce until everything is well blended. Remove the crackling and cut the pork belly into slices. Enjoy!

Per serving: 561 Calories; 34g Fat; 1.7g Carbs; 52.7g Protein; 0.4g Fiber

173. Chinese Pork Shoulder with Gouda Cheese

(Ready in about 20 minutes | Servings 6)

Ingredients

1 ½ pounds pork shoulder, cut into strips
4 ounces gouda cheese, cut into small pieces
1/2 teaspoon cayenne pepper
1 tablespoon tahini (sesame butter)
1 tablespoon soy sauce
1/2 cup shallots, roughly chopped
2 bell peppers, sliced
1/2 teaspoon Sriracha sauce
1 tablespoon sesame oil
1/4 cup cream of onion soup
Himalayan salt and freshly ground black pepper, to taste

Directions

Heat he sesame oil in a wok over a moderately high flame.

Stir-fry the pork strips for 3 to 4 minutes or until just browned on all sides. Add in the spices, shallots and bell peppers and continue to cook for a further 4 minutes.

Stir in the cream of onion soup, Sriracha, sesame butter, and soy sauce; continue to cook for 3 to 4 minutes more.

Top with the cheese and continue to cook until the cheese has melted. Enjoy!

Per serving: 424 Calories; 29.4g Fat; 3.8g Carbs; 34.2g Protein; 0.6g Fiber

174. Pork and Kale Bowl

(Ready in about 25 minutes | Servings 4)

Ingredients

1 bunch kale, trimmed and roughly chopped
1 cup onions, sliced
1/4 cup port wine
2 cloves garlic, pressed
1 teaspoon sea salt
1/4 cup tomato puree
1 cup chicken bone broth
2 tablespoons olive oil
1 bell pepper, chopped
1/4 teaspoon black pepper, or more to taste
1 chili pepper, sliced
1 ½ pounds ground pork

Directions

Heat 1 tablespoon of the olive oil in a cast-iron skillet over a moderately high heat. Now, sauté the onion, garlic, and peppers until they are tender and fragrant; reserve.

Heat the remaining tablespoon of olive oil; once hot, cook the ground pork and approximately 5 minutes until no longer pink.

Add in the other ingredients and continue to cook for 15 to 17 minutes or until cooked through.

Bon appétit!

Per serving: 349 Calories; 13g Fat; 4.4g Carbs; 45.3g Protein; 1.2g Fiber

175. Wine-Braised Pork Butt Steak

(Ready in about 30 minutes | Servings 4)

Ingredients

1/4 cup dry red wine
4 pork butt steaks
1 red onion, peeled and chopped
1 teaspoon celery seeds
1/2 teaspoon salt
1/2 teaspoon freshly ground black pepper
1/2 teaspoon cayenne pepper
1 garlic clove, minced
2 tablespoons lard, room temperature

Directions

Melt 1 tablespoon of lard in a cast-iron skillet that is preheated over a moderate heat. Cover the skillet and sear the butt steaks for 10 minutes on each side.

Add a splash of red wine to deglaze the skillet. Season with celery seeds, cayenne pepper, salt and black pepper; cook an additional 8 to 12 minutes; reserve.

Warm the remaining 1 tablespoon of lard in the same skillet; cook the onions and garlic until tender and aromatic.

Bon appétit!

Per serving: 305 Calories; 20.6g Fat; 3.7g Carbs; 22.5g Protein; 0.6g Fiber

176. Spicy Ground Pork with Swiss Chard

(Ready in about 25 minutes | Servings 4)

Ingredients

1 ½ pounds ground pork
1 bunch Swiss chard, trimmed and roughly chopped
1/4 cup tomato puree
1/4 cup dry sherry wine
1 cup leeks, sliced
1 Serrano pepper, sliced
1 bell pepper, chopped
1 teaspoon sea salt
2 cloves garlic, pressed
1 cup beef bone broth
2 tablespoons vegetable oil
1/4 teaspoon lemon pepper, or more to taste

Directions

Heat 1 tablespoon of the vegetable oil in a pan over a moderately high heat. Now, sauté the garlic, leeks, and peppers until they are just softened; reserve.

Heat the remaining tablespoon of vegetable oil; add the ground pork and cook, stirring frequently, for 3 to 4 minutes more.

Add the remaining ingredients along with the sautéed vegetables. Cook, covered, an additional 10 minutes or until everything is thoroughly cooked.

Uncover and cook for a further 5 minute or until the liquid has evaporated. Bon appétit!

Per serving: 349 Calories; 13g Fat; 6.5g Carbs; 45.3g Protein; 1.8g Fiber

177. Tangy Pork Stew with Avocado

(Ready in about 25 minutes | Servings 4)

Ingredients

3/4 pound boneless pork shoulder, cubed
2 shallots, chopped
1 teaspoon habanero pepper, deveined and minced
1 carrot, chopped
1/2 teaspoon ground bay leaf
1/2 teaspoon ground cloves
1 avocado, pitted, peeled and diced
1/2 cup sour cream, full-fat
1/2 tablespoon garlic paste
1 ½ cups bone broth
Himalayan salt and ground black pepper, to taste
1 tablespoon fresh parsley, chopped
1 tablespoon butter

Directions

Melt the butter in a heavy-bottomed pot that is preheated over a moderate heat.

Now, sauté the shallots, carrot, and habanero pepper for 3 minutes or until they are tender.

After that, add the cubed pork; cook an additional 5 minutes, stirring frequently.

Then, add the garlic paste, broth, bay leaf powder ground cloves, salt, and pepper; turn the heat to a medium-high and bring it to a boil.

Next, decrease the heat to a simmer. Cook an additional 15 minutes or until thoroughly heated.

Garnish with fresh parsley, avocado and sour cream.

Bon appétit!

Per serving: 295 Calories; 19.6g Fat; 6.7g Carbs; 20.3g Protein; 4.4g Fiber

178. Pork Medallions with Scallions and Herbs

(Ready in about 20 minutes | Servings 4)

Ingredients

A bunch of scallions, roughly chopped
1 thyme sprig, minced
Coarse salt and ground black pepper, to taste
2 rosemary sprigs, minced
1 tablespoon butter
1 teaspoon dried sage, crushed
1/2 teaspoon garlic powder
1/2 teaspoon red pepper flakes, crushed
1 pound pork tenderloin, cut crosswise into 12 medallions

Directions

Season each pork medallion with salt, black pepper, garlic powder and red pepper flakes.

Then, melt the butter in a saucepan over medium-high heat. Cook the pork tenderloin about 3 minutes per side.

Add the scallions, thyme, and rosemary; cook until heated through, an additional 3 minutes. Garnish with dried sage.

Bon appétit!

Per serving: 192 Calories; 6.9g Fat; 0.9g Carbs; 29.8g Protein; 0.4g Fiber

179. Mexican Pork Spare Rib Soup

(Ready in about 20 minutes | Servings 6)

Ingredients

A pinch of dried Mexican oregano
1 medium-sized avocado, pitted and sliced
1 teaspoon habanero pepper, seeded and minced
1 teaspoon garlic, crushed
3 cups beef broth, less-sodium
1 ¼ pounds pork spare ribs, boneless and cut into chunks
2 vine-ripened tomatoes, undrained
1 celery, chopped
1 onion, peeled and chopped
1/4 cup fresh coriander, roughly chopped
2 tablespoons butter, room temperature
Sea salt and ground black pepper, to taste

Directions

Melt the butter in a heavy-bottomed pot over a moderate heat. Sauté the onion, garlic, pepper and celery approximately 3 minutes.

Then, sear the pork for 4 to 5 minutes, stirring continuously to ensure even cooking. Add in the broth, salt, black pepper, oregano, tomatoes, and coriander.

Continue to simmer, partially covered, for about 12 minutes.

Serve with avocado. Bon appétit!

Per serving: 423 Calories; 31.8g Fat; 6g Carbs; 25.9g Protein; 3.2g Fiber

180. Roasted Pork with Marinara Sauce

(Ready in about 2 hours | Servings 8)

Ingredients

2 pounds pork butt
1 teaspoon hot sauce
1/3 teaspoon hot paprika
1/2 cup marinara sauce
1 teaspoon stone-ground mustard
1 teaspoon fresh garlic, halved
A few drops of liquid smoke
1/3 teaspoon ground cumin
2 tablespoons olive oil
Sea salt and freshly ground black pepper, to taste

Directions

Rub the pork with the olive oil and garlic. Sprinkle with salt, pepper, and hot paprika.

Roast the pork at 410 degrees F for 20 minutes. Turn the heat to 340 degrees F and roast for about 1 hour.

In a mixing bowl, whisk the remaining ingredients. Spoon the sauce over the pork and continue to roast an additional 20 minutes.

Bon appétit!

Per serving: 561 Calories; 34g Fat; 1.7g Carbs; 52.7g Protein; 0.4g Fiber

181. Meatballs with Double Cream Sauce

(Ready in about 30 minutes | Servings 6)

Ingredients

For the Meatballs:
1 pound ground pork
1/2 pound ground turkey
1 tablespoon scallions, minced
2 eggs
1 tablespoon green garlic, minced
1 tablespoon steak seasoning
For the Sauce:
1 cup double cream
1/2 teaspoon dried rosemary
3 teaspoons ghee
1 cup cream of onion soup
Salt and pepper, to your liking

Directions

Preheat your oven to 365 degrees F.

In a mixing bowl, combine all ingredients for the meatballs. Roll the mixture into 20 to 24 balls and place them on a parchment-lined baking sheet.

Roast for about 25 minutes or until your meatballs are golden-brown on the top.

While your meatballs are roasting, melt the ghee in a preheated sauté pan over a moderate flame. Gradually add in the remaining ingredients, whisking constantly, until the sauce has reduced slightly.

Bon appétit!

Per serving: 378 Calories; 29.9g Fat; 2.9g Carbs; 23.4g Protein; 0.3g Fiber

182. New Orleans Pork Gumbo

(Ready in about 35 minutes | Servings 6)

Ingredients

8 ounces New Orleans spicy sausage, sliced
2 tablespoons olive oil
1/2 cup celery, chopped
1/4 cup flaxseed meal
3/4 pound okra
2 bell peppers, deveined and thinly sliced
5 cups bone broth
1 medium-sized leek, chopped
1 tablespoon Cajun spice mix
1 teaspoon gumbo file
1 pound pork tenderloin, cubed

Directions

In a heavy-bottomed pot, heat the oil until sizzling. Sear the pork tenderloin and New Orleans sausage for about 8 minutes or until browned on all sides; set aside.

In the same pot, cook the leek and peppers until they softened. Add in the gumbo file, Cajun spice and broth. Bring it to a rolling boil.

Turn the heat to medium-low and add in celery. Let it simmer for 18 to 20 minutes longer.

Stir in the flax seed meal and okra along with the reserved meat. Then, continue to simmer for 5 to 6 minutes or until heated through. Enjoy!

Per serving: 427 Calories; 16.2g Fat; 3.6g Carbs; 33.2g Protein; 4.4g Fiber

183. Pork Stew with Serrano Pepper and Cheese

(Ready in about 25 minutes | Servings 4)

Ingredients

3/4 pound boneless pork shoulder, cubed
1 teaspoon Serrano pepper, deveined and minced
2 garlic cloves, minced
1 carrot, chopped
1 tablespoon lard, room temperature
1 tablespoon fresh coriander, chopped
1 ½ cups vegetable stock
1/2 teaspoon ground cloves
1 onion, chopped
2 ounces cream cheese, full-fat
Himalayan salt and ground black pepper, to taste

Directions

Melt the lard in a soup pot over medium-high heat.

Now, sauté the onion, carrot, and Serrano pepper for about 4 minutes or until tender and fragrant.

Add in the boneless pork butt and cook for a father 5 to 6 minutes, stirring continuously to ensure even cooking.

Add in the garlic, vegetable stock, ground cloves, salt, black pepper, and coriander; bring to a rapid boil. Now, reduce the temperature to medium-low.

Cook for 15 to 20 minutes or until everything is thoroughly cooked.

Serve in individual bowls, dolloped with cream cheese.

Per serving: 295 Calories; 15.6g Fat; 6.3g Carbs; 17.3g Protein; 1.1g Fiber

184. Carrot and Meat Loaf Muffins

(Ready in about 35 minutes | Servings 6)

Ingredients

1 pound pork, ground
1/2 pound turkey, ground
1 cup carrots, shredded
2 ripe tomatoes, pureed
1 ounce envelope onion soup mix
1 tablespoon Worcestershire sauce
1 tablespoon Dijon mustard
1/2 teaspoon dry basil
1 teaspoon dry oregano
Kosher salt and ground black pepper, to taste
2 cloves of garlic, minced
1 eggs, whisked
1 cup mozzarella cheese, shredded

Directions

Start by preheating your oven to 350 degrees F.

Then, thoroughly combine all ingredients until everything is blended.

Spoon the mixture into a muffin tin that is previously coated with a non-stick cooking spray.

Bake for 30 minutes; allow them to cool slightly before removing from the tin. Bon appétit!

Per serving: 220 Calories; 6.3g Fat; 5.4g Carbs; 33.8g Protein; 1.7g Fiber

185. Roasted Pork Shoulder with Asiago Cheese

(Ready in about 25 minutes | Servings 4)

Ingredients

2 tablespoons lard
2 shallots, sliced
2 tablespoons rice vinegar
1 tablespoon fish sauce
2 tablespoons Kalamata olives, pitted and sliced
1 tablespoon tamarind paste
1 cup bone broth
2 cloves garlic, smashed
1 rosemary sprig
1 thyme sprig
1/2 cup Asiago cheese, freshly grated
1 pound pork shoulder, cut into 1-inch-thick pieces
Salt and cayenne pepper, to taste

Directions

Start by preheating your broiler. Sprinkle your pork with salt and cayenne pepper on all sides.

Melt the lard in a pan that is preheated over a moderately high flame. Sweat the shallots and garlic for about 5 minutes; reserve.

Warm the remaining 1 tablespoon of lard. Sear the pork for 7 to 8 minutes, turning once; reserve.

Now, cook the garlic, thyme, rosemary, tamarind paste, fish sauce, olives, vinegar, and bone broth in pan drippings. Cook until the sauce is reduced by about half. Transfer to an oven-safe dish.

Add the reserved pork along with the shallot mixture; sprinkle with grated Asiago cheese. Lastly, broil until everything is thoroughly heated, about 5 minutes.

Enjoy!

Per serving: 476 Calories; 35.3g Fat; 6.2g Carbs; 31.1g Protein; 1.2g Fiber

186. Pork and Pepperoncini Soup

(Ready in about 1 hour | Servings 4)

Ingredients

1 ½ pounds pork stew meat, cubed
1 carrot, thinly sliced
1 Italian pepper, thinly sliced
Salt and black pepper, to taste
1 shallot, chopped
1 teaspoon green garlic, minced
1 Pepperoncini, seeded and cut into very thin strips with scissors
1 tablespoon Italian herb mix
1/2 cup Marsala wine
2 tablespoons olive oil
4 cups beef bone broth
1 tomato, crushed

Directions

In a soup pot, heat the oil over a moderately high flame. Brown the pork for about 6 minutes until no longer pink; set aside.

In the same pot, cook the shallot until tender and fragrant. Stir in the garlic and continue to sauté for 30 seconds more or until aromatic. Add in wine to deglaze the bottom of the soup pot.

Add in the remaining ingredients along with the reserved pork; bring to a rapid boil. Reduce the heat to medium-low; continue to simmer, partially covered, for about 45 minutes. Bon appétit!

Per serving: 331 Calories; 17.6g Fat; 4.4g Carbs; 37.4g Protein; 0.9g Fiber

187. Pork and Romano Cheese Muffins

(Ready in about 35 minutes | Servings 6)

Ingredients

1 pound pork, ground
1/2 pound turkey, ground
1 cup Romano cheese, grated
1 tablespoon stone-ground mustard
Kosher salt and ground black pepper, to taste
1 cup tomato puree
1 tablespoon coconut aminos
1 ½ teaspoons dry basil
2 cloves of garlic, minced
1 cup carrots, shredded
1 egg, whisked
1 ounce envelope onion soup mix

Directions

In a mixing bowl, combine all ingredients until everything is well incorporated. Press the mixture into a lightly-oiled muffin tin.

Bake in the preheated oven at 355 degrees F for 30 to 33 minutes; let it cool slightly before unmolding and serving.

Bon appétit!

Per serving: 303 Calories; 17g Fat; 6.2g Carbs; 29.6g Protein; 1.7g Fiber

188. Mustard Pork Cutlets with Veggies

(Ready in about 30 minutes + marinating time | Servings 4)

Ingredients

1 tablespoon yellow mustard
1/2 teaspoon sea salt
2 carrots, sliced
1 cup leeks, sliced
2 tablespoons cider vinegar
2 tablespoons lard, melted
1/2 teaspoon freshly ground black pepper
4 pork cutlets
1 celery stalk, diced
1 teaspoon garlic paste

Directions

In a mixing bowl, combine the garlic paste, salt, black pepper, mustard and cider vinegar until well mixed. Add the pork cutlets and let them marinate for 2 hours.

Now, melt the lard in an oven-safe pan over a moderate heat. Brown the pork cutlets for 5 minutes on each side. Add the celery, carrots, and leeks.

Cook an additional 5 minutes, stirring periodically.

Transfer the pan to the oven; roast the pork with the vegetables for about 13 minutes.

Bon appétit!

Per serving: 452 Calories; 34.8g Fat; 5.7g Carbs; 26.3g Protein; 0.7g Fiber

189. Roasted Sherry Ribs with Peppers

(Ready in about 2 hours | Servings 4)

Ingredients

1 pound baby back ribs
2 roasted red bell peppers, chopped
2 roasted chile peppers, chopped
1 red onion, chopped
2 rosemary sprigs
1/2 cup dry sherry
1/2 cup soy sauce
1 tablespoon garlic paste
1 tablespoon crushed sage
1 tablespoon tamarind paste
1 cup beef broth
2 tablespoons olive oil
Salt and pepper, to your liking

Directions

Start by preheating your oven to 340 degrees F. Spritz a roasting pan with a non-stick cooking spray.

Heat the oil in an ovenproof pan over a moderately high heat. Now, brown the meat on all sides for 10 minutes; sprinkle with salt and pepper.

Add the garlic paste, onion, rosemary and sage. Cook an additional 4 minutes or until heated through. Stir in the remaining ingredients.

Bake for 1 hour 30 minutes in the middle of the preheated oven. Bon appétit!

Per serving: 370 Calories; 21.3g Fat; 6.3g Carbs; 33.7g Protein; 2.7g Fiber

190. Classic Wine-Braised Pork Chops

(Ready in about 30 minutes | Servings 4)

Ingredients

4 pork chops
1/2 teaspoon fresh ginger root, grated
2 tablespoons Worcestershire sauce
3 cloves garlic, minced
4 allspice berries, lightly crushed
2 tablespoons lard, melted
1/2 cup red onion, thinly sliced
1/4 cup dry white wine
1 teaspoon dried thyme

Directions

Melt the lard in a saucepan over medium heat. Sauté the onions and garlic until aromatic and just browned.

Add the pork and cook 15 to 20 minutes, turning once or twice. Add the dry white wine, Worcestershire sauce, thyme, crushed allspice berries and fresh ginger.

Cook an additional 8 minutes or until everything is thoroughly heated.

Bon appétit!

Per serving: 335 Calories; 26.3g Fat; 2.5g Carbs; 18.3g Protein; 0.3g Fiber

191. Spicy Pork Soup with Roma Tomatoes

(Ready in about 1 hour | Servings 4)

Ingredients

1 ½ pounds pork stew meat, cubed
1 ripe Roma tomato, crushed
1 Anaheim chile, seeded and cut into very thin strips with scissors
2 carrots, thinly sliced
2 parsnips, thinly sliced
1 onion, chopped
2 thyme sprigs
Fresh cilantro, for garnish
2 rosemary sprigs
2 garlic cloves, crushed
1/2 cup dry white wine
4 cups beef bone broth
1/2 teaspoon dried basil
2 tablespoons olive oil
Salt and black pepper, to taste

Directions

Heat the olive oil in a heavy-bottomed pot that is preheated over a moderately high flame. Now, sear the pork cubes until they are just browned; reserve.

Then, cook the onions and garlic in pan drippings for 3 to 4 minutes. Pour in wine to deglaze the bottom.

Add the carrots, parsnip, and beef bone broth, bringing to a boil. Turn the heat to medium-low and simmer 6 to 7 more minutes.

Add the tomato, chile, basil, thyme, and rosemary; let it simmer an additional 50 minutes, partially covered. Garnish with chopped cilantro.

Bon appétit!

Per serving: 341 Calories; 12.9g Fat; 5.8g Carbs; 45.4g Protein; 3g Fiber

192. Crock Pot Ribs with Wine

(Ready in about 8 hours | Servings 4)

Ingredients

1 pound pork ribs
1/4 cup dry red wine
1 teaspoon grated orange peel
1/4 cup Worcestershire sauce
1 garlic clove, crushed
1/2 teaspoon ground oregano
1/2 teaspoon smoked cayenne pepper
1/2 teaspoon ground cloves
1 teaspoon Ancho chiles, minced
1 bell pepper, thinly sliced
1 tablespoon lard

Directions

Treat the sides and bottom of your Crock pot with melted lard. Arrange the pork chops and peppers on the bottom.

Drizzle Worcestershire sauce and wine over everything. Sprinkle with cayenne pepper, garlic, oregano and ground cloves.

Slow cook on Low setting approximately 8 hours. Garnish with grated orange peel.

Bon appétit!

Per serving: 192 Calories; 6.9g Fat; 0.9g Carbs; 29.8g Protein; 0.4g Fiber

193. Pork in Chilorio Sauce

(Ready in about 30 minutes | Servings 6)

Ingredients

6 pork chops
1 tablespoon olive oil
For the Sauce:
2 teaspoons olive oil
1/2 teaspoon red pepper flakes, crushed
2 garlic cloves, minced
1 teaspoon dried basil
1/2 teaspoon ground cumin
1/2 cup bone broth
Salt and ground black pepper, to taste
2 Ancho chiles, chopped

Directions

Heat 1 tablespoon of the olive oil in a saucepan that is preheated over a moderately high flame. Sear the pork chops until they're well browned and their juices run clear.

To make the sauce, in a pot, boil the Ancho chiles and bone broth for a couple of minutes. Now, remove your pot from the heat; allow the chiles to stand in the hot water for 15 to 25 minutes.

Add the chiles along with the liquid to a blender or food processor; add the remaining ingredients for the sauce.

Puree until creamy, smooth and uniform. Bon appétit!

Per serving: 347 Calories; 29.2g Fat; 0.2g Carbs; 20.2g Protein; 0.2g Fiber

194. Pork and Bacon Meatloaf

(Ready in about 1 hour 10 minutes | Servings 6)

Ingredients

1 ¼ pounds ground pork
6 strips bacon
1 egg, beaten
1/2 pound pork sausage, broken up
2 ounces half-and-half
1 teaspoon celery seeds
1/4 teaspoon cayenne pepper
1 yellow onion, chopped
1 teaspoon garlic, finely minced
1 bunch cilantro, roughly chopped
1 teaspoon lard, melted
Salt and ground black pepper, to taste

Directions

Preheat your oven to 395 degrees F. Lightly grease a baking dish and set it aside.

Heat the lard in a cast-iron skillet over a medium heat. Next, sauté the onions and garlic until they are tender and fragrant, for 2 to 4 minutes.

Stir in the pork and cook until it is no longer pink, about 2 minutes.

In a mixing bowl, thoroughly combine the egg, half-and-half, celery seeds, salt, black pepper, cayenne pepper, pork sausage and cilantro.

Add the reserved pork mixture; stir to combine well. Lastly, shape the mixture into a loaf.

Place the bacon on the top of your meatloaf. Bake about 1 hour. Bon appétit!

Per serving: 405 Calories; 24.6g Fat; 2.8g Carbs; 40.6g Protein; 0.4g Fiber

195. Milk Braised Pork Loin with Sage

(Ready in about 1 hour 35 minutes | Servings 8)

Ingredients

2 pounds pork loin
2 cup full-fat milk
1 tablespoon dried sage, crushed
1/2 cup shallots, sliced
2 bell peppers, deveined and thinly sliced
Salt and cayenne pepper, to taste
1 teaspoon dried thyme
3 teaspoons olive oil

Directions

Start by preheating your oven to 330 degrees F.

Heat the oil in a pan over a moderate flame. Sear the pork loin in a pan until just browned.

Transfer the loin to a baking pan. Season with salt, pepper, and thyme. Scatter the sliced shallot and peppers around the meat.

Pour in the milk and cover the pan tightly with a piece of foil. Roast for 1 hour 30 minutes, turning the loin once or twice.

Carve the pork loin and transfer to a serving plate along with the roasted vegetables as well as the cooking liquid. Garnish with sage leaves.

Bon appétit!

Per serving: 293 Calories; 15.4g Fat; 5.4g Carbs; 31.4g Protein; 0.4g Fiber

BEEF

196. Beef Meatloaf with Halloumi Cheese

(Ready in about 55 minutes | Servings 8)

Ingredients

8 slices of bacon
6 ounces Halloumi cheese, crumbled
1 red onion, finely chopped
1/4 cup half-and-half
1 tablespoon Greek red wine
1 tablespoon Dijon mustard
2 eggs, beaten
2 teaspoons Greek seasoning mix
1/2 cup Greek black olives, chopped
2 ½ pounds ground beef
3 teaspoons olive oil

Directions

In a frying pan, heat the oil over a moderate flame. Once hot, cook the onion and beef until the onion is tender and the beef is no longer pink or 5 to 6 minutes.

Then, thoroughly combine half-and-half, cheese eggs, seasoning mix, mustard, wine and olives; add in sautéed mixture. Mix until everything is well combined.

Press the mixture into a loaf pan. Top the meatloaf with the bacon slices and cover with a piece of foil.

Bake in the preheated oven at 385 degrees F for 35 to 40 minutes. Remove the foil and bake for a further 13 minutes. Bon appétit!

Per serving: 442 Calories; 20.6g Fat; 4.9g Carbs; 56.3g Protein; 0.7g Fiber

197. Thai-Style Porterhouse Steak

(Ready in about 15 minutes + marinating time | Servings 4)

Ingredients

1 teaspoon Sriracha sauce
1 tablespoon ginger-garlic paste
1 teaspoon celery seeds
1 tablespoon fresh cilantro, chopped
1/2 teaspoon dried rosemary
1/2 cup green onions, chopped
1/2 tablespoon lard, melted
Salt and pepper, to taste
2 tablespoons coconut aminos
1 ½ pounds Porterhouse steak, cubed

Directions

In a ceramic bowl, thoroughly combine the coconut aminos, Sriracha sauce, ginger-garlic paste, salt, pepper, celery seeds, rosemary, and green onions.

Add in the cubed beef and allow it to marinate in your refrigerator for 1 hour.

Melt the lard in a frying pan over medium-high heat. Cook the Porterhouse steak for 5 to 6 minutes until it is fall-apart-tender. Add in the cilantro and remove from the heat. Bon appétit!

Per serving: 292 Calories; 14.3g Fat; 3.9g Carbs; 36.9g Protein; 0.6g Fiber

198. Bacon Meatballs with Parsley Sauce

(Ready in about 30 minutes | Servings 6)

Ingredients

For the Meatballs:
1/2 cup onion, chopped
1/2 cup crushed pork rinds
2 cloves garlic, smashed
1 ½ pounds ground chuck
1 egg, beaten
Sea salt and ground black pepper, to your liking
1 ½ tablespoons sesame oil
6 slices bacon, cut into thirds lengthwise
For the Parsley Sauce:
1/2 tablespoon olive oil
1 cup fresh Italian parsley
2 tablespoons sunflower seeds, soaked
Flaky salt, to taste

Directions

Thoroughly combine all ingredients for the meatballs. Roll the mixture into 18 balls and wrap each of them with a slice of bacon; secure with a toothpick.

Bake the meatballs in the preheated oven at 385 degrees F for about 30 minutes, rotating the pan once or twice.

Pulse all ingredients for the parsley sauce in your blender or food processor until your desired consistency is reached.

Serve with the parsley sauce on the side. Bon appétit!

Per serving: 399 Calories; 27g Fat; 1.8g Carbs; 37.7g Protein; 0.9g Fiber

199. Beef and Ale Stew

(Ready in about 1 hour | Servings 6)

Ingredients

1 ½ pounds chuck roast, cut into small chunks
1 cup red onions, chopped
1/4 cup basil leaves, snipped
1 cup ale beer
1 bay leaf
1 celery with leaves, chopped
1 parsnip, chopped
1 ½ tablespoons olive oil
1/2 teaspoon mustard seeds
3 cups beef bone broth
1 ½ cups tomato puree

Directions

Heat the olive oil in a heavy-bottomed pot or Dutch oven over medium-high flame. Cook the chuck roast for about 6 minutes or until it is browned; set aside.

Sauté the vegetables in the same pot for about 8 minutes or until tender and fragrant, stirring occasionally.

Add in the remaining ingredients and bring to a boil. Turn the heat to a simmer and continue to cook, partially covered, for about 45 minutes.

Bon appétit!

Per serving: 444 Calories; 14.2g Fat; 6.1g Carbs; 66.3g Protein; 2g Fiber

200. Hungarian Marha Pörkölt

(Ready in about 1 hour 25 minutes | Servings 4)

Ingredients

1 tablespoon Hungarian paprika
2 tablespoons lard, room temperature
1 cup leeks, peeled and chopped
1/2 cup dry white wine
2 bell pepper, deveined and chopped
1 tablespoon flaxseed meal
4 cups beef broth
1 celery with leaves, chopped
Salt and pepper, to taste
1 ¼ pounds beef roast, diced

Directions

In a heavy-bottomed pot, melt the lard over moderate heat. Cook the beef and leeks for about 5 minutes. Sprinkle with salt, pepper, and Hungarian paprika.

Add in wine to deglaze the bottom of your pot. Add in the beef broth, celery, and peppers. Turn the heat to a simmer and continue to cook for a further 1 hour 10 minutes.

Stir in the flaxseed meal; continue stirring for about 4 minutes to thicken the liquid. Bon appétit!

Per serving: 357 Calories; 15.8g Fat; 5g Carbs; 40.2g Protein; 2.2g Fiber

201. Lasagna with Beef and Cheddar Cheese

(Ready in about 1 hour 30 minutes | Servings 6)

Ingredients

For the Lasagna Sheets:
6 ounces cream cheese, at room temperature
1/2 teaspoon dried Mediterranean spice mix
3 eggs, whisked
1 1/2 cup Romano cheese, grated
For the Filling:
2 slices bacon, chopped
1 cup Cheddar cheese
1 teaspoon fresh garlic, smashed
1 onion, chopped
1 tablespoon butter, room temperature
2 cups cream cheese
1 ½ pounds ground beef
1 cup marinara sauce

Directions

Begin by preheating your oven to 365 degrees F. Line a baking sheet with parchment paper.

Combine the eggs and 6 ounces of cream cheese with a hand mixer. Stir in the remaining ingredients for the lasagna sheets and continue to mix until everything is well combined.

Spread the mixture onto a baking sheet and bake in the preheated oven for 17 to 20 minutes. Let it cool and then, place in your refrigerator for about 30 minutes. Slice into lasagna sheets and reserve.

In a saucepan, melt the butter over a moderately high heat. Cook the ground beef for about 4 minutes or until no longer pink.

Stir in the onion, garlic and bacon; continue to cook an additional 4 minutes. Add in the marinara sauce and continue to simmer an additional 12 minutes.

Pour 1/4 cup of the beef sauce into the bottom of a lightly greased baking dish. Top with the first lasagna sheet. Repeat until you run out of ingredients, ending with a sauce layer.

Bake for about 20 minutes or until heated through.

Top with the cheese and place under the preheated broiled for 6 to 7 minutes or until the top is hot and bubbly. Enjoy!

Per serving: 494 Calories; 41g Fat; 3.8g Carbs; 24.1g Protein; 1.1g Fiber

202. Beef Sausage Vegetable Stir-Fry

(Ready in about 25 minutes | Servings 4)

Ingredients

2 smoked beef sausage links, sliced
2 bell peppers, sliced
1 teaspoon fajita seasoning
1 carrot, sliced
1 piquillo pepper, minced
1 teaspoon crushed garlic
2 zucchinis, sliced
1/2 teaspoon saffron
1 tablespoon lard

Directions

Warm the lard in a wok that is preheated over a moderate heat.

Now, brown the chicken sausage along with the garlic approximately 8 minutes.

Add the other ingredients and cook, stirring periodically, for 13 minutes more.

Bon appétit!

Per serving: 227 Calories; 18g Fat; 6.2g Carbs; 7.1g Protein; 0.7g Fiber

203. Spanish-Style Beef Tenderloin

(Ready in about 20 minutes + marinating time | Servings 4)

Ingredients

1 Spanish pepper, deseeded and chopped
1 pound beef tenderloin, cut into bite-sized strips
1 cup cabbage, shredded
1/2 teaspoon dried rosemary
2 tablespoons olive oil
1/2 teaspoon dried marjoram
1/2 teaspoon dried basil
1 red onion, chopped
1 teaspoon garlic, minced
1 tablespoon fish sauce
Sea salt and pepper, to taste

Directions

Toss the beef tenderloin with the fish sauce and spices. Allow it to marinate in your refrigerator for at least 2 hours.

In a Dutch oven, heat the olive oil over a moderately high heat. Cook the marinated beef for about 5 minutes, stirring periodically to ensure even cooking.

Add in the onions and garlic and cook for 2 minutes more. Now, stir in the cabbage and pepper; turn the heat to a simmer.

Continue to simmer, partially covered, for 10 to 12 minutes more. Bon appétit!

Per serving: 321 Calories; 14g Fat; 5.3g Carbs; 36.7g Protein; 1.4g Fiber

204. French Ventrèche and Beef Soup

(Ready in about 2 hours 10 minutes | Servings 4)

Ingredients

4 ounces ventrèche, chopped
1 tablespoon flaxseed meal, dissolved in 2 tablespoons of cold water
2 cloves garlic, minced
1 bell pepper, deveined and chopped
2 tablespoons dry red wine
1 small-sized ripe tomato, crushed
2 tablespoons fresh chives, chopped
1 celery rib, chopped
4 cups vegetable broth
1 yellow onion, chopped
2 sprigs rosemary
1 pound beef stew meat, cubed
2 tablespoons butter
1 tablespoon cider vinegar

Directions

In a heavy-bottomed pot, melt 1 tablespoon of butter over a moderate heat. Cook the ventrèche for about 4 minutes and reserve.

Melt another tablespoon of butter. Once hot, sauté the onions, garlic, pepper, and celery for 3 to 4 minutes until they have softened. Add in the beef and continue to cook until browned.

Stir in the rosemary, tomato, vinegar, red wine, and broth. Turn the heat to a simmer, cover and continue to cook for a further 2 hours.

Add in the flaxseed slurry and continue to cook an additional 3 to 4 minutes or until thoroughly cooked. Add in the reserved ventrèche. Serve with fresh chives. Bon appétit!

Per serving: 340 Calories; 19.6g Fat; 6.5g Carbs; 30.2g Protein; 2g Fiber

205. Montreal Meatballs with Thyme-Butter Sauce

(Ready in about 30 minutes | Servings 6)

Ingredients

For the Meatballs:
2 small-sized eggs
2 cloves garlic, minced
1 pound ground pork
1 tablespoon Montreal steak seasoning
1/2 pound ground beef
1 tablespoon beef bouillon granules
For the Sauce:
1 cup heavy whipping cream
Salt and pepper, to taste
1 cup bone broth
3 teaspoons butter
1/2 teaspoon dried thyme

Directions

Begin by preheating an oven to 360 degrees F.

Thoroughly combine all ingredients for the meatballs in a mixing bowl. Shape into 20 balls with oiled hands.

Arrange the meatballs on a cookie sheet that is previously greased with a non-stick cooking spray.

Bake for 18 to 22 minutes or until the meatballs are thoroughly cooked. Now, place your meatballs under the broiler for a couple of minutes to achieve a browned, crispy crust.

Meanwhile, make the sauce in a pan. Firstly, melt the butter over a moderate heat. Slowly and gradually stir in the other ingredients for the sauce, whisking constantly.

Bring to a boil and cook until the sauce has thickened. Bon appétit!

Per serving: 284 Calories; 14.8g Fat; 1.3g Carbs; 34.4g Protein; 0.4g Fiber

206. Sloppy Joes with Mustard and Paprika

(Ready in about 30 minutes | Servings 6)

Ingredients

2 teaspoons lard, room temperature
1 teaspoon paprika
1 teaspoon mustard
1/2 cup tomato sauce
1/2 teaspoon hot sauce
1 large onion, chopped
2 garlic cloves, minced
Salt and ground pepper, to taste
1 tablespoon red wine vinegar
1 ½ pounds ground beef

Directions

Melt 1 teaspoon of the lard in a saucepan over a moderately high heat.

Once hot, sauté the onion and garlic until tender and translucent; reserve.

In the same skillet, melt another teaspoon of the lard. Cook the ground beef, breaking apart with a fork, until well browned.

Add the sautéed vegetables back to the saucepan; stir in the spices, vinegar, tomato sauce, and hot sauce. Reduce the heat to simmer and continue to cook for 17 to 20 minutes. Bon appétit!

Per serving: 313 Calories; 20.6g Fat; 3.5g Carbs; 26.6g Protein; 2.1g Fiber

207. Easy Spicy Sloppy Joes

(Ready in about 30 minutes | Servings 6)

Ingredients

1 ½ pounds ground chuck
1/2 cup pureed tomatoes
Salt and ground pepper, to taste
1 teaspoon deli mustard
1 tablespoon coconut vinegar
1 teaspoon cayenne pepper
1 teaspoon garlic, minced
2 shallots, finely chopped
1 teaspoon chipotle powder
2 teaspoons tallow, room temperature
1 teaspoon celery seeds

Directions

Melt 1 tablespoons of tallow in a heavy-bottomed skillet over a moderately high flame.

Now, sauté the shallots and garlic until tender and aromatic; reserve.

In the same skillet, melt another tablespoon of the tallow. Now, brown the ground chuck, crumbling with a spatula.

Add the vegetables back to the skillet; stir in the remaining ingredients. Turn the heat to medium-low; simmer for 20 minutes, stirring periodically.

Bon appétit!

Per serving: 313 Calories; 20.6g Fat; 3.5g Carbs; 26.6g Protein; 0.8g Fiber

208. Rib Eye Steak with Herbs and Wine

(Ready in about 20 minutes | Servings 6)

Ingredients

2 pounds rib eye steaks
1 thyme sprig, chopped
1/2 teaspoon chipotle powder
2 rosemary sprigs, chopped
1 teaspoon dried sage, crushed
2 tablespoons Swerve sweetener
2 garlic cloves, smashed
2 tablespoons dry red wine
2 tablespoons olive oil
1 tablespoon oyster sauce
1 tablespoon Worcestershire sauce
Celery salt and ground black pepper, to taste

Directions

In a mixing bowl, thoroughly combine the oyster sauce, Worcestershire sauce, Swerve, garlic, thyme, rosemary, sage, chipotle powder, salt, pepper, wine and olive oil.

Now, marinate the rib eye steaks in your refrigerator overnight.

Preheat your grill that is previously lightly greased. Grill the rib eye steaks over direct heat for 4 to 5 minutes on each side for medium-rare.

Bon appétit!

Per serving: 314 Calories; 11.4g Fat; 1g Carbs; 48.2g Protein; 0.1g Fiber

209. Cheesy and Marsala Beef Brisket

(Ready in about 6 hours | Servings 8)

Ingredients

1 cup Provolone cheese, sliced
2 tablespoons fresh coriander, chopped
1/3 cup Marsala wine
2 garlic cloves, minced
1 rosemary springs
1 onion, cut into wedges
2 tablespoons soy sauce
1 thyme sprig
2 tablespoons lard, room temperature
1/2 cup beef bone broth
Salt and pepper, to season
2 pounds beef brisket

Directions

Place all ingredients, except for the Provolone cheese, in your Slow Cooker.

Cook on High settings about 6 hours. Cut the beef brisket into eight portions.

Top the beef brisket with the slices of Provolone cheese and place under the preheated broiler for 5 to 6 minutes or until cheese melts. Enjoy!

Per serving: 519 Calories; 39.6g Fat; 2.7g Carbs; 34.4g Protein; 0.6g Fiber

210. Guinness Beef Stew with Mint

(Ready in about 1 hour | Servings 6)

Ingredients

1 cup Guinness beer
1 ½ pounds chuck shoulder, cut into bite-size cubes
1/4 cup mint leaves, chopped, to serve
1 tablespoon beef bouillon granules
1 parsnip, chopped
3 cups boiling water
2 carrots, chopped
1 ½ cups tomato puree
1 cup leeks, chopped
1 celery stalk, chopped
1 bay leaf
1/2 teaspoon caraway seeds
1 ½ tablespoons canola oil

Directions

Heat the oil in a stockpot over medium-high heat. Now, sauté the chuck shoulder cubes until they are browned; reserve.

Then, sauté the vegetables in the pan drippings for 8 minutes, stirring periodically.

Throw in the remaining ingredients, except for the mint leaves, and bring to a rapid boil. Now, turn the heat to medium-low; let it simmer about 50 minutes; garnished with mint leaves.

Bon appétit!

Per serving: 444 Calories; 14.2g Fat; 6.3g Carbs; 66.3g Protein; 2.2g Fiber

211. Ground Beef and Cheese-Stuffed Tomatoes

(Ready in about 35 minutes | Servings 4)

Ingredients

3/4 cup Cotija cheese, shredded
1 pound ground beef
8 tomatoes, scoop out the pulp and chop it
1 teaspoon mild paprika
1/2 teaspoon cumin seeds
1 cup scallions, chopped
2 cloves garlic, minced
1 teaspoon dried coriander leaves
1/2 cup beef broth
1 tablespoon olive oil
2 tablespoons tomato paste, sugar-free
Salt and pepper, to your liking

Directions

Start by preheating your oven to 350 degrees F. Lightly grease a casserole dish with a cooking spray.

Heat the oil in a saucepan over a moderately high heat. Sauté the scallions and garlic until aromatic.

Stir in the ground meat; cook for 5 minutes, crumbling with a spatula. Add the tomato paste and cook until heated through. Season with salt, pepper and cumin seeds.

Fill the tomatoes with the beef mixture and transfer them to the prepared casserole dish.

In a mixing bowl, whisk tomato pulp with paprika, coriander and broth. Pour the mixture over the stuffed tomatoes.

Bake until the tomatoes are tender, about 20 minutes. Top with the Cotija cheese and bake an additional 5 minutes.

Bon appétit!

Per serving: 244 Calories; 9.6g Fat; 6g Carbs; 28.9g Protein; 4.2g Fiber

212. Beef, Tomato and Wine Mélange

(Ready in about 1 hour 40 minutes | Servings 6)

Ingredients
- 2 pounds boneless beef sirloin steak, cubed
- 2 ripe Roma tomatoes, pureed
- 1 tablespoon dry white wine
- 2 thyme sprigs
- 1 tablespoon fish sauce
- 1 tablespoon smoked paprika
- 1 teaspoon caraway seeds, crushed
- 6 cups bone broth
- 1/2 teaspoon mustard seeds
- 1 rosemary sprig
- 1 cup yellow onions, chopped
- 2 cloves garlic, minced
- 2 bay leaves
- Seasoned salt and cayenne pepper, to taste
- 1/2 teaspoon black peppercorns, crushed
- 3 teaspoons tallow, room temperature

Directions
Heat 1 teaspoon of the tallow in a heavy-bottomed pot over a moderate heat. Now, brown the beef until it is no longer pink.

Season with salt, cayenne pepper, and black peppercorns; reserve.

In the same pot, heat remaining 2 teaspoons of tallow over a moderate heat. Cook the onions and garlic until they're softened, stirring continuously.

Now, add the paprika, caraway seeds, mustard seeds, thyme, and rosemary; cook an additional minute or until they are fragrant.

Add the remaining ingredients. Cook, partially covered, for 1 hour 30 minutes more. Discard the bay leaves. Bon appétit!

Per serving: 375 Calories; 13.3g Fat; 5.6g Carbs; 55.1g Protein; 1.5g Fiber

213. Beef and Vegetable Soup with Lemon-Chili Drizzle

(Ready in about 1 hour 10 minutes | Servings 6)

Ingredients
- 2 pounds beef chuck (well-marbled), boneless and cubed
- 1/2 cup ripe olives, pitted and halved
- 1/2 teaspoon ground cumin
- 1/2 cup frozen green peas
- 1 celery with leaves, chopped
- 2 tablespoons instant bouillon granules
- 2 carrots, chopped
- 6 cups water
- 2 onions, peeled and chopped
- 1 parsnip, chopped
- 1/2 teaspoon ground bay leaf
- 1 tablespoon canola oil
- 1 ripe tomato, pureed
- For the chili drizzle:
- 2 tablespoons lemon juice
- 2 red chilies
- 1 tablespoon extra-virgin olive oil
- Salt, to taste

Directions
Heat the oil in a stockpot over a moderately high heat. Now, brown the beef cubes for 3 to 5 minutes, stirring often; reserve.

Next, in the pan drippings, cook the onions, parsnip, celery and carrots until just tender. Add the olives, tomato, water, bouillon granules, ground bay leaf and cumin.

Stir in the reserved beef and bring the soup to a boil.

Turn the heat to medium-low; let it simmer, partially covered, about 50 minutes. Add the green peas and cook for a further 15 minutes.

Meanwhile, make the chili drizzle by blending all ingredients in your food processor. Afterwards, top with the chili drizzle. Bon appétit!

Per serving: 375 Calories; 14.4g Fat; 5.8g Carbs; 47.6g Protein; 2.4g Fiber

214. Pot Roast with Scallion Sauce

(Ready in about 50 minutes | Servings 4)

Ingredients
- 1 ½ pounds chuck pot roast, cubed
- 1 bunch scallions, chopped
- 1 tablespoon garlic paste
- 1 teaspoon mustard seeds
- 1/2 teaspoon dried marjoram
- 1/4 teaspoon celery seeds
- 1 tablespoon fresh parsley, roughly chopped
- 1/2 tablespoon tallow
- 1/4 teaspoon cumin
- 2 tablespoons soy sauce
- 1 teaspoon Sriracha sauce
- Salt and crushed mixed peppercorns, to taste

Directions
Whisk the soy sauce, Sriracha sauce and garlic paste in a mixing bowl. Add the salt, crushed peppercorns, mustard seeds, marjoram, and scallions.

Add the cubed beef and let it marinate for 40 minutes in your refrigerator.

Melt the tallow in a frying pan over a moderately high heat. Cook the marinated beef for 5 to 6 minutes, stirring frequently; work in batches to cook the beef cubes through evenly.

Season with cumin and celery seeds. Garnish with fresh parsley. Bon appétit!

Per serving: 292 Calories; 14.3g Fat; 3.9g Carbs; 36.9g Protein; 0.5g Fiber

215. Authentic Hungarian Pörkölt

(Ready in about 1 hour 25 minutes | Servings 4)

Ingredients
- 1 tablespoon Hungarian paprika
- 1 ¼ pounds chuck-eye roast, diced
- 2 onions, peeled and chopped
- 1 celery with leaves, chopped
- 4 cups water
- 1 tablespoon flaxseed meal
- 2 tablespoons beef bouillon granules
- 1/4 teaspoon ground bay leaf
- 2 carrots, peeled and cut into 1/4-inch rounds
- 1/2 cup Cabernet Sauvignon
- 2 tablespoons olive oil
- 1 tablespoon pear cider vinegar
- Celery salt and ground black pepper, to taste

Directions
Heat the oil in a heavy-bottomed pot. Then, cook the meat until no longer pink, for 3 to 4 minutes; work in batches and set aside. Season with celery salt, pepper, and Hungarian paprika.

Now, pour the vinegar and Cabernet Sauvignon to deglaze the bottom of the pot. Add the water, beef bouillon granules and reserved beef to the pot.

Stir in the ground bay leaf, onions, celery and carrots and cook an additional 1 hour 15 minutes over medium-low heat.

Add the flaxseed meal to thicken the liquid; stir constantly for 3 minutes. Bon appétit!

Per serving: 357 Calories; 15.8g Fat; 6g Carbs; 40.2g Protein; 3.5g Fiber

216. Marsala Steak with Brussels Sprouts

(Ready in about 1 hour 40 minutes | Servings 4)

Ingredients

1 ½ pounds top round steak, cut into 4 serving-size pieces
1 ½ cups Brussels sprouts, quartered
1/4 teaspoon freshly ground black pepper
1 tablespoon dried sage, crushed
1 cup broth
1 garlic clove, pressed
1 teaspoon ground bay leaf
1/2 teaspoon dried basil
2 tablespoons olive oil
1 shallot, chopped
1/2 teaspoon sea salt
For the Sauce:
3/4 teaspoon Dijon mustard
1 cup double cream
1/4 teaspoon freshly grated nutmeg
1/2 cup Marsala wine
1/2 cup chicken broth

Directions

Begin by preheating your oven to 340 degrees F. Flatten each top round steak with a meat tenderizer.

Heat the olive oil in an oven-safe pan over medium-high heat. Now, cook the steak until just browned; reserve.

Next, cook the shallots and garlic in pan drippings in the same pan until they're softened. After that, cook the Brussels sprouts until tender and smell good.

Add the round steak back to the pan. Season with ground bay leaf, basil, sage, salt, and pepper. Pour in 1 cup of broth. Wrap with foil and roast for 1 hour 10 minutes.

Add the wine, 1/2 cup chicken cup of broth and nutmeg to the same roasting pan. Let it simmer for 15 to 18 minutes or until the sauce is reduced to half.

Now, stir in the mustard and double cream; cook an additional 15 minutes or until everything is heated through. Bon appétit!

Per serving: 339 Calories; 21.7g Fat; 6.2g Carbs; 35g Protein; 1.7g Fiber

217. Chuck Roast with Horseradish Mayo

(Ready in about 2 hours | Servings 6)

Ingredients

1 tablespoon Italian seasoning mix
1/3 cup dry red wine
1 ½ tablespoons whole grain mustard
1/4 teaspoon black pepper, to taste
1/2 teaspoon cayenne pepper, or more to taste
2 bay leaves
1/4 cup vegetable oil
1 garlic clove, minced
1 teaspoon sea salt
1 ½ pounds chuck
For the Sauce:
2 tablespoons mayonnaise
1/4 cup sour cream
2 tablespoons prepared horseradish

Directions

Toss the chuck with bay leaves, vegetable oil, garlic, Italian seasoning, mustard, red wine, salt, black pepper and cayenne pepper.

Let it marinate overnight in the refrigerator. Place your chuck in a baking dish that is lined with a piece of foil; pour the marinade over it.

Wrap with the foil. Then, bake at 375 degrees F for 2 hours or until a thermometer registers 125 degrees F.

In the meantime, mix all ingredients for the sauce. Slice your chuck across the grain. Bon appétit!

Per serving: 493 Calories; 39.4g Fat; 2.9g Carbs; 27.9g Protein; 0.7g Fiber

218. Cheesy Saucy Corned Beef Brisket

(Ready in about 8 hours | Servings 6)

Ingredients

1 ½ pounds corned beef brisket
6 ounces blue cheese, crumbled
1/4 cup soy sauce
1/3 teaspoon ground coriander
1 shallot, chopped
1/2 tablespoon garlic paste
1/4 teaspoon cloves, ground
2 tablespoons olive oil
1 cup water

Directions

Heat a sauté pan with the olive oil over medium heat. Cook the shallot until it is softened.

Add the garlic paste and cook an additional minute; transfer to your Crock pot that is previously greased with a non-stick cooking spray.

Sear the brisket until it has a golden-brown crust. Transfer to the Crock pot. Add the remaining ingredient, except for the blue cheese.

Cover and cook on Low heat setting for 6 to 8 hours or until the meat is very tender. Garnish with blue cheese.

Bon appétit!

Per serving: 397 Calories; 31.4g Fat; 3.9g Carbs; 23.5g Protein; 0.3g Fiber

219. Tender Filet Mignon Steaks

(Ready in about 30 minutes | Servings 4)

Ingredients

1 red bell pepper, deveined and chopped
2 rosemary sprigs
1 cup scallions, chopped
2 garlic cloves, minced
1/2 cup dry red wine
1 tablespoon deli mustard
Celery salt and freshly ground pepper, to taste
1 thyme sprigs
2 tablespoons lard, room temperature
4 (6-ounce) filet mignon steaks

Directions

Rub the filet mignon steaks with mustard. Sprinkle the filet mignon steaks with salt, pepper, rosemary and thyme.

Heat the lard in a heavy-bottomed skillet over a moderate heat. Cook the filet mignon steaks for 10 minutes on each side or until a thermometer registers 120 degrees F.

Now, cook the scallions, garlic, and pepper in pan drippings about 3 minutes. Pour in the wine to scrape up any browned bits from the bottom of the skillet.

Now, cook until the liquid is reduced by half.

Bon appétit!

Per serving: 451 Calories; 34.4g Fat; 3.6g Carbs; 29.7g Protein; 1g Fiber

220. Ground Beef and Sauerkraut

(Ready in about 20 minutes | Servings 4)

Ingredients

1 ¼ pounds ground beef
18 ounces sauerkraut, rinsed and well drained
2 onions, chopped
1 bay leaf
2 garlic cloves, smashed
1 teaspoon mustard powder
1 teaspoon chili pepper flakes
1 tablespoon tallow, melted
Sea salt and ground black pepper, to taste

Directions

Heat a saucepan over a moderately high heat. Now, warm the tallow and cook the onions and garlic until aromatic.

Stir in the ground beef and cook until it is slightly browned.

Add the remaining ingredients. Reduce the heat to medium. Cook about 6 minutes or until everything is thoroughly cooked.

Bon appétit!

Per serving: 330 Calories; 12.2g Fat; 6.7g Carbs; 44.4g Protein; 4.1g Fiber

221. Hamburger, Cabbage and Cream Soup

(Ready in about 35 minutes | Servings 4)

Ingredients

3/4 pound ground chuck
1 cup cabbage, shredded
1 cup sour cream
1 tomato, pureed
1 carrot, diced
1 bay leaf
1 celery with leaves, diced
6 cups chicken broth
1/2 cup scallions, chopped
2 cloves garlic, minced
Seasoned salt and ground black pepper, to taste
2 tablespoons lard, melted

Directions

Melt the lard in a stockpot. Cook the chuck until it is no longer pink; reserve.

Then, cook the scallions, garlic, carrot, cabbage, and celery in the pan drippings, stirring constantly.

Stir in the other ingredients along with the reserved chuck, bringing to a rapid boil. Turn the heat to a simmer. Cook another 27 minutes, partially covered.

Taste and adjust the seasonings. Ladle into individual bowls; garnish with full-fat sour cream.

Bon appétit!

Per serving: 307 Calories; 23.6g Fat; 7.1g Carbs; 14.8g Protein; 2.4g Fiber

222. Strip Steak Omelet

(Ready in about 30 minutes | Servings 6)

Ingredients

2 Spanish peppers, deveined and chopped
6 eggs
1/2 teaspoon smoked paprika
1/2 cup scallions, chopped
1 ½ pounds New York strip, cut into cubes
Flaky sea salt and pepper, to season
2 garlic cloves, pressed
2 tablespoons butter, at room temperature

Directions

Ina frying pan, melt the butter over a moderately high heat. Cook the beef until browned on all sided or for 10 to 12 minutes. Season with salt, pepper, and paprika; reserve.

In the same pan, cook the scallions, garlic, and pepper until just tender and aromatic.

Add in the eggs and gently stir to combine. Continue to cook, covered, for 10 minutes more or until the eggs are set. Bon appétit!

Per serving: 429 Calories; 27.8g Fat; 3.2g Carbs; 39.1g Protein; 0.8g Fiber

223. Keto Tortilla with Spicy Ground Beef

(Ready in about 40 minutes | Servings 6)

Ingredients

2 ripe Roma tomatoes, crushed
1/2 cup dry sherry wine
1/2 teaspoon dried basil
2 shallots, chopped
1/2 teaspoon dried thyme
1/2 teaspoon paprika
1/2 teaspoon salt
1/2 teaspoon ground black pepper
2 garlic cloves, minced
1 ½ pounds ground chuck
1/4 teaspoon caraway seeds, ground
1 teaspoon habanero pepper, minced
2 tablespoons tallow, at room temperature
1/2 teaspoon ground bay leaf
1 teaspoon fennel seeds
For Ketogenic Tortillas:
1/3 teaspoon baking powder
6 tablespoons water
A pinch of table salt
A pinch of Swerve
4 egg whites
1/4 cup coconut flour

Directions

Melt the tallow in a wok that is preheated over a moderately high heat.

Now, brown the ground chuck for 4 minutes, crumbling it with a fork. Add all seasonings along with the shallots, garlic, and habanero pepper. Continue to cook 9 minutes longer.

Now, stir in the tomatoes and sherry. Now, turn the heat to medium-low, cover, and let it simmer an additional 20 minutes.

Meanwhile, make the tortillas by mixing the eggs, coconut flour and baking powder in a bowl. Add the water, salt and Swerve and mix until everything is well incorporated.

Preheat a non-stick skillet over a moderate flame. Bake the tortillas for a couple of minutes on each side. Repeat until you run out of batter.

Bon appétit!

Per serving: 361 Calories; 21.9g Fat; 6.4g Carbs; 29g Protein; 1.4g Fiber

224. Mediterranean Barbecued Flank Steak

(Ready in about 20 minutes + marinating time | Servings 6)

Ingredients

2 tablespoons BBQ sauce
1 teaspoon Mediterranean spice mix
1 tablespoon fish sauce
2 tablespoons dry sherry
2 tablespoons olive oil
2 garlic cloves, smashed
1 tablespoon coconut aminos
2 pounds flank steak
Celery salt and ground black pepper, to taste

Directions

In a ceramic bowl, thoroughly combine the fish sauce, coconut aminos, BBQ sauce, garlic, Mediterranean spice mix, salt, pepper, dry sherry, and olive oil.

Add in the flank steaks and let it marinate for 2 hours in your refrigerator.

Grill the flank steaks over direct heat for about 5 minutes per side (a meat thermometer should read 135 degrees F). Bon appétit!

Per serving: 314 Calories; 11.4g Fat; 1g Carbs; 48.2g Protein; 0.7g Fiber

225. San Diego-Style Beef Tacos

(Ready in about 40 minutes | Servings 6)

Ingredients

1 teaspoon Fresno pepper, minced
1 cup tomato puree
1/2 cup port wine
1/4 teaspoon mustard seeds, ground
1/2 teaspoon dried rosemary
2 tablespoons butter, room temperature
1 onion, chopped
1/2 teaspoon dried thyme
1/2 teaspoon red pepper flakes
1 bay laurel
1 teaspoon garlic, minced
1 ½ pounds ground beef
Sea salt and ground black pepper, to taste
For Ketogenic Tortillas:
1/4 cup almond meal
6 tablespoons water
4 egg whites
1/4 teaspoon granulated Swerve
A pinch of salt
1 tablespoon flaxseed meal
1/3 teaspoon baking powder

Directions

Melt the butter in a large saucepan over a moderately high flame.

Brown the ground beef for about 5 minutes, stirring and crumbling it with a wide spatula. Stir in all seasonings, onion, garlic, and Fresno pepper. Continue to cook for a further 10 minutes.

Add in the tomato puree and port wine. Turn the heat to a simmer, partially cover, and continue to cook for 15 to 20 minutes.

To make the tortillas, whisk the eggs, almond meal, flaxseed meal, and baking powder until well combined. Add in water, Swerve and salt and whisk until everything is well combined.

Cook the tortillas in a lightly oiled skillet that is previously preheated over medium-high heat. Repeat until you run out of ingredients. Assemble your tacos and enjoy!

Per serving: 361 Calories; 21.9g Fat; 6.4g Carbs; 29g Protein; 2g Fiber

226. Beef and Mexican Cheese-Stuffed Tomatoes

(Ready in about 35 minutes | Servings 4)

Ingredients

1 tablespoon butter
1 pound ground chuck
3/4 cup Mexican cheese blend, crumbled
2 tablespoons tomato sauce
2 cloves garlic, minced
1 teaspoon dried parsley flakes
1 cup onions, chopped
1/2 cup vegetable broth
1 teaspoon ancho chili powder
8 tomatoes, scoop out the pulp and chop it
1/2 teaspoon caraway seeds
Flaky salt and pepper, to taste

Directions

Start by preheating your oven to 350 degrees F. Lightly grease a casserole dish with cooking spray.

In a sauté pan, melt the butter over a moderately high flame. Now, cook the onion and garlic until tender and fragrant.

Add in the ground chuck and continue to cook for 5 to 6 minutes, breaking apart with a wide spatula.

Add in the tomato sauce, salt, and pepper. Divide the filling between the prepared tomatoes.

Place the stuffed tomatoes in a lightly oiled baking dish. Mix the scooped tomato pulp with the ancho chili powder and caraway seeds; salt to taste and pour it into the baking dish.

Bake in the preheated oven at 360 degrees F for about 25 minutes until the tomatoes have softened and everything is thoroughly cooked.

Top with cheese and place under preheated broiled for 5 minutes until hot and bubbly. Enjoy!

Per serving: 244 Calories; 9.6g Fat; 6g Carbs; 28.9g Protein; 3.2g Fiber

227. Classic Chunky Cheeseburger Soup

(Ready in about 25 minutes | Servings 4)

Ingredients

1 cup cream cheese
1 tablespoon fresh parsley, chopped
1 tablespoon fresh basil, chopped
1/2 cup sour cream
1 celery with leaves, chopped
4 cups chicken broth
1 cup scallions, chopped
2 tablespoons butter, softened
1/2 pound ground chuck

Directions

Ina heavy-bottomed pot, melt the butter over a moderately high heat. Cook the ground chuck for about 5 minutes, crumbling with a fork; set aside.

Add in the scallions and celery and continue to cook for a further 4 minutes, adding a splash of broth if needed.

Add in the parsley, basil, and broth; bring to a boil. Immediately reduce heat to a simmer. Add the cooked meat back to the pot, partially cover, and continue to cook for 8 to 10 minutes.

Add in the sour cream and let it cook for 3 minutes more until cooked through.

Add in the cheese and simmer for 5 to 6 minutes until the cheese has melted completely. Serve in individual bowls. Bon appétit!

Per serving: 326 Calories; 20.5g Fat; 4.5g Carbs; 26.8g Protein; 0.7g Fiber

228. Beef Sausage and Tomato-Mayo Sauce

(Ready in about 15 minutes | Servings 4)

Ingredients

1 pound beef sausage, crumbled
2 tablespoons cilantro, minced
1/3 teaspoon red pepper flakes
1/2 teaspoon salt
1/2 teaspoon dried marjoram
1 red onion, chopped
1 garlic clove, finely minced
1 tablespoon lard, at room temperature
For the Sauce:
1 tablespoon tomato puree
1/4 cup mayonnaise
1 teaspoon cayenne pepper
1 ½ teaspoon mustard
A pinch of salt

Directions

Melt the lard over medium-high heat. Add the onion and garlic and cook for 2 minutes or until tender and fragrant.

Stir in the beef and continue to cook for about 3 minutes more. Stir in the salt, red pepper, marjoram and cilantro; cook for 1 more minute.

Then, make the sauce by whisking all the sauce ingredients. Enjoy!

Per serving: 549 Calories; 49.3g Fat; 6.7g Carbs; 16.2g Protein; 0.8g Fiber

229. Keto Z'paghetti Bolognese

(Ready in about 1 hour 35 minutes | Servings 4)

Ingredients

For Bolognese:
1/2 cup water
1 pound ground chuck
1 cup tomato puree
1 tablespoons Greek spice mix
1 cup celery with leaves, finely chopped
2 slices bacon, chopped
1 shallot, finely chopped
1 teaspoon garlic, thinly sliced
1/2 cup Sauvignon blanc wine
2 tablespoons sesame oil
Salt and ground black pepper, to taste
For Zucchini Spaghetti:
4 zucchinis, peeled and jullianed (tagliatelle shape)

Directions

In a saucepan, heat the sesame oil over a moderately high flame. Sweat the shallot until just tender and translucent; add in the garlic and celery and continue to cook until they are just tender and fragrant.

Stir in the bacon and ground chuck; continue to cook for 6 to 7 more minutes, breaking up lumps with a fork.

Stir in the tomato puree, wine, water, and spices and continue to simmer, partially covered, for 1 hour 10 minutes.

Meanwhile, cook your zucchini in a lightly buttered wok for about 2 minutes or until they've softened.

Fold in the prepared Bolognese sauce and stir to combine well. Enjoy!

Per serving: 477 Calories; 25.6g Fat; 6.3g Carbs; 41.8g Protein; 1.4g Fiber

230. Chuck Roast with Provolone Cheese

(Ready in about 6 hours | Servings 8)

Ingredients

1 cup Provolone, sliced
3 garlic cloves, minced
1/3 cup dry red wine
2 tablespoons Worcestershire sauce
2 rosemary springs
1 thyme sprig
1/2 cup beef broth
2 tablespoons olive oil
1 large-sized white onion, cut into wedges
2 tablespoons fresh parsley, chopped
2 pounds beef chuck roast
Salt and pepper to taste

Directions

Add the beef, olive oil, onion, garlic, rosemary and thyme to your Crock pot.

Now, add the dry red wine, salt, pepper, Worcestershire sauce, beef broth.

Cover and cook on High settings until meat is tender, about 6 hours.

Garnish with fresh parsley and sliced Provolone cheese. Bon appétit!

Per serving: 519 Calories; 39.6g Fat; 2.7g Carbs; 34.4g Protein; 0.1g Fiber

231. Country-Style Beef Stew

(Ready in about 1 hour 35 minutes | Servings 6)

Ingredients

3 teaspoons lard, room temperature
6 cups roasted vegetable broth
1 tablespoon oyster sauce
1 tablespoon paprika
1 bay laurel
1 teaspoon celery seeds, crushed
1/2 teaspoon mustard seeds
Salt and pepper, to taste
1 cup leeks, chopped
1 teaspoon ginger-garlic paste
1 teaspoon dried parsley flakes
2 vine-ripened tomatoes, pureed
2 pounds beef rib-eye steak, cubed

Directions

Melt 1 teaspoon of lard in a large stock pot over a moderately high heat. Now, brown the rib-eye steak until it is no longer pink or about 6 minutes.

Season with salt and pepper to taste; reserve.

Heat the remaining 2 teaspoons of lard and sauté the leeks until tender and fragrant.

Now, add in the remaining ingredients. Continue to cook, partially covered, for 1 hour 20 minutes. Bon appétit!

Per serving: 375 Calories; 13.3g Fat; 5.6g Carbs; 55.1g Protein; 1.2g Fiber

232. Tangy Rib-Eye Steak

(Ready in about 25 minutes | Servings 6)

Ingredients

1 ½ pounds rib-eye steak
2 tablespoons apple cider vinegar
2 garlic cloves, minced
1/2 cup Worcester sauce
1 tablespoon vegetable oil
1 teaspoon sea salt
1/2 teaspoon ground black pepper

Directions

Preheat your oven to 350 degrees F. Grease a roasting pan with a non-stick cooking spray.

Heat the vegetable oil in a skillet that is preheated over a medium-high heat. Season the steak with salt and black pepper; sear the steak until just browned or about 3 minutes.

Place the steak in the prepared roasting pan. In a mixing bowl, combine the garlic, Worcester sauce and apple cider vinegar. Pour this mixture over the steak.

Afterwards, cover tightly with a piece of foil. Roast the steak about 20 minutes or until it is tender and well browned.

Bon appétit!

Per serving: 343 Calories; 27.3g Fat; 3g Carbs; 20.1g Protein; 0.4g Fiber

233. Cheese and Beef Sausage Dip

(Ready in about 20 minutes | Servings 8)

Ingredients

1 cup Ricotta cheese, at room temperature
2 garlic cloves, minced
2 tablespoons fresh Italian parsley, roughly chopped
1 ½ cups Swiss cheese, shredded
1 ½ cups beef sausages, crumbled
1 tablespoon olive oil
1 shallot, chopped

Directions

In a saucepan, heat the olive oil over a moderately high flame. Cook the shallot until tender and translucent or about 4 minutes.

Stir in the garlic and continue to cook for 30 seconds more until fragrant. Add in the sausage, cheese and parsley.

Bake in the preheated oven at 320 degrees F for 15 to 18 minutes. Enjoy!

Per serving: 333 Calories; 29.2g Fat; 2.9g Carbs; 14.7g Protein; 0.1g Fiber

234. Greek-Style Beef Sausage Souffle

(Ready in about 45 minutes | Servings 4)

Ingredients

2 tablespoons Greek-style yogurt
1 pound beef sausages, sliced
6 eggs
1 onion, chopped
1/2 teaspoon caraway seeds
2 garlic cloves, minced
2 Greek pepper, thinly sliced
1 teaspoon rosemary
1 cup cauliflower, broken into florets
Salt and black pepper, to taste

Directions

In a preheated saucepan, cook the beef sausage over a moderately high flame.

Add in the peppers, onion, cauliflower, garlic, and spices; continue to sauté for 10 minutes more or until the cauliflower is crisp-tender.

Spoon the sautéed mixture into a lightly oiled casserole dish. Whisk the eggs until pale and frothy; add in yogurt and whisk to combine well.

Pour the eggs/yogurt mixture over the top and bake at 365 degrees F for 30 to 35 minutes. Enjoy!

Per serving: 289 Calories; 19.7g Fat; 6.3g Carbs; 19.8g Protein; 1.4g Fiber

235. Flank Steak with Port Wine

(Ready in about 2 hours 15 minutes | Servings 4)

Ingredients

1 pound flank steak, thinly sliced
1/3 cup port wine
1 teaspoon fresh ginger root, minced
1 ½ cups beef stock
1 heaping teaspoon garlic, thinly sliced
1 cup leeks, sliced
1/2 teaspoon paprika
1 parsnip, chopped
1/2 teaspoon cardamom
1 tablespoon lard, room temperature

Directions

Melt the lard in a heavy-bottomed skillet over a moderately high heat. Cook the beef for about 12 minutes until no longer pink; reserve.

In the pan drippings, cook the leeks, parsnip and garlic approximately 3 minutes until they are tender and fragrant.

Add in the other ingredients and bring to a boil. Immediately reduce the heat to a simmer. Partially cover and continue to cook about 2 hours. Enjoy!

Per serving: 238 Calories; 9.2g Fat; 6.3g Carbs; 27.4g Protein; 0.6g Fiber

236. Ground Beef and Broccoli Bowl

(Ready in about 20 minutes | Servings 4)

Ingredients

1 pound ground beef
1 head broccoli, cut into small florets
1/2 teaspoon salt
1/2 ground black pepper
1/4 teaspoon cayenne pepper
1/2 teaspoon dill weed
1 teaspoon garlic, minced
1 cup red onion, sliced
1/2 teaspoon turmeric
2 teaspoons avocado oil
1/2 cup beef bone broth
2 tablespoons Marsala wine

Directions

Heat 1 teaspoon of the avocado oil in a pan that is preheated over a moderate flame. Then, cook the broccoli for 3 to 4 minutes, stirring often.

Now, stir in the garlic and onion; cook until aromatic and just tender, or about 2 minutes. Reserve.

Heat another teaspoon of the avocado oil. Stir in the beef and cook until it is well browned.

Add the reserved broccoli mixture, lower the heat and add the remaining ingredients. Cook covered, until everything is heated through or about 10 minutes. Bon appétit!

Per serving: 241 Calories; 7.6g Fat; 6g Carbs; 36g Protein; 0.7g Fiber

237. Cheeseburger Soup with A Twist

(Ready in about 30 minutes | Servings 6)

Ingredients

1 cup Cheddar cheese, shredded
1 tablespoon butter, room temperature
2 tablespoons plum vinegar
Salt and pepper, to your liking
2 Roma tomatoes, pureed
2 garlic cloves, chopped
2 cups vegetable broth
1 bay laurel
1 leek, chopped
1 ½ pounds ground beef

Directions

Melt the butter in a soup pot over a moderately-high flame. Cook the beef until it is no longer pink, breaking apart with a fork. Reserve.

In the pan drippings, cook the leeks and garlic until they've softened, for 5 to 6 minutes.

Add in the vegetable broth, tomatoes, salt, pepper, and bay laurel. Cover and continue to cook for 18 to 20 minutes more.

Add in the cheese and simmer for 5 to 6 minutes until the cheese has melted completely. Serve in individual bowls garnished with plum vinegar. Bon appétit!

Per serving: 238 Calories; 12.6g Fat; 5.6g Carbs; 25.1g Protein; 0.9g Fiber

238. Dijon Garlicky Beef Brisket

(Ready in about 3 hours 30 minutes | Servings 8)

Ingredients

1 tablespoon Dijon mustard
2 garlic cloves, halved
1/4 cup dry red wine
1 teaspoon dried marjoram
1 teaspoon shallot powder
1 teaspoon dried rosemary
2 pounds beef brisket, trimmed
1 teaspoon sea salt
1/2 teaspoon freshly ground black pepper

Directions

Start by preheating an oven to 375 degrees F. Rub the raw brisket with the garlic and Dijon mustard.

Then, make a dry rub by mixing the remaining ingredients. Season the brisket on both sides with the rub. Pour the wine into the pan.

Lay the beef brisket in a baking pan. Roast in the oven for 1 hour.

Decrease the oven temperature to 300 degrees F; roast an additional 2 hours 30 minutes. Afterwards, slice the meat. Enjoy!

Per serving: 219 Calories; 7.2g Fat; 0.6g Carbs; 34.6g Protein; 0.1g Fiber

239. Spicy Sausage and Vegetable Bake

(Ready in about 30 minutes | Servings 4)

Ingredients

1 tablespoon butter
1 cup cauliflower, broken into small florets
1 teaspoon paprika
1 celery stalk, chopped
2 garlic cloves, finely chopped
1 yellow onion, sliced
1 ½ cups vegetable broth
4 beef sausages, sliced
2 Spanish peppers, sliced
1 teaspoon dry chili pepper, crushed
Salt and pepper, to taste

Directions

In a frying pan, melt the butter over a moderately high heat. Brown the sausage until browned on all sides or about 5 minutes; reserve.

Sauté the onion, cauliflower, peppers, celery, and garlic for about 8 minutes or until the vegetables have softened.

Place the sautéed vegetables in a lightly buttered baking dish. Season with salt, pepper, and paprika. Nestle the reserved sausages within the vegetables.

Pour in the vegetable broth and bake in the preheated oven at 360 degrees F for 10 to 12 minutes.

Enjoy!

Per serving: 424 Calories; 32.4g Fat; 6g Carbs; 23.7g Protein; 1.6g Fiber

240. Mexican Tacos with Bacon and Beef

(Ready in about 30 minutes | Servings 4)

Ingredients

1 ½ cups Mexican cheese blend, shredded
1 cup tomato puree
1/2 teaspoon shallot powder
1/2 teaspoon ground cumin
2 teaspoon white vinegar
2 chili peppers, minced
1/2 cup cream of onion soup
1 ½ cups ground beef
6 slices bacon, chopped
Salt and pepper, to taste

Directions

Place 6 piles of the Mexican cheese on a parchment-lined baking pan; bake in the preheated oven at 385 degrees F for 13 to 15 minutes and let them cool slightly.

Then, in a frying pan, cook the ground beef until no longer pink or about 5 minutes. Add in the tomato puree, salt, pepper, shallot powder, and ground cumin; continue to cook for 5 minutes more.

In another pan, cook the bacon along with the remaining ingredients for about 3 minutes or until cooked through.

Assemble your tacos. Divide the meat mixture among the 6 taco shells; top with the bacon sauce. Enjoy!

Per serving: 258 Calories; 19.3g Fat; 5g Carbs; 16.3g Protein; 1.9g Fiber

241. Meatballs with Cheese and Peppers

(Ready in about 1 hour | Servings 4)

Ingredients

1/2 cup Cheddar cheese, crumbled
1 ½ cups chicken broth
2 garlic cloves
1 jalapeno pepper, deveined and minced
3 tablespoons Romano cheese, grated
4 Spanish peppers, deveined and chopped
1/2 teaspoon mustard seeds
1 pound ground chuck
1 cup onions, chopped
1 cup tomato puree
1 egg
Salt and ground black pepper, to taste

Directions

Place the Spanish peppers under the preheated broiler for about 15 minutes. Peel the peppers and discard the seeds.

Thoroughly combine the jalapeno pepper, onion, garlic, Romano cheese, egg, salt, black pepper, and ground chuck; add in roasted peppers. Roll the mixture into balls.

In a lightly oiled skillet, sear the meatballs until browned on all sides about 8 to 10 minutes.

In a saucepan, heat the tomato puree, chicken broth, and mustard seeds; bring to a boil. Turn the heat to a simmer and continue to cook until cooked through. Fold in the prepared meatballs.

Serve topped with Cheddar cheese. Bon appétit!

Per serving: 348 Calories; 13.7g Fat; 5.9g Carbs; 42.8g Protein; 2.7g Fiber

242. Summer Steak Medallions

(Ready in about 50 minutes | Servings 4)

Ingredients

2 tablespoons fresh lime juice
1 teaspoon celery seeds
1 tablespoon ginger root, freshly grated
1 tablespoon cayenne pepper
1/2 teaspoon chipotle powder
1 teaspoon fennel seeds
1 teaspoon sea salt
1/2 teaspoon ground black pepper
4 steak medallions, 1 1/2 inches thick

Directions

Place the steak medallions in a large-sized resealable bag. Then, thoroughly combine the remaining ingredients to make the marinade.

Marinate the steak medallions for 40 minutes at room temperature.

Preheat your grill to medium-high. Remove the medallions from marinade and grill on each side to the desired doneness, about 5 to 6 minutes.

Bon appétit!

Per serving: 326 Calories; 11.1g Fat; 1.6g Carbs; 52g Protein; 0.8g Fiber

243. Grandma's Beef Brisket and Vegetables

(Ready in about 6 hours + marinating time | Servings 6)

Ingredients

1 tablespoon Cajun seasonings
1 teaspoon garlic, smashed
2 celery stalks, chopped
1 cup stock
2 tablespoons vegetable oil
2 yellow onions, sliced into half moons
2 tablespoons dry red wine
2 tablespoons Worcestershire sauce
2 carrots, sliced
1 ½ pounds beef brisket
Ground black pepper, to taste

Directions

Rub the beef brisket with garlic, black pepper and Cajun seasonings. Add the wine, Worcestershire sauce and 1 tablespoon of vegetable oil.

Wrap with foil and place in the refrigerator for 3 hours.

Heat 1 tablespoon of the vegetable oil in your slow cooker. Now, sauté the onions until just tender.

In a pan, sear the brisket until it has a golden brown crust. Transfer to your slow cooker. Add the carrots, celery and stock

Cover and cook on Low heat setting for 6 hours or until the beef brisket is as soft as you want it.

Bon appétit!

Per serving: 296 Calories; 12g Fat; 7g Carbs; 35.2g Protein; 0.3g Fiber

244. Ground Chuck, Cabbage and Cheese Bake

(Ready in about 55 minutes | Servings 6)

Ingredients

1 ½ cups Ricotta cheese, crumbled
8 slices Colby cheese
1/2 teaspoon mustard seeds
2 eggs
1/2 teaspoon fennel seeds
1 cup tomato sauce
2 slices bacon, chopped
1 head of cabbage, cut into quarters
1 yellow onion, chopped
1 teaspoon dried rosemary
1 pound ground chuck
Salt and black pepper, to taste

Directions

Parboil the cabbage in a pot of a lightly salted water for 4 to 5 minutes; drain and reserve.

Then, cook the ground chuck for about 5 minutes until it is no longer pink. Add in the onion and bacon and continue to sauté for 4 minutes more.

Stir in the spices and tomato sauce; bring it to a boil. Turn the heat to simmer; partially cover, and continue to cook an additional 7 minutes.

Spoon 1/2 of the mixture into the bottom of a lightly oiled casserole dish. Top with a layer of the boiled cabbage leaves. Repeat the layers one more time.

Then, thoroughly combine the eggs, Ricotta cheese, and Colby cheese. Top your casserole with the cheese mixture; bake at 390 degrees F for 25 to 30 minutes or until cooked through.

Bon appétit!

Per serving: 467 Calories; 37g Fat; 4.9g Carbs; 27.1g Protein; 3.1g Fiber

245. Roasted Short Ribs with Tomato and Wine

(Ready in about 2 hours 35 minutes | Servings 8)

Ingredients

1 vine-ripened tomato
1 tablespoon butter, at room temperature
1/2 cup dry red wine
2 garlic cloves, minced
1/2 teaspoon red pepper flakes
2 pounds chuck short ribs
Sea salt and black pepper, to taste

Directions

Start by preheating your oven to 325 degrees F.

Toss the beef ribs with salt, pepper and red pepper flakes until well coated.

In a large frying pan, melt the butter over medium-high heat. Sear the short ribs until browned, about 9 minutes.

Place the ribs in a lightly-oiled baking pan. Add in the remaining ingredients.

Cover with foil and roast in the preheated oven at 330 degrees F for 2 hours. Remove the foil and roast an additional 30 minutes. Bon appétit!

Per serving: 231 Calories; 8.9g Fat; 1.3g Carbs; 34.7g Protein; 0.2g Fiber

246. Chuck Roast with Serrano Pepper

(Ready in about 2 hours 10 minutes | Servings 4)

Ingredients

1 Serrano pepper, finely minced
2 bell peppers, chopped
1 celery with leaves, chopped
1 teaspoon garlic, minced
1 tablespoon flaxseed meal, dissolved in 2 tablespoons of water
1 teaspoon mustard seeds
1/4 teaspoon cardamom, ground
2 tablespoons butter
4 cups vegetable broth
1 large onion, chopped
Salt and pepper, to taste
1 ½ pounds chuck roast, cut into small chunks

Directions

In a Dutch oven, melt 1 tablespoon of butter and brown the beef, breaking apart with a fork; set aside.

Then, melt the remaining tablespoon of butter and sauté the vegetables until they've softened.

Add the reserved beef to the Dutch oven along with the vegetable broth. Add the seasonings and bring to a boil.

Reduce the heat to a simmer and continue to cook approximately 2 hours.

Stir in the flaxseed slurry. Let it cook, stirring continuously, until the cooking liquid has thickened about 2 minutes.

Bon appétit!

Per serving: 467 Calories; 18.7g Fat; 3.7g Carbs; 58g Protein; 2.1g Fiber

247. Spiced Beef Sauerkraut Goulash

(Ready in about 20 minutes | Servings 4)

Ingredients

1 tablespoon lard, melted
1 ¼ pounds ground chuck roast
1 medium leek, chopped
1 teaspoon fresh garlic, minced
1 teaspoon celery powder
1 bay laurel
18 ounces sauerkraut, rinsed and well drained
1 teaspoon hot paprika

Directions

In a saucepan, melt the lard over a moderately high heat. Sauté the leek and garlic until tender and fragrant.

Add in the ground chuck and continue to cook until slightly browned or about 5 minutes.

Add in the remaining ingredients. Reduce the heat to a simmer. Cover and continue to cook for a further 7 minutes until everything has cooked through. Bon appétit!

Per serving: 342 Calories; 22g Fat; 7.7g Carbs; 29.4g Protein; 4.3g Fiber

248. Ancho Marinated Steak

(Ready in about 1 hour 20 minutes + marinating time | Servings 4)

Ingredients

1/2 teaspoon ancho chile powder
1 teaspoon fresh ginger root, minced
1 ½ pounds flank steak
1 teaspoon celery seeds
Sea salt and black pepper, to taste

Directions

Place all ingredients in a ceramic dish and let it marinate for 1 hour in your refrigerator.

Preheat your grill to medium-high.

Then, grill the flank steak for about 15 minutes, basting them with the reserved marinade. Bon appétit!

Per serving: 326 Calories; 11.1g Fat; 1.6g Carbs; 52g Protein; 0g Fiber

249. Cheesy Blead Roast with Vinegar

(Ready in about 8 hours | Servings 6)

Ingredients

6 ounces goat cheese, crumbled
1 tablespoon red wine vinegar
2 tablespoons coconut aminos
1 ¼ cups water
2 cloves garlic, minced
1 Italian pepper, deveined, and sliced
1/3 teaspoon ground mustard seeds
2 tablespoons butter, room temperature
1 large onion, chopped
1 ½ pounds blade roast

Directions

Brush the sides and bottom of your Crock pot with a non-stick spray.

Melt the butter in a large saucepan over a moderate heat. Now, sauté the onion, garlic, and pepper until they've softened.

Transfer the sautéed mixture to your Crock pot. Add in the blade roast coconut aminos, vinegar, mustard seeds, and water.

Cover with the lid; cook on Low heat setting for 7 hours.

Top with cheese and place under the preheated broiler for 6 to 7 minutes or until thoroughly warmed. Enjoy!

Per serving: 439 Calories; 33.4g Fat; 4.2g Carbs; 25.5g Protein; 0.6g Fiber

250. Curried Ground Beef with Broccoli

(Ready in about 20 minutes | Servings 4)

Ingredients

1/2 teaspoon curry paste
1/2 teaspoon red pepper flakes, crushed
1/2 cup vegetable broth
1 pound ground beef
2 teaspoons olive oil
1 large onion, sliced
1 head broccoli, cut into small florets
2 garlic cloves, minced
Kosher salt and black pepper, to season

Directions

In a cast-iron skillet, heat 1 teaspoon of the olive oil over a moderately high flame. Cook the broccoli for 3 to 4 minutes until crisp-tender.

Stir in the garlic and onion and continue to cook for 2 to 3 minutes more until tender and aromatic. Reserve.

In the same skillet, heat another teaspoon of the oil and cook the beef until it is well browned, crumbling with a fork.

Add in the sautéed broccoli mixture, turn the heat to a simmer, and stir in the other ingredients. Cover and continue to cook for 12 minutes more. Bon appétit!

Per serving: 241 Calories; 7.6g Fat; 6g Carbs; 36g Protein; 3.9g Fiber

251. Wine-Marinated Skirt Steak

(Ready in about 20 minutes + marinating time | Servings 6)

Ingredients

2 tablespoons sesame oil
1/4 cup Pinot Noir
2 garlic cloves, minced
1 teaspoon dried parsley flakes
2 tablespoons coconut aminos
1 teaspoon dried marjoram
1/2 cup onions, chopped
2 pounds skirt steak
Salt and pepper, to taste

Directions

Place the skirt steak along with other ingredients in a ceramic dish. Let it marinate in your refrigerator overnight.

Preheat a lightly oiled frying pan over a moderately high heat. Cook your skirt steaks for 8 to 10 minutes per side. Bon appétit!

Per serving: 350 Calories; 17.3g Fat; 2.1g Carbs; 42.7g Protein; 0.8g Fiber

252. Roasted Skirt Steak with Wine

(Ready in about 25 minutes + marinating time | Servings 6)

Ingredients

1 tablespoon olive oil
2 tablespoons green garlic, chopped
1/2 cup dry red wine
1 tablespoon stone-ground mustard
Sea salt and black pepper, to taste
1 ½ pounds skirt steak

Directions

Remove the connective tissue from one side of your steak using a knife.

Place the skirt steak, mustard, salt, black pepper, green garlic, and red wine in a ceramic dish. Let it marinate in your refrigerator at least 1 hour.

Brush the marinated steak with olive oil and place on a parchment-lined baking pan. Bake in the preheated oven at 360 degrees F for about 20 minutes, basting with the reserved marinade.

Bon appétit!

Per serving: 343 Calories; 27.3g Fat; 3g Carbs; 20.1g Protein; 0.9g Fiber

253. Marinated Beef Shoulder with Mustard and Wine

(Ready in about 6 hours + marinating time | Servings 6)

Ingredients

- 1 ½ pounds beef shoulder
- 1 teaspoon Dijon mustard
- 2 celery stalks, chopped
- 1 cup chicken stock
- 1 teaspoon garlic, smashed
- Salt and black pepper, to taste
- 2 tablespoons Marsala wine
- 2 tablespoons olive oil
- 1 large-sized leek, chopped
- 2 tablespoons coconut aminos

Directions

Rub the beef shoulder with the garlic, mustard, salt, and black pepper. Add in the Marsala wine and coconut aminos. Let it marinate for 3 hours in your refrigerator.

Heat the olive oil in your slow cooker and sauté the leeks until they've softened.

Then, cook the beef shoulder until it is golden-brown on top. Add in the celery and stock and stir to combine.

Cover with the lid and cook on Low heat setting for 5 to 6 hours. Bon appétit!

Per serving: 296 Calories; 12g Fat; 5g Carbs; 35.2g Protein; 0.6g Fiber

254. Homemade Beef Soup

(Ready in about 1 hour 10 minutes | Servings 6)

Ingredients

- 2 pounds beef chuck-eye roast, cubed
- 1 celery with leaves, chopped
- 1 medium leek, chopped
- 1 bay laurel
- 1 tablespoon ghee
- 1/2 cup bell peppers, chopped
- 1 cup tomato sauce
- 1/2 cup green peas, frozen
- 6 cups beef bone broth
- 1 parsnip, chopped
- For the Lime-Chili Drizzle:
- 2 tablespoons lemon juice
- 1 tablespoon olive oil
- 2 jalapenos

Directions

In a heavy-bottomed pot, melt the ghee over a moderately high heat. Sear the beef for about 5 minutes, stirring continuously, until well browned on all sides; set aside.

In the same pot, cook the leek, parsnip, celery, and peppers until they've softened. Add in the tomato sauce, beef bone broth and bay laurel; bring to a boil.

Turn the heat to simmer; partially cover and continue to cook for 45 to 50 minutes. Add in the green peas and continue to cook for about 12 minutes longer.

Make the lime-chili drizzle by whisking the ingredients. Garnish with the lemon-chili drizzle and serve hot!

Per serving: 375 Calories; 14.4g Fat; 4.8g Carbs; 47.6g Protein; 2.8g Fiber

255. Beef, Cheese and Mustard Sauce

(Ready in about 20 minutes | Servings 4)

Ingredients

- 4 (1 ½-inch) thick sirloin steaks
- 1/3 cup cream cheese, room temperature
- 1 tablespoon fresh basil, finely chopped
- 1 tablespoon deli mustard
- 1 sprig rosemary, chopped
- 1 tablespoon olive oil
- Seasoned salt and black pepper, to taste

Directions

Season the sirloin steaks with salt, pepper, and rosemary. Heat the olive oil in a large grill pan over medium-high flame.

Sear the sirloin steaks in the grill pan for 5 minutes; flip them over and cook for 4 to 5 minutes on the other side.

Combine together the cream cheese, mustard, and basil. Place in your refrigerator until ready to serve. Bon appétit!

Per serving: 321 Calories; 13.7g Fat; 1g Carbs; 45g Protein; 0.4g Fiber

256. Mini Mushroom Meatloaves

(Ready in about 40 minutes | Servings 6)

Ingredients

- 1/2 pound button mushrooms, chopped
- 1/4 cup almond meal
- 1/2 cup tomato puree
- 1 shallot, chopped
- 2 eggs, lightly beaten
- 1/2 cup pork rinds, crushed
- 1 tablespoon lard, room temperature
- 2 garlic cloves, minced
- 3/4 cup mozzarella cheese, grated
- 1 ¼ pounds ground chuck
- Salt and pepper, to taste

Directions

Melt the lard in a saucepan over a moderately high flame. Sauté the shallot and mushrooms until they are just tender and aromatic.

Add in the remaining ingredients and mix to combine well.

Press the mixture into a lightly greased muffin pan. Bake in the preheated oven at 380 degrees F for 25 to 30 minutes. Bon appétit!

Per serving: 404 Calories; 22.8g Fat; 6.2g Carbs; 44g Protein; 1.3g Fiber

257. Filet Mignon with Marsala Wine

(Ready in about 3 hours 30 minutes | Servings 8)

Ingredients

- 1/4 cup Marsala wine
- 1 teaspoon porcini powder
- 1 heaping teaspoon garlic, sliced
- Sea salt and pepper, to taste
- 1 teaspoon dried thyme
- 1 tablespoon brown mustard
- 2 pounds filet mignon

Directions

Rub the filet mignon with mustard and garlic. Toss with the spices and place on a lightly oiled baking pan. Pour in the Marsala wine.

Roast in the preheated oven at 370 degrees F for 1 hour 30 minutes.

Turn the oven temperature to 310 degrees F and roast an additional 2 hours. Bon appétit!

Per serving: 219 Calories; 7.2g Fat; 0.6g Carbs; 34.6g Protein; 0.3g Fiber

258. Roast Beef with Horseradish-Cheese Sauce

(Ready in about 2 hours + marinating time | Servings 6)

Ingredients

1/4 cup olive oil
1/2 teaspoon paprika
1 garlic clove, minced
1/3 cup Merlot
1 sprig thyme
1 ½ tablespoons Dijon mustard
1 sprig rosemary
1 teaspoon dried marjoram
1 ½ pounds top sirloin roast
For the Sauce:
1/4 cup cream cheese
2 tablespoons prepared horseradish
2 tablespoons mayonnaise

Directions

Place all ingredients for the roast beef in a ceramic bowl; let it marinate in your refrigerator for 3 to 4 hours.

Transfer the top sirloin roast along with the marinade to a lightly oiled baking pan.

Wrap with the foil and bake in the preheated oven at 370 degrees F approximately 1 hour. Rotate the pan and continue to roast for 1 hour longer (a meat thermometer should register 125 degrees F).

Whisk all ingredients for the horseradish sauce. Bon appétit!

Per serving: 493 Calories; 39.4g Fat; 2.9g Carbs; 27.9g Protein; 0.5g Fiber

259. Cheese and Beef Stuffed Avocado Boats

(Ready in about 20 minutes | Servings 6)

Ingredients

3/4 cup Swiss cheese, shredded
1/2 cup mayonnaise
1 tablespoon butter, room temperature
1 large tomato, chopped
Salt and pepper, to taste
1/2 cup onions, sliced
3/4 pound ground chuck
1/3 cup vegetable broth
3 ripe avocados, pitted and halved
3 tablespoons green olives, pitted and sliced

Directions

Melt the butter in a non-stick skillet over a moderate heat; cook the ground chuck for about 3 minutes, crumbling it with a fork.

Add in the broth and onions. Continue to sauté until the onions are tender translucent. Season with salt and pepper to taste.

Scoop out some of the middle of your avocados. Combine the avocado flesh with the chopped tomatoes and green olives. Add in the reserved beef mixture and stuff your avocado.

Place the stuffed avocado in a parchment-lined baking pan. Bake in the preheated oven at 350 degrees F for about 10 minutes.

Serve with mayonnaise. Bon appétit!

Per serving: 407 Calories; 28.8g Fat; 16.4g Carbs; 23.4g Protein; 6.1g Fiber

260. Thai-Style Spicy Steak Salad

(Ready in about 15 minutes | Servings 4)

Ingredients

1 Bird's eye chili, minced
1/4 cup sunflower seeds
1 bunch fresh Thai basil
2 tablespoons olive oil
1 cup scallions, chopped
1 avocado, pitted, peeled and sliced
1 bell pepper, sliced
1 teaspoon coconut aminos
2 tablespoons white wine
1 garlic clove, minced
Salt and black pepper, to season
1/2 pound flank steak, trimmed

Directions

Toss the flank steak with the salt, pepper and coconut aminos.

In a frying pan, heat 1 tablespoon of olive oil over a moderate heat. Cook the scallions and garlic until tender for 3 to 4 minutes; reserve.

In the same pan, heat another tablespoon of the olive oil. Once hot, cook the flank steak for about 5 minutes per side; add in the sautéed mixture.

Toss the remaining ingredients in a nice salad bowl; toss to combine well.

Serve the flank steak on top of the salad and enjoy!

Per serving: 288 Calories; 21.5g Fat; 8.6g Carbs; 15.8g Protein; 5g Fiber

261. Colby Cheese, Beef and Tomato Quiche

(Ready in about 25 minutes | Servings 4)

Ingredients

1 cup Colby cheese, grated
1 pound ground chuck
1 tablespoon lard, room temperature
1/2 teaspoon mustard powder
1/2 tablespoon dill relish
3/4 cup Ricotta cream
1/2 cup onions, finely chopped
2 garlic cloves, minced
2 tomatoes, chopped
Sea salt and ground black pepper to taste
2 tablespoons sun-dried tomatoes, chopped

Directions

Start by preheating your oven to 395 degrees F.

Melt the lard in a saucepan over medium-high flame. Once hot, brown the ground chuck, breaking apart with a spatula.

Add in the garlic and onions and cook until they are tender and aromatic. Stir in the tomatoes, dill relish and seasonings.

Spoon the sautéed mixture into a lightly-oiled baking dish. Top with the cheese. Bake in the preheated oven for about 20 minutes. Enjoy!

Per serving: 509 Calories; 29.6g Fat; 6.1g Carbs; 45.2g Protein; 1.6g Fiber

262. Beef and Mushroom Stew with Egg

(Ready in about 40 minutes | Servings 6)

Ingredients

1 tablespoon olive oil
1 bay leaf
1 teaspoon garlic, chopped
Salt and pepper, to taste
4 cups beef bone broth
1 egg, lightly whisked
1 tablespoon white mushrooms, thinly sliced
1 teaspoon dried caraway seeds
1/4 teaspoon hot paprika
1 cup onions, thinly sliced
1 ½ pounds beef shoulder, cubed

Directions

In a heavy-bottomed pot, heat the olive oil over a moderately high flame.

Sear the beef for about 7 minutes until it's just browned; reserve.

In the same pot, cook the onions for about 3 minutes or until fragrant. Stir in the garlic and mushrooms and continue to cook for a minute or so.

Stir in the remaining ingredients, cover, and cook for 35 minutes more. Add in the egg, remove from the heat, and stir to combine. Bon appétit!

Per serving: 259 Calories; 10.1g Fat; 4.1g Carbs; 35.7g Protein; 0.5g Fiber

263. Shish Kebab with Garlic-Mustard Relish

(Ready in about 20 minutes | Servings 6)

Ingredients

2 teaspoons stone-ground mustard
1 large zucchini, sliced
1 jalapeno pepper, minced
2 bell peppers, sliced
3 tablespoons olive oil
2 ½ tablespoons apple cider vinegar
1 cup shallots, cut into wedges
2 garlic cloves, minced
2 pounds beef shoulder, cut into cubes
Salt and ground black pepper, to taste

Directions

Season the meat and vegetables with the salt and pepper to taste. Brush them with a non-stick cooking spray.

Thread the meat cubes and vegetables onto bamboo skewers. Grill the beef kabobs for about 10 minutes, flipping them occasionally to ensure even cooking.

Make the relish by whisking the mustard, garlic, jalapeno pepper, olive oil and apple cider vinegar. Bon appétit!

Per serving: 413 Calories; 21.1g Fat; 5.8g Carbs; 45.3g Protein; 1g Fiber

264. Greek-Style Sausage with Aioli

(Ready in about 15 minutes | Servings 4)

Ingredients

2 tablespoons coriander
1/2 cup onion, chopped
1 teaspoon garlic, finely minced
1 tablespoon olive oil
1 pound beef sausage, crumbled
Kosher salt and pepper, to taste
For the Sauce:
1 ½ teaspoon mustard
1/4 cup aioli
1 teaspoon paprika

Directions

In a frying pan, heat the olive oil over a moderate heat. Stir in the onion and garlic and continue to cook for 2 to 3 minutes or until they've softened.

Stir in the beef sausage; continue to cook for 3 to 4 minutes or until no longer pink. Add in the salt, pepper, and coriander and stir to combine well.

Make the sauce by whisking all the sauce ingredients. Enjoy!

Per serving: 549 Calories; 49.3g Fat; 4.7g Carbs; 16.2g Protein; 0.8g Fiber

265. Mediterranean Steak Salad

(Ready in about 20 minutes | Servings 6)

Ingredients

1/2 teaspoon dried Mediterranean spice mix
1 Lebanese cucumber, sliced
2 tablespoons fresh lime juice
1/4 cup extra-virgin olive oil
1 onion, peeled and thinly sliced
1 cup cherry tomatoes, halved
2 bell peppers, thinly sliced
Salt and pepper, to taste
1 head of butter lettuce, leaves separated and torn into pieces
1 Serrano pepper, thinly sliced
1 ½ pounds rib-eye steak, 1-inch thick piece

Directions

Brush a frying pan with a non-stick cooking spray. One hot, cook the steak for about 3 to 4 minutes on each side for medium rare.

After that, thinly slice the steak across the grain.

In a salad bowl, mix the remaining ingredients; toss to coat. Place the steak on top of your salad and serve. Bon appétit!

Per serving: 315 Calories; 13.8g Fat; 6.4g Carbs; 37.5g Protein; 0.9g Fiber

266. Italian-Style Peppery Tenderloin

(Ready in about 30 minutes | Servings 4)

Ingredients

1 teaspoon Mediterranean seasoning mix
1/2 cup dry red wine
Kosher salt and black pepper, to taste
1 cup red onions, chopped
2 garlic cloves, minced
1 Italian pepper, deveined and chopped
2 tablespoons olive oil
1 tablespoon Dijon mustard
1 ½ pounds tenderloin

Directions

Rub the tenderloin steak with the mustard, salt, pepper, and Mediterranean seasoning mix.

Heat the olive oil in a non-stick skillet over moderately high heat. Cook the tenderloin steak for 9 to 10 minutes per side.

Sauté the onion, garlic, and Italian pepper for 3 to 4 minutes more until they've softened. Add in red wine to scrape up any browned bits from the bottom of the skillet.

Continue to cook until the cooking liquid has thickened and reduced by half. Bon appétit!

Per serving: 451 Calories; 34.4g Fat; 3.6g Carbs; 29.7g Protein; 1.1g Fiber

267. Italian Wine-Braised Sausage and Vegetables

(Ready in about 40 minutes | Servings 4)

Ingredients

2 Italian peppers, deveined and chopped
1 ½ cups vegetable broth
1 teaspoon dried parsley flakes
1/4 cup dry red wine
2 rosemary sprigs
1 teaspoon fresh garlic, smashed
1 celery rib, chopped
Salt and pepper, to taste
1 cup tomato sauce
1 large onion, chopped
2 tablespoons olive oil
4 beef sausages, sliced

Directions

In a saucepan, heat the oil over a moderately high heat. Brown the sausage for about 3 minutes, stirring periodically to ensure even cooking.

Stir in the onion, garlic, peppers, and celery rib; season with salt and pepper to taste. Continue to cook for 6 to 7 minutes or until they've softened.

Add in the other ingredients, bringing it to a rolling boil. Turn the heat to a simmer and continue to cook for 20 to 25 minutes or until heated through. Enjoy!

Per serving: 250 Calories; 17.5g Fat; 5.4g Carbs; 6.8g Protein; 2.8g Fiber

268. Sea Scallop Salad and Olives

(Ready in about 10 minutes | Servings 4)

Ingredients

1 cup cherry tomatoes, halved
1 Lebanese cucumber, sliced
1/4 cup extra-virgin olive oil
2 tablespoons fresh lime juice
1/2 tablespoon Dijon mustard
1 teaspoon garlic, chopped
1/2 cup Kalamata olives, pitted and sliced
2 cups arugula
1 pound sea scallops, halved horizontally
Sea salt and pepper, to season

Directions

Boil the scallops in a pot of a lightly salted water for about 3 minutes or until opaque; place them in a serving bowl.

To make the salad, toss the remaining ingredients until everything is well combined.

Top your salad with the prepared scallops. Enjoy!

Per serving: 260 Calories; 13.6g Fat; 5.9g Carbs; 28.1g Protein; 1.5g Fiber

269. Marsala Fish Stew

(Ready in about 25 minutes | Servings 4)

Ingredients

1/2 cup Marsala wine
1/2 pound sole, cut into 2-inch pieces
1 cup tomato sauce
1 cup shallots, chopped
1 teaspoon garlic, smashed
2 thyme sprigs, chopped
1/3 pound halibut, cut into 2-inch pieces
4 cups chicken bone broth
1/8 teaspoon hot sauce, or more to taste
1 tablespoon lard, room temperature
Sea salt and black pepper, to taste

Directions

In a large-sized pot, melt the lard over medium-high heat. Cook the shallots and garlic until they've softened.

Add in the salt, black pepper, chicken bone broth, tomato sauce, and thyme and; continue to cook an additional 15 minutes.

Add in the fish, wine and hot sauce; bring to a boil. Reduce the heat to simmer. Let it simmer for 4 to 5 minutes longer, stirring periodically. Enjoy!

Per serving: 296 Calories; 8.6g Fat; 5.5g Carbs; 41.4g Protein; 4.3g Fiber

270. Ground Beef, Cabbage and Pepper Soup

(Ready in about 35 minutes | Servings 4)

Ingredients

1 ½ tablespoons tallow, room temperature
1 cup green cabbage, shredded
1 celery with leaves, diced
4 cups vegetable broth
1 cup tomato sauce
1/2 cup onions, chopped
1 bell pepper, diced
2 cloves garlic, minced
1 cup sour cream
1 sprig thyme
Salt and pepper, to taste
3/4 pound ground beef

Directions

In a large soup pot, melt the tallow until sizzling. Once hot, cook the ground beef for about 5 minutes, falling apart with a fork; reserve.

Add in the onions, garlic, bell pepper, cabbage, and celery and continue to cook for 5 to 6 minutes more or until the vegetables have softened.

Stir in the remaining ingredients along with the reserved ground beef; bring to a boil. Reduce the heat to a simmer and continue to cook an additional 20 minutes until everything is thoroughly cooked.

Serve dolloped with chilled sour cream. Enjoy!

Per serving: 307 Calories; 23.6g Fat; 5.4g Carbs; 14.8g Protein; 2.9g Fiber

271. Rum-Mustard Marinated Tilapia

(Ready in about 15 minutes + marinating time | Servings 4)

Ingredients

1/2 cup dark rum
1 teaspoon Dijon mustard
1 pound tilapia fish, cubed
1 cup white onions, chopped
1 teaspoon garlic, pressed
2 chili peppers, deveined and minced
1 cup heavy cream
1 tablespoon butter, room temperature
Sea salt and ground black pepper, to taste

Directions

Toss the tilapia with the salt, pepper, onions, garlic, chili peppers and rum. Let it marinate for 2 hours in your refrigerator.

In a grill pan, melt the butter over a moderately high heat. Sear the fish in hot butter, basting with the reserved marinade.

Add in the mustard and cream and continue to cook until everything is thoroughly cooked, for 2 to 3 minutes. Bon appétit!

Per serving: 228 Calories; 13g Fat; 6.5g Carbs; 13.7g Protein; 1.1g Fiber

272. Steak and Brussels Sprout Skillet

(Ready in about 1 hour 40 minutes | Servings 6)

Ingredients

1 ½ cups Brussels sprouts, quartered
2 tablespoons olive oil
1 cup roasted vegetable broth
1 red onion, chopped
1/2 teaspoon fresh garlic, minced
1/2 teaspoon dried oregano
1 tablespoon dried marjoram
1 ½ pounds Porterhouse steak, cut into 6 serving-size pieces
Kosher salt and black pepper, to taste
For the Sauce:
1/2 cup roasted vegetable broth
1/4 teaspoon ground cardamom
3/4 teaspoon yellow mustard
1 cup heavy cream
1/2 cup dry red wine

Directions

Heat the olive oil in an oven-proof skillet over medium-high flame. Sear the steak until just browned, 4 to 5 minutes per side; reserve.

In the same skillet, cook the onion and garlic until they've softened. Add in the Brussels sprouts and continue to cook until just tender.

Add the Porterhouse steak back to the skillet. Add all spices along with 1 cup of vegetable broth. Cover with foil and roast at 350 degrees F for 1 hour 15 minutes. Reserve.

Add the remaining ingredients to the pan and continue to simmer for about 15 minutes until the sauce has thickened and reduced. Bon appétit!

Per serving: 339 Calories; 21.7g Fat; 5.2g Carbs; 35g Protein; 1.5g Fiber

273. Creamy Herby Meatloaf

(Ready in about 50 minutes | Servings 6)

Ingredients

1/3 cup heavy cream
1 egg, slightly beaten
1 large onions, chopped
1 ½ teaspoons coconut aminos
2 pounds ground beef
2 tablespoons flaxseed meal
1 tablespoon yellow mustard
1 teaspoon Italian seasoning mix
1/3 cup almond meal
2 garlic cloves, minced
For the Tomato Sauce:
1 tablespoon dried parsley flakes
Salt and pepper, to taste
2 vine-ripened tomatoes, pureed

Directions

In a mixing bowl, combine all ingredients for the meatloaf. Press the meatloaf mixture into a lightly greased loaf pan.

In a saucepan, over a moderate heat, cook all ingredients for the sauce until reduced slightly, about 4 minutes. Pour the sauce over the top of your meatloaf.

Bake at 365 degrees F for 40 to 45 minutes. Bon appétit!

Per serving: 163 Calories; 8.4g Fat; 5.6g Carbs; 12.2g Protein; 1.9g Fiber

FISH & SEAFOOD

274. Cottage Cheese and Tuna Pâté

(Ready in about 10 minutes | Servings 6)

Ingredients

1/2 cup Cottage cheese
2 (6-ounce) cans tuna in oil, drained
1 ounce sesame seeds, ground
1 ounce sunflower seeds, ground
1/2 teaspoon mustard seeds
1 tablespoon fresh Italian parsley, chopped

Directions

Add all of the above ingredients to the bowl of your blender or food processor.

Blend until everything is well combined.

Serve with keto veggie sticks.

Per serving: 181 Calories; 10.4g Fat; 2.1g Carbs; 19g Protein; 1g Fiber

275. Sherry Prawns with Garlic

(Ready in about 10 minutes + marinating time | Servings 4)

Ingredients

2 tablespoons dry sherry
1/2 teaspoon mustard seeds
1 ½ tablespoons fresh lemon juice
1 tablespoon garlic paste
1/2 stick butter, at room temperature
1 teaspoon dried basil
1 teaspoon cayenne pepper, crushed
1 ½ pounds king prawns, peeled and deveined

Directions

Whisk the dry sherry with cayenne pepper, garlic paste, basil, mustard seeds, lemon juice and prawns. Let it marinate for 1 hour in your refrigerator.

In a frying pan, melt the butter over a medium-high flame, basting with the reserved marinade.

Sprinkle with salt and pepper to taste. Enjoy!

Per serving: 294 Calories; 14.3g Fat; 3.6g Carbs; 34.6g Protein; 1.4g Fiber

276. Stuffed Tomatoes with Salmon and Cheese

(Ready in about 30 minutes | Servings 6)

Ingredients

1/2 cup aioli
2 tablespoons coriander, chopped
1 teaspoon Dijon mustard
10 ounces salmon
1 cup scallions, finely chopped
1 ½ cups Ricotta cheese
2 garlic cloves, minced
Sea salt and ground black pepper, to taste
6 tomatoes, pulp and seeds removed

Directions

Grill your salmon for about 10 minutes until browned and flakes easily with a fork. Cut into small chunks.

Thoroughly combine the salmon, scallions, garlic, coriander, aioli, mustard, salt, and pepper in a bowl.

Spoon the filling into tomatoes. Bake in the preheated oven at 390 degrees F for 17 to 20 minutes until they are thoroughly cooked.

Top with the Ricotta cheese and place under the preheated broiled for 5 minutes until hot and bubbly. Enjoy!

Per serving: 303 Calories; 22.9g Fat; 6.8g Carbs; 17g Protein; 1.6g Fiber

277. Greek Halibut Salad

(Ready in about 15 minutes | Servings 4)

Ingredients

1 pound halibut steak
1 cup Halloumi cheese
1/2 head butterhead lettuce
2 tablespoons sunflower seeds
1 Lebanese cucumbers, thinly sliced
1/2 cup radishes, thinly sliced
1 onion, thinly sliced
1 tablespoon lemon juice
1 ½ tablespoons extra-virgin olive oil
1 cup cherry tomatoes, halved
Sea salt and pepper, to taste

Directions

Cook the halibut steak on preheated grill for 5 to 6 minutes per side. until the fish flakes easily with a fork.

Grill the halloumi cheese and slice into small pieces.

Toss the grilled halloumi cheese with the remaining ingredients and set aside.

Serve with chilled salad and enjoy!

Per serving: 199 Calories; 10.6g Fat; 6.1g Carbs; 14.2g Protein; 1.1g Fiber

278. Traditional Louisiana-Style Gumbo

(Ready in about 25 minutes | Servings 4)

Ingredients

1/2 pound tilapia, cut into chunks
20 sea scallops
1 cup tomatoes, pureed
1/3 cup port wine
1 tablespoon fish sauce
2 breakfast sausages, cut crosswise into 1/2-inch-thick slices
2 garlic cloves, finely minced
1 yellow onion, chopped
3/4 cup fish consommé
2 tablespoons fresh coriander, chopped
2 tablespoons lard, melted

Directions

In a stock pot, melt the lard over medium-high heat. Cook the sausages for about 5 minutes until no longer pink; reserve.

Now, sauté the onion and garlic until they've softened; reserve.

Add in the pureed tomatoes, fish sauce, fish consommé and wine; let it simmer for another 15 minutes.

Add in the tilapia, scallops, coriander, and reserved sausages. Continue to simmer, partially covered, for 5 to 6 minutes.

Garnish with coriander and enjoy!

Per serving: 481 Calories; 26.9g Fat; 5g Carbs; 46.6g Protein; 1.3g Fiber

279. Creamed Mint and Mackerel Chowder

(Ready in about 30 minutes | Servings 6)

Ingredients

2 ½ cups hot water
1 tablespoon peanut oil
1/2 cup white onions, sliced
1 garlic clove, smashed
1 bell pepper, deveined and sliced
3/4 cup heavy cream
1/4 cup fresh mint, chopped
1 teaspoon Five-spice powder
1 celery rib, diced
1 chili pepper, deveined and sliced
1 tablespoon coconut aminos
1 ¼ pounds mackerel, cut into small pieces

Directions

Heat the oil in a large pot over a moderately high heat. Cook the onion and garlic until they are just tender or about 3 minutes.

Stir in the celery, peppers, coconut aminos, water, and Five-spice powder. Reduce to a simmer, and cook, partially covered, for 15 minutes.

Fold in the fish chunks and continue to simmer an additional 15 minutes or until cooked through. Add in the heavy cream and remove from the heat.

Serve with fresh mint leaves and enjoy!

Per serving: 165 Calories; 5.5g Fat; 4g Carbs; 25.4g Protein; 0.5g Fiber

280. Tuna Salad with Bocconcini and Olives

(Ready in about 10 minutes | Servings 4)

Ingredients

1 head Romaine lettuce
8 ounces bocconcini
2 garlic cloves, minced
1/2 cup black olives, pitted and sliced
1/2 teaspoon chili pepper, finely chopped
1 teaspoon balsamic vinegar
1 tablespoon fish sauce
2 bell peppers, sliced
1 Lebanese cucumber, sliced
1 teaspoon sesame oil
1/2 cup radicchio, sliced
1 tomato, diced
2 teaspoons tahini paste
1/2 cup onion, thinly sliced
1 pound tuna steak

Directions

Grill the tuna over medium-high heat for about 4 minutes per side. Flake the fish with a fork.

Mix the vegetables in a salad bowl. In a small mixing dish, thoroughly combine the tahini, sesame oil, vinegar, and fish sauce.

Dress the salad. Garnish with the bocconcini and serve well-chilled. Enjoy!

Per serving: 273 Calories; 11.7g Fat; 6.7g Carbs; 34.2g Protein; 4.1g Fiber

281. Easy Fish Kabobs

(Ready in about 15 minutes | Servings 4)

Ingredients

1 cup cherry tomatoes
1 red onion, cut into wedges
2 tablespoons coconut aminos
1/2 teaspoon basil
2 tablespoons olive oil
1 zucchini, diced
1 pound haddock, cut into small cubes
Salt and pepper, to taste

Directions

Start by preheating your grill on high.

Toss the haddock and vegetables with salt, pepper, basil, olive oil, and coconut aminos.

Alternate the seasoned haddock, onion, zucchini and tomatoes on bamboo skewers.

Grill your skewers for 5 minutes for medium-rare, flipping them occasionally to ensure even cooking. Bon appétit!

Per serving: 257 Calories; 12.5g Fat; 7g Carbs; 27.5g Protein; 0.9g Fiber

FISH & SEAFOOD

282. Fisherman's Stew with Sauvignon Blanc

(Ready in about 25 minutes | Servings 4)

Ingredients

1/2 cup Sauvignon blanc
1/8 teaspoon Tabasco sauce, or more to taste
1/3 pound halibut, cut into 2-inch pieces
1/2 pound sea bass, cut into 2-inch pieces
1 cup fresh tomato, pureed
4 cups water
1 tablespoon chicken bouillon granules
1 cup onions, chopped
1 teaspoon garlic, smashed
2 rosemary sprigs, chopped
1 tablespoon sesame oil
Sea salt, to taste

Directions

Heat the oil in a large stockpot that is preheated over medium heat. Now, sauté the onions and garlic until they're softened and aromatic.

Add the salt, water, tomato and chicken bouillon granules; cook an additional 13 minutes.

Stir in the remaining ingredients and bring to a rolling boil.

After that, turn the heat to medium-low and let it simmer until the fish easily flakes apart, about 4 minutes.

Taste and adjust the seasonings. Bon appétit!

Per serving: 296 Calories; 8.6g Fat; 5.5g Carbs; 41.4g Protein; 1g Fiber

283. Lemon Tuna with Brussels Sprouts

(Ready in about 25 minutes | Servings 4)

Ingredients

1 pound tuna
2 garlic cloves, crushed
1/3 cup pine nuts, chopped
1 teaspoon dried rosemary
1/2 pounds Brussels sprouts
1/4 cup extra-virgin olive oil
1 tomato, chopped
1/2 cup fish stock
1 tablespoon fresh lemon juice
1/4 cup parsley
Sea salt and freshly ground black pepper, to taste

Directions

Brush a non-stick skillet with cooking spray. Once hot, cook the tuna steaks for about 4 minutes per side; sprinkle with salt, pepper, and rosemary; set aside.

In the same skillet, cook the Brussels sprouts; adding the fish stock to prevent over cooking. Then, sauté for about 5 minutes or until the Brussels sprouts are crisp-tender.

Add in the chopped tomatoes and continue to cook for 3 minutes more. Fold in the reserved tuna steaks.

Process the parsley, garlic, pine nuts, lemon juice, and olive oil in your food processor or blender until it reaches a paste consistency.

Top your fish with the sauce and serve. Bon appétit!

Per serving: 372 Calories; 27.8g Fat; 5.6g Carbs; 26.5g Protein; 2.2g Fiber

284. Mackerel with Mushroom Coulis

(Ready in about 35 minutes | Servings 4)

Ingredients

For the Fish:
2 tablespoons avocado oil
2 tablespoons coconut aminos
1/3 cup Shaoxing wine
1/2 teaspoon cayenne pepper
1 pound mackerel fillets
Sea salt and ground black pepper, to taste
For the Mushroom Coulis:
2 ounces button mushrooms, chopped
1 Spanish pepper, deveined and chopped
1/2 shallot, peeled and chopped
1/4 teaspoon cardamom
3 tablespoons Shaoxing wine
1 ½ ounces sesame oil
Salt and ground black pepper, to taste

Directions

In a wok, heat the avocado oil over a moderately high heat. Season the fish with salt, black pepper, and cayenne pepper.

Cook the fish for about 10 minutes until golden brown; reserve.

Add in 1/3 cup of Shaoxing wine and coconut aminos; bring to a boil. Turn the heat to simmer and continue to cook for 4 to 5 minutes.

Add the mackerel fillets back to the pan, and continue to cook for 4 minutes longer.

To make the mushroom coulis, heat sesame oil in a wok that is preheated over a moderate flame. Now, cook the shallots until tender and translucent or about 3 minutes.

Turn the heat to simmer and stir in the peppers and mushrooms along with 3 tablespoons of Shaoxing wine; cook for 10 minutes longer or until the vegetables have softened. Add in salt, black pepper, and cardamom.

Puree the sautéed mixture in your blender until creamy and uniform. Enjoy!

Per serving: 415 Calories; 28g Fat; 4.4g Carbs; 34.5g Protein; 1.8g Fiber

285. Baked Cod with Cilantro and Mustard

(Ready in about 30 minutes | Servings 4)

Ingredients

4 cod fillets
1/4 cup fresh cilantro, chopped
1/2 tablespoon yellow mustard
1 teaspoon garlic paste
Salt and ground black pepper, to taste
1/2 teaspoon red pepper flakes, crushed
2 tablespoons olive oil
1/2 tablespoon fresh lemon juice
1/2 teaspoon shallot powder

Directions

Start by preheating your oven to 420 degrees F. Lightly grease a baking dish with a non-stick cooking spray.

In a small mixing dish, thoroughly combine the oil, mustard, garlic paste, lemon juice, shallot powder, salt, black pepper and red pepper.

Rub this mixture on all sides of your fish.

Bake 15 to 22 minutes in the middle of the preheated oven. Garnish with fresh cilantro.

Bon appétit!

Per serving: 195 Calories; 8.2g Fat; 0.5g Carbs; 28.7g Protein; 0.3g Fiber

286. Shrimp with Classic Mignonette

(Ready in about 15 minutes | Servings 4)

Ingredients

1 ½ pounds shrimp, shelled and deveined
1 teaspoon garlic, minced
2 tablespoons dry sherry
1 large onion, chopped
1 cup tomato puree
Salt and pepper, to taste
1 ½ tablespoons butter, melted
For Mignonette Sauce:
1 teaspoon black pepper, coarsely ground
1/2 cup white wine vinegar
1/2 cup onion, chopped

Directions

Melt the butter in a sauté pan over a moderately high heat. Then, cook the onion and garlic until they are tender and fragrant.

Add in the tomato puree and season with salt and pepper to taste; add in the shrimp and continue to cook until thoroughly cooked.

Remove from the heat and add in the dry sherry. Wisk all ingredients for the Mignonette sauce. Bon appétit!

Per serving: 252 Calories; 7.3g Fat; 5.3g Carbs; 36.6g Protein; 2.5g Fiber

287. Creamed Prawn Salad with Mayonnaise

(Ready in about 10 minutes | Servings 6)

Ingredients

1/2 cup mayonnaise
1 celery rib, sliced
1/4 cup capers, drained
1/2 head Iceberg lettuce, torn into pieces
1/4 cup fresh basil, chopped
1 cup white onions, chopped
1 Lebanese cucumber, chopped
Juice from 1 fresh lime
2 pounds tiger prawns, peeled leaving tails intact
Sea salt and freshly ground black pepper, to taste

Directions

Boil the tiger prawns in a large pot of salted water for about 3 minutes. Drain well and let it cool completely.

Toss the remaining ingredients in a large bowl; toss to combine well.

Top your salad with the tiger prawns and serve immediately!

Per serving: 196 Calories; 8.3g Fat; 6.5g Carbs; 21.4g Protein; 1.6g Fiber

288. Swordfish Cutlets with Greek Cauliflower Puree

(Ready in about 35 minutes | Servings 4)

Ingredients

1 pound swordfish cutlets, about 3/4 inch thick
1 ½ teaspoons Greek herb mix
1 pound cauliflower, broken into florets
1/4 cup Romano cheese, freshly grated
1/4 cup double cream
2 tablespoons butter
1/2 cup fresh basil, roughly chopped
Flaky sea salt and ground black pepper, to taste
1 ½ tablespoons extra-virgin olive oil
1 tablespoon freshly squeezed lemon juice

Directions

Whisk the extra-virgin olive oil with the lemon juice.

Grill the fish cutlets for about 15 minutes, basting them with the lemon mixture. Season with salt, black pepper, and Greek herb mix. Reserve, keeping them warm.

Boil the cauliflower in a lightly salted water until crisp-tender. Mash the cauliflower with a potato masher.

Fold in the other ingredients and stir to combine well. Enjoy!

Per serving: 404 Calories; 22.2g Fat; 5.7g Carbs; 43.5g Protein; 3g Fiber

289. Italian Seafood Stew with Wine

(Ready in about 20 minutes | Servings 4)

Ingredients

1 leek, chopped
2 garlic cloves, pressed
1/2 teaspoon lime zest
3 cups fish stock
2 tablespoons port wine
1/2 pound scallops
1 teaspoon Italian seasonings blend
Salt and ground black pepper, to taste
1/2 pound shrimp
1 cup tomato puree
1 celery stalk, chopped
2 tablespoons lard, room temperature

Directions

Melt the lard in a large pot over a moderately high heat. Sauté the leek and garlic until they've softened.

Stir in the pureed tomatoes and continue to cook for about 10 minutes.

Add in the remaining ingredients and bring to a boil. Turn the heat to a simmer and continue to cook for 4 to 5 minutes. Enjoy!

Per serving: 209 Calories; 12.6g Fat; 6.6g Carbs; 15.2g Protein; 2g Fiber

FISH & SEAFOOD

290. Old Bay Pollock Soup

(Ready in about 30 minutes | Servings 4)

Ingredients

3 teaspoons butter
1/4 cup dry white wine
1 teaspoon Old Bay seasonings
2 carrots, chopped
3 cups boiling water
1/2 cup full-fat milk
1 parsnip, chopped
2 shallots, chopped
1 celery with leaves, chopped
1/2 cup clam juice
1 ¼ pounds pollock fillets, skin removed
Sea salt and ground black pepper, to taste

Directions

Chop the pollock fillets into bite-sized pieces.

Warm the butter in a pan over a moderately high flame. Cook the vegetables until they're softened. Season with salt, pepper and Old Bay seasonings.

Stir in the chopped fish and cook for 12 to 15 minutes more. Add the boiling water and clam juice. Afterwards, pour in the white wine and milk.

Bring to a boil. Reduce the heat and cook for 15 minutes longer. Bon appétit!

Per serving: 170 Calories; 5.8g Fat; 6.7g Carbs; 20g Protein; 2.3g Fiber

291. Shrimp Salad with Avocado and Aioli

(Ready in about 10 minutes + chilling time | Servings 6)

Ingredients

1 pound shrimp, peeled and deveined
1 avocado, pitted and sliced
1/2 cup aioli
1 shallot, thinly sliced
1 tablespoon soy sauce
2 teaspoons fresh lemon juice
1 cup butterhead lettuce
1/2 cup cucumber, chopped

Directions

Cook your shrimp in a pot of salted water for about 3 minutes. Drain and reserve.

In a salad bowl, mix all ingredients, except for the lettuce leaves. Gently stir to combine.

Mound the salad onto the lettuce leaves and top each portion with shrimp. Enjoy!

Per serving: 236 Calories; 14.3g Fat; 5.3g Carbs; 16.3g Protein; 3g Fiber

292. Cod Fritters with Romano Cheese

(Ready in about 20 minutes | Servings 5)

Ingredients

3 tablespoons olive oil
1 teaspoon butter, room temperature
1/2 cup Romano cheese, preferably freshly grated
3 cups broccoli, cut into rice-sized chunks
2 eggs, whisked
Sea salt and pepper, to taste
1/2 teaspoon dried oregano
1/2 cup almond flour
1/2 teaspoon dried thyme
1/4 cup onion, chopped
2 ½ cups cod fish, cooked

Directions

Melt the butter in a pan over medium-high flame. Once hot, cook the broccoli for 5 to 6 minutes, until crisp-tender. Let it cool completely.

Add in the cooked fish, salt, pepper, oregano, thyme, onion, eggs, almond flour, and cheese; mix until everything is well incorporated.

Form the mixture into 10 patties.

In a frying pan, heat the oil over a moderately high heat. Cook your fritters for 4 to 5 minutes per side. Bon appétit!

Per serving: 326 Calories; 21.7g Fat; 5.8g Carbs; 25.6g Protein; 1g Fiber

293. Creamed Shrimp Pate

(Ready in about 10 minutes + chilling time | Servings 8)

Ingredients

1 tablespoon Cholula
2 teaspoons green garlic, finely minced
Sea salt and ground black pepper, to taste
1/2 cup mayonnaise
1/2 teaspoon dried rosemary
12 ounces shrimp, canned and drained
1 teaspoon cayenne pepper

Directions

In a mixing bowl, stir all ingredients until well incorporated.

Cover and transfer to your refrigerator until thoroughly chilled. Bon appétit!

Per serving: 108 Calories; 5.4g Fat; 5g Carbs; 8.2g Protein; 0.5g Fiber

294. Cod with Broccoli and Tomato Chutney

(Ready in about 30 minutes | Servings 4)

Ingredients

1 ½ pounds cod fish
1 onion, thinly sliced
1 teaspoon paprika
2 tablespoons sesame oil
2 Spanish peppers, thinly sliced
1 pound broccoli, cut into florets
Sea salt and freshly ground black pepper, to taste
For Tomato Chutney:
2 garlic cloves, sliced
1 teaspoon sesame oil
1 cup tomatoes, chopped
Sea salt and ground black pepper, to taste

Directions

In a frying pan, heat 2 tablespoons of sesame oil over a moderately high flame.

Stir in the broccoli florets, Spanish peppers, and onion until they've softened; season with salt, black pepper, and paprika; reserve.

In the same pan, sear the fish for 4 to 5 minutes per side.

To make the chutney, heat 1 teaspoon of sesame oil in a frying pan over a moderately high heat. Sauté the garlic until just browned or about 1 minute.

Add in the chopped tomatoes and continue to cook, stirring periodically, until cooked through. Season with salt and pepper to taste. Serve the broccoli and cod fish with the tomato chutney. Enjoy!

Per serving: 291 Calories; 9.5g Fat; 3.5g Carbs; 42.5g Protein; 3g Fiber

295. Italian Zuppa Di Pesce

(Ready in about 20 minutes | Servings 4)

Ingredients

1/2 pound mussels
2 tomatoes, pureed
1 celery stalk, chopped
2 onions, chopped
1/2 teaspoon lemon zest
1/2 pound shrimp
2 cups shellfish stock
1 teaspoon Italian seasonings
1 teaspoon saffron threads
2 garlic cloves, pressed
1 cup hot water
2 tablespoons dry white wine
1/2 stick butter, at room temperature
Salt and ground black pepper, to taste

Directions

Melt the butter in a stockpot over a moderate heat. Cook the onion and garlic until aromatic.

Now, stir in the pureed tomatoes; cook for 8 minutes or until heated through.

Add the remaining ingredients and bring to a rapid boil. Reduce the heat to a simmer and cook an additional 4 minutes. Bon appétit!

Per serving: 209 Calories; 12.6g Fat; 6.6g Carbs; 15.2g Protein; 2g Fiber

296. Classic Fish Cakes

(Ready in about 30 minutes | Servings 6)

Ingredients

1/2 cup Cottage cheese, at room temperature
1/4 cup almond meal
2 eggs, lightly beaten
1/4 tablespoons flax meal
2 teaspoons brown mustard
2 tablespoons sesame oil
1 ½ pounds tilapia fish, deboned and flaked
Sea salt and pepper, to taste
2 tablespoons fresh basil, chopped

Directions

Mix the flakes fish with the eggs, almond and flax meal, cheese, mustard, salt, pepper, and basil. Form the mixture into 12 patties.

Now, place the patties on a parchment-lined baking sheet. Spritz them with sesame oil.

Bake in the preheated oven at 395 degrees F approximately 25 minutes, rotating the pan occasionally. Bon appétit!

Per serving: 234 Calories; 10.6g Fat; 2.5g Carbs; 31.2g Protein; 0.2g Fiber

297. Salmon with Herbs and Wine

(Ready in about 40 minutes | Servings 4)

Ingredients

4 salmon fillets
1/4 teaspoon ground black pepper
2 garlic cloves, minced
1/4 teaspoon onion powder
1/4 teaspoon white pepper
3 teaspoons avocado oil
1 teaspoon lemon thyme
1/3 cup Worcestershire sauce
1 teaspoon dried oregano
1/3 cup fresh lime juice
1/4 cup fresh chives, chopped

Directions

To make the marinade, thoroughly mix the lime juice, Worcestershire sauce, avocado oil, fresh chives, garlic, and onion powder.

Place the salmon fillets in the marinade; place in the refrigerator for 20 to 25 minutes. Season the salmon fillets with lemon thyme, black pepper, white pepper and oregano.

Place the salmon fillets on the preheated grill and reserve the marinade.

Cook your salmon for 10 to 12 minutes, turning once and brushing with the reserved marinade. Bon appétit!

Per serving: 266 Calories; 11.5g Fat; 5.6g Carbs; 34.9g Protein; 0.4g Fiber

298. Rich Salmon Dipping Sauce

(Ready in about 10 minutes | Servings 10)

Ingredients

4 hard-boiled egg yolks, finely chopped
5 ounces Ricotta cheese
Salt and freshly ground black pepper, to your liking
1/2 teaspoon hot paprika
1/4 cup fresh scallions, chopped
5 ounces full-fat cream cheese
10 ounces salmon

Directions

Grill the salmon for about 10 minutes until browned and easily flakes with a fork. Cut into small chunks.

Mix all ingredients until everything is well incorporated.

Per serving: 109 Calories; 6.3g Fat; 1.3g Carbs; 11.4g Protein; 0.1g Fiber

299. Thai-Style Fish Curry

(Ready in about 25 minutes | Servings 6)

Ingredients

2 pounds blue grenadier, cut into large pieces
8 fresh curry leaves
1 tablespoon ground coriander
2 green cardamom pods
1 teaspoon dried basil
2 green chilies, minced
1 cup coconut milk
2 tablespoons olive oil
1 cup shallots, chopped
1/2 tablespoon fresh ginger, grated
4 Roma tomatoes, pureed
2 tablespoons fresh lime juice
2 garlic cloves, finely chopped
Salt and black pepper, to taste

Directions

Drizzle the blue grenadier with the lime juice.

Heat the oil in a non-stick skillet over a moderate flame. Cook the curry leaves and shallots until the shallot has softened, about 4 minutes.

After that, add the chilies, ginger and garlic and cook an additional minute or until fragrant. Add the remaining ingredients, except for coconut milk, and simmer for 10 minutes or until heated through.

Now, stir in the fish; pour in 1 cup of coconut milk and cook, covered, for 6 minutes longer. Bon appétit!

Per serving: 270 Calories; 16.9g Fat; 6.6g Carbs; 22.3g Protein; 1.4g Fiber

300. Keto "Breaded" Cod Fillets

(Ready in about 15 minutes | Servings 4)

Ingredients

3/4 cup grated Parmesan cheese
1 pound cod fillets, cut into 4 servings
Flaky sea salt and ground black pepper, to taste
2 tablespoons olive oil
1/2 teaspoon paprika

Directions

In a shallow mixing dish, combine the salt pepper, paprika, and Parmesan cheese,

Press the cod fillets into this Parmesan mixture.

Heat the olive oil in a non-stick skillet over medium-high flame. Cook the cod fillets for 12 to 15 minutes or until opaque.

Bon appétit!

Per serving: 222 Calories; 12.6g Fat; 0.9g Carbs; 27.9g Protein; 0.3g Fiber

301. Grilled Clams in Tangy Sauce

(Ready in about 25 minutes | Servings 4)

Ingredients

40 littleneck clams
For the Sauce:
2 tablespoons olive oil
1/2 teaspoon paprika
2 garlic cloves, pressed
1/2 lemon, cut into wedges
1 shallot, chopped
1/3 cup port wine
2 tomatoes, pureed
Sea salt and freshly ground black pepper, to taste

Directions

Grill the clams until they are open, for 5 to 6 minutes.

In a frying pan, heat the olive oil over moderate heat. Cook the shallot and garlic until tender and fragrant.

Stir in the pureed tomatoes, salt, black pepper and paprika and continue to cook an additional 10 to 12 minutes or until thoroughly cooked.

Heat off and add in the port wine; stir to combine. Garnish with fresh lemon wedges.

Bon appétit!

Per serving: 134 Calories; 7.8g Fat; 5.9g Carbs; 8.3g Protein; 1g Fiber

302. Keto Fish Pie

(Ready in about 45 minutes | Servings 6)

Ingredients

For the Crust:
2 eggs
2 teaspoons ground psyllium husk powder
2 tablespoons almond milk
1/2 stick butter
1 cup almond meal
3 tablespoons flaxseed meal
1 teaspoon baking powder
Flaky salt, to taste
For the Filling:
1 ½ cups Colby cheese, shredded
1/2 cup cream cheese
1/2 cup mayonnaise
10 ounces cod fish, chopped
1 teaspoon stone-ground mustard
2 eggs
1 teaspoon Mediterranean spice mix

Directions

Thoroughly combine all the crust ingredients. Press the crust into a parchment-lined baking pan.

Bake the crust in the preheated oven at 365 degrees F for about 15 minutes.

In a mixing dish, combine the ingredients for the filling. Spread the mixture over the pie crust and bake for a further 25 minutes. Enjoy!

Per serving: 416 Calories; 34.2g Fat; 5.5g Carbs; 19.5g Protein; 1.5g Fiber

303. Spanish-Style Salad with Crab Mayonnaise

(Ready in about 15 minutes | Servings 4)

Ingredients

For the Crab Mayo:
2 egg yolks
1/2 teaspoon basil
1/2 teaspoon Sriracha sauce
2 tablespoons fresh lime juice
1 teaspoon garlic, pressed
1/2 tablespoon Dijon mustard
3/4 cup extra-virgin olive oil
Coarse sea salt and ground black pepper, to season
1 pound crabmeat
For the Salad:
1 Spanish pepper, julienned
1 cup radishes, sliced
1 head Romaine lettuce
1 cup arugula
A bunch of scallions, chopped

Directions

Mix the egg yolks and mustard in your blender; pour in the oil in a tiny stream, and continue to blend.

Now, add in the Sriracha sauce, lime juice, salt, black pepper, garlic, basil, and crabmeat.

Toss the remaining ingredients in a salad bowl. Add in the prepared crab mayo sauce and gently stir to combine.

Serve well-chilled.

Per serving: 293 Calories; 27.1g Fat; 6.3g Carbs; 9.3g Protein; 3.3g Fiber

304. Indonesian Pollock Curry

(Ready in about 25 minutes | Servings 6)

Ingredients

1 cup coconut milk
8 fresh curry leaves
2 tablespoons fresh lime juice
2 green chilies, minced
1/2 tablespoon fresh ginger, grated
1 teaspoon mustard seeds
1 cup white onions, chopped
1 tablespoon ground coriander
2 pounds pollock, cut into large pieces
4 Roma tomatoes, pureed
2 tablespoons sesame oil
1 teaspoon fresh garlic, minced
Salt and black pepper, to taste

Directions

Drizzle the fish with lime juice.

Heat the sesame oil in a frying pan over a moderately high flame. Cook the onion, curry leaves and garlic for 3 to 4 minutes until tender and aromatic.

Add in the ginger, salt, pepper, tomatoes, mustard seeds, and ground coriander. Let it simmer for 12 minutes or until thoroughly cooked.

Add in the fish and coconut milk and continue to cook, partially covered, for 6 to 7 minutes longer. Bon appétit!

Per serving: 270 Calories; 16.9g Fat; 5.6g Carbs; 22.3g Protein; 1.5g Fiber

305. Lime Herb Halibut Steaks

(Ready in about 35 minutes | Servings 2)

Ingredients

1/3 cup freshly squeezed lime juice
1 teaspoon dry thyme
1 teaspoon dry rosemary
2 teaspoons sesame oil, room temperature
4 tablespoons fresh chives, chopped
1 teaspoon garlic, finely minced
Flaky sea salt and white pepper, to taste
2 halibut steaks

Directions

Place the fresh lime juice, sesame oil, salt, white pepper, rosemary, thyme, chives, garlic, and halibut steak in a ceramic dish; let it marinate for about 30 minutes.

Grill the halibut steaks approximately 15 minutes, turning occasionally and basting with the reserved marinade. Bon appétit!

Per serving: 308 Calories; 10.9g Fat; 2g Carbs; 46.5g Protein; 0.8g Fiber

306. Seafood Chowder with Cream and Wine

(Ready in about 15 minutes | Servings 5)

Ingredients

1 teaspoon Mediterranean spice mix
3/4 pound prawns, peeled and deveined
1/2 pound crab meat
2 cups double cream
1/3 cup port wine
2 garlic cloves, minced
1 quart chicken bone broth
2 tablespoons scallions, chopped
1 tablespoon tomato sauce
1 egg, lightly beaten
1/2 stick butter

Directions

In a heavy bottomed pot, melt the butter over a moderately high flame. Sauté the scallions and garlic until they've softened.

Add in the prawns, crab meat, wine, and chicken bone broth. Continue to cook until thoroughly heated for 5 to 6 minutes.

Decrease the heat to low; add in the remaining ingredients and continue to simmer for 5 minutes more.

Enjoy!

Per serving: 404 Calories; 30g Fat; 5.3g Carbs; 23.9g Protein; 0.3g Fiber

307. Dijon Tuna Steaks with Spinach and Lemon

(Ready in about 20 minutes | Servings 6)

Ingredients

2 pounds tuna steaks
1 tablespoon Dijon mustard
1 fresh lemon, sliced
1 cup green onions, thinly sliced
Salt and pepper, to season
1/2 cup radishes, thinly sliced
3 tablespoons peanut oil
3 cups spinach

Directions

Brush each tuna steak with peanut oil and season them with salt and pepper.

Arrange the tuna steaks on a foil-lined baking pan. Top with lemon slices, cover with foil and roast at 400 degrees F for about 10 minutes.

Serve with spinach, green onions, radishes and mustard mixture. Bon appétit!

Per serving: 444 Calories; 38.2g Fat; 4.7g Carbs; 21.9g Protein; 1g Fiber

308. Amberjack with Romano Cheese Sauce

(Ready in about 20 minutes | Servings 6)

Ingredients

2 tablespoons olive oil, at room temperature
Sea salt and ground black pepper, to taste
6 amberjack fillets
1/4 cup fresh tarragon chopped
For the Sauce:
1/3 cup Romano cheese, grated
3/4 cup double cream
3 teaspoons butter, at room temperature
2 garlic cloves, finely minced
1/3 cup vegetable broth

Directions

In a non-stick frying pan, heat the olive oil until sizzling.

Once hot, fry the amberjack for about 6 minutes per side or until the edges are turning opaque. Sprinkle them with salt, black pepper, and tarragon. Reserve.

To make the sauce, melt the butter in a saucepan over moderately high heat. Sauté the garlic until tender and fragrant or about 2 minutes.

Add in the vegetable broth and cream and continue to cook for 5 to 6 minutes more; heat off.

Stir in the Romano cheese and continue stirring in the residual heat for a couple of minutes more. Bon appétit!

Per serving: 285 Calories; 20.4g Fat; 1.2g Carbs; 23.8g Protein; 0.1g Fiber

FISH & SEAFOOD

309. Creamed Sardine and Mayo Salad

(Ready in about 10 minutes | Servings 4)

Ingredients

1 pound fresh sardines, chopped
1/2 cup cucumber, thinly sliced
1/2 teaspoon smoked paprika
1/4 cup fresh scallions, roughly chopped
1 celery, thinly sliced
1 red onion, chopped
3/4 cup mayonnaise
1 head of Iceberg lettuce
Sea salt and ground black pepper, to taste

Directions

Pat your sardines dry with kitchen paper towel. Place your sardines in a baking dish; roast them in the preheated oven at 390 degrees F for 20 minutes.

Toss the remaining ingredients in a salad bowl.

Top your salad with the sardines and enjoy!

Per serving: 195 Calories; 14.7g Fat; 6g Carbs; 7.8g Protein; 3.1g Fiber

310. Curried Trout with Basil Chimichurri Sauce

(Ready in about 15 minutes | Servings 6)

Ingredients

6 trout fillets
1/2 teaspoon mustard seeds
Sea salt and ground black pepper, to taste
1/2 teaspoon curry powder
2 tablespoons butter
For Basil Chimichurri Sauce:
1 chili pepper, finely chopped
1 tablespoon fresh basil leaves, snipped
1/3 cup olive oil
2 garlic cloves, minced
1/2 cup yellow onion, finely chopped
1/2 cup fresh cilantro, minced
1/3 cup apple cider vinegar
Kosher salt and pepper, to taste

Directions

In a cast-iron skillet, melt the butter over a moderately high heat. Season the trout fillets with salt, pepper, curry powder, and mustard seeds.

Cook the trout fillets for about 5 minutes per side.

To make the Chimichurri sauce, pulse the remaining ingredients in your food processor until well mixed. Serve with the trout fillets and enjoy!

Per serving: 265 Calories; 20.9g Fat; 4g Carbs; 17.1g Protein; 0.7g Fiber

311. Dijon Salad with Snapper and Cheese

(Ready in about 15 minutes | Servings 4)

Ingredients

2 cups arugula
6 ounces Feta cheese, crumbled
1/2 cup black olives, pitted and sliced
10 grape tomatoes, halved
2 tablespoons butter, melted
2 cups lettuce leaves, torn into pieces
1 teaspoon ground mustard seeds
1/2 teaspoon celery seeds
1 carrot, thinly sliced
1 cup spring onions, thinly sliced
4 snapper fillets with skin
Sea salt and ground black pepper, to taste
For the Vinaigrette:
1 teaspoon dried basil
1 lime, juiced and zested
2 tablespoons fresh mint, finely chopped
1/3 cup extra-virgin olive oil
1 teaspoon Dijon mustard
1 teaspoon ginger-garlic paste
Sea salt and ground black pepper, to taste

Directions

In a grill pan, melt the butter over a moderately high flame. Cook the fish for 5 to 6 minutes; flip the fish fillets over and cook them for 5 minutes more.

Toss all ingredients for the salad.

Whisk all ingredients for the vinaigrette and dress the salad.

Top your salad with the fish fillets, serve, and enjoy!

Per serving: 507 Calories; 42.8g Fat; 6g Carbs; 24.4g Protein; 2.7g Fiber

312. Cod Fish with Green Salad

(Ready in about 15 minutes + marinating time | Servings 4)

Ingredients

1 tablespoon olive oil
1 teaspoon garlic, minced
2 tablespoons scallions, chopped
Salt and pepper, to taste
4 white cod fish fillets
2 tablespoons fresh lemon juice
For French Salad:
1/4 cup extra-virgin olive oil
1 cup arugula
1/4 cup red wine vinegar
1 cup chicory
1 cup frissee
1 head Iceberg lettuce
2 tablespoons dandelion
Salt and ground black pepper, to your liking

Directions

Toss the cod fish fillets with the olive oil, lemon juice, garlic, scallions salt, and pepper; allow it to marinate for 2 hours in your refrigerator.

Sear the fish fillets in the preheated skillet over moderately high heat; basting with the marinade.

Toss all ingredients for the salad in a salad bowl. Serve immediately.

Per serving: 425 Calories; 27.2g Fat; 6.1g Carbs; 38.3g Protein; 3g Fiber

313. Old Bay Mackerel Steak

(Ready in about 30 minutes | Servings 4)

Ingredients

1 tablespoon Old Bay seasoning
1 pound mackerel steaks
1 cup mozzarella, shredded
1 cup carrots, thinly sliced
3 tomatoes, thinly sliced
1 cup parsnip, thinly sliced
1/4 cup clam juice
1/2 stick butter
2 cloves garlic, thinly sliced
2 onions, thinly sliced
1/2 cup fresh chives, chopped
Salt and black pepper, to your liking

Directions

Preheat your oven to 450 degrees F.

Melt the butter in a pan that is previously preheated over a moderate flame. Cook the carrots, parsnip, garlic, and onions until they are tender.

Add the clam juice and tomatoes and cook 4 minutes more. Transfer this vegetable mixture to a casserole dish.

Lay the fish steaks on top of the vegetable layer. Sprinkle with the seasonings. Cover with foil and roast for 10 minutes, until the fish is opaque in the center.

Top with the shredded cheese and bake another 5 minutes. Garnish with fresh chopped chives. Bon appétit!

Per serving: 301 Calories; 14g Fat; 7g Carbs; 33.3g Protein; 2.4g Fiber

314. Salmon Stuffed Peppers

(Ready in about 25 minutes | Servings 4)

Ingredients

4 bell peppers
1 pound salmon fillets, boneless
1 onion, finely chopped
1/2 teaspoon garlic, pressed
1/3 cup mayonnaise
1/3 cup black olives, pitted and chopped
Sea salt and pepper, to taste
1/2 teaspoon dried oregano
1/2 teaspoon dried oregano
1 cup cream cheese

Directions

Broil the bell pepper for 5 to 6 minutes until they've softened.

Now, remove the seeds and membranes and cut the peppers in half.

Cook the salmon in a lightly oiled grill pan for 5 to 6 minutes per side until the fish flakes easily with a fork. Add in the other ingredients; stir to combine well.

Divide the salmon mixture between the peppers and bake in the preheated oven at 380 degrees F for about 15 minutes or until heated through. Serve warm.

Per serving: 273 Calories; 13.9g Fat; 5.1g Carbs; 28.9g Protein; 2.1g Fiber

315. Crab Legs with Bacon and Vegetables

(Ready in about 10 minutes | Servings 4)

Ingredients

10 Kalamata olives, pitted and halved
3 tablespoons olive oil
1 tablespoon peanut butter
1/4 cup fresh parsley, chopped
4 cups spinach
1 large-sized tomato, diced
12 ounces lump legs
1/4 cup fresh scallions, chopped
2 ounces thinly sliced bacon, chopped
1/2 lime, zested and juiced
Flaky sea salt and ground black pepper, to your liking

Directions

Start by preheating your grill to 225 degrees F for indirect cooking.

Place the crab legs on the grill grates. Close the lid and grill for about 30 minutes or until done.

To prepare the dressing, whisk the oil, peanut butter, lime juice, salt, and pepper.

Toss the remaining ingredients and dress your salad. Bon appétit!

Per serving: 232 Calories; 15.6g Fat; 6g Carbs; 18.9g Protein; 2g Fiber

316. Clams with Sherry-Tomato Sauce

(Ready in about 25 minutes | Servings 4)

Ingredients

40 littleneck clams
For the Sauce:
1/3 cup dry sherry
1 teaspoon crushed garlic
1 lemon, cut into wedges
1 onion, chopped
2 tomatoes, pureed
2 tablespoons olive oil
Sea salt and freshly ground black pepper, to taste
1/2 teaspoon cayenne pepper

Directions

Heat your grill to medium-high. Cook until the clams open, about 6 minutes.

Heat the oil in sauté pan over a moderate heat. Cook the onion and garlic until aromatic.

Add the pureed tomatoes, salt, black pepper and cayenne pepper and cook an additional 10 minutes or until everything is thoroughly cooked.

Remove from the heat and add the dry sherry; stir to combine. Add the grilled clams and lemon wedges.

Bon appétit!

Per serving: 134 Calories; 7.8g Fat; 5.9g Carbs; 8.3g Protein; 1.2g Fiber

FISH & SEAFOOD

317. Creole Seafood Jambalaya

(Ready in about 25 minutes | Servings 4)

Ingredients

1/2 pound skinned sole, cut into chunks
20 sea scallops
2 andouille sausages, cut crosswise into 1/2-inch-thick slices
2 tomatoes, pureed
2 garlic cloves, finely minced
3/4 cup clam juice
1/3 cup dry white wine
1 shallot, chopped
1 tablespoon oyster sauce
2 tablespoons fresh cilantro, chopped
1/2 stick butter, melted

Directions

Melt the butter in a heavy-bottomed pot over medium-high heat. Cook the sausages until no longer pink; reserve.

Now, sauté the garlic and shallots in pan drippings until they are softened; reserve.

Add the pureed tomatoes, oyster sauce, clam juice and wine; simmer for another 12 minutes.

Add the skinned sole, scallops and reserved sausages. Let it simmer, partially covered, for 6 minutes. Garnished with fresh cilantro. Bon appétit!

Per serving: 481 Calories; 26.9g Fat; 5g Carbs; 46.6g Protein; 0.7g Fiber

318. Mackerel and Vegetable Bake

(Ready in about 30 minutes | Servings 4)

Ingredients

1/2 stick butter
2 shallots, thinly sliced
2 tomatoes, thinly sliced
1/2 cup celery, thinly sliced
1/4 cup fish consommé
1 cup parsnip, thinly sliced
2 cloves garlic, thinly sliced
1 pound mackerel steaks, chopped
1/2 cup fresh scallions, chopped
1 cup goat cheese, shredded
Salt and black pepper, to your liking

Directions

In a frying pan, melt the butter in over a moderately high heat. Cook the vegetables until they are just tender and fragrant.

Add in the clam juice and tomatoes and cook for a further 5 minutes. Place the sautéed vegetables in a lightly-greased casserole dish.

Lower the mackerel steaks on top of the vegetable layer. Sprinkle with salt and pepper. Bake in the preheated oven at 420 degrees F for about 15 minutes.

Top with the shredded goat cheese and bake for a further 5 to 6 minutes or until it is hot and bubbly.

Bon appétit!

Per serving: 301 Calories; 14g Fat; 6g Carbs; 33.3g Protein; 3.2g Fiber

319. Cheese Tuna Mousse

(Ready in about 10 minutes + chilling time | Servings 12)

Ingredients

1/2 cup Ricotta cheese
1/2 teaspoon country Dijon mustard
1/4 cup sour cream
2 tablespoons mayonnaise
1 (14-ounce) tuna in brine, drained
2 ounces cilantro, finely chopped
1/2 teaspoon smoked paprika
Coarse salt and freshly cracked mixed peppercorns, to your liking

Directions

Add all ingredients to a mixing bowl.

Mix with a wide spatula until everything is well incorporated.

Pour into a greased mold; chill for 6 hours or overnight. Bon appétit!

Per serving: 64 Calories; 2.9g Fat; 1.3g Carbs; 7.9g Protein; 0.2g Fiber

320. Halibut Fillets with Mushrooms and Sour Cream

(Ready in about 20 minutes | Servings 4)

Ingredients

1 tablespoon butter
1/2 pound brown mushrooms, thinly sliced
1 cup sour cream
2 tablespoons olive oil
1 medium-sized leek, chopped
2 garlic cloves, chopped
1 ½ cups chicken stock
1/2 cup fresh scallions, chopped
Sea salt and freshly ground black pepper, to taste
4 halibut fillets

Directions

Heat the olive oil in a saucepan over a moderately high heat. Cook the leek until tender and translucent.

Add in the mushrooms, garlic, salt, and black pepper and continue to cook for 5 minutes more or until the mushrooms release liquid.

Add in the halibut fillets and continue to cook over medium-high heat approximately 5 minutes on each side.

Add in the butter, chicken stock, and scallions; bring to a boil. Immediately reduce the heat and let it cook for 10 minutes more or until heated through.

Add in the sour cream, remove from the heat and stir to combine well.

Bon appétit!

Per serving: 585 Calories; 30.5g Fat; 5.5g Carbs; 66.8g Protein; 1.1g Fiber

321. Sea Bass and Port Wine Chowder

(Ready in about 30 minutes | Servings 4)

Ingredients

3 cups boiling water
1/2 cup sour cream
1 teaspoon Old Bay seasonings
3 teaspoons olive oil
1/2 cup fish stock
1/4 cup port wine
Sea salt and ground black pepper, to taste
1 onion, chopped
2 carrots, chopped
1 celery rib, chopped
1 ¼ pounds sea bass, skin removed, cut into small chunks

Directions

In a heavy-bottomed pot, heat the olive oil over a moderately high flame. Once hot, cook the fish for about 10.

Stir in the onion, celery, carrot, spices, water, and fish stock and bring to a boil. Turn the heat to medium-low.

Let it simmer for 15 to 20 minutes more or until thoroughly cooked. Afterwards, add in the port wine and sour cream. Remove from the heat and stir to combine well. Bon appétit!

Per serving: 170 Calories; 5.8g Fat; 5.7g Carbs; 20g Protein; 1.9g Fiber

322. Lemony Tuna Fillets

(Ready in about 40 minutes | Servings 4)

Ingredients

4 tuna fillets
1/4 cup scallions, chopped
2 garlic cloves, minced
1/3 cup fresh lemon juice
1/3 cup coconut aminos
3 teaspoons olive oil
1 teaspoon lemon thyme
Salt and ground black pepper
1 teaspoon dried rosemary

Directions

Place all ingredients in a ceramic dish; cover and let it marinate for about 30 minutes in the refrigerator.

Grill the tuna fillets for about 15 minutes, basting with the reserved marinade. Enjoy!

Per serving: 266 Calories; 11.5g Fat; 5.6g Carbs; 34.9g Protein; 0.7g Fiber

323. Za'atar Salmon with Cheese

(Ready in about 20 minutes | Servings 6)

Ingredients

6 salmon fillets
1 teaspoon Za'atar
1 garlic clove, finely minced
1 cup cauliflower
1 tablespoon fresh lemon juice
2 tablespoons sesame oil
1 cup Nabulsi cheese, crumbled
3 tablespoons mayonnaise
1/2 cup shallots, thinly sliced
Coarse salt and black pepper, to taste

Directions

Toss the salmon fillets with the salt, pepper, and Za'atar. Place the salmon fillets on a parchment-lined baking pan; scatter the cauliflower, shallot, and garlic around the fish fillets.

Wrap with the foil and bake in the preheated oven at 390 degrees F for 10 to 12 minutes or until the salmon fillets flake easily with a fork. Remove the foil.

Mix the Nabulsi cheese, mayonnaise, lemon juice, and sesame oil. Pour the cheese mixture over the fish and vegetables.

Bake for a further 5 minutes or until the top is hot and bubbly. Bon appétit!

Per serving: 354 Calories; 20.2g Fat; 4.5g Carbs; 39.6g Protein; 0.5g Fiber

324. Halibut Fillets with Cheesy Cauliflower

(Ready in about 25 minutes | Servings 4)

Ingredients

1 cup Cheddar cheese, shredded
1 head of cauliflower, broken into florets
1/2 teaspoon dried rosemary
2 tablespoons butter
1/2 teaspoon dried oregano
4 halibut fillets
1 lemon, cut into wedges
Sea salt and ground black pepper, to taste

Directions

Parboil the cauliflower in a pot of lightly salted water until crisp-tender.

Place in a lightly buttered baking pan; brush with melted butter, too. Season with salt and pepper to taste.

Scatter the shredded Cheddar cheese on top of the cauliflower layer and bake at 385 degrees F approximately 15 minutes.

Grill the halibut steaks until golden and crisp on top. Sprinkle with oregano and rosemary; salt to taste.

Serve with lemon wedges.

Per serving: 508 Calories; 22.9g Fat; 4.7g Carbs; 68.6g Protein; 1.4g Fiber

325. Seafood Pickled Pepper Boats

(Ready in about 10 minutes | Servings 4)

Ingredients

8 ounces canned herring, drained
1 celery, chopped
1 cup onions, chopped
4 pickled peppers, slice into halves
1 tablespoon fresh coriander, chopped
1 teaspoon Dijon mustard
Salt and freshly ground black pepper, to taste

Directions

Broil the bell pepper for 5 to 6 minutes until they've softened. Cut into halves and discard the seeds.

In a mixing bowl, thoroughly combine the herring, Dijon mustard, celery, onions, salt, black pepper, and fresh coriander.

Mix to combine well. Spoon the mixture into the bell pepper halves. Enjoy!

Per serving: 120 Calories; 5.4g Fat; 5.8g Carbs; 12.3g Protein; 1.6g Fiber

326. Marsala, Red Snapper and Herb Soup

(Ready in about 20 minutes | Servings 4)

Ingredients

1/4 cup Marsala wine
1/2 stick butter, melted
1 cup tomato puree
2 garlic cloves, minced
1/4 cup fresh parsley, chopped
1 medium leek, finely chopped
3 cups chicken stock
1/2 teaspoon dried rosemary
2 thyme sprigs, chopped
1 pound red snapper, chopped
Sea salt and ground black pepper, to taste

Directions

In a heavy-bottomed pot, melt the butter over a moderately high heat. Cook the leek and garlic for 3 to 4 minutes or until tender and fragrant.

Add in the parsley, tomato puree, chicken stock, wine, red snapper, and rosemary; bring to a rolling boil.

Turn the heat to simmer; continue to simmer until the thoroughly cooked for a further 15 to 20 minutes. Season with salt and pepper to taste. Bon appétit!

Per serving: 316 Calories; 14.3g Fat; 6.6g Carbs; 32.7g Protein; 1.7g Fiber

327. Halibut with Italian Sauce

(Ready in about 20 minutes | Servings 4)

Ingredients

4 halibut steaks
1/4 cup Italian parsley, finely chopped
1/2 cup white onions, chopped
1 tablespoon fish sauce
3 tablespoons fish consommé
2 tablespoons fresh coriander, chopped
2 cloves garlic, finely minced
1 tablespoon soy sauce
1 teaspoon garlic
1 ½ tablespoons extra-virgin olive oil
1 tablespoon fresh lemon juice
2 tablespoons butter, at room temperature
Salt and ground black pepper, to taste

Directions

Melt the butter in a saucepan over medium-high heat.

Once hot, sear the halibut for 6 to 7 minutes until cooked all the way through. Reserve.

In the same pan, sauté the onions and garlic until tender and fragrant. Add in the fish consommé along with the coriander, fish sauce, and reserved halibut steaks; continue to cook, partially covered, for 5 to 6 minutes.

Whisk the remaining ingredients for the herb sauce. Enjoy!

Per serving: 273 Calories; 19.2g Fat; 4.3g Carbs; 22.6g Protein; 0.7g Fiber

328. Creamed Tuna and Avocado Salad

(Ready in about 20 minutes | Servings 4)

Ingredients

1 ½ pounds tuna steaks
1/4 cup mayonnaise
1/2 cup black olives, pitted and sliced
1 cup grape tomatoes, halved
1 shallot, chopped
1 avocado, pitted, peeled and diced
2 tablespoons fresh lemon juice
1 head lettuce
2 Italian peppers, deveined and sliced
Salt and ground black pepper, to taste

Directions

Grill the tuna steaks for about 15 minutes; cut into chunks.

In a salad bowl, mix lettuce, peppers, tomatoes, shallot, and avocado.

Then, make the dressing by mixing the mayonnaise, salt, pepper and lime juice. Dress the salad and toss to combine. Top with black olives.

Top your salad with the tuna chunks and serve!

Per serving: 244 Calories; 12.7g Fat; 5.3g Carbs; 23.4g Protein; 4.4g Fiber

329. Herring Keto Fat Bombs

(Ready in about 5 minutes | Servings 4)

Ingredients

1 can herring
1/2 teaspoon hot paprika
1 teaspoon capers
Salt and black pepper, to taste
3 ounces sunflower seeds
1 avocado, pitted and peeled
1/2 cup scallions, chopped

Directions

In a mixing bowl, combine all ingredients until well incorporated. Roll the mixture into 8 balls.

Bon appétit!

Per serving: 316 Calories; 24.4g Fat; 5.9g Carbs; 17.4g Protein; 4.2g Fiber

330. Sole Fillets with Mustard and Parsley

(Ready in about 30 minutes | Servings 4)

Ingredients

4 sole fillets
1/2 tablespoon Dijon mustard
1/4 cup fresh parsley, chopped
1/2 teaspoon porcini powder
1 teaspoon garlic paste
1/2 tablespoon fresh ginger, minced
1/2 teaspoon paprika
2 tablespoons olive oil
Salt and ground black pepper, to taste

Directions

Combine the oil, Dijon mustard, garlic paste, ginger, porcini powder, salt, black pepper and paprika.

Rub this mixture all over sole fillets. Place the sole fillets in a lightly oiled baking pan.

Bake in the preheated oven at 400 degrees F for about 20 minutes.

Serve with fresh parsley.

Per serving: 195 Calories; 8.2g Fat; 0.5g Carbs; 28.7g Protein; 0.6g Fiber

331. Creamed Spiced Prawn Salad

(Ready in about 10 minutes + chilling time | Servings 6)

Ingredients

2 pounds prawns
1 tablespoon Sriracha sauce
1/2 cup mayonnaise
1 cucumber, sliced
1 ½ cups radishes, sliced
1 tablespoon balsamic vinegar
Salt and black pepper
4 scallion stalks, chopped
1 Italian pepper, sliced
1/2 cup cream cheese
1/2 teaspoon stone-ground mustard
1 tablespoon dry sherry
1 medium-sized lemon, cut into wedges

Directions

Bring a pot of a lightly salted water to a boil over high heat. Add in the lemon and prawns and cook approximately 3 minutes, until they are opaque. Drain and rinse your prawns.

In a salad bowl, toss the remaining ingredients until well combined.

Top with the prepared prawns and serve!

Per serving: 209 Calories; 9.5g Fat; 6.8g Carbs; 20.2g Protein; 0.4g Fiber

VEGETARIAN

332. Spicy Turnips with Peppers

(Ready in about 35 minutes | Servings 6)

Ingredients

3 tablespoons ghee, cubed
1 garlic clove, minced
2 tablespoons olive oil
1 fresh jalapeño, minced
1 bell pepper, sliced
1 teaspoon dried marjoram
1 onion, thinly sliced
1 ½ pounds turnips, cut into wedges
1/2 teaspoon freshly ground black pepper
1/2 teaspoon cayenne pepper
1 teaspoon salt

Directions

Begin by preheating an oven to 425 degrees F. Lightly grease a baking dish with a non-stick cooking spray.

Toss the turnips and bell peppers with the remaining ingredients.

Roast the turnips and peppers for 25 to 35 or until they're softened. Taste and adjust the seasonings.

Bon appétit!

Per serving: 137 Calories; 11.1g Fat; 7.1g Carbs; 1.2g Protein; 3.7g Fiber

333. Blackberry, Hemp and Coconut Pudding

(Ready in about 5 minutes + prep time | Servings 3)

Ingredients

9 blackberries, fresh or frozen
1/4 cup hemp hearts
1/4 teaspoon grated nutmeg
A few drops of liquid Stevia
1/4 cup chia seeds
1/4 teaspoon ground cinnamon
1/4 teaspoon ground cloves
2 cups coconut milk, unsweetened
1/8 teaspoon coarse sea salt

Directions

Thoroughly combine the coconut milk, hemp hearts, chia seeds, ground cloves, nutmeg, cinnamon, salt, and Stevia in an airtight container.

Cover and let it stand in your refrigerator overnight.

Top with blackberries and serve.

Per serving: 153 Calories; 8g Fat; 6.7g Carbs; 6.7g Protein; 2.6g Fiber

334. Stuffed Mushrooms with Vegan Parmesan

(Ready in about 35 minutes | Servings 4)

Ingredients

2 tablespoons coconut oil, melted
2 garlic cloves, minced
1 cup vegan parmesan
1 teaspoon Italian herb mix
Salt and pepper, to taste
1 pound broccoli florets
1 Italian pepper, chopped
1 shallot, finely chopped
1 pound button mushrooms, stems removed

Directions

Parboil the broccoli in a large pot of salted water until crisp-tender, about 6 minutes. Mash the broccoli florets with a potato masher.

In a saucepan, melt the coconut oil over a moderately-high heat. Once hot, cook the shallot, garlic, and pepper until tender and fragrant. Season with the spices and add in the broccoli.

Fill the mushroom cups with the broccoli mixture and bake in the preheated oven at 365 degrees F for about 10 minutes.

Top with the vegan parmesan and bake for 10 minutes more or until it melts. Enjoy!

Per serving: 206 Calories; 13.4g Fat; 5.6g Carbs; 12.7g Protein; 4g Fiber

335. Spicy Braised Cabbage

(Ready in about 15 minutes | Servings 6)

Ingredients

1 Thai bird chili, minced
1/2 cup vegetable broth
1 teaspoon sesame seeds
4 tablespoons sesame oil
1/4 teaspoon cardamom
1/4 teaspoon cinnamon
2 tablespoons fresh chives, chopped
2 pounds Chinese cabbage, cut into wedges
Salt and black pepper, to taste

Directions

In a wok or a large saucepan, heat the sesame oil over medium-high heat. Then, fry the cabbage until crisp-tender.

Stir in the remaining ingredients and continue to cook for 10 minutes more or until heated through. Bon appétit!

Per serving: 186 Calories; 17g Fat; 5.3g Carbs; 2.1g Protein; 2g Fiber

336. Creamed Eggplant Soup

(Ready in about 1 hour 20 minutes | Servings 4)

Ingredients

1 tablespoon peanut oil
1 pound eggplant, sliced
1 cup tomato puree
1 medium onion, chopped
1/2 teaspoon Mediterranean herb mix
3 cups vegetable broth
1/3 cup raw cashews, soaked overnight
1 teaspoon garlic, chopped
Salt and pepper, to season

Directions

Brush the eggplant slices with peanut oil. Roast in the preheated oven at 380 degrees F for about 35 minutes.

Thoroughly combine the eggplant flesh with tomato, onion, garlic, Mediterranean herb mix, and vegetable broth in a heavy-bottomed pot.

Leave the lid slightly ajar and continue to simmer for 35 to 40 minutes or until heated through. Puree the soup in your food processor or blender.

Blend the soaked cashews with 1 cup of water until creamy and smooth. Spoon the cashew cream into the soup and stir until well combined. Season with salt and pepper to taste. Enjoy!

Per serving: 159 Calories; 9.4g Fat; 7.1g Carbs; 4.2g Protein; 4g Fiber

337. Squash and Cocoa Smoothie Bowl

(Ready in about 5 minutes | Servings 2)

Ingredients

2 tablespoons cocoa powder, unsweetened
1/2 cup butterhead lettuce
1 ½ cups almond milk, unsweetened
1/2 cup butternut squash, roasted
1/2 teaspoon pumpkin spice mix

Directions

Blend all ingredients until well combined. Pour into chilled glasses and enjoy!

Per serving: 71 Calories; 2.3g Fat; 4.1g Carbs; 4.3g Protein; 2.4g Fiber

338. Broccoli and Monterey Jack Bake

(Ready in about 25 minutes | Servings 3)

Ingredients

1 head broccoli, cut into small florets
2 ounces Monterey Jack cheese, shredded
1/2 teaspoon turmeric powder
3 eggs, well-beaten
1/2 cup half-and-half
1/2 teaspoon dried basil
1 shallot, minced
1/2 teaspoon garlic, minced
Kosher salt and cayenne pepper, to taste
3 tablespoons avocado oil

Directions

Preheat your oven to 310 degrees F.

Melt the avocado oil in a pan over a moderate heat. Now, sauté the shallots and garlic for a few minutes. Stir in the broccoli florets and cook until they're tender. Transfer the mixture to a lightly greased casserole dish.

In a separate mixing bowl, combine the eggs with the half-and-half, basil, turmeric, salt and cayenne pepper.

Pour the egg mixture over the broccoli mixture. Bake for 20 minutes or until set. Check the temperature with an instant-read food thermometer. Add the Monterey Jack cheese.

Bon appétit!

Per serving: 195 Calories; 12.7g Fat; 6.7g Carbs; 11.6g Protein; 5g Fiber

339. Eggplant Parmigiana Casserole

(Ready in about 1 hour | Servings 4)

Ingredients

1/3 cup Parmigiano-Reggiano cheese, shredded
2 tablespoons extra-virgin olive oil
1 celery, peeled and diced
1 teaspoon Taco seasoning mix
1 tablespoon fresh sage leaves, chopped
1 tomato, diced
1 medium-sized leek, sliced
1/2 garlic head, crushed
1 Habanero pepper, minced
1 large eggplant, cut into thick slices

Directions

Place the eggplant in a medium-sized bowl; sprinkle with salt and let it stand for 30 minutes; now, drain and rinse the eggplant slices.

Meanwhile, preheat your oven to 345 degrees F. Spritz a casserole dish with a non-stick cooking spray.

Mix the vegetables along with the Taco seasoning mix, olive oil, and sage in the prepared casserole dish.

Roast the vegetables approximately 20 minutes. Scatter the shredded cheese over the top and bake an additional 10 minutes.

Bon appétit!

Per serving: 159 Calories; 10.4g Fat; 5.7g Carbs; 6.4g Protein; 5.1g Fiber

340. Vegetarian Chinese Wok

(Ready in about 20 minutes | Servings 4)

Ingredients

1/2 teaspoon Chinese five-spice powder
2 garlic cloves, minced
1/2 cup vegetable broth
2 tablespoons sesame oil
1 cup onions, chopped
6 ounces smoked tofu, pressed, drained and cubed

For the Sauce:
2 tablespoons Shaoxing rice wine
1/2 teaspoon cardamom
1 cup tomatoes, pureed
1 teaspoon Sriracha sauce
1/2 tablespoon sesame oil

Directions

In a wok, heat 2 tablespoons of sesame oil over medium-high flame.

Cook the tofu cubes until they are slightly browned or about 5 minutes. Add in the onions, garlic, vegetable broth, and Chinese five-spice powder.

Stir fry for 5 to 7 minutes more until almost all liquid has evaporated.

To make the Chinese sauce, heat 1/2 tablespoon of sesame oil over a moderate flame. Add in the pureed tomatoes and cook until thoroughly warmed.

Add in the remaining ingredients and turn the heat to a simmer; continue to simmer for 8 to 10 minutes or until the sauce has reduced by half. Fold in the tofu cubes and gently stir to combine. Enjoy!

Per serving: 336 Calories; 22.2g Fat; 5.8g Carbs; 27.6g Protein; 3.4g Fiber

341. Berry Smoothie Bowl

(Ready in about 5 minutes | Servings 2)

Ingredients

1 tablespoon flax seeds, ground
1/2 teaspoon ground cinnamon
2 tablespoons Swerve
1/4 teaspoon ground cloves
1 tablespoon cocoa, unsweetened
1 tablespoon peanut butter
1 cup water
1 cup mixed berries

Directions

Blend all ingredients until smooth, creamy, and uniform.

Serve immediately.

Per serving: 103 Calories; 5.9g Fat; 6.1g Carbs; 4.1g Protein; 2.4g Fiber

342. Vegan Mushroom Stroganoff

(Ready in about 25 minutes | Servings 4)

Ingredients

1 cup fresh brown mushrooms, sliced
1 parsnip, chopped
1/2 teaspoon dried basil
1/2 cup celery rib, chopped
1 teaspoon Hungarian paprika
1/2 teaspoon dried oregano
2 garlic cloves, pressed
3 ½ cups roasted vegetable broth
1 cup tomato puree
1 tablespoon flaxseed meal
2 tablespoons sherry wine
1 rosemary sprig, chopped
2 tablespoons canola oil
1 cup onions, chopped

Directions

In a heavy-bottomed pot, heat the oil over a moderately-high flame. Cook the onion and garlic for 2 minutes or until tender and aromatic.

Add in the celery, parsnip, and mushrooms, and continue to cook until they've softened; reserve.

Add in the sherry wine to deglaze the bottom of your pot. Add in the seasonings, vegetable broth, and tomato puree.

Continue to simmer, partially covered, for 15 to 18 minutes. Add in the flaxseed meal and stir until the sauce has thickened. Bon appétit!

Per serving: 114 Calories; 7.3g Fat; 5.2g Carbs; 2.1g Protein; 3.1g Fiber

343. Greek Vegetables with Halloumi Cheese

(Ready in about 15 minutes | Servings 4)

Ingredients

1/2 pound button mushrooms, chopped
1 cup cauliflower, cut into small florets
1 thyme sprig, leaves picked
1/2 cup tomato sauce
8 ounces Halloumi cheese, cubed
2 garlic cloves, minced
1/2 cup red onion, chopped
1 medium-sized eggplant, chopped
1 rosemary sprig, leaves picked
1/4 cup dry white wine
2 tablespoons olive oil
1 teaspoon dried basil
1 teaspoon dried oregano

Directions

Heat the olive oil in a saucepan over a moderately high heat. Now, sauté the garlic for 1 to 1½ minutes.

Now, stir in the onion, mushrooms, cauliflower, and eggplant; cook an additional 5 minutes, stirring periodically.

Add the seasonings, tomato sauce, and wine; continue to cook for 4 more minutes. Remove from the heat and top with the Halloumi cheese. Bon appétit!

Per serving: 318 Calories; 24.3g Fat; 7.1g Carbs; 15.4g Protein; 7.1g Fiber

344. Chinese-Style Brussels Sprouts

(Ready in about 25 minutes | Servings 4)

Ingredients

1 pound Brussels sprouts, torn into pieces
1/2 head garlic, smashed
2 tablespoons sesame oil
Salt and ground black pe1/2 teaspoon Cassia
1/2 teaspoon jiāng (ginger) pper, to the taste
1/2 teaspoon Sichuan peppercorns, crushed

Directions

Parboil the Brussels sprouts in a pot of a lightly salted water for 15 to 17 minutes over a moderately-high heat. Drain.

In a wok, heat the sesame oil over a moderately-high heat. Then, sauté the garlic for a minute or so.

Add in the reserved Brussels sprouts and spices; continue to cook until everything is cooked through. Enjoy!

Per serving: 118 Calories; 7g Fat; 3.4g Carbs; 2.9g Protein; 4g Fiber

345. Stuffed Avocado Boats

(Ready in about 10 minutes | Servings 4)

Ingredients

5 ounces pine nuts, ground
1/2 teaspoon garlic, minced
1 teaspoon fresh lime juice
1 celery stalk, chopped
1 tablespoon coconut aminos
Salt and pepper, to taste
2 avocados, pitted and halved

Directions

Thoroughly combine the avocado pulp with the pine nuts, celery, garlic, fresh lime juice, and coconut aminos. Season with salt and pepper to taste.

Spoon the filling into the avocado halves. Serve immediately.

Per serving: 263 Calories; 24.8g Fat; 6.5g Carbs; 3.5g Protein; 6.1g Fiber

346. Cream of Cauliflower Soup with Paprika

(Ready in about 20 minutes | Servings 4)

Ingredients

2 heads of cauliflower, broken into florets
1 teaspoon paprika
1 ½ tablespoons vegetable broth
2 tablespoons extra-virgin olive oil
1/4 teaspoon mustard powder
1/4 teaspoon ground cloves
1/2 teaspoon fenugreek

Directions

Parboil the cauliflower florets for about 12 minutes until crisp-tender.

Add in the remaining ingredients and stir to combine.

Let it simmer, partially covered, for about 10 minutes or until cooked through. Puree the mixture using your immersion blender. Enjoy!

Per serving: 94 Calories; 7.2g Fat; 7g Carbs; 2.7g Protein; 2.8g Fiber

347. Asparagus with Parsley and Feta Cheese

(Ready in about 15 minutes | Servings 6)

Ingredients

2 garlic cloves, minced
2 tablespoons butter, melted
1 cup feta cheese, crumbled
1/2 cup fresh parsley, roughly chopped
2 green onions, chopped
Salt and black pepper, to the taste
1 ½ pounds asparagus spears

Directions

Preheat an oven to 420 degrees F.

Drizzle the asparagus with the melted butter. Toss with the green onions, garlic, salt, and black pepper.

Place the asparagus on a lightly-greased baking pan in a single layer. Roast for about 14 minutes.

Scatter the crumbled feta over the warm asparagus spears. Garnish with fresh parsley. Enjoy!

Per serving: 128 Calories; 9.4g Fat; 6.5g Carbs; 6.4g Protein; 3.1g Fiber

348. Traditional Mexican Guacamole

(Ready in about 10 minutes + chilling time | Servings 8)

Ingredients

2 avocados, peeled, pitted, and mashed
1 shallot, chopped
2 tablespoons cilantro, chopped
2 tablespoons fresh lemon juice
1 teaspoon garlic, smashed
1 ancho chili pepper, deveined and minced
2 tomatoes, pureed
Sea salt and pepper, to taste

Directions

Thoroughly combine all ingredients

Keep in your refrigerator until ready to serve. Enjoy!

Per serving: 112 Calories; 9.9g Fat; 6.5g Carbs; 1.3g Protein; 2.4g Fiber

349. Tofu and Pecan Zucchini Boats

(Ready in about 50 minutes | Servings 4)

Ingredients

6 ounces firm tofu, drained and crumbled
1 tablespoon nutritional yeast
2 ounces pecans, chopped
1/4 teaspoon curry powder
1/2 cup onions, chopped
1 tablespoon olive oil
1 cup tomato puree
2 garlic cloves, pressed
4 zucchinis, cut into halves lengthwise and scoop out the pulp
Sea salt and pepper, to taste

Directions

In a saucepan, heat the olive oil over a moderately-high heat; cook the tofu, garlic, and onion for about 5 minutes.

Stir in the tomato puree and scooped zucchini pulp; add all seasonings and continue to cook for a further 5 to 6 minutes.

Spoon the filling into the zucchini "shells" and arrange them in a lightly greased baking dish.

Bake in the preheated oven at 365 degrees F for 25 to 30 minutes. Top with nutritional yeast and pecans nuts; bake for a further 5 minutes. Enjoy!

Per serving: 208 Calories; 14.4g Fat; 8.8g Carbs; 6.5g Protein; 4.3g Fiber

350. Cremini Mushrooms with Enchilada Sauce

(Ready in about 15 minutes | Servings 4)

Ingredients

1 pound cremini mushroom, sliced
1/4 cup enchilada sauce
1 medium-sized avocado, pitted and mashed
1 cup tomatillo, chopped
1/2 teaspoon salt
1/2 teaspoon ground black pepper
2 small-sized shallots, chopped
1 garlic clove, minced
4 eggs
2 tablespoons olive oil

Directions

Heat the olive oil in a saucepan over a moderate flame. Now, cook the shallot and garlic until just tender and fragrant.

Now, add the mushrooms and stir until they're tender. Season with salt and pepper; stir in chopped tomatillo.

Stir in the eggs and scramble them well. Top with the enchilada sauce; top with avocado slices.

Enjoy!

Per serving: 290 Calories; 21.7g Fat; 6.5g Carbs; 10.6g Protein; 6g Fiber

351. Appenzeller and Pepper Quiche

(Ready in about 1 hour | Servings 4)

Ingredients

3/4 pound Appenzeller cheese, shredded
1 teaspoon smoked paprika
6 whole eggs
1/3 cup sour cream
1 garlic clove, crushed
2 red onions, thinly sliced
Sea salt and ground black pepper, to taste
8 bell peppers

Directions

Preheat an oven to 470 degrees F. Arrange the peppers on a baking sheet in a single layer.

Bake the peppers in the preheated oven until the skins are browned and blackened, about 20 minutes.

Turn them over and bake another 10 to 15 minutes. Remove your peppers from the oven; cover with a plastic wrap and allow them to steam for 1 hour.

Then, remove the skins, stems, and seeds. Place 4 peppers in a lightly oiled casserole dish.

Top with half of the shredded Appenzeller; add a layer of the sliced onions and crushed garlic. Place another layer of the roasted peppers, followed by the remaining Appenzeller.

In a mixing dish, whisk the eggs with the sour cream, salt, pepper, and paprika. Pour the mixture over the peppers. Cover tightly with a piece of foil and bake about 20 minutes.

Next, remove the foil and bake another 20 minutes. Bon appétit!

Per serving: 408 Calories; 28.9g Fat; 5.6g Carbs; 24.9g Protein; 1.8g Fiber

VEGETARIAN

352. Zoodles with Classic Cashew Parmesan

(Ready in about 15 minutes | Servings 4)

Ingredients

For Zoodles:
4 zucchinis, peeled and sliced into noodle-shape strands
Salt and pepper, to taste
2 tablespoons canola oil

For Cashew Parmesan:
2 tablespoons nutritional yeast
1 garlic clove, minced
Sea salt and pepper, to taste
1/2 cup raw cashews
1/4 teaspoon onion powder

Directions

In a saucepan, heat the canola oil over medium heat; once hot, cook your zoodles for 1 minute or so, stirring frequently to ensure even cooking.

Season with salt and pepper to taste.

In your food processor, process all ingredients for the cashew parmesan. Toss your zoodles with the cashew parmesan and enjoy!

Per serving: 145 Calories; 10.6g Fat; 5.9g Carbs; 5.5g Protein; 1.6g Fiber

353. Spanish Vegetables with Herbs

(Ready in about 45 minutes | Servings 4)

Ingredients

4 tablespoons cream of mushroom soup
3 Spanish peppers, deveined and sliced
1 teaspoon dried sage, crushed
4 tablespoons olive oil
2 zucchinis, cut into thick slices
1 onion, quartered
4 garlic cloves, halved
1 teaspoon Ñora
1 teaspoon saffron
1/2 head of cauliflower, broken into large florets
Salt and pepper, to taste

Directions

Toss all ingredients in a parchment-lined roasting pan.

Roast in the preheated oven at 420 degrees F for 35 to 40 minutes.

Toss your vegetables halfway through the cooking time. Taste and adjust the seasonings. Enjoy!

Per serving: 165 Calories; 14.3g Fat; 5.6g Carbs; 2.1g Protein; 1.9g Fiber

354. Easy Cheesy Spinach

(Ready in about 10 minutes | Servings 4)

Ingredients

1 cup cottage cheese
2 pounds spinach leaves, rinsed and torn into pieces
1/4 teaspoon turmeric powder
1 teaspoon salt
1/2 teaspoon cayenne pepper
2 garlic cloves, minced
1/2 stick butter

Directions

Melt the butter in a Dutch oven and sauté the garlic until it's just browned.

Add the spinach leaves, salt, cayenne pepper, and turmeric powder; cook another 2 to 3 minutes over a moderate heat, adding a splash of warm water if needed.

Next, turn the heat on high, and cook for 1 to 2 minutes more, stirring often. Taste and adjust the seasonings.

Top with cottage cheese. Enjoy!

Per serving: 208 Calories; 13.5g Fat; 7g Carbs; 14.5g Protein; 5.1g Fiber

355. Mediterranean Fennel in Cherry Tomato Sauce

(Ready in about 20 minutes | Servings 4)

Ingredients

1/2 teaspoon garlic, minced
2 tablespoons olive oil
Salt and pepper, to taste
1/4 cup vegetable broth
1 bay laurel
1 fennel, thinly sliced
For the Sauce:
1 cup cherry tomatoes
1 bunch fresh basil, leaves picked
1 teaspoon rosemary
1/2 cup red onion, chopped
1 teaspoon oregano
2 tablespoons olive oil
1 cloves garlic, minced
1 cayenne pepper, minced
Sat and pepper, to taste

Directions

Heat 2 tablespoons of olive oil in a frying pan over a moderate flame. Sauté the garlic until aromatic.

Add in the fennel, broth, salt, pepper, and bay laurel. Continue to cook until the fennel is just tender.

Puree the sauce ingredients in your food processor until smooth and creamy. Heat the sauce over-medium low flame.

Add in the fennel mixture and continue to cook for 5 to 6 minutes more or until everything is cooked through. Bon appétit!

Per serving: 135 Calories; 13.6g Fat; 3g Carbs; 0.9g Protein; 1.9g Fiber

356. Ultimate Fathead Cauliflower Pizza

(Ready in about 25 minutes | Servings 4)

Ingredients

For the Crust:
1/2 cup Edam cheese
1/4 cup heavy cream
1 tablespoon basil-infused oil
1 pound cauliflower
4 medium-sized eggs
Salt, to taste
A spray coating
For the Topping:
1/4 cup Kalamata olives, pitted and sliced
1 cup mozzarella cheese
2 tablespoons chives, finely chopped
1 cup spring mix
3/4 cup tomato sauce, sugar-free
1 tablespoon fresh sage

VEGETARIAN

Directions

Cook the cauliflower in a large pot of salted water until it is just tender; cut into florets and add the remaining ingredients for the crust.

Then, preheat your oven to 380 degrees F; add an oven rack to the middle of the oven. Lightly grease a baking pan with a thin layer of a spray coating.

Spread the crust mixture onto the bottom of the prepared baking pan. Bake for 15 minutes or until the crust is firm and golden.

Remove from the oven and add the remaining ingredients, ending with mozzarella cheese; bake until the cheese has completely melted.

Add a few grinds of black pepper if desired. Enjoy!

Per serving: 234 Calories; 16.1g Fat; 6.1g Carbs; 13.6g Protein; 6.1g Fiber

357. Garlicky Broccoli Masala

(Ready in about 15 minutes | Servings 4)

Ingredients

1 pound broccoli florets
1 Badi Elaichi (black cardamom)
1 teaspoon garlic, pressed
1/2 teaspoon Garam Masala
1 tablespoon Kasuri Methi (dried fenugreek leaves)
1/4 cup sesame oil
Salt and pepper, to taste

Directions

Parboil the broccoli for 6 to 7 minutes until it is crisp-tender.

Heat the sesame oil in a wok or saucepan until sizzling. Once hot, cook your broccoli for 3 to 4 minutes. Add in the other ingredients and give it a quick stir.

Adjust the spices to suit your taste. Bon appétit!

Per serving: 100 Calories; 8.2g Fat; 4.7g Carbs; 3.7g Protein; 4g Fiber

358. Creamed Broccoli and Spinach Soup

(Ready in about 15 minutes | Servings 4)

Ingredients

8 ounces baby spinach
2 garlic cloves, minced
2 tablespoons parsley, chopped
1/2 cup coconut milk
2 tablespoons olive oil
1 yellow onion, chopped
4 cups roasted vegetable broth
1 pound broccoli, cut into small florets
Salt and pepper, to taste

Directions

Heat the oil in a soup pot over a moderately-high flame. Then, sauté the onion and garlic until they're tender and fragrant.

Add in the broccoli, spinach, and broth; bring to a rolling boil. Immediately turn the heat to a simmer.

Pour in the coconut milk, salt, pepper, and parsley; continue to simmer, partially covered, until cooked through.

Puree your soup with an immersion blender. Enjoy!

Per serving: 252 Calories; 20.3g Fat; 5.8g Carbs; 8.1g Protein; 4.5g Fiber

359. Creamed Kohlrabi with Mushrooms

(Ready in about 25 minutes | Servings 4)

Ingredients

1 ½ cups double cream
1 garlic clove, minced
1/2 pound mushrooms, sliced
1/2 teaspoon ground black pepper
1/2 cup scallions, chopped
1 teaspoon sea salt
3 tablespoons butter
1/4 teaspoon red pepper flakes
3/4 pound kohlrabi, trimmed and thinly sliced

Directions

Parboil the kohlrabi in a large pot of salted water for 7 to 9 minutes. Drain and set aside.

Warm the butter over medium-high heat. Sauté the mushrooms, scallions, and garlic until tender and fragrant.

Season with salt, black pepper, and red pepper flakes.

Slowly stir in the double cream, whisking continuously until the sauce has thickened, about 8 to 12 minutes.

Pour the mushroom sauce over the kohlrabi. Bon appétit!

Per serving: 220 Calories; 20g Fat; 6.3g Carbs; 4g Protein; 4.1g Fiber

360. Movie Night Swiss Chard Chips

(Ready in about 20 minutes | Servings 6)

Ingredients

2 cups Swiss chard, cleaned
1 tablespoon coconut oil
Sea salt and pepper, to taste
Avocado Dip:
2 teaspoons lemon juice
2 garlic cloves, finely minced
2 tablespoons extra-virgin olive oil
Salt and pepper, to taste
3 ripe avocados, pitted and mashed

Directions

Toss the Swiss chard with the coconut oil, salt, and pepper.

Bake the Swiss chard leaves in the preheated oven at 310 degrees F for about 10 minutes until the edges brown but are not burnt.

Thoroughly combine the ingredients for the avocado dip. Enjoy!

Per serving: 269 Calories; 26.7g Fat; 3.4g Carbs; 2.3g Protein; 4.1g Fiber

361. Mediterranean Crunchy Salad with Seeds

(Ready in about 15 minutes | Servings 4)

Ingredients

For Dressing:
1 cup sunflower seeds, soaked overnight
1 lemon, freshly squeezed
1/2 teaspoon Mediterranean herb mix
2 tablespoons onions, chopped
1/2 cup almond milk
1/2 teaspoon paprika
1/2 teaspoon garlic, chopped
Salt and pepper, to taste
For the Salad:
1 head Romaine lettuce, separated into leaves
1 Lebanese cucumbers, sliced
1 tablespoon cilantro leaves, coarsely chopped
2 tablespoons black olives, pitted
1 cup cherry tomatoes, halved

Directions

Process all of the dressing ingredients until creamy and smooth.

Toss all of the salad ingredients in a bowl. Dress your salad and serve right away!

Per serving: 208 Calories; 15.6g Fat; 6.2g Carbs; 7.6g Protein; 6g Fiber

362. Vegan Stuffed Mushrooms

(Ready in about 30 minutes | Servings 4)

Ingredients

1 pound white mushrooms, stems removed
1 cup onions, chopped
1/4 cup raw walnuts, crushed
2 tablespoons cilantro, chopped
1 garlic clove, minced
Salt and black pepper, to taste
2 tablespoons sesame oil

Directions

Begin by preheating an oven to 360 degrees F. Lightly grease a large baking sheet with a non-stick cooking spray.

Heat the sesame oil in a frying pan that is preheated over medium-high heat. Now, sauté the onions and garlic until aromatic.

Then, chop the mushroom stems and cook until they are tender. Heat off, season with salt and pepper; stir in the walnuts.

Stuff the mushroom caps with the walnut/mushroom mixture and arrange them on the prepared baking sheet.

Bake for 25 minutes and transfer to a wire rack to cool slightly. Garnish with fresh cilantro.

Bon appétit!

Per serving: 139 Calories; 11.2g Fat; 6.4g Carbs; 4.8g Protein; 2.2g Fiber

363. Chocolate, Chia and Almond Smoothie

(Ready in about 10 minutes | Servings 2)

Ingredients

1 tablespoon unsweetened cocoa powder
1 tablespoon chia seeds
3/4 cup almond milk
1/4 cup water
4 fresh dates, pitted
8 walnuts
1 ½ cups lettuce
2 teaspoons vegan protein powder, zero carbs

Directions

Process all ingredients in your blender until everything is uniform and creamy.

Pour the smoothie into two glasses and enjoy!

Per serving: 335 Calories; 31.7g Fat; 6.7g Carbs; 7g Protein; 6g Fiber

364. Romano Tomato Chips

(Ready in about 5 hours | Servings 6)

Ingredients

1 ½ pounds Romano tomatoes, sliced
1/4 cup extra-virgin olive oil
1 tablespoon Italian spice mix
For Vegan Parmesan:
1/4 cup sunflower seeds
1/4 teaspoon dried dill weed
1/4 cup sesame seeds
1 tablespoon nutritional yeast
Salt and pepper, to taste
1 teaspoon garlic powder

Directions

Process all ingredients for the vegan parmesan in your food processor.

Toss the sliced tomatoes with the extra-virgin olive oil, Italian spice mix, and vegan parmesan.

Arrange the tomato slices on a parchment-lined baking sheet in a single layer. Bake at 220 degrees F about 5 hours. Enjoy!

Per serving: 161 Calories; 14g Fat; 6.2g Carbs; 4.6g Protein; 2.6g Fiber

365. Celery and Carrot Salad with Sriracha Vinaigrette

(Ready in about 10 minutes | Servings 4)

Ingredients

1/4 cup fresh parsley, chopped
3/4 pound celery, shredded
1/4 pound carrots, coarsely shredded
For the Vinaigrette:
1/2 teaspoon Sriracha sauce
1/3 cup olive oil
2 tablespoons balsamic vinegar
1/2 teaspoon ground allspice
1 lemon, freshly squeezed
2 garlic cloves, smashed
Sea salt and pepper, to taste

Directions

Toss the carrots, celery, and parsley in a bowl until everything is well combined.

Mix all ingredients for a vinaigrette and dress your salad. Serve immediately.

Per serving: 196 Calories; 17.2g Fat; 6g Carbs; 1.2g Protein; 2.2g Fiber

366. Asparagus with Traditional Baba Ghanoush

(Ready in about 45 minutes | Servings 6)

Ingredients

1 ½ pounds asparagus spears, trim and cut off the woody ends
1/2 teaspoon ground black pepper, to taste
1/2 teaspoon paprika
1 teaspoon sea salt
1/4 cup olive oil
For Baba Ghanoush:
1 tablespoon tahini
1/4 cup fresh parsley leaves, chopped
2 tablespoons fresh lemon juice
1/2 teaspoon cayenne pepper
1/2 cup scallions, chopped
2 cloves garlic, minced
Salt and ground black pepper, to taste
3/4 pound eggplant
2 teaspoons olive oil

Directions

Begin by preheating your oven to 390 degrees F. Line a baking sheet with parchment paper.

Place the asparagus spears on the baking sheet.

Toss the asparagus spears with the oil, salt, pepper, and paprika. Bake about 9 minutes or until thoroughly cooked.

Then, make the Baba Ghanoush. Preheat your oven to 425 degrees F.

Place the eggplants on a lined cookie sheet. Set under the broiler approximately 30 minutes; allow eggplants to cool. Now, peel the eggplants and remove the stems.

Heat 2 teaspoons of olive oil in a frying pan over a moderately high flame. Now, sauté the scallions and garlic until tender and aromatic.

Add the roasted eggplant, scallion mixture, tahini, lemon juice, cayenne pepper, salt and black pepper to your food processor. Pulse until the ingredients are evenly mixed. Top with parsley.

Enjoy!

Per serving: 149 Calories; 12.1g Fat; 7g Carbs; 3.6g Protein; 4g Fiber

367. Easy Cauliflower Slaw with Olives

(Ready in about 15 minutes + chilling time | Servings 4)

Ingredients

1 roasted pepper, chopped
1/2 cup black olives, pitted and chopped
1 teaspoon deli mustard
3/4 cup yellow onions, chopped
1 tablespoon balsamic vinegar
1/2 cup almonds, coarsely chopped
1/4 cup olive oil
1 pound cauliflower florets
Salt and pepper, to taste

Directions

Parboil the cauliflower florets in a lightly-salted water for about 5 minutes until crisp-tender; transfer the cauliflower to a bowl.

Toss the cauliflower with the remaining ingredients. Bon appétit!

Per serving: 281 Calories; 26.8g Fat; 5.6g Carbs; 4.2g Protein; 3.4g Fiber

368. Easy Breakfast Smoothie

(Ready in about 5 minutes | Servings 4)

Ingredients

1/2 banana, peeled and sliced
1 tablespoon vegan protein powder, zero carbs
1/2 cup water
1/2 cup fresh blueberries
1 ½ cups coconut milk

Directions

Blend all ingredients until creamy and uniform. Serve immediately.

Per serving: 247 Calories; 21.7g Fat; 9.9g Carbs; 2.6g Protein; 3g Fiber

369. Asian-Style Curried Cauliflower and Peppers

(Ready in about 35 minutes | Servings 4)

Ingredients

1 teaspoon curry powder
1/4 cup extra-virgin olive oil
2 bell peppers, halved
2 pasilla peppers, halved
1 pound cauliflower, broken into florets
1/2 teaspoon cayenne pepper
1/2 teaspoon nigella seeds
1/4 teaspoon freshly ground black pepper, or more to taste
1/2 teaspoon sea salt

Directions

Preheat your oven to 425 degrees F. Line a large baking sheet with a piece of parchment paper.

Drizzle the cauliflower and peppers with extra-virgin olive oil. Sprinkle with salt, black pepper, cayenne pepper, curry powder and nigella seeds

Next, arrange the vegetables on the prepared baking sheet.

Roast the vegetables, tossing periodically, until they are slightly browned, about 30 minutes.

Enjoy!

Per serving: 166 Calories; 13.9g Fat; 6.4g Carbs; 3g Protein; 3.9g Fiber

VEGETARIAN

370. Baked Zucchini Boats

(Ready in about 50 minutes | Servings 4)

Ingredients

4 zucchinis, cut into halves lengthwise and scoop out the insides
1 (12-ounce) block firm tofu, drained and crumbled
1 tablespoon nutritional yeast
2 cups tomato puree
2 ounces cashew nuts, lightly salted and chopped
2 garlic cloves, pressed
1/2 cup scallions, chopped
1/4 teaspoon turmeric
Sea salt and cayenne pepper, to taste
1 tablespoon olive oil
1/4 teaspoon chili powder

Directions

Heat the oil in a pan that is preheated over a moderate heat; now, cook the tofu, garlic, and scallions for 4 to 6 minutes.

Stir in 1 cup of the tomato puree and scooped zucchini flesh; add all seasonings and cook an additional 6 minutes, until tofu is slightly browned.

Next, preheat your oven to 360 degrees F.

Divide the tofu mixture among the zucchini shells. Place the stuffed zucchini shells in a baking dish that is previously greased with a cooking spray. Pour in the remaining 1 cup of tomato puree.

Bake approximately 30 minutes. Sprinkle with nutritional yeast and cashew nuts; bake an additional 5 to 6 minutes. Enjoy!

Per serving: 148 Calories; 10g Fat; 6.8g Carbs; 7.5g Protein; 5.6g Fiber

371. Raspberry and Peanut Shake

(Ready in about 5 minutes | Servings 1)

Ingredients

3/4 cup almond milk, unsweetened
1 tablespoon peanut butter
1/2 cup baby spinach leaves
1 teaspoon Swerve
1/3 cup raspberries

Directions

Place all ingredients in your blender and puree until creamy, uniform and smooth.

Pour your smoothie into a glass and enjoy!

Per serving: 114 Calories; 8.2g Fat; 6.9g Carbs; 4.2g Protein; 3.4g Fiber

372. Keto "Cereal" with Almond Milk

(Ready in about 1 hour | Servings 8)

Ingredients

1/3 cup shredded coconut flakes
1 ½ cups almond milk, unsweetened
2 tablespoons sunflower seeds
1/8 teaspoon allspice, freshly grated
1/4 cup flax seeds
A pinch of Himalayan salt
2 tablespoons sesame seeds
1 teaspoon ground cinnamon
1/2 cup pine nuts, chopped
1/2 cup almonds, slivered
2 tablespoons granulated Swerve
2 tablespoons coconut oil, melted
1 teaspoon grated orange peel

Directions

Toss all ingredients in a parchment-lined baking pan.

Roast in the preheated oven at 290 degrees F for about 70 minutes; check and stir every 20 minutes. Enjoy!

Per serving: 262 Calories; 24.3g Fat; 5.2g Carbs; 5.1g Protein; 2.2g Fiber

373. Peanut and Coconut Candy

(Ready in about 10 minutes + chilling time | Servings 12)

Ingredients

3/4 cup coconut oil
1/2 teaspoon pure almond extract
1/2 cup coconut flakes
1 cup Swerve
1 teaspoon pure vanilla extract
3/4 cup peanut butter

Directions

Combine all ingredients in a pan over a moderate heat; cook, stirring continuously, for 4 to 5 minutes.

Spoon the mixture into a parchment-lined baking sheet. Refrigerate overnight and break your bark into pieces.

Bon appétit!

Per serving: 316 Calories; 31.6g Fat; 4.6g Carbs; 6.6g Protein; 0.7g Fiber

374. Hazelnut Chocolate Bark

(Ready in about 25 minutes | Servings 8)

Ingredients

1/2 cup roasted hazelnuts, chopped
8 tablespoons cocoa powder
1/4 teaspoon grated nutmeg
1/8 teaspoon coarse salt
4 ounces cacao butter
1/4 cup Swerve
1/4 teaspoon hazelnut extract
1 teaspoon pure vanilla extract
1 tablespoon extra-virgin coconut oil

Directions

Melt the cacao butter and coconut oil in a microwave for 1 minute or so.

Now, stir in the cocoa powder, Swerve, hazelnut extract, vanilla extract, salt and nutmeg.

Pour the mixture into an ice cube mold. Add the roasted hazelnuts and place in your freezer for 20 minutes or until solid. Bon appétit!

Per serving: 140 Calories; 14g Fat; 6.1g Carbs; 2g Protein; 2.4g Fiber

375. Butternut Squash Smoothie with Chocolate

(Ready in about 5 minutes | Servings 2)

Ingredients

1/2 cup butternut squash, roasted
2 tablespoons cocoa powder
2 ½ cups almond milk
1/2 cup baby spinach
A pinch of grated nutmeg
A pinch of salt
1/2 teaspoon ground cinnamon

Directions

Mix all ingredients in a blender or a food processor.

Pour your smoothie into two glasses and enjoy!

Per serving: 71 Calories; 2.3g Fat; 6.1g Carbs; 4.3g Protein; 4g Fiber

376. Colorful Roasted Vegetables

(Ready in about 45 minutes | Servings 4)

Ingredients

4 tablespoons olive oil
4 tablespoons tomato puree
2 thyme sprigs, chopped
2 medium-sized leeks, quartered
1 teaspoon dried sage, crushed
1 orange bell pepper, deveined and sliced
1/2 head of cauliflower, broken into large florets
2 zucchinis, cut into thick slices
1 teaspoon mixed whole peppercorns
1 red bell pepper, deveined and sliced
1 green bell pepper, deveined and sliced
4 garlic cloves, halved
Sea salt and cayenne pepper, to taste

Directions

Preheat your oven to 425 degrees F. Sprits a rimmed baking sheet with a non-stick cooking spray.

Toss all of the above vegetables with the seasonings, oil and apple cider vinegar.

Roast about 40 minutes. Flip the vegetables halfway through cook time.

Bon appétit!

Per serving: 165 Calories; 14.3g Fat; 7.2g Carbs; 2.1g Protein; 2.4g Fiber

377. German Savoy Cabbage

(Ready in about 25 minutes | Servings 4)

Ingredients

1 teaspoon garlic, minced
1/2 teaspoon red pepper flakes, crushed
1/2 teaspoon dried basil
Salt and ground black pepper, to the taste
2 tablespoons almond oil
1 ½ pounds Savoy cabbage, torn into pieces

Directions

Cook the Savoy cabbage in a pot of a lightly salted water approximately 20 minutes over a moderate heat. Drain and reserve.

Now, heat the oil in a sauté pan over a medium-high heat. Now, cook the garlic until just aromatic.

Add the reserved Savoy cabbage, basil, red pepper, salt and black pepper; stir until everything is heated through.

Taste and adjust the seasonings.

Bon appétit!

Per serving: 108 Calories; 7g Fat; 8.2g Carbs; 2.9g Protein; 3.7g Fiber

378. Stuffed Berbere Cauli Rice Peppers

(Ready in about 40 minutes | Servings 4)

Ingredients

1 teaspoon Berbere
1/2 pound cauliflower rice
1 teaspoon ancho chili powder
1/2 teaspoon garlic, smashed
1 shallot, chopped
1 cup tomato puree
1 ½ tablespoons avocado oil
4 bell peppers, seeds removed, and halved
Kosher salt and red pepper, to season

Directions

Start by preheating your oven to 365 degrees F.

Roast the peppers for about 15 minutes until the skin is slightly charred.

In a saucepan, heat the avocado oil over medium-high flame. Sauté the shallot and garlic until they are just tender.

Stir in the cauliflower rice, ancho chili powder, and Berbere spice and cook for 5 to 6 minutes.

Spoon the cauliflower mixture into pepper halves. Place the peppers in a lightly greased casserole dish.

Add the tomato, salt and pepper around to the casserole dish and bake for about 15 minutes. Bon appétit!

Per serving: 77 Calories; 4.8g Fat; 5.4g Carbs; 1.6g Protein; 3.1g Fiber

379. Asian-Style Brussels Sprouts

(Ready in about 20 minutes | Servings 4)

Ingredients

1/2 pound Brussels sprouts, quartered
1 tablespoon tomato puree
10 ounces tempeh, crumbled
2 tablespoons water
2 tablespoons soy sauce
2 garlic cloves, minced
1/2 cup leeks, chopped
2 tablespoons olive oil
Sea salt and ground black pepper, to taste

Directions

Heat the oil in a saucepan that is preheated over a moderate heat. Now, cook the garlic and leeks until tender and aromatic.

Now, add the tempeh, water and soy sauce. Cook until the tempeh just beginning to brown, about 5 minutes.

Stir in the tomato puree and Brussels sprouts; season with salt and pepper; turn the heat to low and cook, stirring often, for about 13 minutes.

Bon appétit!

Per serving: 179 Calories; 11.7g Fat; 6.1g Carbs; 10.5g Protein; 2.6g Fiber

380. Roasted Asparagus with Eggplant Dip

(Ready in about 45 minutes | Servings 6)

Ingredients

1 ½ pounds asparagus spears, med
1/4 cup sesame oil
1/2 teaspoon red pepper flakes
Salt and pepper, to taste
For Baba Ghanoush:
3/4 pound eggplant
1 tablespoon sesame paste
1/2 teaspoon allspice
2 tablespoons fresh lime juice
1/4 cup fresh parsley leaves, chopped
Salt and ground black pepper, to taste
2 teaspoons olive oil
1/2 cup onion, chopped
1 teaspoon garlic, minced
1/4 teaspoon ground nutmeg

Directions

Toss the asparagus spears with sesame oil, salt, and pepper. Arrange the asparagus spears on a foil-lined baking pan.

Roast in the preheated oven at 380 degrees F for 8 to 10 minutes.

Meanwhile, make your Baba Ghanoush. Bake the eggplants in the preheated oven at 420 degrees F for 25 to 30 minutes; discard the skin and stems.

In a saucepan, heat the olive oil over a moderately-high heat. Cook the onion and garlic until tender and fragrant; heat off.

Add the roasted eggplant, sautéed onion mixture, sesame paste, lime juice, and spices to your blender or food processor. Pulse until creamy and smooth. Enjoy!

Per serving: 149 Calories; 12.1g Fat; 6.3g Carbs; 3.6g Protein; 4.6g Fiber

381. "No Oats" Oatmeal with Hemp and Berries

(Ready in about 5 minutes + chilling time | Servings 4)

Ingredients

1/4 cup sunflower seeds
1/2 cup coconut milk, unsweetened
1 cup mixed berries
1/2 teaspoon ground cinnamon
8 tablespoons granulated Swerve
1/2 cup hemp hearts
1/2 cup water

Directions

Thoroughly combine the water, milk, hemp hearts, sunflower seeds, Swerve, and cinnamon in an airtight container.

Cover and let it stand in your refrigerator overnight.

Top with mixed berries and serve.

Per serving: 176 Calories; 12.7g Fat; 6g Carbs; 9.7g Protein; 3.2g Fiber

382. Tofu with Garlic, Sesame and Pine Nuts

(Ready in about 13 minutes | Servings 4)

Ingredients

1 ½ tablespoons coconut aminos
3 tablespoons vegetable broth
2 garlic cloves, minced
2 teaspoons lightly toasted sesame seeds
3 teaspoons avocado oil
1/4 cup pine nuts, coarsely chopped
1 teaspoon red pepper flakes
1/2 teaspoon porcini powder
1/2 teaspoon ground cumin
1 cup extra firm tofu, pressed and cubed
Salt and pepper, to season

Directions

In a wok, heat the avocado oil over a moderately-high heat. Now, fry the tofu cubes for 5 to 6 minutes until golden brown on all sides.

Stir in the pecans, coconut aminos, broth, garlic, red pepper, porcini powder, cumin, salt, and pepper and continue to stir for about 8 minutes.

Top with toasted sesame seeds. Bon appétit!

Per serving: 232 Calories; 21.6g Fat; 5.3g Carbs; 8.3g Protein; 2.4g Fiber

383. Masala Broccoli with Sesame Paste

(Ready in about 15 minutes | Servings 4)

Ingredients

1/4 cup extra-virgin olive oil
1/2 teaspoon Garam Masala
1 tablespoon sesame paste
1 tablespoon fresh lime juice
1 garlic clove, smashed
3/4 pound broccoli, broken into florets
Seasoned salt and ground black pepper, to taste

Directions

Steam the broccoli for 7 minutes, until it is crisp-tender but still vibrant green. Pulse in your blender or a food processor until rice-like consistency is achieved.

Now, add the oil, salt, black paper, garlic, sesame paste, fresh lime juice and Garam Masala.

Blend until everything is well incorporated.

Drizzle with some extra olive oil.

Bon appétit!

Per serving: 100 Calories; 8.2g Fat; 4.7g Carbs; 3.7g Protein; 2.6g Fiber

384. Almond Milk and Berry Shake

(Ready in about 5 minutes | Servings 4)

Ingredients

1 ½ cups almond milk
1 tablespoon vegan protein powder, zero carbs
1/3 cup fresh blueberries
1/3 cup frozen cherries
1/4 teaspoon vanilla extract
1/2 cup water

Directions

Mix all ingredients in your blender or a smoothie maker until creamy and uniform.

Pour your smoothie into four glasses and enjoy!

Per serving: 108 Calories; 21.7g Fat; 6.9g Carbs; 2.6g Protein; 1.9g Fiber

385. Crunchy Granola with A Twist

(Ready in about 1 hour | Servings 6)

Ingredients

1 cup pecans, chopped
1/3 cup chia seeds
1/2 cup almonds, chopped
1 teaspoon lime zest
A few drops of Stevia
1/3 cup flax meal
1 teaspoon ground cinnamon
1 teaspoon freshly grated nutmeg
1/3 cup water
1/3 cup pumpkin seeds
1/3 cup almond milk
1/3 cup coconut oil, melted

Directions

Preheat an oven to 310 degrees F. Coat a cookie sheet with parchment paper.

Toss all ingredients together and spread the mixture out in an even layer onto the prepared cookie sheet.

Bake about for 50 to 55 minutes, stirring every 15 to 20 minutes. Store at room temperature for up to a month.

Per serving: 449 Calories; 44.9g Fat; 6.9g Carbs; 9.3g Protein; 2.3g Fiber

386. Oven-Roasted Cabbage with Sesame Seeds

(Ready in about 45 minutes | Servings 6)

Ingredients

2 pounds green cabbage, cut into wedges
1 teaspoon sesame seeds
2 tablespoons fresh chives, chopped
1/4 cup olive oil
Non-stick cooking spray
Coarsely salt and freshly ground black pepper, to taste

Directions

Begin by preheating your oven to 390 degrees F. Brush a rimmed baking sheet with a non-stick cooking spray.

Add the cabbage wedges to the baking sheet. Toss with the olive oil, salt, black pepper and sesame seeds.

Roast for 40 to 45 minutes, until the cabbage is softened. Top with fresh chopped chives. Bon appétit!

Per serving: 186 Calories; 17g Fat; 7g Carbs; 2.1g Protein; 3.3g Fiber

387. Berbere Cauliflower Rice-Stuffed Peppers

(Ready in about 40 minutes | Servings 4)

Ingredients

1 ½ tablespoons oil
4 bell peppers
1 teaspoon Berbere
2 ripe tomatoes, pureed
1 onion, chopped
1 garlic clove, minced
Sea salt and pepper, to taste
1 teaspoon chipotle powder
1 small head cauliflower

Directions

To make the cauliflower rice, grate the cauliflower into the size of rice. Place on a kitchen towel to soak up any excess moisture.

Next, preheat your oven to 360 degrees F. Lightly grease a casserole dish.

Cut off the top of the bell peppers. Now, discard the seeds and core.

Roast the peppers in a parchment lined baking pan for 18 minutes until the skin is slightly browned.

In the meantime, heat the oil over medium-high heat. Sauté the onion and garlic until tender and fragrant.

Add the cauliflower rice, chipotle powder, and Berbere spice. Cook until the cauliflower rice is tender, about 6 minutes.

Divide the cauliflower mixture among the bell peppers. Place in the casserole dish.

Mix the tomatoes, salt, and pepper. Pour the tomato mixture over the peppers. Bake about 10 minutes, depending on the desired tenderness.

Bon appétit!

Per serving: 77 Calories; 4.8g Fat; 6.4g Carbs; 1.6g Protein; 3.3g Fiber

388. Tempeh with Savoy Cabbage

(Ready in about 20 minutes | Servings 4)

Ingredients

6 ounces tempeh, crumbled
2 tablespoons coconut aminos
Sea salt and pepper, to season
1/2 pound savoy cabbage, shredded
2 tablespoons sesame oil
2 tablespoons vegetable broth
1 teaspoon garlic, minced
1/2 cup white onion, chopped

Directions

In a wok, heat the sesame oil over a moderately-high heat. Sauté the garlic and onion until tender and fragrant.

Now, add in the remaining ingredients and cook for 15 minutes or until thoroughly cooked. Bon appétit!

Per serving: 179 Calories; 11.7g Fat; 2.1g Carbs; 10.5g Protein; 2.3g Fiber

VEGETARIAN

389. Tofu and Brussels Sprout Bowl

(Ready in about 25 minutes | Servings 4)

Ingredients

1 (14-ounce) block tofu, pressed and cubed
1 pound Brussels sprouts, trimmed and quartered
1 teaspoon cayenne pepper
1/2 teaspoon dried dill weed
1 teaspoon garlic powder
1/2 teaspoon turmeric powder
1 celery stalk, chopped
1 bunch scallions, chopped
1/4 teaspoon dried basil
2 tablespoons olive oil
2 tablespoons Worcestershire sauce
Salt and black pepper, to taste

Directions

Heat 1 tablespoon of olive oil in a large-sized skillet over a moderately high flame. Add the tofu cubes and cook, gently stirring, for 8 minutes.

Now, add the celery and scallions; cook until they are softened, about 5 minutes

Add the cayenne pepper, garlic powder, Worcestershire sauce, salt, and pepper; continue to cook for 3 more minutes; reserve.

Heat the remaining 1 tablespoon of oil in the same pan. Cook the Brussels sprouts along with the remaining seasonings for 4 minutes.

Add the tofu mixture to the Brussels sprouts. Bon appétit!

Per serving: 128 Calories; 8.3g Fat; 6g Carbs; 5.1g Protein; 5.2g Fiber

390. Easy Traditional Guacamole

(Ready in about 10 minutes + chilling time | Servings 8)

Ingredients

1 red chili, deseeded and finely chopped
1 cup fresh tomatoes, chopped
1/2 teaspoon cumin, ground
1 yellow onion, chopped
2 garlic cloves, minced
2 Haas avocados, peeled, pitted, and mashed
2 tablespoons fresh lime juice
2 tablespoons coriander leaves, chopped
Sea salt and ground black pepper, to taste

Directions

In a bowl, thoroughly combine the avocados, lime juice, salt and black pepper.

Stir in the onion, cilantro, tomatoes, and garlic; sprinkle with paprika.

Bon appétit!

Per serving: 112 Calories; 9.9g Fat; 6.5g Carbs; 1.3g Protein; 3.8g Fiber

391. Fennel with Aromatic Tomato Sauce

(Ready in about 20 minutes | Servings 4)

Ingredients

1 fennel, thinly sliced
1/4 cup vegetable stock
1 garlic clove, crushed
Sea salt and ground black pepper, to taste
2 tablespoons olive oil
For the Sauce:
1 ancho chili, minced
1/2 cup scallions, chopped
1 bunch fresh basil, leaves picked
1 tablespoon fresh cilantro, roughly chopped
1 cloves garlic, minced
Sat and pepper, to taste
2 tomatoes, halved
2 tablespoons extra-virgin olive oil

Directions

Heat the olive oil in a pan over a moderately high heat. Sauté the garlic for 1 to 2 minutes or until aromatic.

Throw the slices of fennel into the pan; add the vegetable stock and continue to cook until the fennel has softened. Season with salt and black pepper to taste. Heat off.

Brush the tomato halves with extra-virgin olive oil. Microwave for 15 minutes on HIGH; be sure to pour off any excess liquid.

Transfer the cooked tomatoes to a food processor; add the remaining ingredients for the sauce. Puree until your desired consistency is reached.

Bon appétit!

Per serving: 135 Calories; 13.6g Fat; 3g Carbs; 0.9g Protein; 2.1g Fiber

392. Peanut Butter Blackberry Delight

(Ready in about 5 minutes | Servings 2)

Ingredients

1 tablespoon peanut butter
1 tablespoon cocoa
1 tablespoon chia seeds
1/4 teaspoon ground nutmeg
Liquid Stevia, to taste
1 cup blackberries
1 cup water

Directions

Add all ingredients to your blender or a food processor.

Mix until creamy and uniform.

Pour your smoothie into two glasses and enjoy!

Per serving: 103 Calories; 5.9g Fat; 7g Carbs; 4.1g Protein; 6.1g Fiber

393. Fried Sticky Oyster Mushrooms

(Ready in about 10 minutes | Servings 4)

Ingredients

1 pound oyster mushrooms, sliced
1 tablespoons Swerve
Salt and white pepper, to taste
3 tablespoons butter
1 tablespoon coconut aminos
1 teaspoon garlic, minced

Directions

Melt the butter in a saucepan over a moderately-high heat. Now, sauté the garlic for a minute or so.

Stir in the mushrooms and continue to cook them for 3 to 4 minutes, until they release the liquid.

Add in the other ingredients and continue to cook until the mushrooms are caramelized. Enjoy!

Per serving: 75 Calories; 5.2g Fat; 3.3g Carbs; 2.9g Protein; 1.1g Fiber

394. Eggs with Parmesan-Kale Pesto

(Ready in about 15 minutes | Servings 4)

Ingredients

1/4 cup full-fat milk
8 eggs, well beaten
Salt and ground black pepper, to your liking
2 tablespoons ghee
For the Kale Pesto:
2 tablespoons fresh lemon juice
2 garlic cloves, minced
1/2 cup olive oil
2 cups kale
1 cup parmesan cheese, grated

Directions

Melt the ghee in a heavy-bottomed sauté pan over moderately high heat. Whisk the eggs with the milk, salt, and pepper.

Now, cook this egg mixture, gently stirring, until the eggs are set but still moist and tender.

Put all ingredients for the pesto, except the olive oil, in your food processor or blender.

Pulse until roughly chopped. With the machine running, slowly pour in the olive oil until you get the desired consistency.

Serve over the warm scrambled eggs. Bon appétit!

Per serving: 495 Calories; 45g Fat; 6.3g Carbs; 19.5g Protein; 0.5g Fiber

395. Cheese and Tomato Omelet

(Ready in about 15 minutes | Servings 2)

Ingredients

4 eggs
1/4 cup Appenzeller cheese, shredded
1 tablespoon sesame oil
1/4 cup Blue cheese, crumbled
1 tomato, thinly sliced
1/4 teaspoon black peppercorns, crushed
Salt, to taste

Directions

Whisk the eggs in a mixing bowl; season with salt and crushed peppercorns.

Heat the oil in a sauté pan over medium-low heat. Now, pour in the eggs and cook, using a spatula to swirl the eggs around the pan.

Cook the eggs until partially set. Top with the cheese; fold your omelet in half to enclose the filling.

Serve warm and enjoy!

Per serving: 307 Calories; 25g Fat; 2.5g Carbs; 18.5g Protein; 0.7g Fiber

396. Spinach and Cheddar Cheese Mini Frittatas

(Ready in about 30 minutes | Servings 6)

Ingredients

8 eggs
1 ½ cups cheddar cheese, grated
1 cup spinach, chopped
2 tablespoons vegetable oil
1/4 teaspoon ground black pepper, or more to the taste
1 cup full-fat milk
1/3 teaspoon salt

Directions

Preheat your oven to 350 degrees F.

In a bowl, mix the milk, with the eggs and oil. Add the remaining ingredients. Mix well to combine.

Add the mixture to a lightly greased muffin tin.

Bake for 25 minutes or until your muffins spring back when lightly pressed.

Bon appétit!

Per serving: 252 Calories; 19.7g Fat; 3g Carbs; 16.1g Protein; 0.1g Fiber

397. The Best Keto Donuts Ever

(Ready in about 25 minutes | Servings 6)

Ingredients

1 egg
A pinch of ground cloves
1 teaspoon pure vanilla extract
1/4 cup xylitol
1 teaspoon baking powder
1/2 stick butter, melted
1/2 teaspoon baking soda
1 teaspoon cinnamon, ground
1/2 cup sour cream
2/3 cup coconut flour
A pinch of salt
For the Frosting:
1 cup sugar-free chocolate, broken into chunks
1 cup double cream

Directions

Begin by preheating your oven to 360 degrees F. Generously spritz a donut pan with a non-stick cooking spray.

In a mixing bowl, thoroughly combine the coconut flour, xylitol, baking powder, baking soda, cinnamon, sea salt and cloves.

In another mixing bowl, mix together the butter, sour cream, egg, and vanilla extract. Add the wet mixture to the dry mixture.

Spoon the batter evenly into the donut pan. Bake approximately 17 minutes or until done.

In the meantime, heat the double cream in a pan over a moderate flame; let it simmer for 2 minutes.

Fold in the chocolate chunks; mix until all the chocolate is melted. Frost your donuts.

Bon appétit!

Per serving: 218 Calories; 20g Fat; 6g Carbs; 4.8g Protein; 2.6g Fiber

VEGETARIAN

398. Creamed Cauliflower Soup with Coriander and Nuts

(Ready in about 25 minutes | Servings 4)

Ingredients

1 pound cauliflower, broken into florets
1 tablespoon fresh coriander, minced
Salt and pepper, to taste
1 cup onions, chopped
1 celery with leaves, chopped
1 teaspoon garlic, smashed
4 cups vegetable broth
1 tablespoon sesame oil
1/4 cup pine nuts, ground

Directions

In a heavy-bottomed pot, heat sesame oil over a moderately-high flame. Sauté the onion, celery and garlic until tender and aromatic.

Add in the cauliflower, vegetable broth, salt, pepper, and pine nuts. Bring to a boil.

Immediately reduce the heat to simmer; continue to cook, partially covered, for about 18 minutes.

Afterwards, add in the fresh coriander and puree your soup with an immersion blender. Enjoy!

Per serving: 114 Calories; 6.5g Fat; 6.4g Carbs; 3.8g Protein; 3.5g Fiber

399. Spicy and Fluffy Eggs with Sour Cream

(Ready in about 15 minutes | Servings 2)

Ingredients

2 tablespoons chervil, chopped
2 medium-sized tomatoes, sliced
2 spring garlic, chopped
1 (8-ounce) carton sour cream, divided
4 eggs, beaten
1 piquillo pepper, minced
2 teaspoons butter
2 spring onions, chopped
Kosher salt and freshly ground black pepper, to taste

Directions

Melt the butter in a pan that is preheated over a moderate flame. Sauté spring onion and garlic until they are just tender and fragrant.

Then, whisk the eggs with the sour cream. Add the egg mixture to the pan and gently smooth its surface with a wide spatula; cook until the eggs are puffy and lightly browned on bottom.

Place the tomatoes, piquillo pepper and chervil on one side of the omelet. Season with salt and pepper.

Fold your omelet in half. Bon appétit!

Per serving: 319 Calories; 25g Fat; 7.1g Carbs; 14.9g Protein; 1.1g Fiber

400. Jaffa Chia Pudding

(Ready in about 35 minutes | Servings 4)

Ingredients

1/2 cup chia seeds
2 tablespoons cocoa powder, unsweetened
1/2 teaspoon maple extract
3 tablespoons orange flower water
1/4 cup water
2 tablespoons almond butter
20 drops liquid stevia
3/4 cup cashew milk, preferably homemade

Directions

Place the cashew milk, almond butter, chia seeds, stevia, maple extract, orange flower water, and cocoa powder in a mixing bowl.

Allow it to stand for 30 minutes, stirring periodically.

Bon appétit!

Per serving: 93 Calories; 5.1g Fat; 5.2g Carbs; 4.4g Protein; 4.7g Fiber

401. Adobo Celery Chips

(Ready in about 35 minutes | Servings 6)

Ingredients

1 tablespoon Adobo seasoning mix
1 ½ pounds celery root, cut into sticks
1/2 teaspoon smoked paprika
2 tablespoons sesame oil
1/4 cup pecans, coarsely ground
Salt and pepper, to taste

Directions

Start by preheating your oven to 395 degrees F. Coat a baking sheet with a Silpat mat.

Toss the celery root with the sesame oil, salt, pepper, paprika, and Adobo seasoning mix.

Place the celery stick on the prepared baking sheet and bake in the preheated oven for 30 to 35 minutes, turning them over once or twice.

Sprinkle with pecans. Bon appétit!

Per serving: 96 Calories; 8.5g Fat; 4.1g Carbs; 1.5g Protein; 2.6g Fiber

402. Keto Crunch Cereal

(Ready in about 10 minutes | Servings 4)

Ingredients

1/3 cup coconut shreds
A pinch of sea salt
A pinch of grated nutmeg
2 tablespoons coconut oil, melted
4 tablespoons Swerve
1/2 cup hemp hearts
16 almonds, roughly chopped
1/2 teaspoon ground cinnamon
2 ½ cups almond milk, full-fat
1/2 cup water

Directions

Place all ingredients, except for the almonds, in a deep saucepan over medium-low heat.

Let it simmer, partially covered, for 5 to 6 minutes or until slightly thickened.

Top each serving with slivered almonds.

Per serving: 279 Calories; 23.6g Fat; 5.9g Carbs; 7.2g Protein; 2.2g Fiber

403. Brown Mushrooms with Cauliflower and Tomato

(Ready in about 30 minutes | Servings 4)

Ingredients

1 cup tomato, pureed
1 head cauliflower, cut into florets
1 teaspoon garlic, smashed
1/4 cup olive oil
1/2 teaspoon turmeric powder
8 ounces brown mushrooms, halved
Salt and pepper, to taste

Directions

Toss all ingredients in a lightly oiled baking pan.

Roast the vegetable in the preheated oven at 380 degrees F for 25 to 30 minutes.

Enjoy!

Per serving: 113 Calories; 6.7g Fat; 6.6g Carbs; 5g Protein; 2.7g Fiber

404. Flambéed Sweet Strawberry Omelet

(Ready in about 10 minutes | Servings 1)

Ingredients

6 fresh strawberries, sliced
2 tablespoons cream cheese
2 tablespoons heavy cream
1 tablespoon coconut oil
1 tablespoon Cognac
1/2 teaspoon ground cloves
2 eggs, beaten

Directions

Whisk the eggs with the heavy cream and ground cloves.

Next, melt the coconut oil in a pan that is preheated over medium-high heat. When hot, add the egg mixture; cook for about 3 minutes until the base is thoroughly cooked.

Tip the omelet out onto a plate; top with the cheese and strawberries. Roll it up; add the warmed Cognac over your omelet and flambé. Bon appétit!

Per serving: 488 Calories; 42g Fat; 8g Carbs; 15.3g Protein; 1.4g Fiber

405. Chocolate, Spinach and Coconut Smoothie

(Ready in about 10 minutes | Servings 2)

Ingredients

1 tablespoon unsweetened cocoa powder
1 ½ cups baby spinach
1/2 cup coconut milk
2 tablespoons Swerve
1/2 cup water
1 tablespoon chia seeds
8 almonds

Directions

Process all ingredients until smooth and creamy. Pour into serving glasses and serve well-chilled!

Per serving: 335 Calories; 31.7g Fat; 5.7g Carbs; 7g Protein; 1.9g Fiber

406. Marinated Spicy Tofu with Peppers

(Ready in about 40 minutes | Servings 2)

Ingredients

1 tablespoon olive oil
1 green bell pepper, deveined and sliced
1 teaspoon shallot powder
1/2 teaspoon ground bay leaf
1 serrano pepper, deveined and sliced
1 ½ tablespoons flaxseed meal
1/2 teaspoon paprika
1 red bell pepper, deveined and sliced
12 ounces extra firm tofu, pressed and cubed
Salt and ground black pepper, to taste
1 teaspoon garlic paste

Directions

Place the tofu, flaxseed meal, salt, black pepper, garlic paste, paprika, shallot powder, and ground bay leaf in a container.

Cover, toss to coat, and let it marinate at least 30 minutes.

Heat the olive oil in a saucepan over a moderate heat. Cook your tofu along with peppers for 5 to 7 minutes, gently stirring.

Bon appétit!

Per serving: 223 Calories; 15.9g Fat; 6.1g Carbs; 15.6g Protein; 4.2g Fiber

407. Ricotta Keto Bites

(Ready in about 10 minutes + chilling time | Servings 6)

Ingredients

1/2 cup fresh cilantro, finely chopped
3 tablespoons butter
1/4 teaspoon red wine vinegar
1 cup Ricotta cheese
Salt and pepper, to taste

Directions

Blend all ingredients, except for the cilantro, in a food processor.

Place the mixture in the refrigerator for 3 hours.

Shape the mixture into 10 to 12 balls; roll them in the chopped cilantro until evenly coated. Bon appétit!

Per serving: 108 Calories; 9g Fat; 2.2g Carbs; 4.8g Protein; 0g Fiber

408. Keto Paprika Chips

(Ready in about 15 minutes | Servings 6)

Ingredients

1 teaspoon paprika powder
3 cups provolone cheese, shredded
4 tablespoons ground flaxseed meal

Directions

Begin by preheating your oven to 420 degrees F.

Then, drop a tablespoon of the shredded cheese into 12 separate piles. Sprinkle the ground flaxseed meal and paprika powder over the top.

Bake in the middle of your oven for roughly 10 to 12 minutes. Bon appétit!

Per serving: 268 Calories; 20.4g Fat; 3.4g Carbs; 18.1g Protein; 2g Fiber

VEGETARIAN

409. Voodles with Avocado Sauce

(Ready in about 15 minutes | Servings 4)

Ingredients

1/2 pound zucchini, spiralized
1/2 pound bell peppers, spiralized
1 avocado, peeled and pitted
1 poblano pepper, deveined and minced
Salt and pepper, to season
1 lime, juiced and zested
3 tablespoons olive oil
1 yellow onion, chopped
2 tablespoons parsley, chopped

Directions

In a saucepan, heat 1 tablespoon of olive oil over a moderately-high heat. Sauté the zucchini and peppers until crisp-tender or about 5 minutes.

In your blender or food processor, pulse the other ingredients until well combined.

Pour the avocado sauce over the vegetable noodles and toss to combine. Enjoy!

Per serving: 233 Calories; 20.2g Fat; 6g Carbs; 1.9g Protein; 4g Fiber

410. Swiss Cheese Cauliflower Cakes

(Ready in about 35 minutes | Servings 6)

Ingredients

1/2 cup Swiss cheese, shredded
1 pound cauliflower, grated
1 garlic clove, minced
2 eggs, beaten
1/2 teaspoon dried dill weed
6 tablespoons almond flour
1 ½ tablespoons olive oil
1 shallot, chopped
1 cup parmesan cheese
Sea salt and ground black pepper, to taste

Directions

Heat the oil in a cast iron skillet over medium heat. Cook the shallots and garlic until they are aromatic.

Add the grated cauliflower and stir with a spatula for another minute or so; set aside to cool to room temperature so you can handle it easily.

Add the remaining ingredients; shape the mixture into balls, then, press each ball to form burger patties.

Bake in the preheated oven at 400 degrees F for 20 minutes. Flip and bake for another 10 minutes or until golden brown on top.

Bon appétit!

Per serving: 199 Calories; 13.8g Fat; 5.9g Carbs; 13g Protein; 1.7g Fiber

411. Squash Stew with Tomatoes and Wine

(Ready in about 35 minutes | Servings 6)

Ingredients

6 ounces butternut squash, chopped
2 shallots, chopped
1 pound ripe tomatoes, chopped
1 celery, chopped
2 tablespoons fresh cilantro, roughly chopped
1/4 teaspoon smoked paprika, or more to the taste
2 tablespoons red wine
1 teaspoon garlic, finely chopped
1/2 teaspoon sea salt
1/4 teaspoon ground black pepper, or more to the taste
1/2 teaspoon chili powder
1/2 stick butter
1 bay leaf

Directions

Melt the butter in a stock pot over a moderate heat. Now, sauté the shallots and garlic until fragrant, about 4 minutes.

Add the eggplant, celery and cilantro; cook an additional 5 minutes.

Stir in the remaining ingredients; reduce the heat to medium-low and let it simmer, covered, for 20 to 25 minutes.

Bon appétit!

Per serving: 113 Calories; 7.9g Fat; 4.7g Carbs; 2.8g Protein; 1.5g Fiber

412. Avocado Boats with Mushrooms

(Ready in about 10 minutes | Servings 8)

Ingredients

4 avocados, halved
1 cup grape tomatoes, diced
2 cups brown mushrooms, chopped
2 garlic cloves, minced
1 shallot, chopped
2 tablespoons sesame oil
1/2 lemon, freshly squeezed
1 tablespoon Dijon mustard
Salt and pepper, to taste

Directions

In a frying pan, heat the sesame oil over a moderately-high heat. Sauté the mushrooms, shallot, and garlic until they are tender and fragrant.

Scoop out about 1 tablespoon of the avocado flesh from each half.

Add the avocado flesh to the mushroom mixture along with the salt, pepper, Dijon mustard, and tomatoes.

Divide the mushroom mixture among the avocado halves. Drizzle each avocado with lemon juice. Bon appétit!

Per serving: 245 Calories; 23.2g Fat; 6.2g Carbs; 2.4g Protein; 4g Fiber

413. Spicy Crispy Fried Tofu

(Ready in about 20 minutes | Servings 2)

Ingredients

6 ounces extra-firm tofu, pressed and cubed
1 tablespoon sesame oil
1/2 teaspoon ground bay leaf
1 chili pepper, deveined and sliced
1 ½ tablespoons almond meal
2 bell peppers, deveined and sliced
Salt and pepper, to taste
1 teaspoon onion powder
1 teaspoon ginger-garlic paste

Directions

Toss your tofu, with the almond meal, salt, pepper, ginger-garlic paste, onion powder, ground bay leaf.

In a sauté pan, heat the sesame oil over medium-high heat.

Fry the tofu cubes along with the peppers for about 6 minutes. Enjoy!

Per serving: 223 Calories; 15.9g Fat; 5.1g Carbs; 15.6g Protein; 3.3g Fiber

414. Peanut Butter Shake with Mixed Berries

(Ready in about 5 minutes | Servings 1)

Ingredients

3/4 cup coconut milk, unsweetened
1/3 cup mixed berries
1 teaspoon Swerve
1/2 cup lettuce
1 tablespoon peanut butter

Directions

Blend all ingredients until creamy and smooth. Pour into a glass and enjoy!

Per serving: 114 Calories; 8.2g Fat; 5.9g Carbs; 4.2g Protein; 1.8g Fiber

415. Tangy Peppery Cabbage Chowder

(Ready in about 25 minutes | Servings 4)

Ingredients

1 cup cabbage, shredded
2 carrots, chopped
1 green pepper, chopped
1 cup sour cream
1 leek, chopped
2 garlic cloves, minced
Fresh tarragon sprigs, for garnish
1 ½ tablespoons butter, melted
4 cups water
2 bouillon cubes

Directions

Warm the butter in a large pot over medium flame. Sauté the leeks until just tender and fragrant. Now, add the remaining vegetables and cook for 5 to 7 minutes, stirring periodically.

Add the water and bouillon cubes; cover partially and cook an additional 13 minutes.

Blend the mixture until creamy, uniform and smooth. Stir in the sour cream; gently heat, stirring continuously, until your soup is hot.

Garnish with fresh tarragon. Bon appétit!

Per serving: 185 Calories; 16.6g Fat; 6.4g Carbs; 2.9g Protein; 1.9g Fiber

416. Stuffed Peppers with Caciocavallo Cheese

(Ready in about 30 minutes | Servings 6)

Ingredients

6 bell peppers, seeds and tops removed
1/2 cup Caciocavallo cheese, grated
3/4 pound button mushrooms, chopped
1 teaspoon Pimento
2 tablespoons fresh chives, chopped
Salt to taste
1/2 cup tomato sauce
2 tablespoons avocado oil
1 shallot, chopped
1 teaspoon caraway seeds
1 teaspoon garlic, minced

Directions

Preheat your oven to 380 degrees F. Heat the oil in a pan that is preheated over a moderately high heat.

Sauté the shallots and garlic until the shallot softens. Stir in the mushrooms and cook an additional 4 minutes or until the mushrooms are fragrant.

Add the pimento, chives, caraway seeds and salt; stir until everything is heated through.

Place the peppers in a foil-lined roasting pan; fill them with the mushroom stuffing. Top each pepper with Caciocavallo cheese.

Afterwards, pour the tomato sauce over everything. Bake for 18 to 23 minutes or until the cheese is lightly browned. Bon appétit!

Per serving: 319 Calories; 8.8g Fat; 5.6g Carbs; 10.3g Protein; 4.2g Fiber

417. Italian Zuppa di Zucchini

(Ready in about 45 minutes | Servings 4)

Ingredients

1 tomato, pureed
1 parsnip, sliced
3 teaspoons olive oil
1 cup scallions, chopped
1 celery, sliced
3 cups zucchini, peeled and chopped
4 cups vegetable broth
1 avocado pitted, peeled and mashed
Salt and black pepper, to taste

Directions

In a soup pot, heat the oil over a moderately-high heat. Sauté the scallion, celery, parsnip, and zucchini until they've softened.

Add in the salt, pepper, vegetable broth, and pureed tomato; bring it to a boil. Turn the heat to a simmer.

Continue to simmer for about 25 minutes. Remove from the heat and fold in the mashed avocado.

Puree your soup with an immersion blender. Bon appétit!

Per serving: 165 Calories; 13.4g Fat; 6.7g Carbs; 2.2g Protein; 6g Fiber

418. Oyster Mushroom Paprikash

(Ready in about 50 minutes | Servings 4)

Ingredients

2 ½ cups oyster mushrooms, chopped
2 vegetable bouillon cubes
1 cup tomato puree
1/2 teaspoon garlic, finely minced
1 cup celery, chopped
1 bay laurel
1 red onion, chopped
1 tablespoon Hungarian paprika
2 thyme sprigs, chopped
2 bell peppers, chopped
1 ½ cups water
2 teaspoons canola oil
Salt and pepper, to taste

Directions

Heat the canola oil in a soup pot over a moderately-high heat. Sauté the onion and garlic until they've softened.

Stir in the celery, peppers, and mushrooms. Now, continue to cook for about 10 minutes, adding a splash of water to prevent sticking.

Add in the remaining ingredients. Turn the heat to a simmer. Continue to cook, partially covered, for a further 30 minutes. Bon appétit!

Per serving: 65 Calories; 2.7g Fat; 6g Carbs; 2.7g Protein; 2.9g Fiber

419. Punjabi Cauliflower Masala

(Ready in about 30 minutes | Servings 4)

Ingredients

1/4 cup sesame oil
1/2 teaspoon nigella seeds
2 bell peppers, halved
1 cup vegetable broth
1 teaspoon fennel seeds
1 tablespoon khus khus
1 garlic clove, minced
2 sprigs curry leaves
1/2 of a star anise
1 pound cauliflower florets
Salt and pepper, to taste

Directions

Parboil the cauliflower in a pot of a lightly-salted water for 5 to 6 minutes until crisp-tender.

Dry roast all the apices on a low flame for about 3 minutes; reserve.

In a wok, or a saucepan, heat the sesame oil until sizzling. Cook the cauliflower, peppers, and garlic for 5 to 6 minutes.

Add in the salt, pepper, and broth and continue to cook for 10 minutes. Bon appétit!

Per serving: 166 Calories; 13.9g Fat; 5.4g Carbs; 3g Protein; 3.1g Fiber

420. Swiss Chard, Tomato and Zucchini Chowder

(Ready in about 25 minutes | Servings 6)

Ingredients

2 cups Swiss chard, torn into pieces
1 zucchini, chopped
1/2 cup scallions, chopped
2 thyme sprigs, chopped
1 cup almond milk, unflavored
1 cup grape tomatoes, chopped
1 teaspoon garlic, minced
2 teaspoons sesame oil
6 cups vegetable broth
2 celery stalks, chopped
1 onion, chopped
2 bay leaves
Sea salt and pepper, to taste

Directions

In a heavy bottomed pot, heat the sesame oil in over a moderately-high heat. Sauté the onion, garlic, and celery, until they've softened.

Add in the zucchini, Swiss chard, salt, pepper, thyme, bay leaves, broth, and tomatoes; bring to a rapid boil. Turn the heat to a simmer.

Leave the lid slightly ajar and continue to simmer for about 13 minutes. Add in the almond milk and scallions; continue to cook for 4 minutes more or until thoroughly warmed. Enjoy!

Per serving: 142 Calories; 11.4g Fat; 5.6g Carbs; 2.9g Protein; 1.3g Fiber

421. Mushrooms with Walnuts and Parsley

(Ready in about 30 minutes | Servings 4)

Ingredients

1/4 cup walnuts, chopped
1 pound button mushrooms, stems removed and chopped
1 cup shallots, chopped
2 tablespoons parsley, chopped
1/2 teaspoon garlic, minced
2 tablespoons olive oil
Salt and pepper, to taste

Directions

Preheat your oven to 365 degrees F. Line a baking pan with a parchment paper.

In a saucepan, heat the olive oil over medium-high flame. Now, sauté the shallot and garlic until tender and aromatic.

Add in the mushrooms stems and continue to cook until they've softened. Remove from the heat and season with salt and pepper.

Stir in the chopped walnuts and parsley; stuff the mushroom caps with the prepared filling. Place your mushrooms on the prepared baking pan.

Bake for 20 to 25 minutes until heated through. Bon appétit!

Per serving: 139 Calories; 11.2g Fat; 5.4g Carbs; 4.8g Protein; 1.8g Fiber

422. Chanterelle Mushroom and Wine Goulash

(Ready in about 25 minutes | Servings 4)

Ingredients

1 cup leeks, chopped
3 ½ cups roasted vegetable stock
2 ripe tomatoes, pureed
1 tablespoon flaxseed meal
2 rosemary sprigs, chopped
1 thyme sprig, chopped
2 garlic cloves, pressed
1 cup fresh Chanterelle, sliced
2 tablespoons dry red wine
1/2 teaspoon cayenne pepper
1/2 cup celery with leaves, chopped
2 carrots, chopped
1 teaspoon Hungarian paprika
2 tablespoons olive oil

Directions

Heat the oil in a stockpot over a moderate flame. Now, cook the leeks until they are tender.

Add the garlic, celery, and carrots and cook for a further 4 minutes or until they are softened.

Now, stir in the Chanterelle mushrooms; cook until they lose their liquid; reserve the vegetables.

Pour in the wine to deglaze the bottom of the stockpot. Now, add the rosemary and thyme.

Add the roasted vegetable stock, cayenne pepper, Hungarian paprika, and tomatoes; stir in the reserved vegetables and bring to a boil.

Reduce heat to a simmer. Let it simmer, covered, an additional 15 minutes. Add the flaxseed meal to thicken the soup.

Bon appétit!

Per serving: 114 Calories; 7.3g Fat; 6g Carbs; 2.1g Protein; 3.8g Fiber

423. Spanish-Style Artichoke with Tofu

(Ready in about 30 minutes | Servings 4)

Ingredients

1 block tofu, pressed and cubed
1 Spanish pepper, chopped
1/4 cup vegetable broth
1 teaspoon fresh garlic, minced
2 tablespoons coconut oil, room temperature
1 teaspoon Cajun spice mix
Salt and pepper, to taste
1 pound artichokes, trimmed and cut into pieces

Directions

Parboil your artichokes in a pot of lightly salted water for 13 to 15 minutes or until they're crisp-tender; drain.

In a large saucepan, melt the coconut oil over medium-high heat; fry the tofu cubes for 5 to 6 minutes or until golden-brown.

Add in the garlic, Cajun spice mix, Spanish pepper, broth, salt, and pepper. Add in the reserved artichokes and continue to cook until for 5 minutes more. Enjoy!

Per serving: 138 Calories; 8.9g Fat; 6.8g Carbs; 6.4g Protein; 5g Fiber

424. Mediterranean Chard Dip

(Ready in about 25 minutes | Servings 6)

Ingredients

1 teaspoon dried Mediterranean spice mix
2 cups Swiss chard
1/2 cup almond milk
2 teaspoons nutritional yeast
1 cup tofu, pressed and crumbled
1 teaspoon fresh garlic, smashed
2 teaspoons sesame oil
Salt and pepper, to taste

Directions

Parboil the Swiss chard in a pot of lightly salted water for about 6 minutes. Transfer the mixture to the bowl of a food processor; add in the other ingredients.

Process the ingredients until the mixture is homogeneous.

Bake in the preheated oven at 390 degrees F for about 10 minutes. Enjoy!

Per serving: 75 Calories; 3g Fat; 6g Carbs; 2.9g Protein; 0.8g Fiber

425. Greek Broccoli Dipping Sauce

(Ready in about 10 minutes | Servings 8)

Ingredients

1 pound broccoli florets
1/2 cup blue cheese
1 teaspoon Mediterranean seasoning mix
Salt and pepper, to taste
1/2 cup Greek-style yogurt
1/3 cup mayonnaise

Directions

Parboil the broccoli florets for about 7 minutes or until crisp-tender. Place the broccoli florets in a bowl of your food processor.

Add in the yogurt, cheese, and spices and blend briefly to combine.

Fold in the well-chilled mayonnaise and continue to blend until everything is well incorporated. Enjoy!

Per serving: 134 Calories; 10.2g Fat; 6.5g Carbs; 5.1g Protein; 1.6g Fiber

426. Oven-Roasted Vegetables with Vegan Parmesan

(Ready in about 40 minutes | Servings 4)

Ingredients

- 1 cup vegan parmesan
- 2 celery stalks, chopped
- Sea salt and pepper, to taste
- 2 tablespoons sesame oil
- 1 cup onions, chopped
- 1 teaspoon porcini powder
- 2 tablespoons fresh parsley, chopped
- 1 cup vegetable broth
- 1/2 pound Brussels sprouts, quartered

Directions

In a frying pan, heat the sesame oil over a moderately-high heat. Cook the onions, celery, and Brussels sprouts until they have softened.

Spoon the vegetable mixture into a lightly greased baking dish.

Whisk the vegetable broth with the salt, pepper, and porcini powder. Pour the mixture over the vegetables.

Top with the vegan parmesan and parsley; bake in the preheated oven at 365 degrees F for 25 to 30 minutes. Bon appétit!

Per serving: 242 Calories; 16.3g Fat; 6.7g Carbs; 16.3g Protein; 3.2g Fiber

427. Fried Tofu with Cabbage and Celery

(Ready in about 25 minutes | Servings 4)

Ingredients

- 8 ounces tofu, pressed, drained and cubed
- 2 garlic cloves, pressed
- 1/2 teaspoon curry paste
- 2 tablespoons coconut aminos
- 1 celery stalk, chopped
- 2 tablespoons sesame oil
- 1 teaspoon red pepper flakes, crushed
- 1/4 teaspoon dried oregano
- 1/2 cup onions, chopped
- 1 pound cabbage, trimmed and quartered
- Salt and pepper, to taste

Directions

Heat the sesame oil in a non-stick skillet over a moderately-high heat. Then, fry the tofu cubes for about 7 minutes or until golden brown on all sides.

Add in the celery and onions, and continue to cook for a further 5 minutes until they are just tender.

Add in the other ingredients and continue to cook, partially covered, for 7 to 8 minutes longer. Fold in the tofu cubes and gently stir to combine.

Bon appétit!

Per serving: 128 Calories; 8.3g Fat; 6.5g Carbs; 5.1g Protein; 3.2g Fiber

428. Spicy Hot Tofu with Vegan Tzatziki

(Ready in about 40 minutes | Servings 4)

Ingredients

- 1 tablespoon schug sauce
- 1/2 teaspoon garlic, minced
- 2 tablespoons olive oil
- 1 cup onions, chopped
- 2 tablespoons balsamic vinegar
- 6 ounces tofu, pressed and cut into 1/4-inch thick slices
- For Vegan Tzatziki:
- 1/2 cucumber, shredded
- 1 teaspoon dill weed, minced
- 2 tablespoons fresh lime juice
- Sea salt and pepper, to taste
- 1 teaspoon garlic, smashed
- 1 cup coconut yogurt

Directions

Place the tofu, garlic, schug sauce, and balsamic vinegar in a ceramic bowl; let your tofu marinate for 30 minutes in your refrigerator.

In a frying pan, heat the olive oil over a moderately-high heat. Cook the tofu with onions for 5 to 6 minutes until it is golden brown.

Then, make the vegan tzatziki by whisking all ingredients in your bowl. Enjoy!

Per serving: 162 Calories; 10.9g Fat; 5.8g Carbs; 9.5g Protein; 3.3g Fiber

EGGS & DAIRY

429. Avocado Boats with Asiago Cheese and Sardines

(Ready in about 25 minutes | Servings 4)

Ingredients

2 large-sized avocados, halved and pitted
4 ounces Asiago cheese, grated
2 ounces canned sardines, flaked
2 tablespoons chives, chopped
2 tablespoons fresh parsley, chopped
1/2 cup cucumbers, diced
Salt and pepper, to taste

Directions

In a mixing bowl, combine the sardines, chives, salt, pepper, parsley, and cucumber. Stuff your avocado halves.

Place the stuffed avocado in a parchment-lined baking pan. Bake in the preheated oven at 355 degrees F for about 20 minutes.

Top with the Asiago cheese and place under the preheated broiler for about 5 minutes or until the cheese is hot and bubbly. Bon appétit!

Per serving: 286 Calories; 23.9g Fat; 6g Carbs; 11.2g Protein; 6g Fiber

430. Italian Eggs with Genoa Salami and Carrot

(Ready in about 25 minutes | Servings 4)

Ingredients

8 eggs, whisked
8 Genoa salami slices
1 carrot, chopped
1/2 cup scallions, chopped
1 serrano pepper, chopped
2 garlic cloves, minced
1/2 teaspoon dried dill weed
1/2 stick butter, at room temperature
Salt and black pepper, to taste

Directions

Melt the butter in a pan that is preheated over a moderately high heat. Now, sauté the scallions for 4 minutes, stirring periodically.

Add the garlic and cook for 1 minute or until it is fragrant. Add serrano pepper and carrot. Cook an additional 4 minutes.

Transfer the mixture to a baking pan that is lightly greased with a non-stick cooking spray. Top with the salami slices.

Pour the eggs over the vegetables and salami; season with salt, pepper, and dill. Bake approximately 18 minutes.

Bon appétit!

Per serving: 310 Calories; 26.2g Fat; 3.9g Carbs; 15.4g Protein; 1.1g Fiber

431. Winter Pancetta and Cheese Bites

(Ready in about 3 hours 15 minutes | Servings 6)

Ingredients

1 cup crushed pork rinds
1/4 teaspoon dried dill weed
1/2 pound pancetta, chopped
2 cloves garlic, crushed
1 cup Colby cheese
1/2 cup dill pickles, chopped and thoroughly squeezed
1 cup grated Parmesan cheese
6 ounces Cottage cheese, curds, 2% fat
6 ounces Ricotta cheese
1/2 teaspoon caraway seeds
Salt and black pepper, to taste
4 cups cauliflower rice
1/2 teaspoon shallot powder
Cooking oil

Directions

Thoroughly combine the cauliflower rice, pancetta, Cottage cheese, Ricotta cheese, Colby cheese, dill pickles, garlic, and 1/2 cup of grated Parmesan.

Stir until everything is well mixed and shape the cauliflower mixture into even balls. Now, transfer to your refrigerator for 3 hours.

Now, in a mixing bowl, thoroughly combine the remaining 1/2 cup of Parmesan cheese, caraway seeds, dill, shallot powder, salt, black pepper and crushed pork rinds.

Roll the cheese ball in the Parmesan mixture until they are completely coated.

Then, heat about 1-inch of oil in a skillet over a moderately high flame. Fry the cheeseballs until they are golden brown on all sides.

Transfer to a paper towel to soak up the excess oil. Bon appétit!

Per serving: 407 Calories; 26.8g Fat; 5.8g Carbs; 33.4g Protein; 1.8g Fiber

432. Breakfast Pancetta Muffins

(Ready in about 30 minutes | Servings 9)

Ingredients

9 eggs
1/2 teaspoon dried dill weed
1/2 cup Monterey Jack cheese, shredded
A bunch of scallions, chopped
1/4 teaspoon garlic powder
9 slices pancetta
Sea salt and ground black pepper, to taste

Directions

Start by preheating your oven to 390 degrees F.

Then, brush a 9-cup muffin pan with oil; line each cup with one slice of pancetta.

In a mixing bowl, thoroughly combine the remaining ingredients.

Divide the egg mixture among the muffin cups. Bake in the preheated oven for 20 minutes.

Bon appétit!

Per serving: 294 Calories; 21.4g Fat; 3.5g Carbs; 21g Protein; 0.1g Fiber

433. Egg Salad with Celery and Hot Sauce

(Ready in about 15 minutes | Servings 8)

Ingredients

1/2 cup celery with leaves, chopped
1 tablespoon Dijon mustard
3/4 cup mayonnaise
1/2 teaspoon fresh lemon juice
2 cups butterhead lettuce, torn into pieces
1 teaspoon hot sauce
10 eggs
1/2 cup onions, chopped
Kosher salt and black pepper, to taste

Directions

Place the eggs in a saucepan and cover them with water by 1 inch. Cover and bring the water to a boil over high heat. Boil for 6 to 7 minutes over medium-high heat.

Peel the eggs and chop them coarsely. Add in the remaining ingredients and toss to combine.

Bon appétit!

Per serving: 174 Calories; 13g Fat; 5.7g Carbs; 7.4g Protein; 0.8g Fiber

434. Scrambled Eggs with Swiss Chard Pesto

(Ready in about 15 minutes | Servings 4)

Ingredients

2 tablespoons butter
8 eggs, well beaten
1/4 cup milk
Salt, to taste
For the Swiss Chard Pesto:
2 cups Swiss chard
2 tablespoons fresh lime juice
A pinch of ground cloves
1 cup Pecorino Romano cheese, grated
1 teaspoon garlic, minced
1/2 cup olive oil

Directions

Melt the butter in a cast-iron skillet over moderately-high flame. Beat the eggs with the milk; salt to taste.

When the butter is just hot, cook the egg mixture, gently stirring to create large soft curds. Cook until the eggs are barely set.

Add all the ingredients for the pesto, except the olive oil, to your blender.

Pulse until your ingredients are coarsely chopped. With the machine running, gradually pour in the olive oil and blend until creamy and uniform. Enjoy!

Per serving: 495 Calories; 45g Fat; 6.3g Carbs; 19.5g Protein; 0.3g Fiber

435. Classic Keto Pan Pizza

(Ready in about 15 minutes | Servings 2)

Ingredients

For the Crust:
1 tablespoon garlic-infused olive oil
1/4 teaspoon cumin seeds, ground
1 teaspoon chipotle pepper
1/2 teaspoon dried coriander leaves
1/4 cup sour cream
2 tablespoons flax seed meal
Salt, to taste
4 eggs, beaten
For the Toppings:
2 ounces 4-cheese Mexican blend, shredded
2 tablespoons tomato paste

Directions

Thoroughly combine all ingredients for the crust, except for the oil.

Heat 1/2 tablespoon of garlic-infused oil in a pan over moderately high heat. Now, spoon 1/2 of the crust mixture into the pan and spread out evenly.

Cook until the edges are set; then, flip the pizza crust and cook on the other side. Turn the broiler on high.

Heat the remaining 1/2 tablespoon of oil in the pan. Repeat with another pizza crust. Spread the tomato paste over the top of each of the prepared pizza crusts.

Divide the Mexican cheese blend among the two pizza crusts.

Broil them on high until the cheese is completely melted. Bon appétit!

Per serving: 397 Calories; 31g Fat; 5.1g Carbs; 22g Protein; 1g Fiber

436. Greek-Style Egg Muffins

(Ready in about 5 minutes | Servings 2)

Ingredients

4 eggs
4 tablespoons Greek-style yogurt
1/4 cup Feta cheese, crumbled
2 tablespoons onions, chopped
Salt and pepper, to taste

Directions

Mix all of the above ingredients in a bowl.

Spoon the mixture into lightly greased mugs.

Microwave for about 70 seconds. Bon appétit!

Per serving: 244 Calories; 17.5g Fat; 2.9g Carbs; 19.2g Protein; 0.9g Fiber

437. Classic Scotch Eggs

(Ready in about 20 minutes | Servings 8)

Ingredients

1 ½ pounds ground beef
1/2 teaspoon cayenne pepper
1 teaspoon dried rosemary, chopped
1/2 teaspoon shallot powder
1/2 cup parmesan cheese, freshly grated
1 teaspoon granulated garlic
8 eggs
Salt and pepper to taste

EGGS & DAIRY

Directions

Boil the eggs until hard-cooked; peel them and rinse under cold, running water. Set aside.

In a mixing bowl, thoroughly combine the other ingredients. Divide the meat mixture among 8 balls; flatten each ball and place a boiled egg on it.

Shape the meat mixture around the egg by using your fingers.

Add the balls to a baking pan that is previously greased with a non-stick cooking spray.

Bake in the preheated oven, at 360 degrees F for 18 minutes, until crisp and golden. Serve right away.

Per serving: 247 Calories; 11.4g Fat; 0.6g Carbs; 33.7g Protein; 0.1g Fiber

438. Sausage and Egg Stuffed Zucchini

(Ready in about 35 minutes | Servings 3)

Ingredients

2 sausages, cooked and crumbled
6 eggs
1/4 teaspoon black pepper, or more to taste
1 tablespoon deli mustard
1/4 teaspoon dried dill weed
3 medium-sized zucchinis, cut into halves
Salt, to taste

Directions

Scoop the flesh from each zucchini halve to make shells; place the zucchini boats on a baking pan.

Spread the mustard on the bottom of each zucchini halve. Divide the crumbled sausage among the zucchini boats.

Crack an egg in each zucchini halve, sprinkle with salt, pepper, and dill.

Bake in the preheated oven at 400 degrees F for 30 minutes or until the zucchini boats are tender.

Bon appétit!

Per serving: 506 Calories; 41g Fat; 4.5g Carbs; 27.5g Protein; 0.4g Fiber

439. Double Cheese Omelet

(Ready in about 15 minutes | Servings 2)

Ingredients

1/2 cup queso fresco cheese, crumbled
2 tablespoons fresh chervil, roughly chopped
1/2 cup Cheddar cheese, grated
2 tablespoons olive oil
1/2 teaspoon habanero pepper, minced
4 eggs, beaten
Salt and pepper, to taste

Directions

In a frying pan, heat the oil over a moderately high heat. Cook the eggs until the edges barely start setting.

Add in the salt, pepper, habanero pepper, and cheese and cook an additional 4 minutes.

Serve with fresh chervil. Bon appétit!

Per serving: 490 Calories; 44.6g Fat; 4.5g Carbs; 22.7g Protein; 0.8g Fiber

440. Baked Egg Zucchini Boats

(Ready in about 35 minutes | Servings 3)

Ingredients

6 eggs
1 tablespoon Dijon mustard
2 sausages, cooked and crumbled
3 medium-sized zucchinis, cut into halves and scoop out the pulp
Salt and pepper, to taste
1/2 teaspoon dried basil

Directions

Place the zucchini boats on a lightly oiled baking sheet. Mix the Dijon mustard, sausages, salt, pepper, and basil.

Spoon the sausage mixture into the zucchini shells. Crack an egg in each zucchini shell.

Bake in the preheated oven at 390 degrees F for 30 to 35 minutes or until tender and cooked through. Enjoy!

Per serving: 506 Calories; 41g Fat; 4.5g Carbs; 27.5g Protein; 0.3g Fiber

441. Sage Pork Sausage Frittata

(Ready in about 35 minutes | Servings 4)

Ingredients

1 teaspoon dried sage, crushed
1/2 pound pork sausages, thinly sliced
8 eggs, beaten
3 tablespoons olive oil
1/2 teaspoon ground black pepper
1/4 teaspoon cayenne pepper
1 cup onion, chopped
1 teaspoon salt
1 teaspoon jalapeno pepper, finely minced
2 garlic cloves, minced

Directions

Heat the oil in a non-stick skillet over a medium-high heat. Now, sauté the onions, peppers and garlic until the onion becomes translucent, about 4 minutes.

Season with salt, black pepper, and cayenne pepper. Then, stir in the sausage and cook, stirring often, until they're no longer pink.

Transfer the mixture to a lightly greased baking dish. Pour the eggs over the top and sprinkle with dried sage.

Bake in the preheated oven at 420 degrees F for 25 minutes.

Bon appétit!

Per serving: 423 Calories; 35.4g Fat; 4.1g Carbs; 22.6g Protein; 0.8g Fiber

442. Spicy Frittata with Asparagus and Cheese

(Ready in about 20 minutes | Servings 4)

Ingredients

3/4 cup Cheddar cheese, grated
1/4 cup fresh parsley, to serve
1 cup asparagus spears, chopped
1 teaspoon curry paste
Salt and pepper, to your liking
2 tablespoons olive oil
8 eggs, beaten
1/2 teaspoon Fresno pepper, minced
1/2 cup onions, chopped

Directions

Begin by preheating your oven to 370 degrees F.

In an oven-proof skillet, heat the oil over a medium heat. Sauté the onions until they are tender and caramelized.

Add in the asparagus and cook until they've softened.

Stir in the eggs, Fresno pepper, curry paste, salt, and pepper. Cook the eggs until the edges barely start setting.

Scatter the cheese over the top of your frittata. Bake your frittata in the preheated oven for about 15 minutes.

Serve with fresh parsley and enjoy!

Per serving: 248 Calories; 17.1g Fat; 6.2g Carbs; 17.6g Protein; 1.6g Fiber

443. Muffin in a Mug

(Ready in about 5 minutes | Servings 2)

Ingredients

1/4 cup Swiss cheese, freshly grated
1/4 teaspoon turmeric powder
1 garlic clove, minced
1/4 cup milk
4 eggs
Salt and pepper, to taste

Directions

Combine the ingredients until well incorporated.

Brush 2 microwave-safe mugs with a non-stick cooking spray (butter-flavored). Spoon the egg mixture into the mugs.

Microwave for about 40 seconds. Stir and microwave for 1 minute more or until they're done. Enjoy!

Per serving: 197 Calories; 13.8g Fat; 2.7g Carbs; 15.7g Protein; 0.1g Fiber

444. American-Style Frittata

(Ready in about 25 minutes | Servings 4)

Ingredients

1/2 stick butter, at room temperature
8 eggs, whisked
1/2 cup onions, chopped
2 garlic cloves, minced
1 habanero pepper, chopped
1 celery rib, chopped
8 pepperoni slices
Salt and pepper, to season

Directions

In a skillet, melt the butter over a moderately high flame. Sauté the onions and garlic for about 3 minutes, stirring continuously to ensure even cooking.

Add in the habanero pepper and celery, and continue to cook for 4 to 5 minutes longer or until just tender and fragrant.

Spoon the mixture into a lightly greased baking dish. Top with the pepperoni slices.

Pour the whisked eggs over the pepperoni layer; season with salt and pepper to taste. Bake for 15 to 18 minutes. Enjoy!

Per serving: 310 Calories; 26.2g Fat; 3.9g Carbs; 15.4g Protein; 0.8g Fiber

445. Crabmeat Scramble with Cheese-Garlic Sauce

(Ready in about 15 minutes | Servings 3)

Ingredients

1 tablespoon butter, room temperature
1/2 teaspoon basil
1 can crabmeat, flaked
1/2 teaspoon rosemary
6 eggs, whisked
For the Sauce:
3 tablespoons mayonnaise
1/2 cup onions, white and green parts, chopped
1/2 teaspoon garlic, minced
3/4 cup cream cheese
Salt and black pepper, to taste

Directions

In a frying pan, melt the butter over a moderately high flame. Cook the eggs, gently stirring to create large soft curds. Cook until the eggs are barely set.

Add in the crabmeat, rosemary and basil, and continue to cook, stirring frequently, until cooked through. Salt to taste.

Make the sauce by whisking all ingredients. Bon appétit!

Per serving: 334 Calories; 26.2g Fat; 4.4g Carbs; 21.1g Protein; 0.4g Fiber

446. Stuffed Avocado with Queso Fresco

(Ready in about 15 minutes | Servings 6)

Ingredients

1/3 cup Queso Fresco, crumbled
1 cup prosciutto, chopped
1 teaspoon stone-ground mustard
1 teaspoon hot paprika
2/3 cup Ricotta cheese
3 avocados, cut into halves and pitted
Salt and pepper, to taste

Directions

Scoop out the avocados; combine the avocado flesh with the remaining ingredients; stir until everything is well incorporated.

Spoon the mixture into the avocado halves.

Place under the preheated broiler for about 5 minutes or until the cheese is hot and bubbly. Bon appétit!

Per serving: 308 Calories; 27g Fat; 6.4g Carbs; 8.8g Protein; 4.9g Fiber

447. Pickled Eggs with Onions

(Ready in about 20 minutes | Servings 5)

Ingredients

10 eggs
1 teaspoon mustard seeds
1 teaspoon fennel seeds
1 tablespoon yellow curry powder
1/2 cup onions, sliced
1 tablespoon sea salt
2 clove garlic, sliced
1 cup white vinegar
1 ¼ cups water

Directions

Place the eggs in a saucepan and cover them with water by 1 inch. Cover and bring the water to a boil over high heat. Boil for 6 to 7 minutes over medium-high heat.

Peel the eggs and add them to a large-sized jar.

Cook the other ingredients in a saucepan pan over moderately-high heat; bring to a boil.

Immediately turn the heat to medium-low and continue to simmer for 5 to 6 minutes. Pour the mixture into the prepared jar. Bon appétit!

Per serving: 145 Calories; 9g Fat; 2.8g Carbs; 11.4g Protein; 0.9g Fiber

448. Pepperoni and Pepper Quiche

(Ready in about 35 minutes | Servings 4)

Ingredients

8 slices pepperoni, chopped
1 cup Asiago cheese, grated
1/2 cup cream cheese
1 chili pepper, deveined and chopped
8 eggs
1 bell pepper, chopped
1 teaspoon yellow mustard
Salt and pepper, to taste

Directions

In a mixing bowl, combine the eggs, salt, pepper, and cheese; spoon the mixture into a lightly greased baking dish.

Add in the other ingredients. Bake in the preheated oven at 365 degrees F for about 30 minutes or until cooked through.

Bon appétit!

Per serving: 334 Calories; 23g Fat; 6.2g Carbs; 25.5g Protein; 4.9g Fiber

449. Keto Burritos with Mushrooms

(Ready in about 20 minutes | Servings 4)

Ingredients

For the Wraps:
6 eggs, separated into yolks and whites
1 tablespoon butter, room temperature
2 tablespoons cream cheese
Sea salt, to taste

For the Filling:
6-8 fresh arugula
1 teaspoon olive oil
4 slices of Swiss cheese
1 large vine-ripened tomatoes, chopped
1 cup Cremini mushrooms, chopped
Salt and pepper, to taste

Directions

Mix all ingredients for the wraps until well combined. Prepare four wraps in a frying pan and set them aside.

Next, heat 1 teaspoon of olive oil over a moderate heat. Cook the mushrooms until they release the liquid; season with salt and pepper.

Assemble the wraps. Divide the sautéed mushrooms, arugula, cheese, and tomatoes between the warm wraps.

Per serving: 172 Calories; 14g Fat; 3.4g Carbs; 9.5g Protein; 1g Fiber

450. Curried Asparagus Frittata

(Ready in about 20 minutes | Servings 4)

Ingredients

1 cup asparagus tips
8 eggs, beaten
3/4 cup Colby cheese, grated
Salt and red pepper, to your liking
1 teaspoon Madras curry paste
2 tablespoons avocado oil
1/2 cup shallots, chopped
1/2 teaspoon jalapeno pepper, minced
1/4 cup fresh cilantro, to serve

Directions

In an ovenproof frying pan, heat the avocado oil over a medium flame. Now, sauté the shallots until they are caramelized.

Add the asparagus tips and cook until they're just tender.

Stir in the eggs, jalapeno pepper and Madras curry paste; season with salt and pepper. Now, cook until the eggs are nearly set.

Scatter the cheese over the top of your frittata. Cook in the preheated oven at 375 degrees F for about 12 minutes, until your frittata is set in the middle. Bon appétit!

Per serving: 248 Calories; 17.1g Fat; 6.2g Carbs; 17.6g Protein; 1.1g Fiber

451. Dijon Mustard and Bacon Deviled Eggs

(Ready in about 20 minutes | Servings 10)

Ingredients

1/2 cup mayonnaise
1 tablespoon Marsala wine
2 teaspoons country-style Dijon mustard
2 teaspoons lemon juice
1/4 teaspoon hot pepper sauce
10 eggs
1/4 cup cooked bacon, chopped
Fresh dill weed sprigs, to serve
Salt and red pepper flakes, to taste

Directions

Place the eggs in a single layer in a pan; cover with 2 inches of water.

Bring to a boil over a high heat; now, reduce the heat and cook, covered, for 1 minute.

Remove from the heat and wait for 15 minutes; rinse.

After that, peel the eggs and halve them lengthwise. Remove the yolks and mash them with a fork. Add the mayonnaise, bacon, lemon juice, wine, mustard, and hot pepper sauce.

Season with salt and crushed red pepper; mix until everything is well combined. Divide the mayonnaise-bacon mixture among the egg whites. Bon appétit!

Per serving: 128 Calories; 9.7g Fat; 3.3g Carbs; 6.8g Protein; 0g Fiber

452. Genoa Salami Mug Muffin

(Ready in about 5 minutes | Servings 3)

Ingredients

1/2 cup American yellow cheese, shredded
1/2 cup cottage cheese
6 eggs
3 slices Genoa salami, chopped
1 teaspoon yellow mustard
3 teaspoons butter, melted
Coarse salt and ground black pepper, to taste

Directions

Grease 3 mason jars with melted butter.

Crack two eggs into each jar. Divide the other ingredients among the two jars.

Cover and shake until everything is well incorporated.

Remove the lids and microwave for 2 minutes on high. Bon appétit!

Per serving: 303 Calories; 22.4g Fat; 3.6g Carbs; 21.6g Protein; 0.1g Fiber

453. Mediterranean-Style Cheese Balls

(Ready in about 10 minutes | Servings 10)

Ingredients

1 ½ cups Cottage cheese, at room temperature
1 ½ cups Colby cheese, shredded
1 teaspoon red pepper flakes
1 ½ tablespoons tomato ketchup, no sugar added
18 fresh basil leaves, snipped
1/3 cup black olives, pitted and chopped
Salt and freshly ground black pepper

Directions

Mix all of the above ingredients until well combined.

Roll the mixture into 18 to 20 balls. Enjoy!

Per serving: 105 Calories; 7.2g Fat; 2.8g Carbs; 7.5g Protein; 0.2g Fiber

454. Gorgonzola Mini Frittatas

(Ready in about 25 minutes | Servings 5)

Ingredients

1 cup gorgonzola cheese, diced
1/2 cup coconut flour
A pinch of kosher salt
A pinch of grated nutmeg
1 teaspoon baking powder
4 slices smoked back bacon
4 eggs, beaten

Directions

Preheat a frying pan over a moderately high heat. Now, cook the bacon, turning with tongs, until it is crisp and browned on both sides; drain your bacon on paper towels.

Chop the bacon and combine it with the other ingredients; stir to combine well.

Grease muffin molds. Fill the prepared molds with batter (3/4 full). Bake in the preheated oven at 390 degrees F for 15 minutes.

Top your muffins with the prepared topping and enjoy!

Per serving: 240 Calories; 15.3g Fat; 6.6g Carbs; 16.1g Protein; 0.3g Fiber

455. Greek Egg and Anchovy Salad

(Ready in about 20 minutes | Servings 8)

Ingredients

1/3 cup Greek-style yogurt
1 cup butterhead lettuces, torn into pieces
1/2 tablespoon deli mustard
8 eggs
2 cans anchovies, drained
1/2 Feta cheese, crumbled
1/2 cup scallions, finely chopped

For Aioli:
1 tablespoon fresh lime juice
2 medium cloves garlic, minced
1 egg
1/2 cup olive oil
Salt, to taste

Directions

Place the eggs in a saucepan and cover them with water by 1 inch. Cover and bring the water to a boil over high heat. Boil for 6 to 7 minutes over medium-high heat.

Peel and chop the eggs. Add in the anchovies, lettuce, scallions, Feta cheese, Greek-style yogurt, mustard.

To make the aioli, blend the egg, garlic, and lemon juice until well combined. Gradually pour in the oil and continue to blend until everything is well incorporated. Salt to taste. Toss the salad with the prepared aioli. Enjoy!

Per serving: 285 Calories; 22.5g Fat; 1.8g Carbs; 19.5g Protein; 0.3g Fiber

456. Grandma's Breakfast Waffles

(Ready in about 20 minutes | Servings 3)

Ingredients

3 ounces Asiago cheese, shredded
1/2 teaspoon dried oregano
3 tablespoons tomato paste
1/2 teaspoon baking powder
1/2 teaspoon baking soda
4 tablespoons ghee
Kosher salt, to taste
3 ounces pancetta, chopped
6 large-sized eggs, separate egg whites and egg yolks

Directions

Thoroughly combine the egg yolks, baking powder, baking soda, ghee, salt, and oregano in a mixing bowl.

Now, beat the egg whites with an electric mixer until pale. Gently mix the egg whites into the egg yolk mixture.

Generously grease a waffle iron. Heat your waffle iron and pour in 1/4 cup of the batter. Cook until golden, about 3 minutes. Repeat until you run out of batter; you will have 6 thin waffles.

Add one waffle back to the waffle iron; spread 1 tablespoon of the tomato paste onto your waffle; top with 1 ounce of pancetta and 1 ounce of shredded cheese.

Top with another waffle; cook until the cheese has melted. Repeat with the remaining ingredients.

Bon appétit!

Per serving: 453 Calories; 37g Fat; 4.5g Carbs; 25.6g Protein; 0.7g Fiber

457. Chinese Dan Hua Tang with Tofu

(Ready in about 15 minutes | Servings 3)

Ingredients

- 1/2 pound extra-firm tofu, cubed
- 1/2 teaspoon curry paste
- 1 tablespoon coconut aminos
- 1 teaspoon butter, softened
- 2 cups vegetable broth
- 1/4 teaspoon cayenne pepper
- 2 eggs, beaten
- Salt and ground black ground, to taste

Directions

In a heavy-bottomed pot, cook the broth, coconut aminos and butter over high heat; bring to a boil.

Immediately turn the heat to a simmer. Stir in the eggs and curry paste, whisking constantly, until well incorporated.

Add in the salt, black pepper, cayenne pepper, and tofu. Partially cover and continue to simmer approximately 2 minutes. Enjoy!

Per serving: 153 Calories; 9.8g Fat; 2.7g Carbs; 15g Protein; 0.5g Fiber

458. Italian Breakfast Roll-Ups

(Ready in about 10 minutes | Servings 5)

Ingredients

- 10 slices Genoa salami
- 10 slices Mortadella
- 4 ounces mayonnaise
- 10 olives, pitted
- 10 slices Provolone cheese

Directions

Spread a thin layer of mayo onto each slice of cheese. Add a slice of Mortadella on top of the mayo.

Top with a slice of the Genoa salami. Roll them up; place olives on top and secure with toothpicks. Bon appétit!

Per serving: 381 Calories; 31.2g Fat; 5.8g Carbs; 17.6g Protein; 0.2g Fiber

459. Omelet with Cherry Tomatoes and Cheese

(Ready in about 15 minutes | Servings 2)

Ingredients

- 1 cup cherry tomatoes, halved
- 1 tablespoon olive oil
- 1/4 teaspoon black peppercorns, crushed
- 1/4 cup goat cheese, crumbled
- 1/4 cup Appenzeller cheese, shredded
- 4 eggs
- Salt, to taste

Directions

In a frying pan, heat the olive oil over a moderate heat. Pour in the eggs; swirl the eggs around using a spatula. Season the eggs with salt and black pepper.

When the eggs are just set and no visible liquid egg remains, top them with the cheese. Fold gently in half with the spatula.

Serve with cherry tomatoes. Bon appétit!

Per serving: 307 Calories; 25g Fat; 2.5g Carbs; 18.5g Protein; 1g Fiber

460. One-Pan Eggs with Chorizo Sausage

(Ready in about 20 minutes | Servings 2)

Ingredients

- 2 tablespoons canola oil
- 4 eggs, whisked
- 1 teaspoon ancho chili pepper, deveined and minced
- 1/2 cup red onions, chopped
- 1/2 cup Hojiblanca olives, pitted and sliced
- 1 teaspoon garlic paste
- 2 rosemary sprigs, leaves picked and chopped
- 6 ounces Chorizo sausage, crumbled
- Salt and black pepper to the taste

Directions

In a frying pan, heat the oil over a moderate flame; cook the red onions until just tender and fragrant, about 4 to 5 minutes.

Add in the garlic, pepper, salt, black pepper, sausage, and olives; continue to cook, stirring constantly, for 7 to 8 minutes.

Stir in the eggs and rosemary leaves; cook for 4 to 5 minutes, lifting and folding the eggs until thickened. Enjoy!

Per serving: 462 Calories; 40.6g Fat; 7.1g Carbs; 16.9g Protein; 2.1g Fiber

461. Egg Salad with Bacon and Scallions

(Ready in about 20 minutes | Servings 4)

Ingredients

- 1/2 cup bacon bits
- 1/3 cup mayonnaise
- 1/2 teaspoon deli mustard
- 2 cups Iceberg lettuce leaves
- 8 eggs
- 1 ½ teaspoons fresh lemon juice
- 1 tablespoon scallions, chopped
- Salt and pepper, to taste

Directions

Place the eggs in a saucepan and cover them with water by 1 inch. Cover and bring the water to a boil over high heat. Boil for 6 to 7 minutes over medium-high heat.

Peel and chop the eggs. Add in the remaining ingredients; gently stir to combine. Bon appétit!

Per serving: 284 Calories; 21.3g Fat; 6.8g Carbs; 16.7g Protein; 0.7g Fiber

462. Italian-Style Fat Bombs

(Ready in about 5 minutes | Servings 6)

Ingredients

- 6 ounces cream cheese
- 2 hard-boiled eggs, chopped
- 1 ½ tablespoons fresh cilantro, chopped
- 6 ounces Genovese salami, chopped
- Salt and pepper, to taste

Directions

Thoroughly combine all ingredients until well incorporated. Shape into 12 balls.

Keep in your refrigerator for up to 3 to 4 days. Enjoy!

Per serving: 156 Calories; 12.2g Fat; 1.6g Carbs; 9.7g Protein; 0g Fiber

463. Greek Yogurt and Apple Muffins

(Ready in about 20 minutes | Servings 6)

Ingredients

3/4 Feta cheese
3 eggs, beaten
4 tablespoons Swerve
1/2 teaspoon vanilla paste
1 apple, sliced
2 tablespoons ground almonds
1/4 cup Greek-style yogurt

Directions

Begin by preheating an oven to 365 degrees F.

Thoroughly combine all ingredients until well mixed. Spoon the batter into lightly buttered muffin cups.

Bake in the preheated oven for about 15 minutes. Place on a wire rack before unmolding. Enjoy!

Per serving: 81 Calories; 3.5g Fat; 6.7g Carbs; 5.5g Protein; 2.1g Fiber

464. Greek-Style Stuffed Tomatoes

(Ready in about 45 minutes | Servings 5)

Ingredients

1/4 cup Greek-style yogurt
5 vine-ripened tomatoes, cut into halves and scoop out the pulp
4 tablespoons fresh shallots, chopped
1 cup Ricotta cheese, at room temperature
1 egg, whisked
1 tablespoon fresh green garlic, minced
1 ½ cups Swiss cheese, shredded
2 teaspoons olive oil
Salt and ground black pepper, to taste

Directions

Start by preheating your oven to 355 degrees F.

Then, thoroughly combine the cheese, yogurt, egg, green garlic, shallots, salt, and pepper. Stuff the tomato halves with this filling.

Brush the stuffed tomatoes with olive oil. Bake in the preheated oven for about 30 minutes.

Per serving: 306 Calories; 27.5g Fat; 4.4g Carbs; 11.3g Protein; 1.3g Fiber

465. Italian Mini Frittatas with Spinach and Bacon

(Ready in about 40 minutes | Servings 5)

Ingredients

1 Italian pepper, chopped
1/2 teaspoon chipotle powder
1 cup spinach, torn into pieces
1 cup Asiago cheese, shredded
1 tablespoon fresh coriander, chopped
1 tablespoon olive oil
1 onion, chopped
3 slices bacon, chopped
8 eggs, whisked
Salt and pepper, to taste

Directions

Begin by preheating your oven to 380 degrees F.

Heat the oil in frying pan over medium-high heat; cook the onion for about 6 minutes or until caramelized.

Add in the pepper and spinach, and continue to sauté for 4 to 5 minutes.

Add in the bacon and continue to cook for 3 to 4 minutes. Stir in the remaining ingredients. Spoon the mixture into a lightly oiled muffin pan.

Bake in the preheated oven for about 22 minutes. Bon appétit!

Per serving: 261 Calories; 16g Fat; 6.6g Carbs; 21.1g Protein; 0.9g Fiber

466. Old-Fashioned Scotch Eggs

(Ready in about 20 minutes | Servings 8)

Ingredients

1/2 cup Romano cheese, freshly grated
1 teaspoon garlic, smashed
1/2 teaspoon onion powder
1 ½ pounds ground pork
8 eggs
1 teaspoon Italian seasoning mix
1/2 teaspoon red pepper flakes, crushed

Directions

Place the eggs in a saucepan and cover them with water by 1 inch. Cover and bring the water to a boil over high heat.

Boil for 6 to 7 minutes over medium-high heat; peel the eggs and rinse them under running water.

Thoroughly combine the remaining ingredients. Divide the mixture into 8 pieces; now, using your fingers, shape the meat mixture around the eggs.

Bake in the preheated oven at 365 degrees F for 20minutes until golden brown. Enjoy!

Per serving: 247 Calories; 11.4g Fat; 0.6g Carbs; 33.7g Protein; 0.1g Fiber

467. Mediterranean Cheese Logs

(Ready in about 10 minutes + chilling time | Servings 15)

Ingredients

14 ounces Swiss cheese, grated
1/2 cup mayonnaise
1 teaspoon lemon juice
14 ounces Ricotta cheese, at room temperature
1/2 cup pine nuts, finely chopped
1 tablespoon Mediterranean spice mix

Directions

Combine all ingredients, except for the pine nut, in a mixing bowl. Place the mixture in your refrigerator for about 4 hours or until firm.

Shape the mixture into two logs and roll them over chopped pine nuts. Enjoy!

Per serving: 209 Calories; 18.9g Fat; 3.7g Carbs; 6.6g Protein; 0.3g Fiber

468. Omelet with Asiago and Boursin Cheese

(Ready in about 15 minutes | Servings 2)

Ingredients

1/2 cup Asiago cheese
1/2 cup Boursin cheese
4 eggs, beaten
1/4 teaspoon Pimenta, ground
1/4 teaspoon cayenne pepper
2 tablespoons fresh chervil, roughly chopped
2 tablespoons avocado oil
Salt and black pepper, to taste

Directions

Heat the oil in a pan that is preheated over a moderately high heat.

Season the eggs with salt, black pepper, ground Pimenta, and cayenne pepper. Add the seasoned eggs to the pan; tilt the pan to spread the eggs out evenly.

Once set, top your eggs with the cheese. Slice the omelet into two halves. Garnish with fresh chervil.

Bon appétit!

Per serving: 490 Calories; 44.6g Fat; 4.5g Carbs; 22.7g Protein; 0.3g Fiber

469. Mediterranean Salad with Almond-Cheese Balls

(Ready in about 20 minutes | Servings 6)

Ingredients

For the Cheese Balls:
1 cup blue cheese, crumbled
1/2 cup Romano cheese, shredded
1 cup almond meal
1 teaspoon baking powder
3 eggs
Salt and pepper, to taste

For the Salad:
1 head Iceberg lettuce
1 teaspoon Mediterranean seasoning blend
1/2 cup scallions, thinly sliced
1/2 cup radishes, thinly sliced
1 cup grape tomatoes, halved
1/3 cup mayonnaise

Directions

Thoroughly combine all ingredients for the cheese balls. Roll the mixture into bite-sized balls. Bake the cheese balls in the preheated oven at 380 degrees F for 8 to 10 minutes.

Toss all the salad ingredients in a large bowl.

Serve the cheese balls over your salad and enjoy!

Per serving: 234 Calories; 16.7g Fat; 5.9g Carbs; 12.4g Protein; 4.3g Fiber

470. Loaded Guacamole Tacos

(Ready in about 10 minutes | Servings 6)

Ingredients

1 cup cream cheese
2 cups arugula
1 teaspoon taco seasoning mix
1 ½ cups guacamole
1 pound Monterey-Jack cheese, grated

Directions

Thoroughly combine the cheese and taco seasoning mix.

On a parchment-lined baking sheet, place 1/4 cup piles of cheese 2 inches apart. Press the cheese down lightly.

Bake at 350 degrees F for about 7 minutes or until the edges of your tacos are brown.

Assemble your tacos. Top with the guacamole, cream cheese and arugula. Enjoy!

Per serving: 370 Calories; 30g Fat; 4.9g Carbs; 19.5g Protein; 4g Fiber

471. Keto Sausage Muffins

(Ready in about 10 minutes | Servings 3)

Ingredients

3 beef sausages, chopped
6 eggs, separated into yolks and whites
1/2 teaspoon smoked paprika
1 cup Asiago cheese, freshly grated
1/2 teaspoon dried sage
1 teaspoon butter, melted
Coarse salt and freshly ground black pepper, to taste

Directions

Begin by preheating your oven to 420 degrees F. Lightly grease a muffin pan with melted butter.

Now, beat the egg whites with an electric mixer until stiff peaks form. Add the seasonings, cheese, and sausage.

Pour into muffin cups and bake for 4 minutes.

Now, add an egg to each cup. Bake for 4 more minutes. Leave the cups to cool. Bon appétit!

Per serving: 423 Calories; 34.1g Fat; 2.2g Carbs; 26.5g Protein; 0.2g Fiber

472. Mediterranean Eggs with Sausage and Herbs

(Ready in about 20 minutes | Servings 2)

Ingredients

4 eggs, whisked
6 ounces sausage, crumbled
1 thyme sprig, chopped
1 teaspoon habanero pepper, deveined and minced
1/2 teaspoon dried marjoram, chopped
1 teaspoon smashed garlic
1/2 cup ripe olives, pitted and sliced
2 tablespoons olive oil
1/2 cup leeks, chopped
Salt and black pepper, to taste

Directions

Heat the oil in a non-stick skillet over medium heat; now, sauté the leeks until they are just tender, about 4 minutes.

Add the garlic, habanero pepper, salt, black pepper, and sausage; cook, stirring frequently, for 8 minutes longer.

Now, pour in the eggs and sprinkle with thyme and marjoram; cook an additional 4 minutes, stirring with a spoon. Garnish with olives.

Bon appétit!

Per serving: 462 Calories; 40.6g Fat; 6.1g Carbs; 16.9g Protein; 2.2g Fiber

473. Provençal Eggs with Bayonne Ham

(Ready in about 20 minutes | Servings 5)

Ingredients

5 eggs
4 slices Bayonne ham, chopped
1/2 cup fire-roasted tomatoes, diced
1 clove garlic, minced
1 ½ cups Comté cheese, shredded
1/2 cup onions, chopped
1 tablespoon butter
1 teaspoon Herbes de Provence
1/4 cup chicken broth

Directions

In an oven-proof pan, melt the butter over medium-high heat. Now, cook the Bayonne ham for about 5 minutes until crisp; reserve.

Then, sauté the onions in the pan drippings. Add in the tomatoes, garlic, Herbes de Provence, and broth; continue to cook for 5 to 6 minutes more.

Now, create 5 holes in the vegetable mixture. Crack an egg into each hole.

Bake in the preheated oven at 350 degrees F for about 18 minutes until the egg whites are completely cooked through. Top with reserved Bayonne ham.

Top with the cheese. Bake the thawed Eggs Provencal at 200 degrees F until they are completely warm. Enjoy!

Per serving: 444 Calories; 35.3g Fat; 2.7g Carbs; 29.8g Protein; 1g Fiber

474. Frittata a La Mexicana

(Ready in about 25 minutes | Servings 6)

Ingredients

1 tablespoon butter, room temperature
1/2 cup Mexican cheese blend, shredded
10 eggs
1 Spanish pepper, chopped
1 ½ cups spinach
1 large onion, chopped
1 teaspoon chipotle paste
2 garlic cloves, minced
Salt and black pepper, to taste
1/3 cup Crema Mexicana

Directions

Preheat your oven to 365 degrees F.

In an oven-proof skillet, melt the butter over a moderately high flame. Sauté the onion until caramelized and fragrant.

Add in the garlic, Spanish peppers, and chipotle paste, and continue to cook for about 4 minutes more.

Add in the spinach and continue to cook for 2 minutes or until it wilts. Whisk the eggs, salt, pepper and Crema Mexicana.

Spoon the egg/cheese mixture into the skillet.

Bake in the preheated oven for 8 to 10 minutes or until your frittata is golden on top.

Top with the Mexican cheese blend and bake an additional 5 minutes or until the cheese is hot and bubbly. Enjoy!

Per serving: 225 Calories; 17g Fat; 5.1g Carbs; 13.2g Protein; 0.9g Fiber

475. Amish Pickled Eggs

(Ready in about 20 minutes | Servings 5)

Ingredients

1 tablespoon yellow curry powder
1 teaspoon yellow mustard seeds
1 cup cider vinegar
1 ¼ cups water
1/2 cup onions, sliced
3 cardamom pods
2 clove garlic, sliced
1 tablespoon salt
10 eggs

Directions

Boil the eggs until hard-cooked; peel them and rinse under cold, running water. Add the peeled eggs to a large-sized jar.

Add all remaining ingredients to a pan that is preheated over a moderately high heat; bring to a rapid boil.

Now, turn the heat to medium-low; let it simmer for 6 minutes. Bon appétit!

Per serving: 145 Calories; 9g Fat; 2.8g Carbs; 11.4g Protein; 0g Fiber

476. Italian-Style Cheeseburger Casserole

(Ready in about 45 minutes | Servings 6)

Ingredients

8 eggs
1/2 cup Colby cheese, grated
1/2 ground pork
1 medium leek, chopped
2 tomatoes, thinly sliced
1/4 cup double cream
1 Italian pepper, chopped
1/2 pound ground beef
1 garlic clove, chopped
2 zucchinis, thinly sliced
Salt and pepper, to taste

Directions

Preheat a lightly greased non-stick skillet over medium-high heat. Now, brown the ground meat, leek, garlic and Italian pepper for about 5 minutes, stirring periodically. Season with salt and pepper to taste.

Spoon the meat layer on the bottom of a lightly greased baking pan. Place the zucchini slices on top. Top with tomato slices.

Beat the cream, eggs and cheese in a mixing dish. Spread this mixture on the top of the vegetables.

Bake in the preheated oven at 360 degrees F for about 45 minutes or until cooked through. Enjoy!

Per serving: 310 Calories; 18.3g Fat; 3.8g Carbs; 30.7g Protein; 0.6g Fiber

477. Egg, Mortadella and Mayo Fat Bombs

(Ready in about 5 minutes + chilling time | Servings 6)

Ingredients

6 slices Mortadella, chopped
1/2 cup cream cheese, softened
1/2 teaspoon cayenne pepper
6 hard-boiled eggs, peeled and chopped
1/2 teaspoon Italian seasonings
1/3 cup mayonnaise
Sea salt and ground black pepper, to taste

Directions

Combine all of the above ingredients in a mixing dish.

Shape the mixture into balls.

Transfer the balls to the refrigerator for 1 hour. Bon appétit!

Per serving: 327 Calories; 25.7g Fat; 5.4g Carbs; 17g Protein; 0.1g Fiber

478. Romano Cheese and Sausage Muffins

(Ready in about 10 minutes | Servings 3)

Ingredients

1 cup Romano cheese, freshly grated
1 tablespoon olive oil
1/2 teaspoon cayenne pepper
6 eggs
1 pound beef sausages, chopped
Sea salt and black pepper, to season

Directions

Whisk the eggs until pale and frothy. Add in the remaining ingredients and stir to combine.

Pour the mixture into a lightly greased muffin pan. Bake in the preheated oven at 400 degrees F for 5 to 6 minutes. Bon appétit!

Per serving: 423 Calories; 34.1g Fat; 2.2g Carbs; 26.5g Protein; 0g Fiber

479. Baked Cheesy Avocado Boats

(Ready in about 20 minutes | Servings 4)

Ingredients

2 ounces Swiss cheese, grated
1 tablespoon fresh parsley, coarsely chopped
2 eggs, beaten
2 ounces goat cheese, crumbled
1/2 teaspoon garlic powder
2 avocados, halved and pitted, skin on
Salt and pepper, to taste

Directions

Start by preheating your oven to 355 degrees F. Place the avocado halves in a baking dish.

In a mixing dish, thoroughly combine the eggs with cheese, salt, pepper, garlic powder, and parsley. Spoon the mixture into the avocado halves.

Bake for about 18 minutes or until everything is cooked through. Bon appétit!

Per serving: 342 Calories; 30.4g Fat; 6.5g Carbs; 11.1g Protein; 4.8g Fiber

480. Folded Omelet with Prosciutto di Parma

(Ready in about 10 minutes | Servings 2)

Ingredients

4 eggs, beaten
4 ounces Asiago cheese, grated
4 slices Prosciutto di Parma, chopped
1 teaspoon Italian herb mix
Sea salt and black pepper, to season

Directions

Preheat a slightly greased frying pan over medium-high heat.

Add in the eggs, Italian herb mix, salt, and black pepper. When the eggs are just set and no visible liquid egg remains, top with Asiago cheese. Fold gently in half with the spatula.

Cook an additional 1 to 2 minutes or until cooked through. Bon appétit!

Per serving: 431 Calories; 33.1g Fat; 2.7g Carbs; 30.3g Protein; 0.3g Fiber

481. Deviled Eggs with Peppers and Cheese

(Ready in about 20 minutes | Servings 5)

Ingredients

2 tablespoons goat cheese, crumbled
2 tablespoons bell peppers, minced
1/2 teaspoon red pepper flakes
1/4 cup mayonnaise
2 tablespoons shallot, finely chopped
2 tablespoons celery, finely chopped
10 eggs
Salt and black pepper, to taste

Directions

Place the eggs in a saucepan and cover them with water by 1 inch. Cover and bring the water to a boil over high heat. Boil for 6 to 7 minutes over medium-high heat.

Peel the eggs and slice them in half lengthwise; mix the yolks with the remaining ingredients.

Divide the mixture between the egg whites and arrange the deviled eggs on a nice serving platter. Enjoy!

Per serving: 177 Calories; 12.7g Fat; 4.6g Carbs; 11.4g Protein; 0.4g Fiber

482. Gorgonzola Cheese and Onion Soup

(Ready in about 20 minutes | Servings 4)

Ingredients

2 tablespoons butter
1 chili pepper, finely chopped
1/2 cup white onions, chopped
1 celery stalk, chopped
1 teaspoon ginger-garlic paste
1 ½ tablespoons flaxseed meal
2 cups water
6 ounces Gorgonzola cheese, shredded
1 ½ cups milk
Salt and pepper, to taste

Directions

Melt the butter in a heavy-bottomed pot over a moderately high heat. Sauté the onions, celery and pepper until tender and fragrant.

Add in the garlic paste, flaxseed meal, water, and milk and bring to a boil; immediately, turn the heat to medium-low. Partially cover, and continue to simmer for 8 to 10 minutes.

Fold in the Gorgonzola cheese and remove from the heat. Season with salt and pepper. Enjoy!

Per serving: 296 Calories; 14.1g Fat; 6.4g Carbs; 14.2g Protein; 1.5g Fiber

FAST SNACKS & APPETIZERS

483. Glazed Portobello Mushrooms

(Ready in about 10 minutes | Servings 4)

Ingredients

1 pound Portobello mushrooms, sliced
2 teaspoons olive oil
1 tablespoon soy sauce
Salt and pepper, to taste
1 tablespoon butter
2 cloves garlic, minced

Directions

Heat the oil and butter in a large skillet that is preheated over a moderate heat. Add the garlic and cook until aromatic, 30 seconds or so.

Stir in the mushrooms and cook them for 3 minutes, allowing them to caramelize.

Now, add the soy sauce, salt and pepper; cook for 4 minutes more or to the desired doneness.

Enjoy!

Per serving: 75 Calories; 5.2g Fat; 3.3g Carbs; 2.9g Protein; 1.8g Fiber

484. Country-Style Meatballs

(Ready in about 15 minutes | Servings 10)

Ingredients

1 egg, beaten
1/3 cup double cream
3/4 pound ground turkey
1/2 pound ground pork
2 garlic cloves, finely minced
1 teaspoon shallot powder
1/2 teaspoon mustard seeds
1 teaspoon hot sauce
1/4 cup pork rinds, crushed
1/3 cup Parmesan cheese, grated
Sea salt and black pepper, to taste
1 teaspoon fresh basil, minced

Directions

In a mixing bowl, combine all ingredients until everything is well incorporated. Roll the mixture into small balls and arrange them on a parchment-lined baking sheet.

Bake in the preheated oven at 390 degrees F for 8 to 10 minutes. Then, flip them over and cook another 8 minutes until they are browned and slightly crisp on top. Bon appétit!

Per serving: 158 Calories; 7.9g Fat; 0.4g Carbs; 20.4g Protein; 0.1g Fiber

485. Rustic Almond and Gorgonzola Balls

(Ready in about 25 minutes | Servings 2)

Ingredients

1 tablespoon fresh cilantro, chopped
1 oz Gorgonzola cheese
2 tablespoons almonds, chopped
1 ounce soft cheese, room temperature
1 cucumber, grated

Directions

Throw the cucumbers into a colander and sprinkle with sea salt. Let it stand for about 30 minutes and then, press your cucumber to drain away the excess liquid.

Add in the cheese and cilantro; stir to combine well. Place the chopped almonds in a shallow dish.

Form the mixture into 4 balls and roll them over the chopped almonds. Bon appétit!

Per serving: 133 Calories; 9.9g Fat; 6.8g Carbs; 6g Protein; 2.6g Fiber

486. Cauliflower Florets with Greek Yogurt Dip

(Ready in about 30 minutes | Servings 6)

Ingredients

1 pound cauliflower florets
1/2 teaspoon garlic, minced
1 shallot, finely chopped
1 ½ cups cheddar cheese, grated
Salt and pepper, to taste
3 eggs, whisked
For Greek Dip:
2 tablespoons mayonnaise
1/2 teaspoon garlic, minced
1 teaspoon lime juice
1/2 cup Greek yogurt
1/2 cup feta cheese

Directions

Parboil the cauliflower in a pot of a lightly-salted water until crisp-tender, for 5 to 6 minutes.

Then, place the cauliflower florets, cheese, eggs, shallot, garlic, salt, and pepper in your food processor. Pulse until well blended.

Roll the cauliflower mixture into bite-sized balls and arrange them in a parchment-lined baking pan.

Bake in the preheated oven at 395 degrees F for about 20 minutes. Meanwhile, make the sauce by whisking the remaining ingredients. Enjoy!

Per serving: 182 Calories; 13.1g Fat; 5.9g Carbs; 11.5g Protein; 1.7g Fiber

487. Camembert and Bacon Fat Bombs

(Ready in about 15 minutes + chilling time | Servings 5)

Ingredients

3 ounces bacon
6 ounces Camembert
1 chili pepper, seeded and minced
1/2 teaspoon red pepper flakes, crushed

Directions

Cook the bacon over a moderately high flame until it is browned on all sides; chop the bacon and set aside.

Mix the remaining ingredients until well blended. Place the mixture in your refrigerator for 1 hour.

Roll the mixture into bite-sized balls; roll the balls over the chopped bacon. Serve well chilled!

Per serving: 206 Calories; 16.5g Fat; 0.6g Carbs; 13.4g Protein; 0.1g Fiber

488. Loaded Cheesy Meatballs

(Ready in about 40 minutes | Servings 5)

Ingredients

2 ounces Romano cheese, grated
1 tablespoon Dijon mustard
1 teaspoon ancho chili powder
2 eggs, whisked
1/3 pound ground beef
1/2 cup ground almonds
2 tablespoons buttermilk
1/2 yellow onion, chopped
2 cloves garlic, minced
Salt and ground black pepper, to taste
1/3 pound ground turkey
1/3 pound ground pork

Directions

Thoroughly combine all of the above ingredients, except for the ground almonds, in a mixing dish.

Grease your hands with oil and roll the mixture into 20 meatballs. Place the ground almond in a shallow bowl.

Toss your meatballs in the ground almond until they're completely coated.

Heat up a non-stick skillet over a moderately high heat. Now, spritz the bottom and sides of the skillet with a non-stick cooking spray.

Cook your meatballs about 13 minutes, until they're golden brown all around

Bon appétit!

Per serving: 244 Calories; 13.3g Fat; 3.7g Carbs; 28.1g Protein; 0.6g Fiber

489. Italian Pizza Dip

(Ready in about 20 minutes | Servings 10)

Ingredients

1 cup marinara sauce
2 ounces Parmesan cheese, shredded
1/2 teaspoon dried oregano
8 ounces cream cheese, room temperature
1 teaspoon dried basil
1/2 cup black olives, to garnish
8 ounces pepperoni, chopped
1/2 teaspoon cayenne pepper
Salt and black pepper, to taste

Directions

Begin by preheating your oven to 365 degrees F.

Mix the cheese, marinara sauce, and spices in a bowl. Place the mixture in a lightly oiled baking dish.

Top with the pepperoni and olives and bake for 15 to 18 minutes or until hot and bubbly on top.

Store in your refrigerator for 3 to 4 days. Enjoy!

Per serving: 160 Calories; 12.7g Fat; 2.4g Carbs; 8.9g Protein; 0.8g Fiber

490. Tuna Deviled Eggs

(Ready in about 20 minutes | Servings 6)

Ingredients

1 can tuna in spring water, drained
12 eggs
2 pickled jalapenos, minced
Salt and black pepper, to taste
1/3 cup mayonnaise
1/2 teaspoon smoked cayenne pepper
1/4 teaspoon fresh or dried dill weed

Directions

Place the eggs in a wide pot; cover with cold water by 1 inch. Bring to a rapid boil.

Decrease the heat to medium-low; let them simmer an additional 10 minutes.

Peel the eggs and rinse them under running water.

Slice each egg in half lengthwise and remove the yolks. Thoroughly combine the yolks with the remaining ingredients.

Divide the mixture among the egg whites. Bon appétit!

Per serving: 203 Calories; 13.3g Fat; 3.8g Carbs; 17.2g Protein; 0.2g Fiber

491. Keto Chips with Guacamole

(Ready in about 20 minutes | Servings 10)

Ingredients

For the chips:
3/4 cup almond meal
2 tablespoons canola oil
2 tablespoons flax seed meal
1/4 teaspoon baking powder
1/4 cup psyllium husk powder
1 tablespoon coconut oil
For the Guacamole:
Juice of 1 fresh lemon
2 tablespoons fresh cilantro, chopped
2 garlic cloves, finely minced
1 cup tomatoes, chopped
2 ripe avocados, seeded and peeled
Salt and pepper, to taste
1 serrano jalapeno pepper, stems and seeds removed, minced
1/2 cup green onions, chopped

Directions

Mix all ingredients for the tortilla chips. Pour in hot water to form a dough.

Place the dough in between two large pieces of parchment pepper; roll it out as thin as possible. Cut the dough into triangles.

Bake your tortilla chips in the preheated oven at 360 degrees F for about 12 minutes until the chips are crisp, but not too browned.

Make your guacamole by mixing the remaining ingredients in your blender or food processor. Enjoy!

Per serving: 109 Calories; 8.4g Fat; 5.3g Carbs; 2.2g Protein; 3.1g Fiber

492. Barbecued Cocktail Wieners

(Ready in about 2 hours 30 minutes | Servings 6)

Ingredients

1 tablespoon Erythritol
1 bottle barbecue sauce, no sugar added
1 teaspoon shallot powder
1 teaspoon porcini powder
1 teaspoon granulated garlic
3 tablespoons deli mustard
1 ½ pounds mini cocktail sausages

Directions

Sear the sausage in a preheated non-stick skillet for 3 to 4 minutes.

Place all ingredients in your slow cooker.

Cook on the Lowest setting for 2 hours. Serve with cocktail sticks or toothpicks. Enjoy!

Per serving: 271 Calories; 22.2g Fat; 4.5g Carbs; 12.3g Protein; 3.2g Fiber

493. Balkan-Style Roll-Ups

(Ready in about 10 minutes | Servings 5)

Ingredients

10 slices bacon
10 slices Cheddar cheese
10 olives, pitted
4 ounces mayonnaise
10 slices Kulen salami

Directions

Spread a thin layer of mayo onto each slice of Cheddar cheese. Add a slice of bacon on top of the mayo.

Top with a slice of salami. Roll them up, garnish with olives and secure with toothpicks.

Enjoy!

Per serving: 381 Calories; 31.2g Fat; 4.8g Carbs; 17.6g Protein; 0.4g Fiber

494. Cheddar Cheese, Artichoke and Chive Dip

(Ready in about 5 minutes | Servings 8)

Ingredients

1/2 cup Cheddar cheese, shredded
1 teaspoon garlic, minced
4 tablespoons chives
1/2 pound cream cheese
1 teaspoon cayenne pepper
2 tablespoons spring onions
1/2 cup mayonnaise
12 ounces canned artichoke hearts, drained
Salt and black pepper, to taste

Directions

In a deep saucepan, combine the artichoke hearts and cream cheese over the lowest heat. Let the cheese melt for a couple of minutes.

Remove from the heat and add in the remaining ingredients.

Taste and adjust the seasonings. Enjoy!

Per serving: 157 Calories; 11g Fat; 5.9g Carbs; 6.5g Protein; 2.7g Fiber

495. Double Cheese, Mayo and Pepper Dip

(Ready in about 35 minutes | Servings 10)

Ingredients

1 ¼ cups Colby cheese, grated
10 ounces cream cheese, room temperature
1 cup mayonnaise
1 jar (17-ounce) roasted red peppers, drained and chopped
1 teaspoon deli mustard
Salt and black pepper, to taste

Directions

In a mixing bowl, combine the ingredients until everything is well combined.

Spoon the mixture into a lightly greased baking pan.

Bake in the preheated oven at 355 degrees F for about 30 minutes, rotating the baking pan halfway through the cook time. Bon appétit!

Per serving: 228 Calories; 17.2g Fat; 5.7g Carbs; 10.2g Protein; 0.5g Fiber

496. Bacon and Cheese-Stuffed Mushrooms

(Ready in about 25 minutes | Servings 6)

Ingredients

2 ounces cheddar cheese, grated
3 slices of bacon, finely chopped
6 large-sized button mushrooms, stems removed
2 tablespoons fresh parsley, minced
1 teaspoon fresh basil, minced
3 teaspoons olive oil
1 tablespoon coconut aminos
Salt and black pepper, to taste

Directions

Toss the mushroom caps with the olive oil, coconut amions, salt, and black pepper.

In a mixing bowl, thoroughly combine the bacon, parsley, basil, and cheese. Divide the filling between the mushroom caps.

Place the stuffed mushrooms on a parchment-lined baking pan. Bake in the preheated oven at 360 degrees F for 18 to 20 minutes or until just tender and fragrant. Enjoy!

Per serving: 98 Calories; 5.8g Fat; 3.9g Carbs; 8.4g Protein; 0.5g Fiber

497. Crispy Zucchini Bites

(Ready in about 40 minutes | Servings 4)

Ingredients

4 zucchinis, cut into thick slices
1/2 teaspoon basil
1/2 teaspoon oregano
2 tablespoons olive oil
2 egg whites
Salt and pepper, to taste

Directions

Toss the zucchini with the remaining ingredients.

Roast in the preheated oven at 410 degrees F for about 30 minutes until the slices are crispy and golden. Enjoy!

Per serving: 91 Calories; 6.1g Fat; 6g Carbs; 4.2g Protein; 0.4g Fiber

498. Roasted Vegetable with Spicy Dip

(Ready in about 45 minutes | Servings 4)

Ingredients

2 celery stalks, cut into sticks
2 bell peppers, sliced
1 onion, sliced
1/4 cup olive oil
2 garlic cloves, minced
1 tablespoon fresh cilantro, minced
1/2 teaspoon cayenne pepper
For the Spicy Sour Cream Dip:
1 ½ cups cream cheese
2 tablespoons aioli
3/4 teaspoon deli mustard
1 chili pepper, finely minced
1 tablespoon lemon juice
Salt and pepper, to taste
2 tablespoons basil, chopped

FAST SNACKS & APPETIZERS

Directions

Begin by preheating your oven to 395 degrees F. Line a baking pan with a piece of parchment paper.

Toss your vegetables with the olive oil, garlic, cilantro, and cayenne pepper.

Arrange the vegetables on the baking pan and roast for 35 to 40 minutes, tossing them halfway through.

Thoroughly combine all ingredients for the dip. Enjoy!

Per serving: 357 Calories; 35.8g Fat; 5.2g Carbs; 3.4g Protein; 1.1g Fiber

499. Cheesy Chouriço Bites

(Ready in about 15 minutes + chilling time | Servings 5)

Ingredients

10 ounces Ricotta cheese, softened
8 Kalamata olives, pitted
1/4 cup mayonnaise
2 teaspoons tomato paste
1/2 teaspoon deli mustard
10 ounces chorizo, chopped

Directions

Heat up the skillet over a moderate flame. Now, cook the chorizo until well browned. Transfer it to a mixing bowl.

Add the remaining ingredients and transfer to your refrigerator until it is well chilled.

Bon appétit!

Per serving: 327 Calories; 25.7g Fat; 6.4g Carbs; 17g Protein; 0.3g Fiber

500. Cheese Sticks with Red Pepper Dip

(Ready in about 40 minutes | Servings 8)

Ingredients

3/4 cup Romano cheese, grated
1/3 teaspoon cumin powder
3 tablespoons almond meal
2 (8-ounce) packages Colby cheese, cut into sticks
1 teaspoon baking powder
1/3 teaspoon dried rosemary
2 eggs
Salt and red pepper flakes, to serve

For Roasted Red Pepper Dip:
1 teaspoon fresh garlic, minced
1 cup Ricotta cheese
1/3 cup sour cream
3/4 cup roasted red peppers, drained and chopped
1 tablespoon yellow mustard
Black pepper to taste

Directions

In a shallow bowl, whisk the eggs until pale and frothy. In a separate shallow bowl, mix the Romano cheese, almond meal, baking powder, and spices.

Dip the cheese stick into the eggs, and then dredge them into dry mixture. Place in your freezer for about 30 minutes.

Deep fry the cheese sticks for 5 to 6 minutes. Prepare the sauce by whisking the ingredients. Enjoy!

Per serving: 200 Calories; 16.9g Fat; 3.7g Carbs; 9.4g Protein; 1.1g Fiber

501. 15-Minute Taco Cheese Chips

(Ready in about 15 minutes | Servings 6)

Ingredients

1 tablespoon Taco seasoning mix
3 cups Mexican blend cheese, shredded

Directions

Toss the shredded cheese with the Taco seasoning mix.

Drop tablespoons of this mixture into small piles. Roast in the preheated oven at 410 degrees F for about 12 minutes.

Enjoy!

Per serving: 268 Calories; 20.4g Fat; 3.4g Carbs; 18.1g Protein; 0g Fiber

502. Paprika Bacon Crisps

(Ready in about 20 minutes | Servings 4)

Ingredients

1 tablespoon smoked paprika
1 tablespoon mustard
12 bacon strips, cut into small squares

Directions

Preheat your oven to 360 degrees F

Toss the bacon strips with the paprika and mustard.

Arrange the bacon squares on a parchment lined baking sheet. Bake for 10 to 15 minutes. Enjoy!

Per serving: 118 Calories; 10g Fat; 1.9g Carbs; 5g Protein; 0.7g Fiber

503. Cottage Cheese Balls

(Ready in about 10 minutes + chilling time | Servings 6)

Ingredients

1/2 cup fresh chives, finely chopped
1/4 teaspoon champagne vinegar
Salt and pepper, to taste
1 cup Cottage cheese
3 tablespoons butter

Directions

Thoroughly combine the cheese, butter, and vinegar. Season with salt and pepper to taste.

Place the cheese mixture in the refrigerator to chill for 2 to 3 hours.

Roll the mixture into bite-sized balls and roll them in the chopped chives. Serve well chilled!

Per serving: 108 Calories; 9g Fat; 2.2g Carbs; 4.8g Protein; 0.2g Fiber

FAST SNACKS & APPETIZERS

504. Old Bay Mushrooms with Neufchâtel Cheese

(Ready in about 25 minutes | Servings 4)

Ingredients

1 cup Neufchâtel cheese
1 tablespoon scallions, minced
1 pound button mushrooms, stems removed
1/2 teaspoon mustard seeds
1 teaspoon garlic, pressed
1/4 cup mayonnaise
1/2 pound mixed seafood
1 teaspoon Old Bay seasoning blend
Salt and pepper, to taste

Directions

Start by preheating your oven to 395 degrees F. Brush a baking pan with a non-stick cooking spray.

Sprinkle the mushrooms with salt, pepper, mustard seeds, and Old Bay seasoning blend.

Mix the remaining ingredients to prepare the filling. Divide the filling mixture between the mushroom caps.

Bake in the preheated oven for about 18 minutes or until cooked through.

Per serving: 221 Calories; 13.5g Fat; 6g Carbs; 19.8g Protein; 1.9g Fiber

505. Classic Rutabaga Chips

(Ready in about 35 minutes | Servings 4)

Ingredients

1 ½ pounds rutabaga, cut into sticks 1/4-inch wide
1/2 teaspoon cayenne pepper
1/2 teaspoon mustard seeds
Salt and ground black pepper, to taste
3 tablespoons olive oil

Directions

Add the rutabaga sticks to a mixing dish. In another small-sized mixing dish, whisk the other ingredients.

Add the oil mixture to the rutabaga sticks and toss to coat well.

Preheat your oven to 440 degrees F. Line a baking sheet with parchment paper.

Place the seasoned rutabaga sticks on the baking sheet. Roast them approximately 30 minutes, turning baking sheet occasionally.

Bon appétit!

Per serving: 134 Calories; 10.8g Fat; 6.9g Carbs; 1.5g Protein; 4g Fiber

506. Oven-Baked Chicken Skin Cracklings

(Ready in about 15 minutes | Servings 4)

Ingredients

2 tablespoons scallions, chopped
1/2 teaspoon mustard seeds
Skin from 4 chicken wings
2 tablespoons Greek-style yogurt
1 tablespoon butter
1/4 cup soft cheese
Salt and pepper, to season

Directions

Bake the chicken skins in the preheated oven at 365 degrees F for about 10 minutes; cut the skin into small pieces.

Meanwhile, mix the remaining ingredients to make the sauce.

Enjoy!

Per serving: 119 Calories; 10.5g Fat; 1.1g Carbs; 5.1g Protein; 0.3g Fiber

507. Parmesan Cauliflower Balls with Greek Sauce

(Ready in about 30 minutes | Servings 6)

Ingredients

1/2 cup Parmesan cheese, grated
1 garlic clove, minced
1 cup Asiago cheese, shredded
1 onion, finely chopped
3 eggs
1 head cauliflower
Salt and black pepper, to taste

For Greek Sauce:
1 tablespoon olive oil
1 garlic clove, minced
1/2 teaspoon dried dill weed
1 teaspoon lemon juice
1 tablespoon mayonnaise
1 cup Greek yogurt

Directions

Cook the cauliflower in a large pot of salted water until tender, about 6 minutes; cut into florets.

Preheat your oven to 400 degrees F. Coat a baking pan with parchment paper.

Mash the cauliflower with the Parmesan, eggs, cheese, onion, garlic, salt and black pepper; shape the mixture into balls.

Bake for 22 minutes or until they are slightly crisp.

To make the sauce, whisk all of the remaining ingredients.

Bon appétit!

Per serving: 182 Calories; 13.1g Fat; 5.9g Carbs; 11.5g Protein; 1.4g Fiber

508. Avocado and Cotija Cheese Balls

(Ready in about 20 minutes + chilling time | Servings 8)

Ingredients

6 ounces Cotija cheese
2 ounces bacon bits
6 ounces avocado flesh
1/4 teaspoon mustard powder
1/2 teaspoon chili powder
1 tablespoon cayenne pepper

Directions

Thoroughly combine all ingredients until everything is well incorporated.

Roll the mixture into eight balls. Place in the refrigerator for about 1 hour.

Bon appétit!

Per serving: 145 Calories; 12.6g Fat; 3.7g Carbs; 5.5g Protein; 1.7g Fiber

509. Chicken Bites with Spicy Tomatillo Dip

(Ready in about 50 minutes | Servings 4)

Ingredients

1 teaspoon coarse sea salt
12 chicken drumettes
1/2 teaspoon ground black pepper, or more to taste
For the Tomatillo Dip:
4 medium tomatillos, crushed
1 cup peppers, chopped
2 tablespoons red wine vinegar
1 onion, finely chopped
1 teaspoon chili pepper, deveined and finely minced
2 tablespoons coriander, finely chopped

Directions

Toss the chicken drumettes with salt and black pepper. Bake them in the preheated oven at 390 degrees F for about 40 minutes or until they are golden and crispy.

In a mixing bowl, thoroughly combine all ingredients for the dip. Enjoy!

Per serving: 161 Calories; 3.5g Fat; 8.4g Carbs; 20.6g Protein; 2g Fiber

510. Caramel Cheesecake Fat Bombs

(Ready in about 5 minutes | Servings 4)

Ingredients

1/2 teaspoon caramel flavoring
1/4 teaspoon ground cinnamon
3 ounces soft cheese
3 ounces walnuts, chopped

Directions

Pulse all ingredients in your blender until well combined.

Roll the mixture into 8 balls. Bon appétit!

Per serving: 180 Calories; 17.3g Fat; 3.4g Carbs; 5.3g Protein; 1.1g Fiber

511. Paprika Bacon Fries

(Ready in about 20 minutes | Servings 4)

Ingredients

12 bacon strips, cut into small squares
1 tablespoon Hungarian paprika
2 tablespoons Erythritol

Directions

Start by preheating your oven to 365 degrees F

Toss the bacon strips with the Erythritol and Hungarian paprika.

Place the bacon squares on a parchment lined baking sheet and bake for 13 to 15 minutes. Enjoy!

Per serving: 118 Calories; 10g Fat; 1.9g Carbs; 5g Protein; 0.4g Fiber

512. Greek-Style Ground Meat and Feta Dip

(Ready in about 10 minutes | Servings 24)

Ingredients

1 pound ground beef
1/2 pound ground turkey
1 cup feta cheese
1 cup black olives, pitted and chopped
3 cups cream cheese
1/2 cup tomato paste
1 teaspoon garlic, minced
1 teaspoon Greek seasoning mix

Directions

Preheat a lightly oiled non-stick pan over a moderately-high heat. Cook the ground meat for 5 to 6 minutes until no longer pink, breaking apart with a fork.

Thoroughly combine the cheese, tomato paste, garlic, and spices. Place 1/2 of meat mixture in a bowl.

Top with 1/2 of the cheese mixture; repeat the layers and top with olives. Enjoy!

Per serving: 153 Calories; 11.2g Fat; 2.2g Carbs; 10.8g Protein; 0.4g Fiber

513. Double Spicy Cheese Crisps

(Ready in about 20 minutes | Servings 6)

Ingredients

1 jalapeño, finely chopped
1 cup Pepper Jack cheese, shredded
1/2 teaspoon ground cumin
1/4 teaspoon cardamom
4 slices bacon, cooked and crumbled
1/4 teaspoon red pepper flakes
1 cup Romano cheese, finely shredded
Salt and pepper, to taste

Directions

Begin by preheating your oven to 400 degrees F. Line a baking sheet with a sheet of parchment paper.

Spoon 1 tablespoon of Romano cheese into a small mound on the parchment paper. Top with about 1 tablespoon of shredded Pepper Jack cheese.

Add the bacon and chopped jalapeño. Sprinkle with red pepper, cumin, cardamom, salt, and pepper; gently flatten each mound.

Bake approximately 12 minutes. Transfer the baking sheet to a wire rack to cool and enjoy!

Per serving: 225 Calories; 19.3g Fat; 0.6g Carbs; 12.1g Protein; 0g Fiber

514. Greek Colorful Skewers

(Ready in about 10 minutes | Servings 6)

Ingredients

1/3 cup olive oil
4 ounces feta cheese, cubed
1/2 cup olives, pitted
1/3 cup balsamic vinegar
1 cup bacon, diced
2 bell peppers, sliced
1/2 teaspoon cumin seeds
6 ounces pickled cornichons, no sugar added

Directions

Toss all ingredients in a mixing bowl.

Thread the pickled cornichons, bell peppers, feta cheese, bacon, and olives onto long wooden skewers, alternating the ingredients. Enjoy!

Per serving: 249 Calories; 19.3g Fat; 6g Carbs; 9.7g Protein; 1.4g Fiber

515. Greek-Style Fat Bombs

(Ready in about 35 minutes | Servings 6)

Ingredients

3 tablespoons aioli
3 slices pancetta, chopped
8 Kalamata olives, pitted and coarsely chopped
2 tablespoons sesame seeds, toasted
1/4 cup butter, softened
3 eggs
Salt and pepper, to taste

Directions

Thoroughly combine the eggs, butter, Kalamata olives, aioli, salt and pepper.

Fold in the chopped pancetta. Roll the mixture into balls.

Place the sesame seeds in a shallow dish; roll your balls over the seeds to coat on all sides.

Bon appétit!

Per serving: 174 Calories; 15.2g Fat; 4.3g Carbs; 5.9g Protein; 0.6g Fiber

516. The Best Lil Smokies Ever

(Ready in about 2 hours 30 minutes | Servings 6)

Ingredients

3 tablespoons wholegrain mustard
1 tablespoon Swerve
1 teaspoon onion powder
1 bottle barbecue sauce
1 ½ pounds cocktail franks

Directions

Heat up a pan over a moderately high heat; now, brown the sausage about 3 minutes.

Treat your crockpot with a non-stick cooking spray. Add all of the above ingredients and stir well.

Cook on Low heat setting for 2 ½ hours. Enjoy!

Per serving: 271 Calories; 22.2g Fat; 4.5g Carbs; 12.3g Protein; 0.4g Fiber

517. Mediterranean-Style Celery Sticks

(Ready in about 10 minutes | Servings 16)

Ingredients

1 teaspoon Mediterranean spice mix
2 tablespoons apple cider vinegar
6 ounces crab meat
1 cup cream cheese
8 celery sticks, cut into halves
Salt and pepper, to taste

Directions

In a mixing bowl, combine the crab meat, apple cider vinegar, cream cheese, salt, pepper, and Mediterranean spice mix.

Divide the crab mixture between the celery sticks.

Bon appétit!

Per serving: 29 Calories; 1.9g Fat; 0.7g Carbs; 2.5g Protein; 1.9g Fiber

518. 15-Minute Bacon Chips

(Ready in about 15 minutes | Servings 6)

Ingredients

1 pound bacon, cut into small squares
1 tablespoon cayenne pepper
1 tablespoon deli mustard

Directions

Toss all ingredients in a rimmed baking pan.

Bake in the preheated oven at 365 degrees F for about 15 minutes.

Bon appétit!

Per serving: 409 Calories; 31.6g Fat; 1.1g Carbs; 28g Protein; 0g Fiber

519. Spicy Cucumber Rounds with Goat Cheese

(Ready in about 10 minutes | Servings 10)

Ingredients

1 cup goat cheese
1 teaspoon ancho chili powder
2 tablespoons ham, chopped
1/4 cup chives, chopped
2 cucumbers, cut into thick slices

Directions

Mix the cheese, ham, chives, and ancho chili powder until well combined.

Divide the mixture between the cucumber slices. Enjoy!

Per serving: 63 Calories; 4.3g Fat; 2.7g Carbs; 4g Protein; 0.1g Fiber

520. Mexican-Style Pork Fat Chips

(Ready in about 2 hours 30 minutes | Servings 6)

Ingredients

Salt, to taste
1 whole pork skin from a pork belly
For Mexican Sauce:
1/2 cup scallions, finely chopped
2 avocados, seeded, peeled and chopped
1 teaspoon garlic, smashed
1/4 teaspoon ground mustard seeds
1 cup tomatillo, chopped
2 tablespoons cilantro, chopped
1 Anaheim pepper, deveined and minced
2 tablespoons fresh-squeezed lemon juice

Directions

Toss the pork skin with salt until well coated.

Bake in the preheated oven at 350 degrees F for 2 hours 30 minutes, until skin is completely dried out.

Meanwhile, make the Mexican sauce by whisking all of the ingredients in the order listed above. Enjoy!

Per serving: 199 Calories; 16.1g Fat; 6.5g Carbs; 7.5g Protein; 3.8g Fiber

521. Zingy Cheesecake Balls

(Ready in about 10 minutes + chilling time | Servings 6)

Ingredients

1 cup soft cheese
1/2 cup fresh parsley, minced
3 tablespoons butter
1/4 teaspoon white vinegar
Salt and pepper, to taste

Directions

Mix all ingredients, except for the parsley, in your blender or food processor.

Place the mixture in the refrigerator until firm.

Shape the mixture into bite-sized balls and roll them in the parsley until coated on all sides. Enjoy!

Per serving: 108 Calories; 9g Fat; 2.2g Carbs; 4.8g Protein; 0.3g Fiber

522. Cheese, Kale and Prosciutto Mini Frittatas

(Ready in about 25 minutes | Servings 6)

Ingredients

1 ½ cups Gruyère cheese, grated
10 ounces kale, cooked and drained
1/2 cup full-fat milk
1/2 teaspoon dried basil
5 eggs
1/2 pound prosciutto, chopped
Sea salt, to taste

Directions

Start by preheating your oven to 360 degrees F. Spritz a muffin tin with a cooking spray.

Whisk the milk, salt, basil and cheese in a mixing bowl. Toss in the kale and prosciutto. Spoon the batter into each muffin cup (3/4 full).

Bake for 20 to 25 minutes.

Bon appétit!

Per serving: 275 Calories; 15.8g Fat; 6.2g Carbs; 21.6g Protein; 1g Fiber

523. Salami, Feta, and Mayo Balls

(Ready in about 5 minutes | Servings 6)

Ingredients

4 ounces Feta cheese, crumbled
1/2 teaspoon paprika
4 ounces salami, chopped
1/4 cup mayonnaise
2 tablespoons cilantro, finely chopped
1/2 cup black olives, pitted and chopped

Directions

In a mixing bowl, thoroughly combine all of the above ingredients.

Roll the mixture into 10 to 12 balls

Enjoy!

Per serving: 217 Calories; 18.7g Fat; 2.1g Carbs; 9.9g Protein; 0.4g Fiber

524. Mexican Wings with Habanero Dip

(Ready in about 50 minutes | Servings 6)

Ingredients

Salt and red pepper, to taste
12 chicken wings
For the Dip:
1 Habanero pepper, minced
4 ripe tomatoes
1 shallot, finely chopped
2 tablespoons coriander, minced
1 cup tomatillos, peeled
2 tablespoons lime juice, freshly squeezed

Directions

Toss the chicken wings with salt and red pepper; brush them with a non-stick spray.

Bake in the preheated oven at 396 degrees F for 45 to 50 minutes or until they're crispy.

In your blender, process the remaining ingredients to make the sauce.

Enjoy!

Per serving: 236 Calories; 13.5g Fat; 6g Carbs; 19.4g Protein; 1.7g Fiber

FAST SNACKS & APPETIZERS

525. Rich and Easy Cheeseburger Sauce

(Ready in about 15 minutes | Servings 10)

Ingredients

1/2 pound ground turkey
6 ounces Cheddar cheese, grated
1/2 teaspoon porcini powder
1/2 teaspoon granulated garlic
1/2 teaspoon cayenne pepper
1/2 pound ground pork
1 teaspoon shallot powder
1/2 teaspoon mustard powder
1 tablespoon olive oil
8 ounces cream cheese, at room temperature
Salt and black pepper, to taste

Directions

Heat the oil in a saucepan over a moderately-high flame. Cook the ground meat for about 5 minutes until no longer pink.

Add in the remaining ingredients and continue to simmer over low heat for about 4 minutes.

Enjoy!

Per serving: 195 Calories; 12g Fat; 1.5g Carbs; 19.5g Protein; 0g Fiber

526. Chorizo and Cream Cheese-Stuffed Peppers

(Ready in about 20 minutes | Servings 4)

Ingredients

4 bell peppers, deveined and quartered
1/2 pound ground turkey
2 ounces chorizo, chopped
1 tablespoon fresh cilantro, finely chopped
1 yellow onion, minced
2 garlic cloves, minced
6 ounces cream cheese, softened
2 tablespoons ghee, softened
Salt and pepper, to taste

Directions

In a frying pan, melt the ghee over a moderately high flame. Once hot, sauté the onion until tender and translucent.

Add in the ground turkey and continue to cook for a further 5 minutes or until no longer pink. Remove from the heat.

Add in the cheese, garlic, cilantro, salt, and pepper. Divide the meat/cheese mixture between your peppers. Top with the chorizo and arrange your peppers on a parchment-lined baking sheet.

Bake in the preheated oven at 370 degrees F for about 15 minutes or until the peppers are tender. Enjoy!

Per serving: 252 Calories; 13.7g Fat; 5.6g Carbs; 26g Protein; 1.4g Fiber

527. Butter Dill Zucchini Chips

(Ready in about 40 minutes | Servings 4)

Ingredients

2 tablespoons butter, melted
1/2 teaspoon dried dill weed
1/2 teaspoon red pepper flakes, crushed
2 egg whites
Coarse salt and crushed black peppercorns, to taste
4 zucchinis, cut into thick slices

Directions

Begin by preheating an oven to 420 degrees F. Coat a rimmed baking sheet with parchment paper or Silpat mat.

In a mixing bowl, whisk the butter with two egg whites. Add the seasonings.

Now, toss the zucchini slices with this mixture.

Arrange the coated zucchini slices on the baking sheet; bake for 35 minutes until the slices are golden, turning once.

Check for doneness and bake another 5 minutes if needed.

Enjoy!

Per serving: 91 Calories; 6.1g Fat; 6g Carbs; 4.2g Protein; 0.1g Fiber

528. Cheesy and Parsley Chicken Wings

(Ready in about 1 hour 10 minutes | Servings 6)

Ingredients

1/2 cup Italian parsley, chopped
1 cup Romano cheese, grated
1 stick butter
2 cloves garlic, smashed
1 tablespoon champagne vinegar
2 pounds chicken wings, bone-in
1 teaspoon hot sauce
Salt and black pepper, to taste

Directions

Line a large rimmed baking sheet with a metal rack.

Preheat an oven to 420 degrees F. Set a metal rack on top of a baking sheet.

Toss the wings with salt and black pepper. Bake in the preheated oven at 410 degrees F until golden and crispy, for 45 to 50 minutes.

Place the garlic, butter, vinegar and hot sauce in a saucepan; cook over low heat until the sauce has thickened slightly.

Remove from the heat and fold in the cheese; toss the wings with the cheese mixture until well coated. Bake an additional 8 minutes and top with parsley. Enjoy!

Per serving: 312 Calories; 23g Fat; 0.9g Carbs; 24.6g Protein; 0.3g Fiber

529. Fat Bombs with Salami

(Ready in about 5 minutes + chilling time | Servings 6)

Ingredients

6 slices genoa salami, chopped
6 hard-boiled eggs, peeled and chopped
1/2 teaspoon Italian seasoning mix
Sea salt and pepper, to taste
1/2 cup Ricotta cheese, softened
1/3 cup mayonnaise
1/2 teaspoon paprika

Directions

Thoroughly combine all ingredients until well combined.

Roll the mixture into balls.

Bon appétit!

Per serving: 327 Calories; 25.7g Fat; 6.4g Carbs; 17g Protein; 0.4g Fiber

530. Mini Frittatas with Spanish-Style Sauce

(Ready in about 30 minutes | Servings 6)

Ingredients

1 head broccoli, grated
5 ounces cooked bacon, chopped
1/2 teaspoon Adobo seasoning mix
1 ½ cups cheddar cheese, freshly grated
1 cup onions, chopped
6 eggs, whisked
Sea salt and pepper, to taste
For the Dipping Sauce:
2 tablespoons sesame oil
1/2 teaspoon garlic, chopped
1/2 shallot, minced
1 teaspoon basil
1 Spanish pepper, chopped
2 vine-ripened tomatoes, chopped

Directions

In a mixing bowl, combine the eggs, bacon, cheese, broccoli, onions, salt, pepper, and Adobo seasoning mix.

Preheat your oven to 385 degrees F.

Spoon the mixture into lightly buttered muffin cups and bake for 20 to 30 minutes, or until golden brown.

In the meantime, place all the sauce ingredients in a saucepan over medium-low heat. Let it simmer until reduced by half. Bon appétit!

Per serving: 375 Calories; 27.6g Fat; 6g Carbs; 24.8g Protein; 1.6g Fiber

531. Italian Cheesy Baby Carrots

(Ready in about 35 minutes | Servings 6)

Ingredients

1/2 cup Asiago cheese, grated
1/4 teaspoon ground black pepper
1/4 teaspoon ground cumin
1/4 teaspoon dried dill weed
1 stick butter, melted
1/2 teaspoon coarse salt
1 ½ pounds baby carrots, florets separated

Directions

Begin by preheating your oven to 400 degrees F.

Coat the baby carrots with the melted butter, salt, pepper, cumin and dill weed.

Bake for 30 minutes in the middle of the preheated oven, stirring once or twice.

Top with the shredded Asiago cheese and bake an additional 5 minutes or until the cheese is slightly browned. Bon appétit!

Per serving: 216 Calories; 18.7g Fat; 6.4g Carbs; 3.5g Protein; 3.1g Fiber

532. Tomato Cheeseburger Pie

(Ready in about 25 minutes | Servings 6)

Ingredients

1 cup sharp Cheddar cheese, shredded
1 cup Monterey-Jack cheese, shredded
1 ½ cups ground turkey
1 teaspoon garlic, crushed
1 cup Colby cheese, shredded
1/2 teaspoon mustard powder
2 tomatoes, crushed
1 shallot, chopped
Salt and black pepper, to your liking

Directions

Preheat your oven to 395 degrees F. Coat a baking sheet with a piece of parchment paper.

Spread the shredded cheese on the bottom of your baking sheet. Bake for 11 to 13 minutes or until golden-browned on top.

Meanwhile, preheat a lightly oiled skillet over a moderately-high heat and cook the shallot until just tender and translucent.

Add in the garlic and continue to sauté until aromatic. Stir in the ground turkey and spices and continue to cook, breaking it up in the pan to cook through.

Top the cheese "crust" with the meat mixture; return it to the oven and bake an additional 7 minutes. Top with the tomatoes. Enjoy!

Per serving: 231 Calories; 16.4g Fat; 3.5g Carbs; 17.3g Protein; 0.7g Fiber

533. Spicy Shrimp Scampi

(Ready in about 15 minutes | Servings 6)

Ingredients

1 pound shrimp, deveined and shelled, tail on
1 teaspoon ancho chili powder
2 tablespoons apple cider vinegar
1/4 cup chicken stock
1/2 cup scallions, chopped
1 teaspoon paprika
1 teaspoon garlic, minced
2 tablespoons coconut oil, room temperature
Salt and ground black pepper, to taste

Directions

Heat the coconut oil in a frying pan over a moderately high flame. Now, cook the shrimp together with the garlic and scallions.

Add the chili powder, vinegar, and chicken stock and continue to cook 3 minutes more. Season with paprika, salt, and pepper to taste. Enjoy!

Per serving: 107 Calories; 4.9g Fat; 1g Carbs; 15.3g Protein; 0.6g Fiber

534. Sriracha Bacon Bites

(Ready in about 15 minutes | Servings 6)

Ingredients

1 teaspoon Sriracha sauce
1 pound bacon, cut into 1-inch squares
1 tablespoon smoked paprika
1 teaspoon lime juice
1 teaspoon lime zest

Directions

Toss all ingredients in a mixing dish.

Bake in the preheated oven at 365 degrees F approximately 15 minutes. Enjoy!

Per serving: 409 Calories; 31.6g Fat; 1.1g Carbs; 28g Protein; 0.4g Fiber

535. Cheese, Salami and Olive Muffins

(Ready in about 20 minutes | Servings 6)

Ingredients

1 cup Swiss cheese, shredded
1/2 cup spicy tomato sauce
12 winter salami slices
1/2 cup black olives, pitted and chopped
1 teaspoon Italian spice mix

Directions

Spritz 12-cup muffin tin with a non-stick cooking spray. Place a salami slice in each muffin cup.

Add in the cheese, tomato sauce, Italian spice mix, and olives.

Bake in the preheated oven at 365 degrees F approximately 16 minutes. Enjoy!

Per serving: 162 Calories; 13.1g Fat; 2.5g Carbs; 8.7g Protein; 1.7g Fiber

536. Spicy Cheese Chips

(Ready in about 10 minutes | Servings 4)

Ingredients

2 cups Monterey-Jack cheese, shredded
1/4 teaspoon onion powder
1/2 teaspoon ancho chili powder
1/2 teaspoon garlic powder
1 thyme sprig, minced

Directions

Begin by preheating your oven to 390 degrees F. Line baking sheets with Silpat mat.

Place small piles of the cheese mixture on the prepared baking sheets.

Bake for 6 to 7 minutes; then, let them cool at room temperature. Enjoy!

Per serving: 205 Calories; 15g Fat; 2.9g Carbs; 14.5g Protein; 0g Fiber

537. Shrimp with Sesame and Wine

(Ready in about 15 minutes | Servings 6)

Ingredients

2 tablespoons sesame seeds
2 garlic cloves, pressed
1 teaspoon chili powder
2 tablespoons dry white wine
1/4 cup fish stock
2 tablespoons sesame oil
1/2 cup onions, chopped
1 pound shrimp, deveined and shelled
Salt and ground black pepper, to taste

Directions

Heat the oil in a saucepan over a moderately-high heat. Cook the shrimp, garlic and onions for about 3 minutes.

Add in the remaining ingredients and cook for 10 minutes more until cooked through.

Enjoy!

Per serving: 107 Calories; 4.9g Fat; 1g Carbs; 15.3g Protein; 0.8g Fiber

538. Greek-Style Cheese and Ham Bites

(Ready in about 10 minutes | Servings 6)

Ingredients

6 slices of Iberian ham, chopped
6 Kalamata olives, pitted and chopped
1 teaspoon dried basil
6 ounces Neufchatel cheese
1 teaspoon dried rosemary
1 teaspoon dried oregano
1/4 cup aioli
1 tablespoon tomato paste

Directions

Thoroughly combine the Neufchatel cheese, aioli, tomato paste, chopped ham and olives in a mixing bowl; mix until everything is homogeneous.

In a shallow dish, combine dried basil, oregano, and rosemary.

Shape the mixture into a ball. Roll the ball in the herb mixture.

Bon appétit!

Per serving: 182 Calories; 15.5g Fat; 3g Carbs; 7.6g Protein; 0.3g Fiber

539. Sticky Carrot Bites

(Ready in about 35 minutes | Servings 6)

Ingredients

1 ½ pounds carrot, cut into sticks
1 teaspoon basil
1 tablespoon Swerve
1/2 cup Colby cheese, grated
Salt and pepper, to taste
1/4 teaspoon mustard seeds
1 stick butter, melted

Directions

Preheat your oven to 390 degrees F.

Toss the carrot sticks with the melted butter, salt, pepper, mustard seeds, Swerve, and basil.

Roast the carrot sticks in the preheated oven for 25 to 30 minutes, stirring every 10 minutes.

Top with the shredded cheese and broil an additional 5 minutes or until the cheese is slightly browned. Bon appétit!

Per serving: 216 Calories; 18.7g Fat; 5.4g Carbs; 3.5g Protein; 3.6g Fiber

540. Sardine and Aioli Egg Bites

(Ready in about 20 minutes | Servings 6)

Ingredients

1 can sardines, drained
1/3 cup aioli
12 eggs
1 tablespoon fresh chives, chopped
1 poblano pepper, minced
1/2 teaspoon smoked paprika
1 teaspoon fresh or dried basil
Salt and pepper, to taste

FAST SNACKS & APPETIZERS

Directions

Place the eggs in a saucepan and cover them with water by 1 inch. Cover and bring the water to a boil over high heat. Boil for 6 to 7 minutes over medium-high heat.

Peel the eggs and slice them in half lengthwise; mix the yolks with the remaining ingredients.

Divide the mixture among the egg whites. Enjoy!

Per serving: 216 Calories; 17.3g Fat; 1.8g Carbs; 12.2g Protein; 0.2g Fiber

541. Turkey Tenders with Sriracha Sauce

(Ready in about 30 minutes | Servings 8)

Ingredients

1 ¼ pounds turkey tenderloin, cut into 20 pieces
3/4 cup almond flour
2 eggs, whisked
1/3 cup flax meal
Salt and black pepper, to season

For the Sauce:
1/3 cup tomato paste
1 teaspoon garlic powder
1 teaspoon deli mustard
1/3 teaspoon cumin
1/2 tablespoon Sriracha sauce
1/2 teaspoon cayenne pepper

Directions

Start by preheating your oven to 365 degrees F. Brush the bottom of a baking pan with cooking spray.

Toss the turkey pieces with salt and pepper. Mix the flax meal with the almond meal.

Dip the turkey pieces in the whisked egg, then, coat them with the meal mixture. Bake for 25 to 28 minutes.

Whisk all the sauce ingredients and reserve. Bon appétit!

Per serving: 153 Calories; 6.7g Fat; 4.6g Carbs; 21.8g Protein; 0.7g Fiber

542. 10-Minute Party Cheese Ball

(Ready in about 10 minutes | Servings 6)

Ingredients

6 ounces cream cheese
1 tablespoon ketchup
1 ounce package Ranch seasoning
1/4 cup mayonnaise
6 slices of ham, chopped
Salt and pepper, to taste
6 black olives, pitted and sliced
1 teaspoon poppy seeds

Directions

Thoroughly combine the cream cheese, Ranch seasoning, mayonnaise, ketchup, chopped ham, salt, pepper, and poppy seeds.

Shape the mixture into a ball. Garnish with black olives. Enjoy!

Per serving: 182 Calories; 15.5g Fat; 3g Carbs; 7.6g Protein; 1.1g Fiber

543. Chicken Wings with Greek Dip

(Ready in about 1 hour 15 minutes | Servings 10)

Ingredients

1 teaspoon olive oil
1 teaspoon mustard seeds
3 pounds chicken wings
Salt and red pepper, to taste
For Feta Cheese Dip:
1 cup feta cheese, shredded
1/3 cup mayonnaise
1/2 teaspoon ground cumin
2 cloves garlic, smashed
1 teaspoon porcini powder
2 tablespoons sour cream
1/4 cup fresh parsley leaves, finely chopped

Directions

Toss the chicken wings with the olive oil, salt, red pepper, and mustard seeds.

Roast in the preheated oven at 380 degrees F approximately 35 minutes.

Turn the oven up to 410 degrees F and bake for a further 35 minutes on the higher shelf until crispy.

In the meantime, mix all ingredients for the cheese sauce. Enjoy!

Per serving: 227 Calories; 10.2g Fat; 0.4g Carbs; 31.5g Protein; 0.2g Fiber

544. Crispy Parmesan Chicken Wings

(Ready in about 1 hour 10 minutes | Servings 6)

Ingredients

1 cup Parmesan cheese
2 tablespoons oyster sauce
1/2 cup fresh chives, chopped
2 teaspoons Sriracha chili sauce
2 cloves garlic, smashed
1 stick butter
1/2 teaspoon smoked cayenne pepper
1 tablespoon balsamic vinegar
2 pounds chicken wings
Coarse salt and freshly ground black pepper, to taste

Directions

Preheat an oven to 420 degrees F. Set a metal rack on top of a baking sheet.

Season the chicken wings with salt, black pepper, cayenne pepper. Now, roast the wings until the skin is crisp, about 45 minutes.

In the meantime, simmer the vinegar, Sriracha, and garlic until the mixture has reduced slightly, about 12 minutes.

In a shallow bowl, combine the softened butter with the parmesan cheese and oyster sauce.

Next, toss the chicken wings with the Sriracha mixture. After that, dredge the chicken wings in the parmesan mixture until fully coated; then place on the baking sheet.

Bake an additional 10 minutes; add freshly chopped chives. Enjoy!

Per serving: 312 Calories; 23g Fat; 0.9g Carbs; 24.6g Protein; 0.3g Fiber

545. Dill Pickle and Cheese Fried Balls

(Ready in about 15 minutes | Servings 6)

Ingredients

1 cup crushed pork rinds
1 teaspoon smoked paprika
1/2 cup dill pickles, chopped and thoroughly squeezed
1/2 teaspoon onion powder
1/2 teaspoon mustard seeds
4 cups broccoli, grated
12 ounces Cottage cheese curds
1 cup Swiss cheese, freshly grated
1 teaspoon garlic, minced
1/2 pound salami, chopped
Salt and black pepper, to taste
1/4 teaspoon dried dill weed

Directions

Thoroughly combine all ingredients, except for the pork rinds and paprika. Roll the mixture into 18 balls.

In a shallow dish, mix the pork rinds with the smoked paprika.

Roll each ball over the paprika mixture until completely coated. Fry these balls in a preheated skillet for 5 to 6 minutes. Enjoy!

Per serving: 407 Calories; 26.8g Fat; 5.8g Carbs; 33.4g Protein; 1.1g Fiber

546. Party Creamy Meatballs with Cheddar Cheese

(Ready in about 25 minutes | Servings 5)

Ingredients

1/3 cup double cream
2 eggs, whisked
1/2 pound ground beef
1 teaspoon garlic, minced
1/2 pound ground pork
1 small onion, minced
1 teaspoon dried marjoram
10 (1-inch) cubes of cheddar cheese
1 tablespoon fresh parsley, roughly chopped
Salt and pepper, to taste

Directions

In a mixing bowl, combine the ground meat, double cream, eggs, parsley, onion, garlic, salt, pepper, and marjoram; mix until everything is well combined.

Now, roll the mixture into 10 balls using your hands. Place a piece of cheese in the center of each ball.

Press the ground meat around the piece of cheese, sealing it tightly around the cheese.

Bake in the preheated oven at 395 degrees F for about 20 minutes.

Bon appétit!

Per serving: 302 Calories; 17.3g Fat; 1.9g Carbs; 33.4g Protein; 0.5g Fiber

547. Easy Chicharrones with Chili Cheese Sauce

(Ready in about 3 hours 10 minutes | Servings 10)

Ingredients

1 ½ pounds pork skin, trimmed of excess fat
2 cups mustard greens, torn into pieces and steamed
1 teaspoon onion powder
1/2 cup mayonnaise
1 teaspoon granulated garlic
12 ounces cream cheese
1 tablespoon olive oil
1/4 teaspoon mustard powder
1 tablespoon chili paste (sambal)
Sea salt and pepper, to taste

Directions

Toss the pork skin with salt until well coated. Place them on a wire rack over a baking sheet.

Bake in the preheated oven at 350 degrees F for about 3 hours, until the skin is completely dried out.

Heat the olive oil in a non-stick skillet and cook your chicharrónes in batches until they puff up, about 5 minutes. Place on a paper towel-lined plate.

Meanwhile, parboil the mustard greens for about 7 minutes. Add in the remaining ingredients and mix to combine well.

Bon appétit!

Per serving: 420 Calories; 43g Fat; 3.1g Carbs; 5g Protein; 0.8g Fiber

548. Swiss Chard and Cheese Dip

(Ready in about 30 minutes | Servings 12)

Ingredients

1 ½ cups Swiss chard, chopped
6 ounces double cream
2 egg yolks
1/2 cup Swiss cheese, grated
2 tablespoons butter
2 cloves garlic, chopped
1 ½ cups Ricotta cheese, softened
1/2 cup Prosciutto, roughly chopped
Salt and pepper, to taste

Directions

Strat by preheating your oven to 355 degrees F.

In a saucepan, melt the butter over medium-low heat. Cook the cream, salt and pepper for about 3 minutes.

Add in the egg yolks and continue to cook for 4 to 5 minutes more, stirring continuously. Spoon the mixture into a baking dish.

Add in the remaining ingredients and stir to combine. Bake in the preheated oven for 18 to 20 minutes. Enjoy!

Per serving: 154 Calories; 13g Fat; 3.3g Carbs; 6.2g Protein; 0.1g Fiber

549. Boozy Fat Bombs

(Ready in about 15 minutes + chilling time | Servings 5)

Ingredients

1 teaspoon tequila
1 teaspoon brown mustard
8 black olives, pitted and chopped
2 teaspoons tomato paste
10 ounces Ricotta cheese, room temperature
1/4 cup mayonnaise
1 teaspoon lime juice, freshly squeezed
5 ounces pepperoni, chopped

Directions

Mix all ingredients in a bowl until well combined. Place in your refrigerator for 2 hours.

Roll the mixture into balls.

Serve well chilled!

Per serving: 323 Calories; 28.4g Fat; 2.6g Carbs; 13.1g Protein; 0.3g Fiber

550. Paprika Crackers with Seeds

(Ready in about 30 minutes | Servings 12)

Ingredients

2 tablespoons flax seeds
1/3 cup pumpkin seeds, ground
1 teaspoon paprika
1 tablespoon pine nuts, ground
1/2 cup sesame seeds
1/4 tablespoons sunflower seeds
1/4 cup psyllium husks
Coarse sea salt, to taste

Directions

Mix all the above ingredients in a bowl. Add in the warm water to form a smooth dough ball.

Then, roll the dough out as thin as possible. Use a pizza cutter to cut the dough into 1-inch squares.

Bake in the preheated oven at 365 degrees F for about 12 minutes or until golden and crispy. Turn your crackers over and bake for further 8 to 10 minutes. Enjoy!

Per serving: 119 Calories; 8g Fat; 4.7g Carbs; 2.6g Protein; 1.1g Fiber

551. Pimentón Cheese Crisps

(Ready in about 18 minutes | Servings 2)

Ingredients

1/2 teaspoon Spanish pimentón
3 cups Manchego cheese, grated
1 teaspoon dried Perejil
1/2 teaspoon granulated garlic
Sea salt and black pepper, to taste

Directions

Start by preheating your oven to 410 degrees F.

Mix all of the above ingredients. Place about 2 tablespoons of the mixture into small mounds on a parchment-lined baking sheet.

Bake for 13 to 15 minutes or until golden and crisp. Enjoy!

Per serving: 100 Calories; 8g Fat; 0g Carbs; 7g Protein; 0.4g Fiber

552. Italian Shrimp and Vegetable Skewers

(Ready in about 15 minutes | Servings 4)

Ingredients

1 pound large shrimp, peeled and deveined
1 teaspoon garlic, minced
1 cup cherry tomatoes
2 tablespoons minced coriander
2 Italian peppers, diced
2 tablespoons fresh scallions, chopped
1 tablespoon Cajun seasoning mix
1 tablespoon white vinegar
1 tablespoon fresh lemon juice
3 tablespoons olive oil

Directions

In a saucepan, heat the olive oil over a moderately-high flame.

Cook the shrimp and scallions for about 4 minutes. Stir in the garlic and Cajun seasoning mix and continue to sauté for a minute or so, until aromatic.

Heat off; toss your shrimp with lemon juice, vinegar and coriander. Tread the prawns onto bamboo skewers, alternating them with Italian peppers and cherry tomatoes. Enjoy!

Per serving: 218 Calories; 11g Fat; 5.1g Carbs; 23.5g Protein; 1.4g Fiber

553. Spicy Pancetta Egg Bites

(Ready in about 20 minutes | Servings 10)

Ingredients

10 eggs
1/4 cup pancetta, chopped
1 tablespoon deli mustard
1/4 teaspoon Sriracha sauce
1/2 cup mayonnaise
1 tablespoon fresh basil, finely chopped
2 teaspoons champagne vinegar

Directions

Place the eggs in a saucepan and cover them with water by 1 inch. Cover and bring the water to a boil over high heat. Boil for 6 to 7 minutes over medium-high heat.

Peel the eggs and slice them in half lengthwise; mix the yolks with the remaining ingredients.

Divide the mixture between the egg whites and arrange the deviled eggs on a nice serving platter.

Enjoy!

Per serving: 128 Calories; 9.7g Fat; 3.3g Carbs; 6.8g Protein; 0.1g Fiber

FAST SNACKS & APPETIZERS

554. Salmon and Avocado Balls with Seeds

(Ready in about 5 minutes | Servings 4)

Ingredients

1 avocado, pitted and peeled
1/2 cup scallions, chopped
1/2 teaspoon dried oregano
8 ounces canned salmon, drained
1 ounce pumpkin seeds, chopped
1 ounce sunflower seeds
1 ounce hemp seeds
Salt and pepper, to taste
1/2 teaspoon cayenne pepper

Directions

Combine all ingredients until well mixed.

Roll the mixture into eight balls and place in your refrigerator until set.

Enjoy!

Per serving: 316 Calories; 24.4g Fat; 5.9g Carbs; 17.4g Protein; 6g Fiber

555. Double Cheese Meatballs

(Ready in about 25 minutes | Servings 10)

Ingredients

1 cup Monterey Jack cheese, cubed
1/3 cup Parmesan cheese, freshly grated
2 eggs
2 cloves garlic, minced
1 teaspoon red pepper flakes, crushed
1 teaspoon oyster sauce
1/2 cup onion, finely chopped
1/2 pound ground turkey
1 pound ground pork
Sea salt and ground black pepper, to taste

Directions

Start by preheating your oven to 390 degrees F. Coat a baking pan with parchment paper.

Thoroughly combine all ingredients, except for the Monterey Jack cheese, in a mixing bowl.

Shape this meat mixture into 40 meatballs. Press 1 cheese cube into the middle of each meatball; be sure to seal it inside.

Gently place the meatballs on the prepared baking pan.

Bake about 20 minutes until they are browned and slightly crisp on top. Bon appétit!

Per serving: 186 Calories; 9.6g Fat; 1.2g Carbs; 23.9g Protein; 0.2g Fiber

556. Romano Cheese Sticks

(Ready in about 15 minutes | Servings 5)

Ingredients

2 eggs
10 pieces mozzarella cheese sticks
1/4 cup almond meal
1/3 cup Romano cheese, grated
2 tablespoons buttermilk
1 teaspoon Italian spice mix
1/4 cup flaxseed meal
Vegetable oil for frying

Directions

Mix the Italian spice mix, almond meal, flaxseed meal, and Romano cheese in a shallow bowl.

In another dish, whisk the buttermilk with the eggs.

Dip each cheese stick into the egg mixture; then, dredge them into the almond meal mixture, then quickly again in the egg mixture and again in the almond meal mixture.

Fill a frying pan with about 2 inches of oil. Heat the oil over high heat.

Deep fry the cheese sticks for 2 minutes per side until the crust is golden brown. Place the fried cheese sticks on paper towels to drain the excess oil. Enjoy!

Per serving: 338 Calories; 26.5g Fat; 3.4g Carbs; 21g Protein; 2.3g Fiber

557. Cajun Celery Fries

(Ready in about 35 minutes | Servings 6)

Ingredients

1 tablespoon Cajun seasoning
1/4 cup pine nuts, coarsely ground
1/2 teaspoon cayenne pepper
2 tablespoons olive oil
1 ½ pounds celery root, cut into sticks
Salt and ground black pepper, to taste

Directions

Preheat your oven to 390 degrees F. Line a baking sheet with a parchment paper or Silpat mat.

Mix the celery root, salt, black pepper, cayenne pepper, olive oil and Cajun seasoning in a mixing dish.

Arrange the celery sticks on the prepared baking sheet and bake for 30 minutes, flipping every 10 minutes to promote even cooking; sprinkle with pine nuts.

Bon appétit!

Per serving: 96 Calories; 8.5g Fat; 4.1g Carbs; 1.5g Protein; 2.1g Fiber

558. Spicy Tomatoes with Chive Sauce

(Ready in about 25 minutes | Servings 6)

Ingredients

1 ½ pounds cherry tomatoes
1/4 cup extra-virgin olive oil
1 Adobo spice mix
For the Sauce:
1 cup cream cheese
1/2 cup aïoli
1/2 cup fresh chives, chopped

Directions

Toss your tomatoes with the Adobo spice mix and olive oil.

Roast in the preheated oven at 420 degrees F for about 20 minutes.

In the meantime, make the sauce by whisking all the sauce ingredients.

Enjoy!

Per serving: 230 Calories; 21g Fat; 6g Carbs; 5.1g Protein; 2.5g Fiber

FAST SNACKS & APPETIZERS

559. Cheesy Paprika Meatballs

(Ready in about 25 minutes | Servings 10)

Ingredients

2 eggs
1 pound ground pork
1 teaspoon paprika
1/2 cup shallots, finely chopped
1/2 pound ground chuck
1 teaspoon fish sauce
1 teaspoon garlic, smashed
1 cup Mozzarella cheese, cubed
1/3 cup Pecorino-Romano cheese, grated
Sea salt and pepper, to taste

Directions

In a mixing dish, combine all ingredients, except for the Mozzarella cheese.

Roll this mixture into golf ball sized meatballs using your hands. Press a Mozzarella cheese cube into the middle of each meatball, fully enclosing it.

Bake in the preheated oven at 395 degrees F for 18 to 22 minutes until they are fully cooked.

Bon appétit!

Per serving: 214 Calories; 12.6g Fat; 1.6g Carbs; 21.9g Protein; 0.4g Fiber

560. Chicken Wingettes with Greek Cheese Dip

(Ready in about 1 hour 15 minutes | Servings 10)

Ingredients

1/4 teaspoon smoked paprika
1 teaspoon dried dill weed
3 pounds chicken wingettes
Salt and black pepper, to taste
Non-stick cooking spray
For Goat Cheese Dip:
1 teaspoon Dijon mustard
1/2 teaspoon ground cumin
1/4 cup fresh coriander leaves, finely chopped
2 tablespoons Greek-style yogurt
2 cloves garlic, smashed
1 teaspoon onion powder
1 cup goat cheese, crumbled
1/3 cup mayonnaise

Directions

Preheat your oven to 390 degrees F. Set a wire rack inside a rimmed baking sheet. Spritz the rack with a non-stick cooking oil.

Toss the chicken wingettes with salt, pepper, paprika, and dill.

Place the chicken wingettes skin side up on the rack. Bake in the lower quarter of the oven for 30 to 35 minutes.

Turn the oven up to 420 degrees F. Bake for a further 40 minutes on the higher shelf, rotating the baking sheet once.

In the meantime, combine the goat cheese, mayo, yogurt, mustard, garlic, onion powder, ground cumin, and coriander.

Enjoy!

Per serving: 227 Calories; 10.2g Fat; 0.4g Carbs; 31.5g Protein; 2.1g Fiber

561. Tangy Chicken Wings

(Ready in about 50 minutes | Servings 6)

Ingredients

12 chicken wings
Salt and pepper, to taste
For the Tomato Dip:
2 heaping tablespoons cilantro, finely chopped
2 tablespoons lime juice
1 cup mango, peeled and chopped
1 teaspoon chili pepper, deveined and finely minced
4 ripe tomatoes, crushed
1 onion, finely chopped

Directions

Start by preheating your oven to 400 degrees F. Set a wire rack inside a rimmed baking sheet.

Season the chicken wings with salt and pepper. Bake the wings approximately 45 minutes or until the skin is crispy.

Then, thoroughly combine all ingredients for the tomato dip. Enjoy!

Per serving: 236 Calories; 13.5g Fat; 7g Carbs; 19.4g Protein; 2.5g Fiber

562. Parmesan Cauliflower Bites

(Ready in about 40 minutes | Servings 6)

Ingredients

1 cup Parmigiano-Reggiano cheese, grated
1/4 cup butter, melted
1 teaspoon hot sauce
1 teaspoon lemongrass, grated
1 ½ pounds cauliflower florets
Sea salt and pepper, to your liking

Directions

Toss the cauliflower with the melted butter, salt, pepper, lemongrass, and hot sauce.

Place the cauliflower florets on a parchment-lined baking pan and roast them in the preheated oven at 420 degrees F.

Roast the cauliflower florets for about 35 minutes. Toss with Parmigiano-Reggiano and roast an additional 5 to 7 minutes or until the top is crispy. Enjoy!

Per serving: 167 Calories; 13.4g Fat; 2.4g Carbs; 7.5g Protein; 2.4g Fiber

563. Pancetta Meatballs with Parsley Sauce

(Ready in about 30 minutes | Servings 6)

Ingredients

1/2 pound pancetta slices
1/2 cup pork rinds, crushed
1/2 pound ground pork
1/4 cup fresh scallions, finely chopped
2 cloves garlic, minced
1 teaspoon paprika
1 egg, whisked
1 ½ tablespoons olive oil
1/2 pound ground beef
Salt and pepper, to taste
For the Parsley Sauce:
1 tablespoon pine nuts, toasted and chopped
1/2 tablespoon olive oil
1 cup fresh parsley
1 tablespoon pumpkin seeds, chopped
Salt and pepper, to taste

Directions

In a mixing bowl, thoroughly combine the ground meat, egg, olive oil, pork rinds, scallions, garlic, salt, pepper, and paprika. Roll the mixture into small meatballs.

Wrap each ball with a slice of pancetta and secure with a toothpick.

Place the meatballs on a baking pan; bake in the preheated oven at 385 degrees F for about 30 minutes.

Meanwhile, make the sauce by mixing all ingredients in your food processor. Bon appétit!

Per serving: 399 Calories; 27g Fat; 1.8g Carbs; 37.7g Protein; 1.9g Fiber

564. Pepperoni Keto Bombs

(Ready in about 10 minutes | Servings 5)

Ingredients

5 ounces cream cheese
2 tablespoons mayonnaise
1 teaspoon deli mustard
4 large egg yolks, hard-boiled
5 ounces Pepperoni, chopped
2 tablespoons hemp hearts
1/2 teaspoon paprika

Directions

Add the Pepperoni, cheese and egg yolks to a mixing dish; stir to combine well.

Now, stir in the mayonnaise, mustard, and paprika; stir again.

Shape the mixture into 10 balls.

Place the hemp hearts on a medium plate; roll each ball through to coat. Arrange these balls on a nice serving platter and serve. Bon appétit!

Per serving: 341 Calories; 30.6g Fat; 3.4g Carbs; 12.8g Protein; 0.2g Fiber

565. Ciauscolo Salami and Mozzarella Bites

(Ready in about 10 minutes | Servings 5)

Ingredients

5 ounces Ciauscolo salami, chopped
5 ounces mozzarella cheese
4 large egg yolks, hard-boiled
2 tablespoons extra-virgin olive oil
1 teaspoon Roman mustard
1/2 teaspoon smoked paprika
2 tablespoons sesame seeds, lightly toasted

Directions

Thoroughly combine all ingredients, except for the sesame seeds, in a mixing dish.

Now, roll your mixture into 10 small balls. Roll each ball over the toasted sesame seeds until well coated on all sides.

Serve well chilled!

Per serving: 341 Calories; 30.6g Fat; 3.4g Carbs; 12.8g Protein; 1g Fiber

566. Soppressata Keto Bombs

(Ready in about 15 minutes | Servings 8)

Ingredients

1 teaspoon baking powder
1/2 teaspoon dried oregano
6 ounces cream cheese
1 teaspoon garlic, minced
1/4 cup almond meal
6 slices Soppressata, chopped
1 egg, whisked
1/2 teaspoon dried basil
6 ounces Parmigiano-Reggiano cheese, grated
Salt and pepper, to taste

Directions

Thoroughly combine all ingredients until well combined.

Roll the mixture into bite-sized balls and arrange them on a parchment-lined cookie sheet.

Bake in the preheated oven at 400 degrees F approximately 15 minutes or until they are golden and crisp. Bon appétit!

Per serving: 168 Calories; 13g Fat; 2.5g Carbs; 10.3g Protein; 0.2g Fiber

567. Swiss Cheese and Beef-Stuffed Avocado

(Ready in about 20 minutes | Servings 6)

Ingredients

3/4 cup Swiss cheese, shredded
3/4 pound beef, ground
3 tablespoons olives, pitted and sliced
Salt and pepper, to taste
1 cup cherry tomatoes, chopped
1/2 cup onions, sliced
1/3 cup roasted vegetable broth
1 tablespoon olive oil
1/2 cup aioli
3 ripe avocados, pitted and halved

Directions

Scoop out the middle of each avocado; mash the avocado flesh.

In a Dutch oven, heat the olive oil until sizzling. Once hot, sear the ground beef for about 3 minutes, breaking apart with a fork.

Then, stir in the onion and continue to cook for about 2 minutes or until just aromatic.

Add in broth to deglaze the pan; add in salt, pepper, tomatoes, and avocado flesh. Spoon this filling into avocado halves.

Bake in the preheated oven at 340 degrees F for about 8 minutes. Top with the cheese, olives and aioli and bake an additional 5 minutes.

Bon appétit!

Per serving: 407 Calories; 28.8g Fat; 6.4g Carbs; 23.4g Protein; 5g Fiber

568. Provençal Muffins with Salami

(Ready in about 20 minutes | Servings 6)

Ingredients

- 1 teaspoon Herbes de Provence
- 10 slices salami, chopped
- 1/8 teaspoon grated nutmeg
- 1/2 teaspoon baking powder
- 2 tablespoons xylitol
- 2 teaspoons psyllium
- 1/8 teaspoon kosher salt
- 1/3 cup flaxseed meal
- 2/3 cup almond flour
- 2 eggs
- 1/2 cup yogurt
- non-stick cooking spray

Directions

Start by preheating your oven to 360 degrees F. Lightly grease a muffin pan with a non-stick cooking spray.

Thoroughly combine the flaxseed meal with the almond flour, xylitol, psyllium, salt, nutmeg, herbes de Provence and baking powder; stir until well combined.

Now, stir in the eggs, yogurt, and salami. Press the mixture into prepared muffin cups.

Bake about 15 minutes and transfer to a wire rack to cool slightly before removing from the muffin pan. Enjoy!

Per serving: 269 Calories; 20.7g Fat; 7g Carbs; 15.5g Protein; 2.2g Fiber

569. Dijon Chorizo Fat Bombs

(Ready in about 15 minutes + chilling time | Servings 5)

Ingredients

- 1/2 teaspoon Dijon mustard
- 2 tablespoons butter
- 2 teaspoons tomato paste, no sugar added
- 2 tablespoons mayonnaise
- 10 ounces soft cheese, softened
- 8 black olives, pitted and chopped
- 10 ounces Chorizo sausage, chopped

Directions

Sear the sausage in the preheated skillet until no longer pink. Add in the remaining ingredients and place it in the refrigerator.

Roll the batter into bite-sized balls and serve. Enjoy!

Per serving: 327 Calories; 25.7g Fat; 6.4g Carbs; 17g Protein; 0.3g Fiber

570. Meatballs with Pecorino Cheese

(Ready in about 40 minutes | Servings 5)

Ingredients

- 2 tablespoons green garlic, minced
- 1/2 cup ground pine nuts
- 2 eggs, whisked
- 1 tablespoon deli mustard
- 1 poblano pepper, deveined and minced
- 2 ounces Pecorino cheese, grated
- 1/2 cup green onions, chopped
- 2 tablespoons buttermilk
- 1/3 pound ground chicken
- 2/3 pound ground pork
- Salt and black pepper, to taste

Directions

In a mixing bowl, combine all of the above ingredients, except for the ground nuts. Shape the mixture into small balls.

Roll these balls over the ground nuts until they're coated on all sides.

Preheat a lightly greased skillet over a moderately-high heat. Fry your meatballs in batches until the juice is clear.

Bon appétit!

Per serving: 244 Calories; 13.3g Fat; 3.7g Carbs; 28.1g Protein; 1.1g Fiber

571. Cheese and Prosciutto Crisps

(Ready in about 20 minutes | Servings 6)

Ingredients

- 1 cup Parmesan cheese, finely shredded
- 1/2 teaspoon allspice
- 1 cup Cheddar cheese, shredded
- 1 poblano pepper, finely chopped
- 1/2 teaspoon cayenne pepper
- 4 slices prosciutto, crumbled
- Salt and pepper, to taste

Directions

Start by preheating your oven to 390 degrees F. Coat a baking sheet with a sheet of parchment paper.

Mix all ingredients until well combined.

Add the mixture in small heaps on the prepared baking sheet; be sure to leave enough room in between your crisps.

Bake in the preheated oven approximately 10 minutes. Let them cool on a cooling rack. Enjoy!

Per serving: 225 Calories; 19.3g Fat; 0.6g Carbs; 12.1g Protein; 0.2g Fiber

572. Herbed Mini Muffins with Hunter Salami

(Ready in about 20 minutes | Servings 6)

Ingredients

- 1/3 cup almond meal
- 2 tablespoons granulated Swerve
- 1/3 cup flaxseed meal
- 1/3 cup coconut flour
- 2 eggs
- 10 slices hunter salami, chopped
- 1/2 cup Greek-style yogurt
- 1/2 teaspoon baking powder
- 1 teaspoon herbes de Provence
- 2 teaspoons psyllium
- Salt and pepper, to taste

Directions

Preheat your oven to 365 degrees F. Brush a muffin tin with a non-stick spray.

Thoroughly combine the almond meal, flaxseed meal, coconut flour, Swerve, baking powder, psyllium, salt, pepper, and herbes de Provence.

Fold in the eggs, Greek-style yogurt, and chopped hunter salami. Spoon the mixture into the prepared muffin tin.

Bake in the preheated oven for 13 to 15 minutes until golden brown. Place on a wire rack to cool slightly before unmolding. Bon appétit!

Per serving: 269 Calories; 20.7g Fat; 5g Carbs; 15.5g Protein; 2.4g Fiber

FAST SNACKS & APPETIZERS

573. German-Style Sausage Fat Bombs

(Ready in about 15 minutes + chilling time | Servings 6)

Ingredients

1/2 pound Frankfurter sausage, sliced
4 ounces soft cheese
4 ounces fontina cheese, crumbled
2 garlic cloves, minced
1/2 shallot, minced
4 ounces Mozzarella cheese
2 tablespoons flaxseed meal
1 cup tomato puree
1 tablespoon lard
Sea salt and black pepper, to taste

Directions

In a frying pan, melt the lard over a moderately-high heat. Sear the sausage for about 5 minutes, crumbling with a fork or spatula.

Add in the tomato puree, garlic, and shallot and continue to sauté for 5 to 6 minutes more. Add in the remaining ingredients; stir until everything is well combined.

Place the mixture in your refrigerator and roll it into bite-sized balls. Enjoy!

Per serving: 353 Calories; 30.7g Fat; 3g Carbs; 16.1g Protein; 2.5g Fiber

574. Mascarpone and Bacon Balls

(Ready in about 10 minutes + chilling time | Servings 6)

Ingredients

3 ounces bacon, chopped
1/2 cup fresh parsley, finely chopped
1/4 teaspoon champagne vinegar
1 cup Mascarpone cheese
Salt and pepper, to season

Directions

In a mixing bowl, thoroughly combine the cheese, bacon, vinegar, salt, and pepper. Cover the bowl and place in your refrigerator for 2 to 3 hours to help firm it up.

Roll the mixture into balls.

Roll the fat bombs over chopped parsley until well coated.

Serve well chilled!

Per serving: 214 Calories; 20.4g Fat; 1.2g Carbs; 5.6g Protein; 0.3g Fiber

575. Herring-Stuffed Pickled Peppers

(Ready in about 10 minutes | Servings 4)

Ingredients

4 red pickled peppers, slice into halves
1 tablespoon fresh cilantro, chopped
1 celery, chopped
1/2 cup onions, chopped
1 teaspoon Dijon mustard
2 tablespoons lemon juice
7 ounces canned herring, chopped
Salt and black pepper, to taste

Directions

Thoroughly combine the herring, Dijon mustard, celery, onions, lemon juice, salt, black pepper, and fresh cilantro.

Mix until everything is well combined.

Spoon the herring mixture into the pickle boats. Bon appétit!

Per serving: 120 Calories; 5.4g Fat; 5.8g Carbs; 12.3g Protein; 1.4g Fiber

576. Baked Stuffed Avocado Boats

(Ready in about 20 minutes | Servings 4)

Ingredients

2 eggs, beaten
1 tablespoon fresh coriander, minced
1 teaspoon garlic, smashed
4 ounces Swiss cheese, grated
2 avocados, halved and pitted
Salt and red pepper, to taste

Directions

Begin by preheating your oven to 365 degrees F. Place the avocado halves in a baking dish.

In a mixing bowl, thoroughly combine the cheese, eggs, garlic, salt, pepper, and coriander. Spoon the mixture into the avocado halves.

Bake for about 16 minutes or until everything is cooked thorough. Bon appétit!

Per serving: 342 Calories; 30.4g Fat; 6.5g Carbs; 11.1g Protein; 4.9g Fiber

DESSERTS

577. Easy Buckeye Candy
(Ready in about 40 minutes | Servings 10)

Ingredients
- 1/2 cup crunchy peanut butter
- 1 tablespoon granular Swerve
- 3 tablespoons heavy cream
- 1/2 cup coconut oil
- 1/2 cup butter

Directions
Simmer all of the above ingredients in a pan over medium-low heat; stir continuously until everything is well incorporated.

Divide the batter among mini muffin cups lined with cupcake wrappers. Allow them to harden at least 30 minutes in your freezer.

Enjoy!

Per serving: 266 Calories; 28.1g Fat; 2.6g Carbs; 3.3g Protein; 0.3g Fiber

578. Greek-Style Chia Pudding
(Ready in about 1 hour | Servings 4)

Ingredients
- 1/2 cup Greek-style yogurt
- 1/3 cup chia seeds
- 1/2 cup coconut milk
- 1/2 teaspoon ground cloves
- 1/4 teaspoon ground cinnamon
- 1 cup coconut cream
- 2 tablespoons Erythritol
- 1/3 teaspoon vanilla extract

Directions
Place all ingredients in a glass jar and let it sit in your refrigerator for 1 hour.

Keep in your refrigerator for 3 days.

Per serving: 270 Calories; 24.7g Fat; 6.5g Carbs; 4.6g Protein; 4g Fiber

579. Easy Chocolate Panache
(Ready in about 15 minutes + chilling time | Servings 8)

Ingredients
- 3/4 Sukrin chocolate, broken into pieces
- 1/2 cup heavy cream
- 2 tablespoons coconut oil
- 4-5 drops Stevia
- 1 stick butter
- 1 cup condensed milk, sugar-free

Directions
Microwave the condensed milk and Sukrin chocolate for 70 seconds; spoon into a baking dish and freeze until firm.

Melt the butter in a small-sized pan; stir in the melted coconut oil, Stevia, and heavy cream; whisk to combine well or beat with a hand mixer.

Spread the cream mixture over the fudge layer in the baking dish. Then, freezer until solid.

Bon appétit!

Per serving: 220 Calories; 20g Fat; 7g Carbs; 1.7g Protein; 0g Fiber

580. Classic Jaffa Dessert
(Ready in about 15 minutes | Servings 4)

Ingredients
- 3/4 cup double cream
- 1 tablespoon orange juice, freshly squeezed
- 2 egg yolks
- 1/4 cup cocoa powder, unsweetened
- 1/4 teaspoon ground cardamom
- 1/4 cup Swerve
- 3 ounces cream cheese, at room temperature
- 1/4 teaspoon grated nutmeg

Directions
Whip the egg yolks using an electric mixer until pale and frothy.

Warm the cream and gradually fold in the hot cream into the beaten eggs.

Let it simmer for about 4 minutes, stirring continuously, until the mixture has reduced and thickened slightly.

In another mixing bowl, beat the remaining ingredients until everything is creamy and uniform. Fold the avocado mixture into the egg/cream mixture; gently stir until well combined.

Enjoy!

Per serving: 154 Calories; 13g Fat; 6.3g Carbs; 5.3g Protein; 1.7g Fiber

581. Nana's Ice Cream
(Ready in about 15 minutes + chilling time | Servings 8)

Ingredients
- 3/4 cup heavy cream
- 1/2 cup coconut milk
- 25 drops liquid stevia
- 1/3 teaspoon pure vanilla extract
- 1 tablespoon butterscotch flavoring
- 1/4 cup sour cream
- A pinch of salt

Directions
Cook the heavy cream and coconut milk in a pan that is preheated over a medium-low flame. Let it simmer, stirring constantly, until there are no lumps.

Allow it to cool at room temperature; mix in the remaining ingredients.

Blend with an electric mixer until your desired consistency is reached.

Bon appétit!

Per serving: 89 Calories; 9.3g Fat; 1.5g Carbs; 0.8g Protein; 0g Fiber

582. Blueberry Protein Smoothie

(Ready in about 10 minutes | Servings 4)

Ingredients

1/2 cup blueberries, frozen
1 cup coconut milk
2 tablespoons coconut cream
1/4 cup coconut shreds
1/2 teaspoon vanilla essence
2 tablespoons collagen protein
1/2 teaspoon Monk fruit powder

Directions

Pulse the frozen blueberries in your blender.

Add in the other ingredients and mix until creamy, smooth and uniform. Spoon into four glasses and enjoy!

Per serving: 274 Calories; 26.8g Fat; 7.5g Carbs; 3.9g Protein; 1.3g Fiber

583. Almond Brownie Cupcakes

(Ready in about 25 minutes | Servings 12)

Ingredients

1/2 cup almonds, ground
5 eggs
1 teaspoon rum extract
3/4 teaspoon baking powder
4 ounces cocoa powder
2 tablespoons Swerve
2/3 cup coconut oil, melted
1/2 teaspoon ground cinnamon
6 ounces sour cream

Directions

Begin by preheating your oven to 365 degrees F. Brush a muffin tin with a non-stick spray.

Mix all ingredients in a bowl and scrape the batter into the muffin cups.

Bake for about 20 minutes; let it cool slightly before unmolding and storing. Enjoy!

Per serving: 251 Calories; 21.5g Fat; 4.6g Carbs; 6.4g Protein; 0.8g Fiber

584. Rum Chocolate Cheesecake

(Ready in about 25 minutes | Servings 12)

Ingredients

5 eggs
2 ounces cocoa powder, unsweetened
1 teaspoon rum extract
1/4 teaspoon ground cinnamon
1 teaspoon vanilla paste
1/4 cup Swerve
1/3 teaspoon baking powder
6 ounces Neufchatel cheese, at room temperature
7 tablespoons coconut oil, melted

Directions

Beat the ingredients using your electric mixer on high speed. Line a mini muffin pan with 12 liners.

Spoon the mixture into the prepared muffins cups.

Bake in the preheated oven at 350 degrees F for about 20 minutes. Bon appétit!

Per serving: 134 Calories; 12.5g Fat; 3.3g Carbs; 4.6g Protein; 0.4g Fiber

585. Classic Pistachio Candy

(Ready in about 25 minutes + chilling time | Servings 6)

Ingredients

1/2 cup toasted pistachios, finely chopped
1/4 teaspoon ground cinnamon
1/2 cup heavy cream
1 teaspoon vanilla essence
3 bars sugar-free chocolate spread

Directions

Melt the chocolate spread with the heavy cream in your microwave for 1 minute or so.

Add the vanilla and ground cinnamon; transfer to your refrigerator for 8 hours or until firm enough to shape.

Shape the chocolate mixture into balls. Freeze for 20 minutes. Afterwards, roll the balls into the chopped pistachios. Bon appétit!

Per serving: 113 Calories; 8.5g Fat; 6.9g Carbs; 1.7g Protein; 1.1g Fiber

586. Iced Cappuccino Toffee

(Ready in about 10 minutes + chilling time | Servings 8)

Ingredients

1/2 teaspoon cappuccino flavor extract
1 cup heavy whipping cream
3 tablespoons erythritol
A pinch of salt
2 tablespoons cocoa powder
A pinch of grated nutmeg
1 cup brewed espresso
1 ½ cups avocado, pitted, peeled and mashed

Directions

Throw all of the above ingredients into your food processor; mix until everything is well combined.

Pour the mixture into an ice cube tray. Freeze overnight, at least 6 hours. Bon appétit!

Per serving: 117 Calories; 11.2g Fat; 5g Carbs; 1.3g Protein; 2.3g Fiber

587. Rustic Walnut Dessert

(Ready in about 2 hours | Servings 8)

Ingredients

1 cup condensed milk, unsweetened
2 ounces toasted walnuts, chopped
1/4 teaspoon orange rind, grated
1/2 teaspoon vanilla paste
1 stick butter
1 cup xylitol
A pinch of salt

Directions

Combine the xylitol and milk in a pan that is preheated over a moderate heat. Simmer, stirring often, for 5 to 6 minutes.

Stir in the butter and vanilla. Cream with an electric mixer at low speed; beat until very creamy.

Fold in the chopped walnuts, orange rind, and salt; stir again. Afterwards, spoon into a baking dish and freeze until firm, about 2 hours. Bon appétit!

Per serving: 167 Calories; 17.1g Fat; 6.8g Carbs; 2.4g Protein; 0.5g Fiber

588. Peanut Butter Custard

(Ready in about 40 minutes + chilling time | Servings 4)

Ingredients

1/2 cup peanut butter
4 eggs
1/2 teaspoon pure almond extract
1 cup coconut cream, unsweetened
1/2 teaspoon pure vanilla extract
1/2 cup granulated Swerve
1/4 teaspoon ground mace

Directions

Begin by preheating your oven to 340 degrees F. Place 4 ramekins in a deep baking pan. Pour boiling water to a depth of about 1 inch.

In a saucepan, bring the coconut cream to a simmer. In a mixing dish, whisk the remaining ingredients until the eggs are foamy.

Slowly and gradually pour the egg mixture into the warm coconut cream, whisking constantly.

Spoon the prepared mixture into ramekins and bake for 35 minutes, or until a tester comes out dry. Bon appétit!

Per serving: 304 Calories; 27.7g Fat; 6.6g Carbs; 11.6g Protein; 2g Fiber

589. Chocolate and Peanut Butter Chewy Cake

(Ready in about 3 hours | Servings 8)

Ingredients

3 tablespoons cocoa nibs, unsweetened and melted
1 stick butter
1/3 cup almond milk
3 tablespoons coconut oil, at room temperature
1 teaspoon vanilla extract
3/4 cup peanut butter, sugar-free, preferably homemade
A pinch of grated nutmeg
1/3 cup Swerve
1/4 teaspoon baking powder
A pinch of salt

Directions

Melt the butter in your microwave. Stir in the milk, 1/4 cup of Swerve, salt, nutmeg, and baking powder.

Spoon the batter into a parchment-lined baking dish. Refrigerate for about 3 hours or until set.

Meanwhile, make the sauce by whisking the remaining ingredients until everything is well incorporated.

Spoon the sauce over your fudge cake. Place in your refrigerator until ready to use.

Per serving: 180 Calories; 18.3g Fat; 4.5g Carbs; 1g Protein; 1.1g Fiber

590. Coconut Raspberry Shake

(Ready in about 10 minutes | Servings 4)

Ingredients

1 cup coconut milk
1/2 cup raspberries, frozen
2 tablespoons hemp seeds
1 teaspoon vanilla paste
4 drops liquid stevia
2 tablespoons almond butter
1/4 cup coconut shreds

Directions

Pulse the frozen berries in your food processor to the desired consistency.

Add the coconut milk, almond butter, coconut, vanilla and stevia. Blend until everything is well incorporated; top with hemp seeds

Pour the smoothie into four glasses and enjoy!

Per serving: 274 Calories; 26.8g Fat; 6.5g Carbs; 3.9g Protein; 1.7g Fiber

591. Mediterranean-Style Chocolate Pudding

(Ready in about 15 minutes + chilling time | Servings 6)

Ingredients

Fresh juice and zest of 1/2 tangerine
1/2 teaspoon crystallized ginger
6 ounces chocolate, unsweetened
2 cups whipped cream
3 tablespoons powdered erythritol
3 1/3 tablespoons Dutch-processed brown cocoa powder
1/4 teaspoon ground cloves

Directions

Using a stand mixer with a whisk attachment, whip the cream until soft peaks form.

Add in the powdered erythritol and cocoa powder and beat again. Add in the remaining ingredients and beat until everything is well incorporated.

Bon appétit!

Per serving: 158 Calories; 15.7g Fat; 7.2g Carbs; 2.2g Protein; 1.6g Fiber

592. Rum and Walnut Truffles

(Ready in about 1 hour | Servings 10)

Ingredients

1 tablespoon rum
4 tablespoons walnuts, coarsely chopped
1/2 cup chocolate, sugar-free
1/4 cup confectioners' Swerve
1/2 coconut oil, room temperature
4 ounces coconut cream
1/2 teaspoon pure vanilla extract
1/2 cup lightly toasted walnuts, chopped

Directions

Melt the coconut oil in a double boiler and fold in the coconut cream and confectioners' Swerve; stir to combine well. Remove from the heat and add in the rum, vanilla extract and chopped walnuts.

Let it cool to room temperature. Roll into 20 balls and chill for about 50 minutes.

Then, melt the chocolate and dip each ball into the chocolate glaze.

Roll your truffles in the chopped walnuts until well coated. Bon appétit!

Per serving: 162 Calories; 14.6g Fat; 5.9g Carbs; 2.3g Protein; 1.7g Fiber

DESSERTS

593. Chia Pudding with Coconut

(Ready in about 20 minutes | Servings 4)

Ingredients

1 cup heavy cream
2 tablespoons erythritol
1/4 teaspoon ground cloves
1/2 teaspoon ground anise star
1 cup coconut milk, unsweetened
1 cup chia seeds
1/4 cup coconut shreds, unsweetened
1 teaspoon vanilla extract
1 cup water

Directions

Thoroughly combine all of the above ingredients in a mixing dish.

Allow it to stand at least 20 minutes, stirring periodically. Let it cool and enjoy!

Per serving: 226 Calories; 17.9g Fat; 6.8g Carbs; 5.9g Protein; 3.3g Fiber

594. Chocolate and Almond Squares

(Ready in about 25 minutes + chilling time | Servings 10)

Ingredients

8 ounces chocolate chunks, sugar-free
1 cup almond meal
2 packets stevia
1 teaspoon vanilla extract
1/4 cup coconut flour
1 ½ cups whipped cream
1/2 teaspoon rum extract
1/4 teaspoon cinnamon
1/4 cup flaxseed meal
1/2 stick butter, cold
A pinch of coarse salt

Directions

Start by preheating your oven to 340 degrees F. Coat a baking dish with a piece of parchment paper.

Add the coconut flour, flaxseed meal, almond meal, stevia, cinnamon, rum extract, vanilla, and salt to your blender. Blend until everything is well incorporated.

Cut in the cold butter and continue to blend until well combined.

Spoon the batter into the bottom of the prepared baking pan. Bake for 12 to 15 minutes and place on a wire rack to cool slightly.

Bring the whipped cream to a simmer; add in the chocolate chunks and whisk to combine. Spread the chocolate filling over the crust and place in your refrigerator until set. Cut into bars. Bon appétit!

Per serving: 119 Calories; 11.7g Fat; 5.2g Carbs; 1.1g Protein; 5g Fiber

595. British Strawberry Dessert

(Ready in about 25 minutes | Servings 10)

Ingredients

1 cup strawberries
1 cup almond flour
2 eggs
1 ½ sticks butter
10 tablespoons liquid stevia
1 teaspoon vanilla extract
1 teaspoon baking powder
A pinch of salt
1 cup heavy cream
1 cup coconut flour

Directions

Start by preheating your oven to 350 degrees F.

In a mixing bowl, thoroughly combine the flour with the baking powder, salt and strawberries.

In another mixing bowl, beat the eggs with the butter and cream. Stir in the liquid stevia and vanilla extract; stir to combine well.

Combine the 2 mixtures and stir until you obtain a soft dough. Knead gently and avoid overworking your dough.

Shape into 16 triangles and arrange on a lined baking sheet; bake for 18 minutes.

Bon appétit!

Per serving: 245 Calories; 21.6g Fat; 7g Carbs; 3.8g Protein; 0.6g Fiber

596. Berry Cheesecake Squares

(Ready in about 30 minutes | Servings 6)

Ingredients

For the Cheesecake Squares:
3 tablespoons Swerve
4 eggs
1/2 cup butter, melted
1 cup soft cheese
1 teaspoon vanilla essence

For the Berry Topping:
3/4 cup, frozen mixed berries
1 ½ tablespoons coconut milk
2 tablespoons Swerve
1/2 teaspoon lime juice

Directions

Start by preheating your oven to 340 degrees F. Line a baking pan with a Silpat mat.

In a mixing bowl, combine all ingredients for the cheesecake squares using an electric mixer. Press the crust into the baking pan.

Bake in the preheated oven for about 23 minutes.

Warm all of the topping ingredients in a saucepan over a moderate flame. Reduce the heat to a simmer and continue to cook until the sauce has reduced by half.

Spoon the berry topping over the chilled cheesecake. Bon appétit!

Per serving: 333 Calories; 28.4g Fat; 6.3g Carbs; 11.7g Protein; 0.1g Fiber

597. Vanilla Rum Cheesecake Cupcakes

(Ready in about 30 minutes + chilling time | Servings 8)

Ingredients

For the Muffins:
2 eggs
1 tablespoon rum
10 ounces Ricotta cheese, at room temperature
1/4 teaspoon ground cinnamon
1/8 teaspoon nutmeg, preferably freshly grated
2 packets stevia
1/8 teaspoon ground cloves
3 tablespoons coconut oil

For the Frosting:
1 ½ tablespoons full-fat milk
1/2 stick butter, softened
1 teaspoon vanilla
1/2 cup confectioners' Swerve

DESSERTS

Directions

Preheat your oven to 360 degrees F; coat muffin cups with cupcake liners.

Thoroughly combine the coconut oil, Ricotta cheese, rum, eggs, stevia, cloves, cinnamon and nutmeg in your food processor.

Scrape the batter into the muffin tin; bake for 13 to 16 minutes. Now, place in the freezer for 2 hours.

In the meantime, combine the confectioners' Swerve with the butter and vanilla with an electric mixer.

Slowly pour in the milk in order to make a spreadable mixture. Frost the chilled cheesecake cupcakes.

Bon appétit!

Per serving: 165 Calories; 15.6g Fat; 6.4g Carbs; 5.2g Protein; 0.1g Fiber

598. Caramel Chocolate Candy

(Ready in about 10 minutes + chilling time | Servings 8)

Ingredients

1 teaspoon sugar-free caramel flavored syrup
3 tablespoons butter
1 teaspoon cold brew coffee concentrate
3 tablespoons cocoa butter
3 ounces dark chocolate, sugar-free
6 drops liquid stevia

Directions

Microwave the cocoa butter, butter, and chocolate for 1 minute or so.

Stir in the remaining ingredients. Pour into candy-safe molds.

Keep in your refrigerator and enjoy!

Per serving: 145 Calories; 12.8g Fat; 6.9g Carbs; 0.9g Protein; 1.2g Fiber

599. Light Peanut Butter Mousse

(Ready in about 15 minutes | Servings 4)

Ingredients

1 tablespoon lime juice
1/2 cup coconut whipped cream
1/2 cup crunchy peanut butter
1 teaspoon pure vanilla extract
50 drops liquid stevia
1/2 cup canned coconut milk
1/4 teaspoon ground cloves
1 cup avocado, peeled, pitted, and diced

Directions

Process the avocados, peanut butter, stevia and coconut milk in a blender.

Now, add the vanilla extract, cloves, and lime juice. Garnish with coconut whipped cream.

Spoon your pudding into four airtight containers; keep in your refrigerator for 5 to 6 days.

Enjoy!

Per serving: 288 Calories; 27.3g Fat; 6.9g Carbs; 6.2g Protein; 5g Fiber

600. Avocado Coffee Popsicles

(Ready in about 10 minutes + chilling time | Servings 8)

Ingredients

1 cup brewed coffee
1 ½ cups avocado, pitted, peeled and mashed
1 cup double cream
1/2 teaspoon cappuccino flavor extract
2 tablespoons cocoa powder
3 tablespoons Swerve

Directions

Using a stand mixer with a whisk attachment, whip the double cream until soft peaks form.

Process all ingredients in your blender or food processor until everything is creamy and smooth.

Pour the mixture into popsicle molds and freeze overnight. Enjoy!

Per serving: 117 Calories; 11.2g Fat; 5g Carbs; 1.3g Protein; 3g Fiber

601. Buttered Whiskey Cupcakes

(Ready in about 30 minutes + chilling time | Servings 8)

Ingredients

1 tablespoon whiskey
10 ounces soft cheese, at room temperature
1/2 teaspoon ground cinnamon
2 packets stevia
3 tablespoons butter, melted
2 eggs

For the Frosting:
1 ½ tablespoons coconut milk, unsweetened
1/2 stick butter, at room temperature
1/2 cup powdered erythritol
1 teaspoon butterscotch extract

Directions

Start by preheating your oven to 365 degrees F.

Mix the butter, soft cheese, whiskey, eggs, stevia, and cinnamon until well combined.

Scrape the batter into the muffin pan and bake approximately 15 minutes; place the muffin pan in the freezer for 2 hours.

In a mixing bowl, beat 1/2 stick of butter with the powdered erythritol and butterscotch extract.

Gradually pour in the milk and mix again. Afterwards, frost the chilled cupcakes. Bon appétit!

Per serving: 165 Calories; 15.6g Fat; 5.4g Carbs; 5.2g Protein; 1.7g Fiber

602. Nutty Fat Bombs

(Ready in about 40 minutes | Servings 12)

Ingredients

10 drops Monk fruit powder
1/4 cup almond flour
1/2 cup coconut oil
1 teaspoon vanilla essence
1/2 cup cashew butter
2/3 cup pecans, chopped
2 tablespoons cocoa powder, unsweetened

Directions

Mix all ingredients in a bowl until well combined.

Drop by teaspoonfuls onto foil-lined baking sheets. Chill in your refrigerator until firm. Bon appétit!

Per serving: 114 Calories; 10.6g Fat; 3.4g Carbs; 3.1g Protein; 1g Fiber

DESSERTS

603. Rum Coconut Candy

(Ready in about 15 minutes + chilling time | Servings 16)

Ingredients

1 tablespoon rum
1/4 cup unsweetened cocoa powder
1 teaspoon vanilla extract
1 ½ cups bakers' chocolate, unsweetened
3 tablespoons Swerve
1/4 cup coconut oil
1 cup whipped cream
4 tablespoons coconut flakes

Directions

Melt the chocolate in your microwave. Add in the coconut flakes, coconut oil, cream, Swerve, vanilla extract, and rum.

Place in your refrigerator until the batter is well-chilled. Roll the mixture into balls and cover with cocoa powder on all sides.

Bon appétit!

Per serving: 90 Calories; 6.3g Fat; 4.9g Carbs; 3.7g Protein; 0.5g Fiber

604. Rustic Almond Cheesecake

(Ready in about 30 minutes + chilling time | Servings 10)

Ingredients

For the Crust:
2 tablespoons almonds, toasted and chopped
1 cup almond meal
4 tablespoons peanut butter, room temperature
For the Filling:
1/2 teaspoon Stevia
1/2 teaspoon sugar-free caramel flavored syrup
1 teaspoon fresh ginger, grated
2 eggs
10 ounces cream cheese, room temperature
A pinch of grated nutmeg
1/2 teaspoon vanilla essence
A pinch of salt

Directions

Begin by preheating your oven to 360 degrees F. Line a baking pan with parchment paper.

Thoroughly combine the peanut butter with the almond meal. Then, press the crust mixture into your baking pan and bake for 7 minutes.

Then, make the filling, by mixing all the filling ingredients with an electric mixer.

Spread the filling onto the prepared crusts; bake for a further 18 minutes.

Transfer it to the refrigerator to chill. Garnish with chopped, toasted almonds. Enjoy!

Per serving: 211 Calories; 19g Fat; 4.4g Carbs; 7g Protein; 0.2g Fiber

605. Dad's Rum Caramels

(Ready in about 10 minutes + chilling time | Servings 8)

Ingredients

3 tablespoons cocoa powder
1/4 cup almond butter
2 tablespoons dark rum
1/2 teaspoon almond extract
1/2 teaspoon rum extract
1 cup bakers' chocolate, sugar-free
1 cup almond milk
1/8 teaspoon ground cloves
1/8 teaspoon cinnamon powder

Directions

Microwave the chocolate, cocoa and almond butter until they have completely melted.

Add in the other ingredients and mix to combine well. Pour the mixture into silicone molds and place in your refrigerator until set.

Bon appétit!

Per serving: 70 Calories; 3.4g Fat; 5.1g Carbs; 2.4g Protein; 1.6g Fiber

606. Fluffy Coconut Cheesecake

(Ready in about 40 minutes + chilling time | Servings 10)

Ingredients

For the Cake Base:
4 eggs
1 ½ cups almond meal
1/2 teaspoon baking powder
1 cup erythritol
1 cup full-fat milk
1 teaspoon vanilla extract
2 ½ tablespoons butter
2/3 cup coconut flour
A pinch of coarse salt
For the Frosting:
10 ounces soft cheese
A few drops coconut flavor
3 ounces coconut oil, at room temperature
1/3 cup erythritol

Directions

Mix all ingredients for the cake base until well combined.

Press the crust into a parchment-lined springform pan. Bake at 365 degrees F for 30 minutes or until a toothpick comes out clean; allow it to cool to room temperature.

Meanwhile, beat the cheese using your electric mixer until creamy. Stir in the remaining ingredients and continue to mix until well combined.

Frost your cake and serve well-chilled. Bon appétit!

Per serving: 241 Calories; 22.6g Fat; 4.2g Carbs; 6.6g Protein; 0.7g Fiber

607. Flourless Chocolate Cake

(Ready in about 15 minutes + chilling time | Servings 8)

Ingredients

1 cup full-fat milk
1/2 cup double cream
4-5 drops Monk fruit sweetener
1/2 cup butter, at room temperature
3/4 cup chocolate chunks, unsweetened
2 tablespoons coconut oil

Directions

Microwave the chocolate and milk until they've completely melted; spoon into a foil-lined pie pan and freeze until firm.

Then, melt the butter, coconut oil, Monk fruit sweetener, and double cream; mix with a wire whisk to combine well.

Spoon the cream mixture over the chocolate layer and freeze until solid.

Enjoy!

Per serving: 220 Calories; 20g Fat; 7g Carbs; 1.7g Protein; 2.1g Fiber

608. Fluffy Brownies with Pecans

(Ready in about 25 minutes | Servings 12)

Ingredients
- 3 ounces sour cream
- 1/4 teaspoon ground cloves
- 2 tablespoons stevia powder
- 3/4 teaspoon baking powder
- 4 ounces cocoa powder
- 1/2 cup pecans, ground
- 3 ounces cream cheese
- 1 teaspoon vanilla paste
- 3/4 cup butter, melted
- 5 eggs

Directions
Preheat your oven to 360 degrees F. Place a baking cup in each of 12 regular-size muffin cups.

Thoroughly combine all ingredients in your food processor. Spoon the batter into the muffin cups.

Bake for 18 to 22 minutes. Transfer to a wire rack to cool and enjoy!

Per serving: 251 Calories; 21.5g Fat; 7.2g Carbs; 6.4g Protein; 1.3g Fiber

609. Rum Cake with Cream Cheese Frosting

(Ready in about 40 minutes + chilling time | Servings 10)

Ingredients
- 4 eggs
- 1/2 teaspoon baking powder
- 1/2 teaspoon Konjac root fiber
- 1 cup Swerve
- 1 teaspoon fresh ginger, grated
- 2 ½ tablespoons ghee
- 1 cup coconut milk, sugar-free
- 1 teaspoon rum extract
- A pinch of salt
- A pinch of grated nutmeg
- 1 ½ cups almond flour
- 1 teaspoon vanilla extract
- 2/3 cup coconut flour
- 1/2 teaspoon baking soda
- For the Cream Cheese Frosting:
- 3 ounces butter, at room temperature
- A few drops chocolate flavor
- 10 ounces cream cheese, cold
- 1/3 cup powdered granular sweetener
- 1 teaspoon vanilla

Directions
Start by preheating your oven to 360 degrees F. Line a baking pan with parchment paper.

In a mixing bowl, combine the coconut flour, almond flour, baking soda, baking powder, salt, nutmeg, Konjac root fiber, Swerve, and ginger.

Microwave the ghee until melted and add to the dry mixture in the mixing bowl. Fold in the eggs, one at a time, and stir until combined.

Lastly, pour in the coconut milk, rum extract, and vanilla extract until your batter is light and fluffy.

Press the mixture into the prepared baking pan. Bake for 28 to 33 minutes or until a cake tester inserted in center comes out clean and dry.

Let it cool to room temperature.

Meanwhile, beat the cream cheese with an electric mixer until smooth. Stir in the powdered granular sweetener and beat again. Beat in the vanilla until it is completely incorporated.

Add the butter, vanilla, and chocolate flavor; whip until light, fluffy and uniform. Frost the cake. Enjoy!

Per serving: 241 Calories; 22.6g Fat; 4.2g Carbs; 6.6g Protein; 0.5g Fiber

610. Light Walnut Pudding

(Ready in about 10 minutes + chilling time | Servings 6)

Ingredients
- 2 tablespoons walnuts, chopped
- 2 tablespoons cocoa powder
- 1/2 teaspoon almond extract
- A few drops Monk fruit powder
- 1/2 stick butter, melted

Directions
Melt the butter in your microwave; add in the almond extract, Monk fruit powder, and cocoa powder.

Spoon the mixture into a parchment-lined baking tray. Scatter the chopped walnuts on top and place in your freezer until set.

Bon appétit!

Per serving: 84 Calories; 8.9g Fat; 1.5g Carbs; 0.8g Protein; 0.7g Fiber

611. Creamy Lemon Jell-O

(Ready in about 45 minutes | Servings 10)

Ingredients
- 1 ¼ cups double cream
- 1 teaspoon vanilla extract
- 5 tablespoons powdered Erythritol
- 1/2 teaspoon ginger, minced
- 3/4 cup boiling water
- 2 envelopes lemon gelatin

Directions
Combine the gelatin, Erythritol, ginger, and vanilla in a heatproof dish. Pour in the boiling water.

Stir until the gelatin has dissolved completely.

Stir in the double cream; continue to stir with a wire whisk. Pour the mixture into molds and transfer to your refrigerator for 30 to 35 minutes or until they are solid. Bon appétit!

Per serving: 56 Calories; 5.5g Fat; 0.4g Carbs; 1.5g Protein; 0g Fiber

612. Old-Fashioned Greek Cheesecake

(Ready in about 30 minutes | Servings 12)

Ingredients
- 1 ounce coconut flakes
- 5 ounces soft cheese
- 4 ounces Swerve
- 1/4 coconut oil
- 10 ounces almond meal
- 1 teaspoon baking powder
- 4 eggs, lightly beaten
- 5 ounces Greek-style yogurt
- 1/4 teaspoon grated nutmeg
- 1 teaspoon lemon zest

Directions
Brush two spring form pans with a non-stick spray.

Mix the almond meal, coconut flakes, nutmeg, and baking powder. Add in the eggs, one at a time, whisking constantly; add in 2 ounces of Swerve.

Spoon the mixture into spring form pans and bake at 360 degrees F for 23 minutes.

In another bowl, combine the coconut oil, lemon zest, yogurt, soft cheese, and the remaining 2 ounces of Swerve. Mix to combine and spoon the filling over the first crust. Spread half of the filling over it.

Top with another crust and spread the rest of the filling over the top. Bon appétit!

Per serving: 246 Calories; 22.2g Fat; 5.7g Carbs; 8.1g Protein; 1.9g Fiber

613. Almond Bar Cookie

(Ready in about 30 minutes | Servings 8)

Ingredients

1/2 cup almonds, chopped
3/4 cup heavy whipping cream
3 eggs
1/2 cup Swerve
1 teaspoon vanilla paste
2 cups almond flour
1 stick butter, melted
1/2 cup Swerve
1/2 teaspoon ground cinnamon
3/4 teaspoon baking powder
A pinch of grated nutmeg
A pinch of sea salt

Directions

Preheat your oven to 360 degrees F. Then, line a baking pan with parchment paper.

In a mixing bowl, thoroughly combine the almond flour, baking powder, Swerve, cinnamon, salt, and nutmeg.

Now, stir in the melted butter, eggs, Swerve, and vanilla paste. Next, stir in the heavy cream to create a soft texture.

Fold in the chopped almonds and gently stir until everything is well incorporated. Spoon the batter into the baking pan.

Bake approximately 27 minutes. Allow it to cool completely and cut into bars. Enjoy!

Per serving: 241 Calories; 23.6g Fat; 3.7g Carbs; 5.2g Protein; 0.1g Fiber

614. Traditional Brigadeiro with Berries

(Ready in about 15 minutes + chilling time | Servings 10)

Ingredients

1 cup freeze-dried mixed berries, crushed
1/2 cup peanut butter
1/4 cup butter
3/4 cup coconut oil
1/2 teaspoon vanilla extract
1/2 teaspoon coconut extract
4 ounces bakers' chocolate chunks, unsweetened

Directions

Melt the butter, peanut butter, and coconut oil in a double boiler over medium-low heat. Fold in the chocolate chunks, mixed berries, vanilla extract, and coconut extract.

Shape the batter into small balls and let them harden in your refrigerator.

Bon appétit!

Per serving: 334 Calories; 37g Fat; 5.3g Carbs; 1.6g Protein; 0.6g Fiber

615. Boozy Walnut Candy

(Ready in about 1 hour | Servings 10)

Ingredients

4 tablespoons walnuts, coarsely chopped
1 tablespoon brandy
1/4 cup Sukrin Icing
1/2 cup chopped toasted walnuts
1/2 cup chocolate chips, sugar-free
1/2 stick butter
1/2 teaspoon pure almond extract
4 ounces heavy cream

Directions

Melt the butter in a double boiler, stirring constantly.

Then, stir in the cream and Sukrin icing; stir to combine well. Remove from the heat and add the brandy, almond extract and chopped walnuts.

Now, allow it to cool at room temperature. Shape into 20 balls and chill for 40 to 50 minutes.

In a double boiler, melt the chocolate chips over medium-low heat. Dip each ball into the chocolate coating.

Afterwards, roll your candy in the chopped walnuts. Bon appétit!

Per serving: 162 Calories; 14.6g Fat; 5.9g Carbs; 2.3g Protein; 1g Fiber

616. Greek-Style Walnut Cheesecake

(Ready in about 1 hour | Servings 14)

Ingredients

The Crust:
8 ounces walnuts, chopped
1 stick butter, melted
1/4 teaspoon ground cloves
1/3 cup Swerve
1/4 teaspoon ground cinnamon
A pinch of salt

For the Filling:
14 ounces Greek-style yogurt
4 eggs
22 ounces Neufchâtel cheese, at room temperature
1 cup Swerve
1 teaspoon pure vanilla extract

Directions

Mix all ingredients for the crust; press the mixture into a baking pan and set it aside.

Whip the Neufchâtel cheese using your electric mixer on low speed.

Add in 1 cup of Swerve and vanilla. Fold in the eggs, one at a time, mixing constantly on low speed. Add in the Greek-style yogurt and gently stir to combine.

Bake in the preheated oven at 290 degrees F for 50 to 55 minutes. Bon appétit!

Per serving: 393 Calories; 38g Fat; 4.1g Carbs; 9.8g Protein; 1.1g Fiber

617. Home-Style Coconut Pastry

(Ready in about 40 minutes + chilling time | Servings 4)

Ingredients

1 teaspoon pure almond extract
1/2 cup granulated Erythritol
4 eggs
1/4 teaspoon ground cinnamon
1/2 cup almond butter
1 cup coconut cream, unsweetened
A pinch of nutmeg
A pinch of salt

Directions

Melt the coconut cream in a sauté pan over medium-low heat. Remove from the heat.

Mix the remaining ingredients until well combined. Now, gradually pour the egg mixture into the warm coconut cream, whisking to combine well.

Spoon the mixture into small tart cases. Bake in the preheated oven at 350 degrees F for about 30 minutes until they are golden and firm. Bon appétit!

Per serving: 304 Calories; 27.7g Fat; 6.6g Carbs; 11.6g Protein; 1.5g Fiber

618. Fluffy Chocolate Cupcakes

(Ready in about 25 minutes | Servings 12)

Ingredients

6 ounces Neufchatel cheese, at room temperature
1 teaspoon pure vanilla extract
1/3 teaspoon baking powder
5 eggs
2 ounces cocoa powder
1/4 cup xylitol
1 teaspoon maple flavor
7 tablespoons butter, melted

Directions

Beat all ingredients with an electric mixer.

Place a paper baking cup in each of 12 muffin cups. Fill each cup 2/3 full.

Bake at 360 degrees F about 23 minutes. Allow your muffins to cool.

Bon appétit!

Per serving: 134 Calories; 12.5g Fat; 3.3g Carbs; 4.6g Protein; 1.4g Fiber

619. Macchiato Chocolate Bark

(Ready in about 10 minutes + chilling time | Servings 8)

Ingredients

3 ounces dark chocolate, unsweetened
6 tablespoons butter
1 tablespoon peanut butter
1 teaspoon liquid Monk fruit
1 teaspoon caramel flavor
1 teaspoon warm coffee

Directions

Microwave the butter and chocolate until they are completely melted.

Fold in the remaining ingredients. Spoon the batter into a foil-lined baking pan, smoothing out the top.

Place in your refrigerator for 30 minutes before cutting. Enjoy!

Per serving: 145 Calories; 12.8g Fat; 6.2g Carbs; 0.9g Protein; 1.2g Fiber

620. Espresso Vanilla Shots

(Ready in about 10 minutes + chilling time | Servings 6)

Ingredients

1 teaspoon espresso powder
1 teaspoon pure vanilla extract
4 ounces coconut milk creamer
4 ounces coconut oil
3 tablespoons powdered Erythritol
2 teaspoons butter, softened
A pinch of grated nutmeg

Directions

Melt the butter and coconut oil in a double boiler over medium-low heat.

Add in the remaining ingredients and stir to combine.

Pour into silicone molds. Enjoy!

Per serving: 218 Calories; 24.7g Fat; 1.1g Carbs; 0.4g Protein; 0.7g Fiber

621. Rich Chocolate and Walnut Dessert

(Ready in about 30 minutes | Servings 10)

Ingredients

2 eggs
1 cup almond meal
1/4 teaspoon ground cinnamon
1/3 cup baker's chocolate chunks, unsweetened
3/4 cup coconut flour
1/2 teaspoon baking powder
1/4 teaspoon ground cardamom
1/2 cup walnuts, chopped
5 drops liquid Monk fruit
1/2 teaspoon almond extract
1/2 cup coconut oil

Directions

Start by preheating your oven to 360 degrees F. Line a baking sheet with a parchment paper.

Melt the coconut oil in a double over low heat.

Thoroughly combine the almond extract, eggs, and Monk fruit. Add in the melted coconut oil along with the remaining ingredients. Stir to combine well.

Scrape the mixture into the prepared baking sheet. Bake in the preheated oven for 25 to 30 minutes. Enjoy!

Per serving: 157 Calories; 14.8g Fat; 3.5g Carbs; 4.5g Protein; 2.2g Fiber

622. Walnut Butter Penuche

(Ready in about 15 minutes + chilling time | Servings 12)

Ingredients

1 ¼ cups walnut butter, sugar-free
1/4 teaspoon grated nutmeg
1/4 teaspoon ground star anise
1/4 teaspoon lemon peel zest
2 tablespoons xylitol
1/8 teaspoon coarse sea salt
3 ounces sugar-free white chocolate
1/3 cup coconut milk, unsweetened
3/4 cup butter, softened

Directions

Microwave the butter, walnut butter, and white chocolate until they are melted. Add the butter mixture to your food processor.

Now, add the other ingredients and mix again until everything is well incorporated. Scrape the mixture into a parchment lined baking pan.

Enjoy!

Per serving: 202 Calories; 21.3g Fat; 2.3g Carbs; 2.4g Protein; 0.8g Fiber

623. Greek-Style Ice Cream

(Ready in about 15 minutes + chilling time | Servings 8)

Ingredients

1/4 cup Greek-style yogurt
24 packets of stevia
A pinch of grated nutmeg
1/2 cup coconut milk
1 tablespoon rum flavoring
3/4 cup double cream
A pinch of salt

Directions

Melt the double cream and coconut milk in a saucepan over a medium-low heat. Stir until there are no lumps.

Allow it to cool and add in the other ingredients.

Beat the ingredients using an electric mixer until creamy and uniform.

Store your ice cream in the very back of the freezer for up to 2 to 4 months. Bon appétit!

Per serving: 89 Calories; 9.3g Fat; 1.5g Carbs; 0.8g Protein; 0g Fiber

624. Chocolate Walnut Teacakes

(Ready in about 30 minutes | Servings 10)

Ingredients

1/3 cup sugar-free baker's chocolate, cut into chunks
1/2 cup walnuts, chopped
1 ¾ cups almond flour
1/2 teaspoon baking powder
15 drops liquid stevia
1/4 teaspoon ground cinnamon
1/2 teaspoon pure almond extract
2 eggs
1 stick butter
1/8 teaspoon kosher salt

Directions

Heat the butter in a pan that is preheated over a moderate flame; stir and cook until it is browned.

In a mixing bowl, beat the pure almond extract with the eggs, stevia, and salt.

Add the melted butter, along with the other ingredients.

Preheat your oven to 350 degrees F. Line a cookie sheet with a parchment paper. Spritz with a non-stick cooking spray.

Bake for 25 minutes and transfer to a wire rack to cool enjoy!

Per serving: 157 Calories; 14.8g Fat; 3.5g Carbs; 4.5g Protein; 0.6g Fiber

625. White Chocolate and Almond Penuche

(Ready in about 15 minutes + chilling time | Servings 12)

Ingredients

2 tablespoons Swerve
1/8 teaspoon coarse sea salt
1 ¼ cups almond butter
3/4 cup coconut oil
3 ounces white chocolate, unsweetened
1/3 cup almond milk

Directions

Microwave the coconut oil, almond butter, and white chocolate until they are melted. Add in the remaining ingredients and process in your blender.

Scrape the mixture into a parchment-lined baking tray. Cut into squares and serve. Enjoy!

Per serving: 202 Calories; 21.3g Fat; 2.3g Carbs; 2.4g Protein; 2.2g Fiber

626. Berry Lemony Macaroons

(Ready in about 2 hours | Servings 10)

Ingredients

3 tablespoons freeze-dried mixed berries, crushed
1 teaspoon lemon rind
3 large egg whites, at room temperature
1/3 cup Erythritol
1 teaspoon vanilla extract

Directions

In a mixing bowl, beat the egg whites until foamy. Add in the vanilla extract, lemon rind, and Erythritol; continue to mix, using an electric mixer until stiff and glossy.

Add the crushed berries and mix again until well combined. Use two teaspoons to spoon meringue onto parchment-lined cookie sheets.

Bake at 220 degrees F for about 1 hour 45 minutes.

Bon appétit!

Per serving: 51 Calories; 0g Fat; 4g Carbs; 12g Protein; 0.1g Fiber

627. Birthday Chocolate Cake

(Ready in about 50 minutes + chilling time | Servings 10)

Ingredients

5 eggs
14 ounces unsweetened chocolate chunks
1/4 teaspoon ground cardamom
2 sticks butter, cold
1/2 teaspoon pure almond extract
1/4 teaspoon ground nutmeg
1/2 cup water
3/4 cup granulated Swerve
A pinch of salt
For Almond-Choc Ganache:
1/4 cup smooth almond butter
9 ounces sugar-free dark chocolate, broken into chunks
3/4 cups double cream
1/2 teaspoon cardamom powder
A pinch of salt
1/2 teaspoon ginger powder

Directions

Begin by preheating your oven to 360 degrees F. Line a baking pan with parchment paper.

Now bring the water to a rolling boil in a deep pan; add the Swerve and cook until it is dissolved.

Microwave the chocolate until melted. Add the butter to the melted chocolate and beat with an electric mixer.

Add the chocolate mixture to the hot water mixture. Now, add the eggs, one at a time, whipping continuously.

Add the almond extract, nutmeg, cardamom, and salt; stir well. Spoon the mixture into the prepared baking pan; wrap with foil.

Lower the baking pan into a larger pan; add boiling water about 1 inch deep.

Bake for 40 to 45 minutes. Allow it to cool completely before removing from the pan.

Meanwhile, place the double cream in a pan over a moderately high heat and bring to a boil. Pour the hot cream over the dark chocolate; whisk until the chocolate has melted.

Add the remaining ingredients for the ganache and whip until it is uniform and smooth. Finally, glaze the cooled cake. Enjoy!

Per serving: 313 Calories; 30.7g Fat; 7.5g Carbs; 7.3g Protein; 2.5g Fiber

628. Favorite Fat Bombs

(Ready in about 40 minutes | Servings 12)

Ingredients

1/4 cup unsweetened peanut flour
1/3 cup walnuts
10 drops liquid stevia
1 teaspoon vanilla extract
1/2 cup cashew butter
1/2 stick butter
2 tablespoons cocoa powder, unsweetened
1/2 cup almonds

Directions

Chop the almonds and walnuts in your food processor.

Transfer to a mixing bowl; add the other ingredients.

Scoop out tablespoons of the batter onto a cookie sheet lined with a wax paper. Place in your freezer approximately 30 minutes to cool completely. Bon appétit!

Per serving: 114 Calories; 10.6g Fat; 3.4g Carbs; 3.1g Protein; 0.6g Fiber

629. Zingy Peanut Buttercream

(Ready in about 15 minutes | Servings 4)

Ingredients

1/2 cup coconut milk
1 teaspoon vanilla extract
1/2 cup coconut cream
1 teaspoon monk fruit powder
1/2 cup peanut butter
1 tablespoon lemon juice
1 ½ cups avocado, peeled, pitted, and diced

Directions

Place all ingredients in your blender or food processor. Process until well combined. Bon appétit!

Per serving: 288 Calories; 27.3g Fat; 6.9g Carbs; 6.2g Protein; 5.2g Fiber

630. Classic Apple Crumble

(Ready in about 30 minutes | Servings 8)

Ingredients

2 eggs, whisked
1/4 cup coconut flour
5 tablespoons coconut oil, melted
1/2 tablespoon fresh lemon juice
1 cup almond flour
3/4 cup xylitol
1/3 teaspoon xanthan gum
2 ½ cups apples, cored and sliced

Directions

Start by preheating your oven to 360 degrees F. Lightly grease a baking dish with a non-stick cooking spray.

Arrange the apples on the bottom of the baking dish. Drizzle with lemon juice and xanthan gum.

Then, in a mixing bowl, mix the flour with the xylitol and eggs until the mixture resembles coarse meal. Spread this mixture over the apples.

Drizzle coconut oil over the topping. Bake for 25 minutes or until dough rises.

Bon appétit!

Per serving: 152 Calories; 11.8g Fat; 5.7g Carbs; 2.5g Protein; 0.9g Fiber

631. Coconut Cheesecake Pudding

(Ready in about 15 minutes+ chilling time | Servings 6)

Ingredients

1 ½ cups avocado, pitted, peeled and mashed
1/2 cup panela cheese
1/2 cup coconut creamer
2 tablespoons powdered Erythritol
1 cup double cream
1/2 cup coconut milk
A pinch of grated nutmeg

Directions

Warm the coconut milk and creamer over low heat. Remove from the heat.

Stir in the avocado and nutmeg; continue to stir until everything is well incorporated.

Add in the remaining ingredients. Beat using an electric mixer on medium-high speed. Place in your refrigerator until firm.

Enjoy!

Per serving: 303 Calories; 30g Fat; 3.1g Carbs; 3.5g Protein; 2.7g Fiber

632. Classic Coconut Cheesecake

(Ready in about 30 minutes | Servings 12)

Ingredients

5 ounces cream cheese
1/2 stick butter
4 eggs, lightly beaten
5 ounces coconut yogurt
10 ounces almond meal
1 ounce coconut, shredded
3 ounces stevia
1 teaspoon baking powder
1/8 teaspoon salt

Directions

Start by preheating your oven to 350 degrees F. Spritz 2 spring form pans with a non-stick cooking spray.

In a mixing bowl, thoroughly combine the almond meal, coconut and baking powder. Stir in the salt, eggs and 2 ounces of stevia.

Combine the 2 mixtures and stir until everything is well incorporated.

Transfer the mixture into 2 spring form pans, introduce in the oven at 350 degrees F; bake for 20 to 25 minutes.

Transfer to a wire rack to cool completely. In the meantime, mix the other ingredients, including the remaining 1 ounce of stevia.

Place one cake layer on a plate; spread half of the cream cheese filling over it. Now, top with another cake layer; spread the rest of the cream cheese filling over the top. Bon appétit!

Per serving: 246 Calories; 22.2g Fat; 6.7g Carbs; 8.1g Protein; 3.1g Fiber

DESSERTS

633. Coconut Cognac Bon Bons

(Ready in about 15 minutes + chilling time | Servings 16)

Ingredients

4 tablespoons coconut, desiccated
1 cup double cream
3 tablespoons xylitol
1/2 teaspoon pure almond extract
1 tablespoon cognac
1/2 stick butter
1 teaspoon vanilla paste
1 ½ cups bittersweet chocolate, sugar-free, broken into chunks
1/4 cup unsweetened Dutch-processed cocoa powder
A pinch of salt
A pinch of freshly grated nutmeg

Directions

Thoroughly combine the chocolate, coconut, butter, double cream, xylitol, almond extract, vanilla, salt, and grated nutmeg.

Microwave for 1 minute on medium-high; let it cool slightly. Now, stir in the cognac and vanilla.

Place in your refrigerator for 2 hours. Shape the mixture into balls; roll each ball in the cocoa powder. Bon appétit!

Per serving: 90 Calories; 6.3g Fat; 4.9g Carbs; 3.7g Protein; 0.6g Fiber

634. Almond Fudge Cake

(Ready in about 2 hours | Servings 8)

Ingredients

1/2 cup butter, at room temperature
1 cup coconut milk, unsweetened
1/4 teaspoon orange zest
1 cup Swerve
1/2 teaspoon vanilla extract
2 ounces almonds, chopped

Directions

Combine the Swerve and coconut milk in a double boiler over low heat.

Add in the butter and vanilla extract and beat the mixture using an electric mixer at low speed.

Fold in the chopped almond and orange zest. Scrape the batter into a lightly greased baking dish and freeze until firm about 1 hour 50 minutes. Enjoy!

Per serving: 167 Calories; 17.1g Fat; 6.8g Carbs; 2.4g Protein; 0.9g Fiber

635. Peanut Butter Candy

(Ready in about 10 minutes + chilling time | Servings 12)

Ingredients

3/4 cup peanut butter
1/2 cup coconut, shredded
1 cup powdered Erythritol
3/4 cup coconut oil
1/2 teaspoon pure almond extract

Directions

Melt all ingredients in a double boiler over medium-low heat.

Scrape the batter into a parchment-lined baking pan. Place in your freezer for about 1 hour; break your bark into pieces. Bon appétit!

Per serving: 316 Calories; 31.6g Fat; 4.6g Carbs; 6.6g Protein; 2.6g Fiber

636. Old-Fashioned Scones with Berries

(Ready in about 25 minutes | Servings 10)

Ingredients

2 eggs
1 cup almond meal
1 cup coconut flour
1 ½ sticks butter
1 cup Swerve
1 teaspoon vanilla paste
1 cup double cream
A pinch of salt
A pinch of grated nutmeg
1 teaspoon baking powder
1 cup mixed berries

Directions

Thoroughly combine the almond meal, coconut flour, baking powder, salt, nutmeg, and berries.

In another bowl, whisk the eggs with the butter and double cream. Stir in the Swerve and vanilla paste; stir until everything is well combined.

Add the egg mixture to the almond flour mixture; stir until a soft dough forms.

Shape the dough into 16 triangles and place them on a foil-lined baking sheet. Bake in the preheated oven at 360 degrees F for about 20 minutes. Enjoy!

Per serving: 245 Calories; 21.6g Fat; 7.4g Carbs; 3.8g Protein; 0.6g Fiber

637. Old-Fashioned Bourbon Walnut Cheesecake

(Ready in about 30 minutes + chilling time | Servings 10)

Ingredients

For the Crust:
4 tablespoons peanut butter, room temperature
1 cup coconut flour
2 tablespoons walnuts, chopped
For the Filling:
2 eggs
1/2 teaspoon Monk fruit sweetener
2 tablespoons bourbon
1 teaspoon fresh ginger, grated
10 ounces cream cheese, room temperature
1/2 teaspoon vanilla essence

Directions

Mix all of the crust ingredients. Press the crust into a parchment-lined springform pan and bake at 330 degrees F for about 10 minutes.

Place the springform pan in a deep baking tray filled with 2 inches of warm water to help create steam during the baking.

Make the cheesecake filling by mixing all the ingredients using an electric mixer. Spread the filling onto the crusts and bake an additional 20 minutes.

Bon appétit!

Per serving: 211 Calories; 19g Fat; 4.4g Carbs; 7g Protein; 0.5g Fiber

638. Mint and Hazelnut Clusters

(Ready in about 35 minutes | Servings 8)

Ingredients

1/2 cup hazelnuts, chopped
1/4 cup Erythritol
1 tablespoon coconut oil
8 tablespoons cocoa powder
1 teaspoon peppermint oil
4 ounces cacao butter
1/4 teaspoon grated nutmeg
1 teaspoon vanilla paste

Directions

Microwave the cacao butter and coconut oil for about 1 minute.

Now, stir in the cocoa powder, Erythritol, peppermint oil, vanilla, and nutmeg.

Spoon the mixture into an ice cube tray. Fold in the chopped hazelnuts and place in your freezer for about 30 minutes until set.

Bon appétit!

Per serving: 140 Calories; 14g Fat; 5.9g Carbs; 2g Protein; 2.4g Fiber

639. Classic Chocolate Cake

(Ready in about 50 minutes + chilling time | Servings 10)

Ingredients

2 sticks butter, cold
5 eggs
1/2 cup water
14 ounces chocolate, unsweetened
3/4 cup erythritol
1/2 teaspoon ground cinnamon
A pinch of coarse salt
For Peanut-Choc Ganache:
1/4 cup smooth peanut butter
A pinch of coarse salt
3/4 cups whipped cream
9 ounces chocolate, unsweetened

Directions

In a medium-sized pan, bring the water to a boil; add in the erythritol and let it simmer until it has dissolved.

Melt the chocolate and butter; beat the mixture with an electric mixer.

Add the chocolate mixture to the hot water mixture. Fold in the eggs, one at a time, beating continuously.

Add in the cinnamon and salt, and stir well to combine. Spoon the mixture into a parchment-lined baking pan and wrap with foil.

Lower the baking pan into a larger pan that is filled with hot water about 1 inch deep. Bake in the preheated oven at 365 degrees F for about 45 minutes.

Meanwhile, place the whipped cream in a pan over a moderately-high heat and bring to a boil. Pour the hot cream over the chocolate and whisk to combine.

Add in the peanut butter and salt; continue to mix until creamy and smooth. Glaze your cake and place in the refrigerator until set.

Enjoy!

Per serving: 313 Calories; 30.7g Fat; 7.5g Carbs; 7.3g Protein; 1.9g Fiber

640. 10-Minute Creamy Cupcakes

(Ready in about 10 minutes + chilling time | Servings 10)

Ingredients

4 tablespoons heavy cream
1 cup peanut butter
1 tablespoon Erythritol
1 stick butter

Directions

Place a bowl over a saucepan of simmering water. Add in all of the above ingredients and stir continuously until well melted and blended.

Spoon the batter into muffin cups lined with cupcake wrappers.

Allow them to harden for about 1 hour in your freezer. Enjoy!

Per serving: 266 Calories; 28.1g Fat; 2.6g Carbs; 3.3g Protein; 0.5g Fiber

641. Easy Crème Brûlée

(Ready in about 45 minutes + chilling time | Servings 5)

Ingredients

1 teaspoon orange juice
1/2 teaspoon star anise, ground
1 teaspoon orange rind, grated
1 ½ cups double cream
3/4 cup water
3/4 cup Erythritol
6 eggs

Directions

In a saute pan, melt the Erythritol until it has caramelized. Spoon the caramelized Erythritol into 5 ramekins.

Bring the cream along with water to a boil.

Whisk the eggs until pale and frothy; add in the remaining ingredients and stir to combine well. Add the mixture to the warm cream mixture and stir to combine well.

Spoon the egg/cream mixture over the caramelized Erythritol. Lower the ramekins into a large cake pan. Pour hot water into the pan to come halfway up the sides of your ramekins.

Bake at 325 degrees F for about 45 minutes. Refrigerate for at least 2 hours. Enjoy!

Per serving: 205 Calories; 16.4g Fat; 6.5g Carbs; 7.4g Protein; 0g Fiber

642. Aromatic Chia Pudding

(Ready in about 1 hour 5 minutes | Servings 4)

Ingredients

1 teaspoon coconut extract
2 tablespoons Swerve
1/2 teaspoon ground star anise
1 cup chia seeds
1 cup water
1/4 cup coconut flakes
1 cup double cream
1 cup unsweetened coconut milk

Directions

Mix the ingredients until everything is well incorporated. Place in your refrigerator for about 1 hour.

Enjoy!

Per serving: 226 Calories; 17.9g Fat; 7g Carbs; 5.9g Protein; 4.6g Fiber

643. Vanilla Avocado Pudding

(Ready in about 1 hour | Servings 6)

Ingredients

1 tablespoon vanilla extract
3 avocados, pitted, peeled and mashed
1 teaspoon lemon juice
1 cup full-fat milk
1 cup buttermilk
1 cup xylitol
1/8 teaspoon xanthan gum

Directions

Mix all ingredients in your blender or a food processor until creamy, smooth and uniform. Enjoy!

Per serving: 248 Calories; 20.8g Fat; 8g Carbs; 4.6g Protein; 6g Fiber

644. Homemade Hazelnut Brittle

(Ready in about 30 minutes | Servings 8)

Ingredients

1/2 cup hazelnuts, chopped
3/4 cup heavy cream
1/2 teaspoon ground cinnamon
1/4 teaspoon ground cardamom
A pinch of sea salt
1/2 cup coconut oil, at room temperature
1 teaspoon almond extract
3/4 teaspoon baking powder
1 cup Erythritol
2 cups almond meal
3 eggs

Directions

Start by preheating your oven to 365 degrees F. Coat the bottom of your baking pan with parchment paper.

Thoroughly combine the almond meal, baking powder, Erythritol, cinnamon, cardamom, and salt.

After that, stir in the coconut oil, eggs, almond extract, and heavy cream; whisk until everything is well incorporated.

Stir in the chopped hazelnuts. Scrape the batter into the prepared baking pan.

Bake in the preheated oven for about 25 minutes. Enjoy!

Per serving: 241 Calories; 23.6g Fat; 3.7g Carbs; 5.2g Protein; 1g Fiber

645. 10-Minute Homemade Ice Cream

(Ready in about 10 minutes + chilling time | Servings 4)

Ingredients

17 drops liquid stevia
1/2 teaspoon xanthan gum
1/2 cup peanuts, chopped
1/3 cup whipped cream
1 ¼ cups almond milk

Directions

Combine all of the above ingredients, except for the xanthan gum, with an electric mixer.

Now, stir in the xanthan gum, whisking constantly, until the mixture is thick. Then, prepare your ice cream in a machine following manufacturer's instructions. Bon appétit!

Per serving: 305 Calories; 18.3g Fat; 4.5g Carbs; 1g Protein; 2.2g Fiber

646. Harvest Pear Crisp

(Ready in about 30 minutes | Servings 8)

Ingredients

3/4 cup almond meal
3/4 cup granulated Swerve
5 tablespoons butter
1/2 cup coconut flour
1/2 tablespoon fresh lime juice
2 eggs, whisked
1/3 teaspoon xanthan gum
2 ½ cups pears, cored and sliced

Directions

Preheat your oven to 365 degrees F. Brush the sides and bottom of a baking dish with a non-stick spray.

Arrange your pears on the bottom of the baking dish. Drizzle the lime juice and xanthan gum over them.

In a mixing dish, thoroughly combine the almond meal, coconut flour, and Swerve. Fold in the eggs, one at a time, mixing constantly until your mixture resembles coarse meal.

Spread this mixture over the pear layer.

Cut in the cold butter and bake in the preheated oven for 20 to 23 minutes or until golden brown on the top.

Bon appétit!

Per serving: 152 Calories; 11.8g Fat; 6.2g Carbs; 2.5g Protein; 1.7g Fiber

647. Chocolate and Walnut Toffee

(Ready in about 15 minutes + chilling time | Servings 8)

Ingredients

1/2 cup walnuts, chopped
1/2 cup coconut oil, at room temperature
1/4 cup cocoa powder, unsweetened
1/4 cup Erythritol
A pinch of coarse salt

Directions

Melt the coconut oil in your microwave; add in the cocoa powder and Erythritol. Remove from the heat and stir well.

Add in the ground walnuts and coarse salt and stir until everything is well combined.

Drop by teaspoonfuls onto foil-lined baking sheets. Chill in your refrigerator until firm.

Bon appétit!

Per serving: 166 Calories; 17.2g Fat; 2.2g Carbs; 1.2g Protein; 1.1g Fiber

648. Traditional Greek Frappé

(Ready in about 2 hours | Servings 2)

Ingredients

2 tablespoons coconut whipped cream
1/2 cup prepared instant espresso, cooled
1/2 teaspoon Monk fruit powder
1 tablespoon cacao butter
1 cup almond milk

Directions

In your blender, mix the cacao butter, almond milk, instant espresso, and Monk fruit powder until well combined.

Serve topped with coconut whipped cream. Enjoy!

Per serving: 222 Calories; 15.8g Fat; 7.1g Carbs; 5.9g Protein; 0.3g Fiber

649. Iced Cocoa Candy

(Ready in about 10 minutes + chilling time | Servings 6)

Per serving: 84 Calories; 8.9g Fat; 1.5g Carbs; 0.8g Protein; 0.6g Fiber

Ingredients

2 tablespoons cocoa powder
2 tablespoons almonds, chopped
1/2 stick butter, melted
10 drops liquid stevia
1/2 teaspoon vanilla paste

Directions

Melt the butter, vanilla paste, and liquid stevia in a pan that is preheated over a moderate heat.

Stir in the cocoa powder and stir well to combine.

Spoon the mixture into 12 molds of a silicone candy mold tray. Scatter chopped almonds on top. Freeze until set.

Bon appétit!

650. Vanilla Pecan Pralines

(Ready in about 25 minutes + chilling time | Servings 6)

Ingredients

3 bars chocolate, sugar-free
1/2 cup double cream
1/4 teaspoon ground cardamom
1/4 teaspoon ground cinnamon
1 teaspoon vanilla paste
1/4 teaspoon coarse salt
1/2 cup toasted pecans, finely chopped

Directions

In a medium stainless steel bowl set over a pot of gently simmering water, melt the chocolate and cream.

Add in the vanilla, cardamom, cinnamon, and salt and place in your refrigerator for 7 to 8 hours or until firm.

Shape the mixture into balls and roll the balls into the chopped pecans. Bon appétit!

Per serving: 113 Calories; 8.5g Fat; 5.9g Carbs; 1.7g Protein; 3.3g Fiber

651. Grandma's Homemade Chocolate Bars

(Ready in about 25 minutes + chilling time | Servings 10)

Ingredients

8 ounces bittersweet chocolate chips, sugar-free
1 teaspoon pure vanilla extract
1/2 stick butter, cold
1 cup almond flour
1/2 teaspoon star anise, ground
1/2 teaspoon coconut extract
1 tablespoon rum
1 ½ cups double cream
2 packets stevia
1/4 teaspoon cardamom
1/2 cup coconut flour
A pinch of table salt

Directions

Preheat an oven to 330 degrees F. Now, line a baking dish with parchment paper.

Add the flour, stevia, cardamom, anise, coconut extract, vanilla extract, rum and salt to your food processor. Blitz until everything is well combined.

Cut in the cold butter and process to combine again.

Press the batter into the bottom of the prepared baking dish. Bake about 13 minutes; transfer to a wire rack to cool slightly.

To make the filling, bring the double cream to a simmer in a pan. Add the chocolate and whisk until uniform. Spread over the crust and cut into squares.

Bon appétit!

Per serving: 119 Calories; 11.7g Fat; 7.2g Carbs; 1.1g Protein; 4.2g Fiber

652. Orange Butterscotch Popsicles

(Ready in about 1 hour | Servings 6)

Ingredients

1 tablespoon butterscotch extract
1 cup Swerve
1/8 teaspoon xanthan gum
1 cup buttermilk
1 cup coconut milk
3 avocados, pitted, peeled and mashed
1 teaspoon orange juice

Directions

Place all ingredients in your blender. Process until well combined.

Spoon the pudding into plastic cups and insert wooden pop sticks into the center of each cup. Freeze and enjoy!

Per serving: 248 Calories; 20.8g Fat; 7g Carbs; 4.6g Protein; 4.1g Fiber

653. Italian Panna Cotta

(Ready in about 10 minutes + chilling time | Servings 10)

Ingredients

1/2 cup almond milk
1 ½ teaspoons gelatins powder, unsweetened
1 teaspoon vanilla extract
1 cup double cream
1 teaspoon lemon rind, grated
1/4 cup erythritol
1 teaspoon lemon juice

Directions

Place the gelatin and milk in a saucepan and let it sit for 2 minutes. Add in the other ingredients and stir to combine.

Let it simmer for 3 to 4 minutes until the gelatin has dissolved completely. Pour the mixture into 4 ramekins and transfer to your refrigerator; cover and let it sit overnight or at least 6 hours.

Enjoy!

Per serving: 221 Calories; 21.5g Fat; 3.8g Carbs; 4.3g Protein; 0g Fiber

DESSERTS

654. Skinny Curd Pudding

(Ready in about 10 minutes + chilling time | Servings 6)

Ingredients

2 eggs + 1 egg yolk, well whisked
1/2 cup butter, at room temperature
1 ½ cups Erythritol
A pinch of nutmeg
4 ounces fresh lemon juice
A pinch of salt

Directions

In a sauté pan, beat the eggs over a low heat.

Add in the remaining ingredients and cook for about 5 minutes, whisking constantly.

Turn the heat to the lowest setting and continue to stir with a wire whisk for 1 to 2 minutes longer.

Cover with a plastic wrap. Enjoy!

Per serving: 180 Calories; 17.6g Fat; 5.2g Carbs; 2.8g Protein; 0.1g Fiber

655. Homemade Coconut Ice Cream

(Ready in about 10 minutes + chilling time | Servings 4)

Ingredients

1/2 cup coconut flakes
A few drops Monk fruit
1/3 cup double cream
1/2 teaspoon xanthan gum
1 ¼ cups coconut milk

Directions

In a mixing bowl, combine the coconut milk, double cream, Monk fruit, and coconut flakes.

Add in the xanthan gum, whisking constantly, until the mixture has thickened.

Then, prepare your ice cream in the ice cream maker according to manufacturer's instructions.

Bon appétit!

Per serving: 305 Calories; 18.3g Fat; 4.5g Carbs; 1g Protein; 2.7g Fiber

KETO FAVORITES

656. Easy Bacon Chips

(Ready in about 15 minutes | Servings 6)

Ingredients

1 teaspoon mustard seeds
1 pound smoked bacon, cut into small squares
1 tablespoon paprika

Directions

Preheat an oven to 360 degrees F.

Bake the smoked bacon for 12 to 15 minutes. Season with mustard seeds and paprika.

Bon appétit!

Per serving: 409 Calories; 31.6g Fat; 1.1g Carbs; 28g Protein; 0g Fiber

657. Swiss Cheese Balls and Celery Fries

(Ready in about 25 minutes | Servings 8)

Ingredients

1/2 cup Greek-style yogurt
2 tablespoons tomato paste
1 teaspoon Italian herb mix
2 tablespoons chili pepper, minced
1 cup Parmesan cheese, freshly grated
1 cup Swiss cheese, shredded
Salt and pepper, to taste
For Celery Chips:
1 pound celery, cut into sticks
2 tablespoons avocado oil
Salt and pepper, to taste

Directions

Mix the Swiss cheese, Parmesan cheese, Greek-style yogurt, tomato paste, Italian herb mix, chili pepper, salt, and pepper in a bowl.

Roll the mixture into balls and place in your refrigerator.

Toss the celery with avocado oil, salt, and pepper. Roast in the preheated oven at 420 degrees F for about 20 minutes.

Per serving: 177 Calories; 12.9g Fat; 6.8g Carbs; 8.8g Protein; 1.3g Fiber

658. Creamy Almond Porridge

(Ready in about 25 minutes | Servings 2)

Ingredients

1 ½ tablespoons butter
1/2 cup sour cream
1/4 cup almonds
3 eggs
1/2 teaspoon star anise
3 tablespoons erythritol

Directions

Whisk the eggs, erythritol, and sour cream until well combined.

Melt the butter and add in the egg mixture along with star anise; continue to cook on medium-low heat until thoroughly warmed.

Top with slivered almonds. Bon appétit!

Per serving: 430 Calories; 41.1g Fat; 5.8g Carbs; 11.4g Protein; 0.1g Fiber

659. Easy Homemade Cheeseburgers

(Ready in about 20 minutes | Servings 6)

Ingredients

2 tablespoons olive oil
1 teaspoon garlic, chopped
1/2 pound ground beef
1/2 pound ground lamb
1/2 cup onions, chopped
2 ounces soft cheese
3 ounces Cheddar cheese, grated
1/2 teaspoon red pepper flakes
Se salt and black pepper, to taste

Directions

Thoroughly combine the ground meat, onions, garlic, salt, black pepper, and red pepper.

Roll the mixture into six balls; flatten them using your hands to make 6 burgers.

In a separate bowl, combine soft cheese with Cheddar cheese. Place the cheese into the center of each ball, and enclose inside the meat mixture.

Heat the olive oil in a frying pan over a moderately-high flame. Cook your burgers approximately 5 minutes per side. Bon appétit!

Per serving: 252 Calories; 15.5g Fat; 1.2g Carbs; 26g Protein; 0.3g Fiber

660. French Rum Crêpes

(Ready in about 25 minutes | Servings 6)

Ingredients

For Crêpes:
1/4 cup almond flour
6 eggs
1 teaspoon baking powder
1/2 teaspoon apple pie spice mix
1 ½ tablespoons granulated Swerve
1 teaspoon baking soda
6 ounces cream cheese, softened
For the Syrup:
1 tablespoon rum extract
3/4 cup Swerve, powdered
1/2 teaspoon xanthan gum
3/4 cup water
1 tablespoon butter

Directions

Combine all ingredients for the crepes using an electric mixer. Mix until everything is well incorporated.

Grease a frying pan with melted butter; fry your crepes over a moderate heat until the edges begin to brown.

Flip and fry on the other side until it is slightly browned.

Whisk the water, butter, and Swerve in a pan over medium heat; simmer about 6 minutes, stirring continuously.

Add the mixture to a blender along with the rum extract and 1/4 teaspoon of xanthan gum; mix to combine.

Add the remaining 1/4 teaspoon of xanthan gum and let it stand until the syrup has thickened. Bon appétit!

Per serving: 243 Calories; 19.6g Fat; 5.5g Carbs; 11g Protein; 3g Fiber

661. Keto Breakfast in a Jar

(Ready in about 5 minutes | Servings 3)

Ingredients

1/2 cup Chèvre cheese, shredded
3 slices salami, chopped
6 eggs
1/2 cup soft cheese
3 teaspoons olive oil
1 teaspoon deli mustard
Salt and pepper, to taste

Directions

Brush three mason jars with olive oil.

Crack two eggs into each jar. Add the other ingredients to your jars and cover them.

Shake until everything is well combined. Uncover and microwave for 2 minutes on high.

Per serving: 303 Calories; 22.4g Fat; 3.6g Carbs; 21.6g Protein; 0.4g Fiber

662. Baked Eggs, Cheese and Pancetta in Ramekins

(Ready in about 20 minutes | Servings 6)

Ingredients

6 eggs, whisked
Salt and pepper, to season
1/4 cup scallions, chopped
2 ounces soft cheese
2 ounces Gorgonzola cheese, diced
12 small thin slices of pancetta

Directions

Line 6 ramekins with 2 slices of pancetta each. Mix the remaining ingredients until everything is well incorporated.

Divide the egg mixture between the ramekins. Cover with a double layer of foil.

Bake in the preheated oven at 395 degrees F for 15 to 18 minutes or until the top is golden brown. Enjoy!

Per serving: 268 Calories; 18.3g Fat; 0.7g Carbs; 26.2g Protein; 0.3g Fiber

663. Decadent Rum and Cheese Pancakes

(Ready in about 25 minutes | Servings 6)

Ingredients

6 eggs
1 ½ teaspoons baking powder
1/2 teaspoon ground cinnamon
4 tablespoons Erythritol
6 ounces soft cheese
1/4 cup almond meal

For the Syrup:
1 tablespoon rum extract
3/4 cup water
1 tablespoon ghee
3/4 cup Erythritol

Directions

Thoroughly combine the soft cheese, eggs, Erythritol, almond meal, baking powder, and cinnamon.

Brush a frying pan with non-stick cooking oil and cook your pancakes over a moderate flame until the edges begin to brown.

Flip and cook your pancake on the other side for about 3 minutes more.

Whisk the water, ghee, Erythritol, and rum extract in a saucepan over medium heat; let it simmer for 5 to 6 minutes or until thickened and reduced. Bon appétit!

Per serving: 243 Calories; 19.6g Fat; 5.5g Carbs; 11g Protein; 0.1g Fiber

664. Herbed Keto Bread

(Ready in about 40 minutes | Servings 6)

Ingredients

1 tablespoon poppy seeds
2 cups almond flour
1 teaspoon dried basil
1/2 teaspoon dried oregano
1/2 stick butter, melted
3 teaspoons baking powder
1 teaspoon sea salt
1/2 teaspoon cream of tartar
2 tablespoons sesame seeds
5 eggs, separated

Directions

Preheat your oven to 360 degrees F. Lightly oil a loaf pan with a non-stick cooking spray.

Mix the eggs with the cream of tartar on medium-high speed until stiff peaks form.

Add the flour, butter, baking powder and salt to your food processor; blitz until everything is well mixed.

Now, stir in the egg white mixture; gently stir to combine well. Spoon the batter into the prepared loaf pan.

Sprinkle dried basil, oregano, poppy seeds and sesame seeds on the loaf and bake for 35 minutes.

Bon appétit!

Per serving: 109 Calories; 10.2g Fat; 1g Carbs; 3.9g Protein; 0.7g Fiber

665. Country-Style Porridge with Pecans

(Ready in about 25 minutes | Servings 2)

Ingredients

1/4 cup pecans, chopped
3 eggs
1/2 teaspoon star anise
1 ½ tablespoons coconut oil
1/4 teaspoon turmeric powder
3 tablespoons Swerve
1/2 cup double cream

Directions

Thoroughly combine the eggs with the Swerve and double cream in a mixing bowl.

Melt the coconut oil in a pot over moderately high heat; stir in the egg/cream mixture and cook until they are warmed through.

Take off the heat and stir in the star anise and turmeric. Add the chopped pecans to the top.

Bon appétit!

Per serving: 430 Calories; 41.1g Fat; 5.8g Carbs; 11.4g Protein; 1.4g Fiber

666. Gorgonzola Cheese and Bacon Gofres

(Ready in about 20 minutes | Servings 3)

Ingredients

4 tablespoons butter
3 ounces bacon, chopped
1 teaspoon Italian seasoning mix
3 ounces Gorgonzola cheese, shredded
1 teaspoon baking powder
6 large-sized eggs, separated
3 tablespoons tomato paste
Salt and pepper, to taste

KETO FAVORITES

Directions

Combine the egg yolks, baking powder, butter, salt, pepper, and Italian seasoning mix.

Beat the egg whites with an electric mixer until pale and frothy. Fold in the egg whites into the egg yolk mixture.

Heat you waffle iron. Cook 1/4 cup of the batter until golden. Repeat with the remaining ingredients; you will have six waffles.

Spread your toppings onto three waffle; top with remaining waffles and cook until the cheese is melted. Enjoy!

Per serving: 453 Calories; 37g Fat; 4.5g Carbs; 25.6g Protein; 1.8g Fiber

667. Comte Cheese and Chanterelle Mousse

(Ready in about 45 minutes | Servings 6)

Ingredients

4 ounces Comté cheese, crumbled
4 ounces Chanterelle mushrooms, chopped
1 ½ cups double cream
1/2 teaspoon fresh garlic, minced
3 eggs, whisked
1 tablespoon ghee, room temperature
Salt and pepper, to taste

Directions

Melt the cream and add in the cheese; stir until melted. Add in the whisked eggs, salt, and pepper; continue to stir for about 2 minutes or until well combined.

Spoon the mixture into 6 ramekins; place the ramekins into a large pan with hot water (depth of about 1-inch).

Bake in the preheated oven at 310 degrees F for about 35 minutes or until set.

Sauté the mushrooms in hot ghee until they release liquid; add in the garlic and continue to sauté a minute more or until aromatic. Top each custard with the sautéed chanterelles. Enjoy!

Per serving: 263 Calories; 22.4g Fat; 6.1g Carbs; 10g Protein; 0.2g Fiber

668. Old-School Meatballs

(Ready in about 35 minutes | Servings 5)

Ingredients

1 egg, beaten
1 teaspoon garlic, minced
1 cup Swiss cheese, shredded
1 yellow onion, chopped
2 tablespoons olive oil
1 celery, grated
1 pound ground beef
Salt and pepper, to taste
1 teaspoon Fajita seasoning mix

Directions

Mix all ingredients, except for the cheese, until everything is well incorporated.

Roll the mixture into small meatballs and bake at 365 degrees F for about 30 minutes.

Scatter the cheese over the balls and place under the preheated broil for about 6 minutes. Bon appétit!

Per serving: 342 Calories; 23.7g Fat; 4.3g Carbs; 31.7g Protein; 0.6g Fiber

669. Italian Salami Pizza Muffins

(Ready in about 20 minutes | Servings 6)

Ingredients

12 Genoa salami slices
1/2 cup green olives, pitted and chopped
1/2 teaspoon dried basil
1 teaspoon dried oregano
1 cup Cheddar cheese, shredded
1/2 cup marinara

Directions

Preheat an oven to 360 degrees F; spritz a muffin pan with a non-stick cooking spray.

Divide 1/2 cup of cheddar cheese among the muffin cups. Divide the marinara sauce among the muffin cups.

Sprinkle each cup with oregano, basil, and chopped olives. Add a salami slice to each muffin cup. Top with the remaining 1/2 cup of cheese.

Bake approximately 17 minutes. Allow them to cool slightly before removing from the muffin pan.

Bon appétit!

Per serving: 162 Calories; 13.1g Fat; 2.5g Carbs; 8.7g Protein; 0.5g Fiber

670. Gofres Belgas Caseros

(Ready in about 30 minutes | Servings 6)

Ingredients

1 cup Colby cheese, shredded
3 fully-cooked breakfast sausage links, chopped
6 tablespoons whole milk
1 teaspoon Belgian spice mix
6 eggs
Non-stick cooking spray
Sea salt and ground black pepper, to taste

Directions

In a mixing bowl, beat the eggs, milk, Spanish spice mix, salt, and black pepper.

Now, stir in the chopped sausage and shredded cheese.

Spritz a waffle iron with a non-stick cooking spray.

Cook the egg mixture about 5 minutes, until it is golden. Bon appétit!

Per serving: 316 Calories; 25g Fat; 1.5g Carbs; 20.2g Protein; 0.4g Fiber

671. Sour Cream and Crab Meat Frittata

(Ready in about 25 minutes | Servings 3)

Ingredients

1/2 cup sour cream
6 eggs, slightly beaten
4 ounces crabmeat, flaked
1 yellow onion, chopped
1 teaspoon garlic, minced
1 tablespoon butter, melted
1 teaspoon Old Bay seasoning mix

Directions

Begin by preheating your oven to 360 degrees F.

Heat the oil in an oven-proof skillet over moderately-high heat.

Sauté the onions until they are tender and translucent; add the crabmeat and garlic and continue to cook for 2 minutes or until fragrant.

Mix the eggs and sour cream until well combined; pour the egg mixture into the skillet.

Bake for 18 to 20 minutes or until the eggs are puffed and opaque.

Per serving: 265 Calories; 15.8g Fat; 7.1g Carbs; 22.9g Protein; 0.6g Fiber

672. Cauliflower Mash with Goat Cheese

(Ready in about 15 minutes | Servings 4)

Ingredients

2 cups goat cheese, crumbled
1 teaspoon garlic, minced
2 tablespoons butter, softened
1 thyme sprig, chopped
1/2 teaspoon dried oregano
1 teaspoon dried basil
1 ½ pounds cauliflower florets
Salt and pepper, to taste

Directions

Steam the cauliflower florets for about 10 minutes or until they are crisp-tender.

Puree the cauliflower in your blender or food processor, adding the cooking liquid periodically.

Add in the remaining ingredients and pulse until everything is well combined. Enjoy!

Per serving: 230 Calories; 17.7g Fat; 7.2g Carbs; 11.9g Protein; 3.5g Fiber

673. Greek-Style Cheesecake Apple Muffins

(Ready in about 20 minutes | Servings 6)

Ingredients

1/4 cup Greek-style yogurt
3/4 cream cheese
1 apple, cored and sliced
1/3 teaspoon ground cinnamon
2 tablespoons hazelnuts, ground
4 tablespoons erythritol
1/2 teaspoon vanilla essence
3 eggs, beaten

Directions

Preheat your oven to 360 degrees F. Treat a muffin pan with a non-stick cooking spray.

Then, thoroughly combine all of the above ingredients. Divide the batter among the muffin cups.

Bake for 12 to 15 minutes. Transfer to a wire rack to cool slightly before serving. Garnish with apples.

Bon appétit!

Per serving: 81 Calories; 3.5g Fat; 6.7g Carbs; 5.5g Protein; 1.1g Fiber

674. Fluffy Russian-Style Cheese Pancakes

(Ready in about 20 minutes | Servings 4)

Ingredients

For the Batter:
5 eggs
6 ounces soft cheese
1 teaspoon baking powder
2 tablespoons canola oil
1/2 cup sour cream
1 cup fresh blueberries
2 tablespoons Swerve
For the Topping:

Directions

In a mixing bowl, whisk all the batter ingredients.

Brush your pan with a small amount of oil.

Once hot, spoon the batter onto the pan and form into circles. Cover and cook until bubbles start to form. Flip and cook on the other side until browned. Repeat with the rest of the batter.

To serve, divide the fresh berries among the prepared pancakes; sprinkle with Swerve, and top with a dollop of sour cream.

Per serving: 237 Calories; 16.3g Fat; 5.5g Carbs; 14.5g Protein; 0.9g Fiber

675. Decadent Sopressata Wafers

(Ready in about 20 minutes | Servings 2)

Ingredients

4 slices Sopressata, chopped
1/2 teaspoon parsley flakes
1/2 teaspoon chili pepper flakes
1/2 cup blue cheese, crumbled
2 tablespoons butter, melted
4 eggs
Salt and black pepper, to your liking

Directions

Combine all ingredients, except for the fresh chives, in a mixing bowl. Preheat your waffle iron and grease with a cooking spray.

Add the omelet mixture and close the lid. Fry about 5 minutes or until the desired consistency is reached. Repeat with the remaining batter.

Bon appétit!

Per serving: 470 Calories; 40.3g Fat; 2.9g Carbs; 24.4g Protein; 0.2g Fiber

676. Jaffa Chia Pudding

(Ready in about 35 minutes | Servings 4)

Ingredients

2 tablespoons peanut butter
1/2 cup chia seeds
1/4 cup water
3 tablespoons orange flower water
2 tablespoons chocolate chunks, unsweetened
1 teaspoon liquid Monk fruit
3/4 cup coconut milk, preferably homemade

Directions

Thoroughly combine the coconut milk, water, peanut butter, chia seeds, Monk fruit, and orange flower water.

Let the mixture stand for 30 minutes in your refrigerator. Scatter the chopped chocolate over the top of each serving. Enjoy!

Per serving: 93 Calories; 5.1g Fat; 7.2g Carbs; 4.4g Protein; 0.7g Fiber

677. Greek Mezze Board

(Ready in about 20 minutes | Servings 4)

Ingredients

1 ½ cups avocado, pitted and sliced
1 tablespoon olive oil
6 eggs
1 cup grape tomatoes, halved
3 teaspoons olive oil
1 teaspoon Greek seasoning blend
4 tablespoons Kalamata olives
12 ounces Halloumi cheese, cut into 1/4-1/3-inch slices
Sea salt and ground black pepper, to taste

Directions

Preheat a grill pan over medium-high heat, about 395 degrees F.

Grill your halloumi for about 3 minutes or until golden brown grill marks appear.

Heat the oil in a non-stick skillet over moderately-high plate; scramble the eggs with a wide spatula.

Season with sea salt, black pepper, and Greek seasoning blend. Garnish with avocado, tomatoes, and olives. Enjoy!

Per serving: 542 Calories; 46.4g Fat; 6.2g Carbs; 23.7g Protein; 4g Fiber

678. Italian-Style Ribs

(Ready in about 15 minutes | Servings 4)

Ingredients

1 tablespoon lard, at room temperature
1 teaspoon garlic, minced
1 pound ribs, cut into small chunks
2 Italian peppers, deveined and thinly sliced
2 tablespoons scallions, chopped
Salt and black pepper, to taste

Directions

Melt the lard in a saucepan over medium-high heat. Cook the ribs for about 5 minutes or until the meat reaches an internal temperature of 160 degrees F.

Add in the other ingredients and cook for 2 minutes more.

Place under the preheated broiler until it is crispy on top. Bon appétit!

Per serving: 490 Calories; 44g Fat; 5.5g Carbs; 16.9g Protein; 0.6g Fiber

679. Classic Salmon Spread

(Ready in about 10 minutes + chilling time | Servings 12)

Ingredients

12 ounces smoked salmon, skinned, deboned, and flaked
1/2 teaspoon cayenne pepper
2 tablespoons butter
1/2 teaspoon deli mustard
3/4 cup soft cheese
2 ounces coriander, finely chopped
Salt and pepper, to taste

Directions

Pulse all of the above ingredients in your food processor and place in your refrigerator.

Enjoy!

Per serving: 64 Calories; 2.9g Fat; 1.3g Carbs; 7.9g Protein; 0.2g Fiber

680. Famous Keto Coffee with MCT Oil

(Ready in about 10 minutes | Servings 4)

Ingredients

4 teaspoons MCT oil
4 tablespoons coconut whipped cream
1/4 teaspoon ground cinnamon
1/4 cup almond milk
1 teaspoon vanilla liquid stevia
4 cups coffee, chilled

Directions

Blend the coffee with the remaining ingredients, except for the heavy cream.

Spoon your coffee along with ice cubes into four chilled glasses.

Serve topped with coconut whipped cream. Enjoy!

Per serving: 161 Calories; 13.7g Fat; 4.4g Carbs; 0.7g Protein; 0.4g Fiber

681. Savory Panna Cotta with Mushrooms and Herbs

(Ready in about 15 minutes + chilling time | Servings 6)

Ingredients

1/4 cup almonds, slivered
1 cup Greek-style yogurt
2 teaspoons powdered gelatin
1 1/3 cups double cream
1 tablespoon canola oil
1 teaspoon Italian herb mix
8 ounces goat cheese
2 ounces button mushrooms, chopped

Directions

Heat the oil in a saucepan over medium-high heat; once hot, sauté the mushrooms for 4 to 5 minutes until they release the liquid.

Add in the gelatin and cream and continue to cook for 3 to 4 minutes more. Remove from the heat.

Add in the remaining ingredients and transfer to your refrigerator until set. Enjoy!

Per serving: 489 Calories; 47.4g Fat; 6.9g Carbs; 12.7g Protein; 1.6g Fiber

682. Taco Vegetables with Sausage

(Ready in about 25 minutes | Servings 4)

Ingredients

2 zucchinis, sliced
2 Spanish peppers, sliced
1 celery, sliced
1 teaspoon Taco seasoning mix
1 poblano pepper, minced
2 cloves garlic, minced
1 tablespoon olive oil
2 chorizo sausages, sliced

Directions

In a large skillet, heat the olive oil over a moderately-high heat. Sear the sausage for 7 to 8 minutes.

Add in the other ingredients and continue to cook, partially covered, for about 15 minutes. Enjoy!

Per serving: 227 Calories; 18g Fat; 7g Carbs; 7.1g Protein; 0.7g Fiber

683. Mascarpone Keto Balls

(Ready in about 15 minutes | Servings 4)

Ingredients

1/2 cup mascarpone cheese
1/2 teaspoon garlic powder
1/2 teaspoon smoke flavor
1/4 teaspoon apple cider vinegar
1 teaspoon paprika
4 bacon slices, chopped
1 teaspoon onion powder

Directions

Thoroughly combine all ingredients until well combined.

Roll the mixture into bite-sized balls.

Serve well chilled!

Per serving: 88 Calories; 6.5g Fat; 0.7g Carbs; 6.5g Protein; 0.3g Fiber

684. Rich and Easy Spanish Tortilla

(Ready in about 15 minutes | Servings 2)

Ingredients

For the Crust:
1 tablespoon extra-virgin olive oil
2 tablespoons flax seed meal
1 teaspoon chili pepper, deveined and minced
1/2 teaspoon coriander, minced
1/4 cup cream cheese
4 eggs, beaten
Salt and pepper, to taste
For the Toppings:
2 tablespoons tomato paste
2 ounces Manchego cheese, shredded

Directions

In a mixing bowl, combine the ingredients for the crust. Divide the batter into two pieces.

Cook in a frying pan for about 5 minutes; flip your tortilla and cook on the other side until crisp and golden-brown on their edges.

Repeat with another tortilla. Spread the tomato paste and cheese over the top of each of the prepared tortillas.

Place under the preheated broiler for about 5 minutes until the cheese is hot and bubbly. Enjoy!

Per serving: 397 Calories; 31g Fat; 6.1g Carbs; 22g Protein; 1.4g Fiber

685. Prosciutto Baked Rolls

(Ready in about 30 minutes | Servings 9)

Ingredients

9 slices prosciutto, chopped
1/2 cup cheddar cheese, shredded
1/2 teaspoon cayenne pepper
1/4 teaspoon garlic powder
9 eggs
1/2 cup green onions, chopped
Sea salt and pepper, to taste

Directions

Thoroughly combine all ingredients in a mixing bowl. Spoon the batter into a lightly oiled muffin pan.

Bake in the preheated oven at 395 degrees F for about 25 minutes. Bon appétit!

Per serving: 294 Calories; 21.4g Fat; 3.5g Carbs; 21g Protein; 0.2g Fiber

686. Omelet with Cheese and Blueberries

(Ready in about 10 minutes | Servings 1)

Ingredients

2 tablespoons soft cheese
6 fresh blueberries, sliced
1/2 teaspoon ground cardamom
1 tablespoon coconut oil
2 tablespoons double cream
2 eggs, whisked

Directions

Beat the eggs with the cream and cardamom until well combined.

In a saucepan, melt the coconut oil over a medium-high flame. Now, cook the egg mixture for 3 to 4 minutes.

Serve with soft cheese and blueberries. Bon appétit!

Per serving: 488 Calories; 42g Fat; 8g Carbs; 15.3g Protein; 0.3g Fiber

687. Spring Omelet with Greek-Style Yogurt

(Ready in about 15 minutes | Servings 2)

Ingredients

2 tomatoes, chopped
1 teaspoon spring garlic, minced
2 spring onions, chopped
8 ounces Greek-style yogurt
2 teaspoons olive oil
1 chili pepper, minced
Salt and black pepper, to taste
4 eggs, beaten

Directions

In a frying pan, heat the olive oil over a moderate flame. Once hot, cook the spring onion and garlic until they've softened or about 2 minutes.

Beat the eggs with the Greek-style yogurt. Pour the egg mixture into the pan; cook until the eggs are puffy and golden-brown.

Place the tomatoes and pepper on one side of the omelet. Sprinkle with salt and pepper and fold the omelet in half.

Per serving: 319 Calories; 25g Fat; 7.4g Carbs; 14.9g Protein; 2.7g Fiber

688. Cheese Custard with Anchovies and Scallions

(Ready in about 20 minutes + chilling time | Servings 5)

Ingredients

2 ounces soft cheese
1 garlic clove, minced
1 teaspoon poblano pepper, deveined and minced
3 tablespoons mayonnaise
1/4 cup scallions, chopped
1 ½ teaspoons gelatin, powdered
3 ounces anchovies, chopped
Sea salt and pepper, to taste
3 tablespoons water

Directions

Dissolve the gelatin in water for about 10 minutes.

Warm the soft cheese over low heat heat; fold in the gelatin and whisk until it is well incorporated.

Let it cool to room temperature. Add in the other ingredients and mix to combine.

Spoon the mixture into ramekins and place in your refrigerator until set. Enjoy!

Per serving: 100 Calories; 5.8g Fat; 4.1g Carbs; 8g Protein; 0.5g Fiber

689. Mascarpone Cheese-Stuffed Avocado

(Ready in about 25 minutes | Servings 4)

Ingredients

1 teaspoon olive oil
8 black olives, pitted and sliced
1/2 cup tomatoes, chopped
3 ounces mascarpone cheese
2 avocados, halved and pitted

Directions

Mix the olive oil, tomatoes, cheese and black olives in a bowl. Spoon the mixture into the avocado halves.

Bake in the preheated oven at 365 degrees F for about 20 minutes or until everything is cooked through.

Bon appétit!

Per serving: 264 Calories; 24.4g Fat; 6g Carbs; 3.7g Protein; 5g Fiber

690. Traditional Homemade Aioli

(Ready in about 10 minutes | Servings 8)

Ingredients

1 egg yolk, at room temperature
1/2 teaspoon garlic, crushed
1 teaspoon dried dill weed
1/2 cup olive oil
1 tablespoon white vinegar
Salt and pepper, to taste

Directions

In your blender, process the vinegar, egg yolk, garlic, salt, and pepper; pulse until smooth and uniform. Turn to low setting.

Gradually drizzle in the olive oil and continue to mix until well blended.

Add in the dried dill and place in your refrigerator.

Per serving: 116 Calories; 13.2g Fat; 0.2g Carbs; 0.4g Protein; 0.1g Fiber

691. Chicken Tenders with Cheese and Garlic

(Ready in about 20 minutes | Servings 4)

Ingredients

1 cup Cheddar cheese, shredded
1 teaspoon garlic, minced
2 tablespoon tomato paste
1 tablespoon butter
1/3 cup chicken stock
1/2 cup double cheese
1 pound chicken tenders

Directions

In a frying pan, melt the butter over a moderately-high flame; cook the chicken for 5 to 6 minutes until no longer pink.

Add in the garlic and continue to sauté for 1 minuet or so; reserve.

Cook the cream, stock, and tomato paste until it has reduced by half.

Remove from the heat. Add in the reserved chicken and garlic; scatter the cheese over the top. Cover and let it sit for about 10 minutes.

Bon appétit!

Per serving: 416 Calories; 26g Fat; 3.2g Carbs; 40.7g Protein; 0.3g Fiber

692. Creamy Almond Bars

(Ready in about 20 minutes | Servings 4)

Ingredients

1/2 cup almonds, chopped
1 cup whipped cream
1/4 teaspoon cinnamon
2 tablespoons butter
2 tablespoons almond butter
1/4 teaspoon nutmeg

Directions

Beat the cream with the nutmeg and cardamom, and spread the mixture on the bottom of a foil-lined baking pan.

Then, mix the regular butter and almond butter. Spread this mixture over the creamed mixture.

Scatter the chopped almonds over the top. Cut into bars.

Enjoy!

Per serving: 278 Calories; 30.1g Fat; 2.2g Carbs; 2.2g Protein; 0.1g Fiber

693. Grandma's Mini Meatloaves

(Ready in about 30 minutes | Servings 6)

Ingredients

1 teaspoon Dijon mustard
2 tablespoons scallions, chopped
2 garlic cloves, smashed
4 ounces Teleme cheese, cubed
1 teaspoon Italian herb mix
1/2 ground pork
1 egg, beaten
1/2 pound ground beef
Sea salt and pepper, to taste
2 ounces pancetta, chopped

Directions

Begin by preheating your oven to 360 degrees F.

In a mixing bowl, thoroughly combine the scallions, garlic, ground meat, pancetta, egg and mustard.

Season with salt, black pepper, and Italian herb mix.

Mix until well combined. Spoon the mixture into muffin cups. Insert one cube of the cheese into each cup; seal the top to cover the cheese.

Bake in the preheated oven for 18 to 20 minutes or until the internal temperature reaches 165 degrees F.

Bon appétit!

Per serving: 276 Calories; 18.3g Fat; 1.2g Carbs; 29.2g Protein; 0.1g Fiber

694. Hemp Heart Porridge

(Ready in about 20 minutes | Servings 4)

Ingredients

1/4 cup hemp hearts
4 eggs, lightly whisked
1/4 cup flax seed, freshly ground
2 teaspoons liquid Monk fruit
1/4 teaspoon pinch psyllium husk powder
1/4 teaspoon coarse salt
8 walnuts, chopped
2 tablespoons butter, softened
1 teaspoon coconut extract

Directions

Mel the butter in a sauté pan over medium-low heat. Add in the remaining ingredients and continue to cook until the mixture starts to boil.

Remove from heat and stir in the chopped walnuts; stir to combine.

Bon appétit!

Per serving: 405 Calories; 37g Fat; 6.6g Carbs; 14.8g Protein; 2.3g Fiber

695. Seed and Egg Bread

(Ready in about 40 minutes | Servings 6)

Ingredients

1 tablespoon poppy seeds
1/4 cup psyllium husk flour
1 tablespoon flax seeds
1 teaspoon baking soda
1 3/4 cups almond flour
1 tablespoon sesame seeds
1/4 cup butter, softened
1 teaspoon baking powder
5 eggs whites
1/2 teaspoon cream of tartar
1/2 teaspoon sea salt

Directions

Start by preheating your oven to 365 degrees F.

Beat the eggs with the cream of tartar using your electric mixer until stiff peaks form.

Add in the flour, butter, baking powder, baking soda, and salt; blend until everything is well combined.

Add the egg mixture to the flour mixture; add in the seeds and stir again. Spoon the batter into a lightly buttered loaf pan.

Bake in the preheated oven for about 30 minutes. Enjoy!

Per serving: 109 Calories; 10.2g Fat; 1g Carbs; 3.9g Protein; 0.8g Fiber

696. Rustic Pumpkin Mousse

(Ready in about 15 minutes + chilling time | Servings 6)

Ingredients

1 ¼ cups pumpkin puree
1/8 teaspoon grated nutmeg
3 eggs
1/4 teaspoon ground cloves
1/2 teaspoon ground cinnamon
1 cup cream cheese
1/2 cup Swerve
1 cup double cream
1/2 teaspoon ground ginger
1/8 teaspoon kosher salt

Directions

Melt the cream, cheese, and Swerve in a sauté pan, whisking frequently.

Whisk the eggs in a mixing bowl.

Add in the eggs, whisking constantly and continue to cook for about 3 minutes, or until the mixture has reduced slightly.

Remove from the heat and fold in the pumpkin puree and spices. Spoon the mixture into serving bowls and place in your refrigerator. Enjoy!

Per serving: 368 Calories; 33.7g Fat; 5.6g Carbs; 13.8g Protein; 1.7g Fiber

697. Tomato and Cheese Fondue

(Ready in about 15 minutes | Servings 10)

Ingredients

1/3 pound goat cheese, shredded
3/4 cup dry white wine
1/2 cup Parmesan, freshly grated
1 tomato, pureed
1 tablespoon xanthan gum
1/3 pound soft cheese, chopped
1/2 tablespoon lime juice
1/2 teaspoon garlic, minced
1 teaspoon onion powder
Cayenne pepper, to taste

Directions

Melt the cheese in a double boiler; add in the remaining ingredients and stir to combine.

Then, place the cheese mixture under the preheated broiler for about 7 minutes, until the cheese is hot and bubbly.

Bon appétit!

Per serving: 148 Calories; 10.2g Fat; 1.5g Carbs; 9.3g Protein; 0.2g Fiber

698. Pancetta and Goat Cheese Cups

(Ready in about 25 minutes | Servings 5)

Ingredients

1 cup goat cheese, diced
4 eggs, beaten
1/2 cup almond flour
1 teaspoon baking powder
4 slices pancetta
Sea salt and black pepper, to taste

Directions

Preheat a non-stick skillet over a moderately-high heat. Cook the pancetta for about 4 minutes until it is browned; place the pancetta on paper towels.

Chop the pancetta and add in the remaining ingredients; stir to combine. Now, spoon the batter into paper-lined muffin cups (3/4 full).

Bake in the preheated oven at 395 degrees F for 15 to 17 minutes.

Bon appétit!

Per serving: 240 Calories; 15.3g Fat; 7g Carbs; 16.1g Protein; 0.2g Fiber

699. German-Style Turkey Rinderrouladen

(Ready in about 50 minutes | Servings 6)

Ingredients

1 tablespoon olive oil
3 tablespoons Dijon mustard
2 garlic cloves, chopped
1/2 teaspoon chili pepper, chopped
2 tablespoons fresh cilantro, roughly chopped
6 slices bacon
6 (4-ounce) turkey fillets
Salt and pepper, to taste

Directions

Rub the olive oil and Dijon mustard all over the turkey fillets.

Place the fresh cilantro, garlic, chili pepper, salt, and pepper on each turkey fillet. Roll the fillets in the bacon and secure with a toothpick.

Bake in the preheated oven at 395 degrees F for about 40 minutes.

Bon appétit!

Per serving: 275 Calories; 9.5g Fat; 1.3g Carbs; 44.5g Protein; 0.5g Fiber

700. Chocolate-Glazed Donuts

(Ready in about 25 minutes | Servings 6)

Ingredients

1/3 cup coconut flour
1 egg
1/3 cup almond flour
1/4 cup Swerve
1 ½ teaspoons baking powder
1/2 teaspoon cinnamon, ground
1/4 teaspoon grated nutmeg
1/4 cup coconut oil, room temperature
1/2 cup soft cheese
1 teaspoon vanilla extract
A pinch of coarse sea salt
For the Frosting:
1 cup bakers' chocolate chunks, unsweetened
1 cup whipping cream

Directions

Thoroughly combine the coconut flour, almond flour, Swerve, baking powder, cinnamon, nutmeg, and salt.

In a separate bowl, thoroughly combine the coconut oil with the cheese, egg, and vanilla. Beat until everything is well mixed. Add the cheese mixture to the dry flour mixture.

Scrape the batter evenly into a lightly buttered donut pan. Bake in the preheated oven at 365 degrees F approximately 20 minutes.

Meanwhile, warm the cream in a saucepan; then, fold in the chocolate chunks and whisk to combine well. Frost the prepared donuts. Enjoy!

Per serving: 218 Calories; 20g Fat; 6g Carbs; 4.8g Protein; 0.3g Fiber

701. Dilled Double Cheese Sauce

(Ready in about 15 minutes | Servings 6)

Ingredients

1/2 teaspoon dried dill
1/2 cup Roquefort cheese
1/3 cup Brie, grated
1/2 teaspoon garlic powder
1 ½ tablespoons butter
3 tablespoons coconut milk
1 teaspoon onion powder
1/3 teaspoon cayenne pepper
1/3 cup double cream

Directions

Melt the double cream and butter in a sauté pan over moderate heat. Once hot, add in the cheese along with the other ingredients.

Cook for 4 to 5 minutes, stirring continuously. Enjoy!

Per serving: 110 Calories; 10.5g Fat; 0.7g Carbs; 3.4g Protein; 0.2g Fiber

702. Rustic Pecan Pie

(Ready in about 30 minutes + chilling time | Servings 6)

Ingredients

For the Crust:
1/4 cup coconut oil
1/3 cup coconut flour
1/3 cup Swerve
3/4 cup almond meal
For the Custard:
1 ¼ cups whipping cream
1/2 teaspoon ground cinnamon
1 teaspoon vanilla essence
1/3 cup Swerve
3/4 cup water
3 egg yolks
1/3 cup almond meal
For the Topping:
2 tablespoons pecans, chopped
1 cup whipping cream

Directions

Microwave the coconut oil; add in 1/3 cup of Swerve and whisk until it has dissolved completely.

Stir in the almond meal and coconut flour and mix again. Press the crust mixture into the bottom of a parchment-lined baking pan. Place in your refrigerator to harden.

Melt the whipping cream and egg yolks until everything is well incorporated.

Whisk in the remaining ingredients for custard. Spread the custard mixture over the crust and place in your refrigerator for at least 1 hour.

Beat 1 cup of whipping cream using an electric mixer until peaks are completely stiff. Top your pie with the cream and garnish with chopped pecans. Bon appétit!

Per serving: 305 Calories; 30.6g Fat; 4.7g Carbs; 4.6g Protein; 0.5g Fiber

703. Nut and Seed Crunch

(Ready in about 35 minutes | Servings 8)

Ingredients

1/4 cup sunflower seeds
1/4 cup pepitas seeds
1 cup coconut flakes
1/4 cup flaxseeds
3/4 cup almonds, chopped
1 tablepsoon Monk fruit powder
3 tablespoons coconut oil
1 teaspoon pumpkin pie spice mix
1/2 cup cashews, chopped
2 tablespoons hemp hearts

Directions

Toss all ingredients in a rimmed baking pan.

Bake in the preheated oven 290 degrees F, tossing once or twice.

Keep at room temperature for up to a month.

Per serving: 281 Calories; 26.6g Fat; 7.7g Carbs; 5.4g Protein; 3.3g Fiber

704. 15-Minute Keto Pizza

(Ready in about 15 minutes | Servings 4)

Ingredients

1 3/4 cups soft cheese
2 tablespoons sour cream
1 cup tomatoes, chopped
2 tablespoons butter, melted
1/2 cup Colby cheese, shredded
2 bell peppers, chopped
1 teaspoon garlic, minced
Salt and pepper, to season

Directions

In a large pan, melt the butter over medium heat.

Spread the cheese on the bottom and cook for 4 to 5 minutes until it is crispy on top.

Add the sour cream, garlic, bell peppers and tomatoes. Season with salt and pepper, and continue to cook for 2 to 3 minutes more.

Per serving: 266 Calories; 23.6g Fat; 6.6g Carbs; 9g Protein; 1g Fiber

705. Flatbread with Kulen and Romano Cheese

(Ready in about 30 minutes | Servings 6)

Ingredients

12 large slices of kulen
2 ½ cups Romano cheese, shredded
2 teaspoons baking powder
4 large eggs, beaten
1/2 cup pork rinds, crushed
3 tablespoons butter
1/2 cup tomato paste
1/4 teaspoon sea salt
10 ounces soft cheese, melted

Directions

Thoroughly combine the cheese, eggs, butter, pork rinds, baking powder, and salt. Preheat a frying pan over a moderately-high flame.

Cook your flatbread for about 5 minutes.

Spread the tomato paste over the flatbread and top with the kulen. Bon appétit!

Per serving: 464 Calories; 33.6g Fat; 5.1g Carbs; 31.1g Protein; 1.2g Fiber

706. Traditional Keto Quesadilla

(Ready in about 15 minutes | Servings 4)

Per serving: 323 Calories; 24g Fat; 7.4g Carbs; 18.8g Protein; 2.3g Fiber

Ingredients

1/2 cup Muenster cheese, shredded
2 garlic cloves, minced
2 tablespoons white vinegar
1 cup whipping cream
1 tablespoon butter
1/2 pound bacon, cut into strips
1 pound cauliflower florets

Directions

In a preheated sauté pan, cook the bacon for 2 to 3 minutes and reserve.

Melt the butter in the same pan. Sauté the cauliflower florets in the pan drippings until they are crisp-tender.

Pour the whipping cream into the pan. Add in the garlic and vinegar and continue to cook for 3 minutes longer, stirring frequently.

Add in the reserved bacon along with the cheese; continue to cook for 2 to 3 minutes, or until the cheese has melted.

MORE KETO RECIPES

707. Homemade Coconut Ice Cream

(Ready in about 10 minutes + chilling time | Servings 4)

Ingredients

1/2 cup coconut flakes
1/2 teaspoon xanthan gum
1/3 cup double cream
1 ¼ cups coconut milk
17 drops liquid Monk fruit

Directions

Thoroughly combine all ingredients, except for the xanthan gum, using your electric mixer.

Add in the xanthan gum, mixing constantly, until the mixture has thickened.

Prepare your ice cream in a machine following the manufacturer's instructions.

Bon appétit!

Per serving: 260 Calories; 24.3g Fat; 6.5g Carbs; 2.5g Protein; 2.7g Fiber

708. Mustard Greens with Cheese

(Ready in about 25 minutes | Servings 5)

Ingredients

1 cup Cheddar cheese, shredded
2 pounds mustard greens, trimmed and torn into pieces
1 tablespoon white vinegar
1 teaspoon red pepper flakes
1 tablespoon olive oil
1/4 cup vegetable broth
1 teaspoon garlic, minced
1 red onion, finely chopped
Sea salt and ground black pepper, to taste

Directions

In a saucepan, heat the oil over a moderately-high flame. Sauté the garlic and onions for 2 to 3 minutes or until fragrant.

Stir in the mustard greens and vegetable broth; continue to cook until the leaves have wilted and all liquid has evaporated, about 15 minutes.

Now, add in the vinegar, red pepper, salt and black pepper. Remove from the heat.

Top with the Cheddar cheese and reheat until melted. Enjoy!

Per serving: 160 Calories; 10g Fat; 7.1g Carbs; 11g Protein; 6g Fiber

709. Loaded Hamburger Muffins

(Ready in about 25 minutes | Servings 6)

Ingredients

1 pound ground pork
1 teaspoon dried marjoram
1/4 cups flaxseed meal
1 teaspoon baking powder
1 stick butter
1/2 pound ground beef
1 tablespoon olive oil
1 cup almond meal
3 eggs, lightly beaten
2 tablespoons whipped cream
Salt and pepper, to season

Directions

In a saucepan, heat the olive oil over a moderate flame. Sear the ground meat for about 5 minutes until the juices run clear.

Add in the remaining ingredients and mix to combine well.

Spoon the mixture into lightly greased muffin cups. Bake in the preheated oven at 365 degrees F for about 17 minutes.

Bon appétit!

Per serving: 600 Calories; 42.3g Fat; 6.5g Carbs; 27.9g Protein; 4.1g Fiber

710. Cream of Cabbage Soup

(Ready in about 25 minutes | Servings 4)

Ingredients

1 ½ tablespoons olive oil
1 medium-sized leek, chopped
1 celery with leaves, chopped
1 cup sour cream
1 bay leaf
1 cup cabbage, shredded
1 bell pepper, chopped
4 cups broth
1 teaspoon garlic, minced

Directions

Heat the oil in a heavy-bottomed pot over a moderate flame. Sauté the leek until tender and aromatic. Add in the remaining vegetables and continue to cook for about 6 minutes, stirring occasionally to ensure even cooking.

Add in the broth and bay leaf, leave the lid slightly ajar, and cover partially. Continue to cook for 12 to 15 minutes.

Puree the mixture with an immersion blender.

Serve dolloped with chilled sour cream. Enjoy!

Per serving: 185 Calories; 16.6g Fat; 2.4g Carbs; 2.9g Protein; 1.2g Fiber

711. Italian Pizzelle with Prosciutto

(Ready in about 20 minutes | Servings 2)

Ingredients

4 slices prosciutto, chopped
4 eggs
1/2 cup gorgonzola cheese, crumbled
2 tablespoons ghee, room temperature
1/2 teaspoon red pepper flakes
Salt and pepper, to taste

Directions

Start by preheating your waffle iron to the desired temperature.

Thoroughly combine all ingredients in a mixing bowl. Spray your waffle iron with a non-stick cooking spray.

Ladle the batter into the preheated waffle iron; cook your waffles until golden and crisp.

Bon appétit!

Per serving: 470 Calories; 40.3g Fat; 2.9g Carbs; 24.4g Protein; 0.5g Fiber

712. Chunky Cheesy Beef Chowder

(Ready in about 20 minutes | Servings 4)

Ingredients

1/2 cup celery with leaves, chopped
4 cups vegetable broth
1 cup Cheddar cheese, shredded
2 tablespoons olive oil
1 tablespoon fresh basil, chopped
1 cup onion, chopped
1/2 cup whipped cream
1/2 pound ground beef

Directions

In a soup pot, heat olive oil over moderate heat. Now, cook the ground beef until it is no longer pink; reserve.

In the same pot, cook the onion until tender and translucent. Add a splash of vegetable broth to scrape up any browned bits from the bottom of the skillet.

Add in the celery and vegetable broth and bring to a boil. Leave the lid slightly ajar and continue to cook for 8 to 10 minutes, partially covered.

Slowly add in the cream, whisking constantly until well combined. Continue to simmer an additional 5 to 6 minutes.

Serve with fresh basil leaves. Bon appétit!

Per serving: 326 Calories; 20.5g Fat; 4.5g Carbs; 26.8g Protein; 0.8g Fiber

713. Peanut Butter Penuche

(Ready in about 3 hours | Servings 8)

Ingredients

1/3 cup almond milk
3 tablespoons cocoa powder, unsweetened
1 tablespoon liquid Stevia
3 tablespoons coconut butter, melted
1 teaspoon vanilla
1/2 cup ghee
3/4 cup peanut butter
1/4 cup Swerve
1/8 teaspoon salt

Directions

Melt the peanut butter and ghee in your microwave.

Add in the almond milk, 1/4 cup Swerve, and salt; stir to combine well and scrape the base into a foil-lined baking pan.

Refrigerate for about 3 hours or until set.

Now, make the sauce by whisking the other ingredients until well combined. Spread the sauce over your fudge. Cut into squares. Enjoy!

Per serving: 180 Calories; 18.3g Fat; 4.5g Carbs; 1g Protein; 1.1g Fiber

714. Old-Fashioned Beef Stew with Egg

(Ready in about 40 minutes | Servings 6)

Ingredients

1 ½ pounds chuck, cubed
1 egg, lightly whisked
1 cup brown mushrooms, thinly sliced
1 teaspoon garlic, minced
4 cups beef bone broth
1 cup onion, thinly sliced
Salt and pepper, to taste
1 tablespoon Steak dry rub
1 tablespoon lard, at room temperature

Directions

Melt the lard in a heavy-bottomed pot over a moderately-high flame.

Brown the beef for about 8 minutes or until no longer pink.

In the same pot, cook the onion and garlic until they are just tender and aromatic. Stir in the mushrooms and cook until they release the liquid.

Add in the other ingredients, and continue to cook, covered, approximately 35 minutes. Fold in the whisked egg and stir for 1 minute or until completely dissolved.

Serve with fresh cilantro. Bon appétit!

Per serving: 259 Calories; 10.1g Fat; 4.1g Carbs; 35.7g Protein; 0.6g Fiber

715. Rustic Tuna and Walnut Pâté

(Ready in about 10 minutes | Servings 6)

Ingredients

1/2 cup soft cheese
1/2 teaspoon curry paste
1 tablespoon fresh coriander, chopped
A bunch of fresh scallions
2 ounces walnuts, ground
6 ounces tuna in oil, drained
1 teaspoon stone-ground mustard

Directions

Process all ingredients in your blender or food processor until smooth and creamy.

Place the tuna pâté in an airtight container; keep in the refrigerator for a week. Enjoy!

Per serving: 384 Calories; 20.4g Fat; 2.5g Carbs; 45.9g Protein; 0.8g Fiber

716. Creamed Green Cabbage Coleslaw

(Ready in about 10 minutes + chilling time | Servings 4)

Ingredients

1 large-sized celery stalk, grated
1/2 red onion, sliced
1 cup mayonnaise
1 teaspoon Dijon mustard
1/2 teaspoon cumin seeds
2 tablespoons pumpkin seeds
3/4 pound green cabbage, cored and shredded
1/2 cup fresh cilantro leaves, coarsely chopped
Salt and pepper, to taste

Directions

Add the green cabbage, celery, and onion to a bowl. Add in the mayonnaise, Dijon mustard, cilantro, cumin seeds, salt, and pepper.

Gently stir to combine and place in your refrigerator. Serve sprinkled with pumpkin seeds.

Per serving: 242 Calories; 20.5g Fat; 6.2g Carbs; 1g Protein; 2.5g Fiber

717. Traditional Creole Jambalaya

(Ready in about 35 minutes | Servings 6)

Ingredients

- 1 teaspoon gumbo file
- 1 ½ tablespoons lard
- 1 cup boiling water
- 1 pound pork butt, cubed
- 1 (14-ounce) can diced tomatoes
- 8 ounces andouille sausage, sliced
- 1 onion, chopped
- 4 cups roasted vegetable broth
- 1/4 cup flaxseed meal
- 1 green bell peppers, deveined and thinly sliced
- 1 parsnip, chopped
- 1 teaspoon cayenne pepper
- Sea salt and black pepper, to taste
- 1 tablespoon Creole spice mix

Directions

In a soup pot, melt the lard over a moderately-high heat. Sear the pork and sausage until just browned on all sides and set aside.

Stir in the onion and continue to cook until tender and translucent. Add in the remaining ingredients, except for the flaxseed meal, and bring it to a boil.

Turn to a simmer and continue to cook for a further 20 minutes.

Afterwards, add in the flax seed meal and let it simmer for 4 to 5 minutes or until the liquid has thickened. Enjoy!

Per serving: 427 Calories; 26.2g Fat; 7.6g Carbs; 35.2g Protein; 4.1g Fiber

718. Omelet with Brown Mushrooms, Avocado and Salsa

(Ready in about 15 minutes | Servings 4)

Ingredients

- 1/4 cup salsa
- 1 cup tomatoes, crushed
- 2 tablespoons butter, melted
- 1 medium-sized avocado, pitted and mashed
- 1 large onion, finely chopped
- 4 eggs
- 1 pound brown mushroom, chopped
- 1/2 teaspoon garlic, smashed
- Sea salt and ground black pepper, to taste

Directions

In a frying pan, melt the butter over a moderately-high flame. Sauté the onion and garlic until they've softened.

Add in the brown mushrooms, tomatoes, salt, and pepper; continue to cook for 2 minutes more.

Stir in the eggs and scramble them; top with the salsa sauce.

Serve warm with avocado slices.

Per serving: 290 Calories; 21.7g Fat; 6.5g Carbs; 10.6g Protein; 5g Fiber

719. Skirt Steak in Wine

(Ready in about 20 minutes + marinating time | Servings 6)

Ingredients

- 1/4 cup dry red wine
- 2 pounds skirt steak
- 2 garlic cloves, minced
- 1/2 cup white onions, chopped
- 1 tablespoon white vinegar
- 1 ½ tablespoons canola oil
- 2 tablespoons coconut aminos
- Salt and pepper, to taste
- 1/2 teaspoon ground bay leaf

Directions

Combine the oil, coconut aminos, garlic, onions, vinegar, and red wine in a ceramic dish. Add in the steak, ground bay leaf, salt, and pepper.

Let it marinate overnight.

Sear the steak in a non-stick skillet over a moderately-high flame. Sear the steak for 8 to 11 minutes per side. Bon appétit!

Per serving: 350 Calories; 17.3g Fat; 2.1g Carbs; 42.7g Protein; 0.4g Fiber

720. Pasta with Green Beans

(Ready in about 15 minutes | Servings 4)

Ingredients

- 1 pound green beans
- 1/2 teaspoon garlic, minced
- 1/2 teaspoon cayenne pepper
- 1 tablespoon olive oil
- 1 cup celery, shredded
- Salt and black pepper, to taste
- For Pasta Elias:
- 3 tablespoons extra-virgin olive oil
- 2 anchovy fillets
- 1 tablespoon lime juice
- 1/2 cup Greek olives, pitted
- 1 ½ tablespoons Italian parsley leaves

Directions

Steam the green beans for about 4 minutes or until just tender.

Heat the olive oil in a sauté pan over a moderately-high heat. Add in the celery and garlic and continue to sauté for 3 to 4 minutes, stirring occasionally to ensure even cooking.

Season with cayenne pepper, salt, and black pepper.

In your blender or food processor, pulse all ingredients for the Pasta Elias. Serve with the green beans.

Per serving: 183 Calories; 16.1g Fat; 8.4g Carbs; 3.2g Protein; 3.4g Fiber

721. Crispy Roasted Chicken

(Ready in about 35 minutes | Servings 4)

Ingredients

- 1/2 cup olive oil
- 6 black olives, pitted and halved
- 1 tablespoon lime juice
- 1 cup feta cheese, cubed
- 2 garlic cloves, minced
- 1 hard-boiled egg yolk, mashed
- Sea salt and pepper, to taste
- 2 tablespoons fresh cilantro, roughly chopped
- 4 chicken drumsticks
- 1 ½ tablespoons butter, room temperature
- Sea salt and ground black pepper, to taste

Directions

Begin by preheating your oven to 390 degrees F.

In a frying pan, melt the butter over medium-high heat.

Sprinkle the chicken drumsticks with salt and pepper; now, sear the chicken for about 4 minutes or until no longer pink.

Arrange the chicken on a foil-lined baking sheet and place the fresh cilantro and black olives on top.

Meanwhile, make the sauce by blending the remaining ingredients, except for the feta cheese. Spread the sauce over the chicken and bake for 20 to 25 minutes.

Top with the cheese and place under the preheated broiler for about 6 minutes or until hot and bubbly.

Per serving: 562 Calories; 43.8g Fat; 2.1g Carbs; 40.8g Protein; 0.6g Fiber

722. Cheesy Roast Beef

(Ready in about 8 hours | Servings 6)

Ingredients

- 6 ounces goat cheese, crumbled
- 1 onion, chopped
- 1 teaspoon coriander seeds
- 1/2 teaspoon mustard seeds
- 1/4 cup red wine
- 1 cup chicken stock
- 1 teaspoon garlic, minced
- 1 ½ pounds boneless blade roast
- 2 tablespoons olive oil

Directions

In a frying pan, heat the oil over medium-high heat. Cook the onion until tender and translucent.

Add in the garlic and continue to sauté for a further 30 seconds; transfer the sautéed mixture to your slow cooker.

Sear the beef until golden-brown and transfer to the slow cooker. Add in the remaining ingredients, except for the cheese.

Cover and cook on Low heat setting for about 7 hours or until the meat has softened.

Serve topped with goat cheese.

Per serving: 397 Calories; 31.4g Fat; 3.9g Carbs; 23.5g Protein; 0.5g Fiber

723. Classic Keto Taco Shells

(Ready in about 10 minutes | Servings 6)

Ingredients

- 1 cup sour cream
- 1 ½ cups salsa
- 2 cups lettuce, torn into pieces
- 1 pound Mexican cheese blend, grated
- 1 teaspoon taco seasoning mix

Directions

Thoroughly combine the cheese and taco seasoning mix. Scatter the cheese all over the preheated pan, covering the bottom.

Cook for about 3 minutes, flip them over, and continue to cook for 2 to 3 minutes more until the bubbles start to form.

Top with the salsa, sour cream and lettuce; roll them up and serve immediately. Bon appétit!

Enjoy!

Per serving: 346 Calories; 25.7g Fat; 6.9g Carbs; 20.5g Protein; 1.4g Fiber

724. Pork and Avocado Soup

(Ready in about 20 minutes | Servings 6)

Ingredients

- 1 avocado, pitted, peeled and sliced
- 1 celery stalk, chopped
- 3 cups roasted vegetable broth
- 1 teaspoon garlic, peeled and minced
- 2 tablespoons olive oil
- 1 cup tomato puree
- 1 onion, peeled and chopped
- 1 teaspoon chili pepper, seeded and minced
- 1/4 cup fresh cilantro, roughly chopped
- 1 ¼ pounds pork butt, cut into bite-sized pieces
- Sea salt and black pepper, to taste

Directions

In a heavy-bottomed pot, heat the oil until sizzling. Once hot, sauté the onion, garlic, pepper and celery for about 3 minutes or until the vegetables have softened.

Stir in the pork and continue to cook for 4 minutes longer or until no longer pink. Add in the remaining ingredients.

Turn the heat to a simmer, partially cover, and continue to cook for about 15 minutes.

Serve topped with fresh avocado. Bon appétit!

Per serving: 423 Calories; 31.8g Fat; 6g Carbs; 25.9g Protein; 2.6g Fiber

725. Blueberry Mocha Cappuccino

(Ready in about 2 hours | Servings 2)

Ingredients

- 16 blueberries, frozen
- 2 teaspoons instant coffee
- 1/4 cup cold water
- 1 cup coconut milk
- 2 tablespoons whipped cream
- 4 drops liquid Monk fruit
- 1 tablespoon cacao butter

Directions

Combine the instant coffee, Monk fruit, cacao butter and cold water. Shake for about 30 seconds.

Divide the frozen blueberries between two glasses. Pour the coffee mixture over them. Add in the coconut milk.

Serve topped with coconut whipped cream.

Per serving: 371 Calories; 37.8g Fat; 7.1g Carbs; 3.4g Protein; 0.3g Fiber

726. Vegetables with Sour Cream Dip

(Ready in about 45 minutes | Servings 4)

Ingredients

- 2 garlic cloves, minced
- 1 onion, sliced
- 1/4 cup olive oil
- 2 celery stalks, cut into sticks
- 2 bell peppers, sliced
- 1 tablespoon fresh cilantro, minced
- 1/2 teaspoon cayenne pepper
- For the Spicy Sour Cream Dip:
- 1 chili pepper, finely minced
- 2 tablespoons basil, chopped
- 3/4 teaspoon deli mustard
- 1 tablespoon lemon juice
- 1 ½ cups cream cheese
- 2 tablespoons aioli
- Salt and pepper, to taste

Directions

Begin by preheating your oven to 395 degrees F. Line a baking pan with a piece of parchment paper.

Toss your vegetables with the olive oil, garlic, cilantro, and cayenne pepper.

Arrange the vegetables on the baking pan and roast for 35 to 40 minutes, tossing them halfway through.

Thoroughly combine all ingredients for the dip. Enjoy!

Per serving: 357 Calories; 35.8g Fat; 5.2g Carbs; 3.4g Protein; 1.1g Fiber

727. Roasted Mexican-Style Vegetable Medley

(Ready in about 30 minutes | Servings 4)

Ingredients

4 Mexican sausages, sliced
1 teaspoon garlic, finely chopped
1 celery stalk, chopped
1 onion, sliced
1 bell pepper, sliced
1 chili pepper, finely chopped
1 cup broccoli florets
1 parsnip, sliced
Salt and pepper, to season
1 ¼ cups vegetable broth
1 tablespoon lard, softened

Directions

Melt the lard in a frying pan over a moderately-high heat. Cook the sausage until no longer pink and reserve.

In the pan drippings, cook the onion, broccoli, parsnip, celery, peppers, and garlic until they've softened.

Season with salt and pepper to taste and spoon the mixture into a lightly buttered baking dish. Nestle the sausages within the sautéed vegetables.

Pour in the vegetable broth and bake in the preheated oven at 360 degrees F for 15 minutes.

Bon appétit!

Per serving: 424 Calories; 32.4g Fat; 6.8g Carbs; 23.7g Protein; 2.9g Fiber

728. Italian Wine-Braised Steaks

(Ready in about 30 minutes | Servings 4)

Ingredients

2 tablespoons butter, room temperature
1 teaspoon garlic, smashed
1 tablespoon Dijon mustard
2 Italian peppers, deveined and chopped
2 thyme sprigs
1 cup onions, chopped
1 tablespoon Dijon mustard
1 ½ pound rib-eye steaks
1/2 cup port wine
Salt and pepper, to taste

Directions

Rub the steaks with the mustard, salt, pepper, and thyme.

Melt the butter in a non-stick skillet over a moderately high heat. Sear your steaks for 8 to 10 minutes per side.

In the same skillet, cook the onions, garlic, and Italian pepper for 3 to 4 minutes. Pour in the wine and scrape up any browned bits from the bottom of the skillet.

Continue to simmer until the liquid has reduced and thickened.

Bon appétit!

Per serving: 451 Calories; 34.4g Fat; 3.6g Carbs; 29.7g Protein; 1.2g Fiber

729. Panna Cotta with Chive Cream Cheese

(Ready in about 40 minutes | Servings 8)

Ingredients

1/4 cup fresh parsley, chopped
2 teaspoons powdered gelatin
4 bell peppers, sliced
1 tablespoon olive oil, room temperature
1/2 teaspoon mustard seeds
1 ½ cups double cream
1 cup chive cream cheese
1/2 teaspoon paprika
Salt and pepper, to taste

Directions

Strat by preheating your oven to 450 degrees F.

Brush the bell peppers with olive oil and roast them for about 30 minutes, until the skin is charred in spots.

Peel the peppers and chop them.

In the meantime, cook the remaining ingredients for about 10 minutes until thoroughly warmed.

Fold in the chopped peppers and stir to combine. Divide the mixture between eight lightly oiled ramekins. Place in your refrigerator overnight.

Enjoy!

Per serving: 155 Calories; 12.7g Fat; 6.2g Carbs; 4.6g Protein; 0.4g Fiber

730. Pork Meatloaf with Tangy Sauce

(Ready in about 45 minutes | Servings 6)

Ingredients

For the Meatloaf:
2 cloves garlic, finely minced
1/4 cup pork rinds, crushed
1 teaspoon chili powder
1/2 pound ground beef
1 large onion, chopped
1/3 cup flaxseed meal
1 pound ground pork
1 egg, whisked
Sea salt and black pepper, to taste
For the Sauce:
1 ½ tablespoons erythritol
1 teaspoon dried coriander
1 cup marinara sauce
1 tablespoon balsamic vinegar

Directions

Mix all ingredients for the meatloaf until well combined. Press the mixture into a lightly greased baking pan.

In another bowl, mix all the sauce ingredients until well combined. Spoon the sauce over the meatloaf.

Bake in the preheated oven at 365 degrees F for 40 to 45 minutes or until a meat thermometer registers 165 degrees F. Bon appétit!

Per serving: 251 Calories; 7.9g Fat; 6.5g Carbs; 34.6g Protein; 4g Fiber

731. Creamed Greek Salad

(Ready in about 15 minutes + chilling time | Servings 4)

Ingredients

1 cup Greek-style yogurt
12 cherry tomatoes, halved
1 onion, thinly sliced
1 tablespoon lemon juice
4 large lettuce leaves
1 teaspoon garlic, minced
2 cucumbers, sliced
1 teaspoon Greek seasoning mix
Sea salt and black pepper, to taste

Directions

Thoroughly combine the Greek-style yogurt, garlic, lemon juice, and Greek seasoning mix.

Toss the onions, cucumbers, and tomatoes in a bowl; dress the salad and season with salt and pepper to taste.

Mound your salad onto each lettuce leaf.

Per serving: 318 Calories; 24.3g Fat; 4.1g Carbs; 15.4g Protein; 1.1g Fiber

732. Creamiest Chicken Salad Ever

(Ready in about 20 minutes | Servings 4)

Ingredients

1 avocado, pitted and sliced
1 tablespoon lemon juice
2 egg yolks
1 tablespoon soy sauce
1/2 teaspoon Italian seasoning mix
2 chicken breasts
1/2 teaspoon deli mustard
1/3 cup extra-virgin olive oil
Sea salt and red pepper, to taste

Directions

Toss the chicken breasts with salt, red pepper and Italian seasoning mix. Cook the chicken on the preheated grill for 4 minutes per side.

Cut the chicken into the strips.

Make the dressing by whisking the remaining ingredients.

Place the avocado slices in 4 serving plates. Mound the salad onto the plates. Dress your salad and serve!

Per serving: 408 Calories; 34.2g Fat; 4.8g Carbs; 22.7g Protein; 3.1g Fiber

733. Classic Asparagus Spears with Pancetta

(Ready in about 20 minutes | Servings 4)

Ingredients

1 pound asparagus spears
1/2 teaspoon dried dill weed
1 teaspoon shallot powder
4 tablespoons pancetta, finely chopped
1/4 teaspoon porcini powder
Salt and black pepper, to season

Directions

Toss your asparagus with the salt, pepper, shallot powder, porcini powder, and dill. Place them on a parchment-lined baking sheet.

Bake in the preheated oven at 440 degrees F for about 20 minutes; toss them halfway through the cooking time.

Top with the chopped pancetta, and serve immediately!

Per serving: 48 Calories; 1.6g Fat; 4.4g Carbs; 5.5g Protein; 2.7g Fiber

734. Rainbow Steak Salad

(Ready in about 15 minutes | Servings 4)

Ingredients

2 avocados, pitted, peeled and sliced
1 tablespoon fresh lime juice
1/4 cup sesame seeds, lightly toasted
1 shallot, peeled and sliced
1 poblano chili, minced
2 tablespoons olive oil
1 teaspoon coconut aminos
2 tablespoons lime juice, freshly squeezed
1 celery, sliced
1 tablespoon fresh basil, snipped
1/2 teaspoon ginger-garlic paste
1/2 pound flank steak, cut into strips
1 cucumber, sliced
Sea salt and ground black pepper, to taste

Directions

In a large frying pan, heat the oil over medium-low flame. Sauté the shallot until tender or about 3 minutes.

Add in the steak and cook for 5 to 6 minutes per side. Season the steak with salt and pepper.

Toss the remaining ingredients in a bowl and top your salad with the steak. Enjoy!

Per serving: 404 Calories; 32.9g Fat; 8g Carbs; 12.8g Protein; 6g Fiber

735. Classic Blueberry Crumb Cake

(Ready in about 30 minutes | Servings 8)

Ingredients

3/4 cup almond meal
1/2 tablespoon lime juice
5 tablespoons butter, melted
1/3 teaspoon xanthan gum
3/4 cup Swerve
2 eggs, whisked
2 ½ cups blueberries, cored and sliced
1/2 cup coconut flour

Directions

Preheat your oven to 365 degrees F. Lightly oil a baking pan with a cooking spray.

Arrange the blueberries on the bottom of the baking pan. Drizzle with lime juice and xanthan gum.

Mix the almond meal, coconut flour, xylitol and eggs until the mixture resembles coarse meal. Spread the mixture over the blueberries.

Drizzle melted butter over the topping. Bake for 25 to 30 minutes. Bon appétit!

Per serving: 152 Calories; 11.8g Fat; 6.2g Carbs; 2.5g Protein; 1.5g Fiber

736. Easy Jaffa Popsicles

(Ready in about 15 minutes | Servings 4)

Ingredients

2 egg yolks
1 tablespoon orange juice, freshly squeezed
1/2 teaspoon ground cinnamon
3/4 cup double cream
3 ounces soft cheese, at room temperature
1/4 cup Swerve
1/4 cup cocoa powder, unsweetened

Directions

Beat the egg yolks using your electric mixer until frothy.

Warm the cream in a saucepan over a moderate heat. Stir in the hot cream into the egg yolks.

Turn the heat to a simmer and continue to cook for 5 to 6 minutes, stirring constantly, until your mixture has thickened.

Beat in the remaining ingredients using your electric mixer until creamy and uniform.

To freeze, pour the mixture into ice-pop molds. Cover and insert sticks. Freeze until firm, at least 4 hours. Dip the molds briefly in hot water to release pops. Enjoy!

Per serving: 154 Calories; 13g Fat; 6.3g Carbs; 5.3g Protein; 1.8g Fiber

737. Sausage with Spicy Tomato Sauce

(Ready in about 15 minutes | Servings 4)

Ingredients

4 turkey sausages, sliced
1 cup cherry tomatoes, chopped
2 cloves garlic, smashed
2 teaspoons olive oil, at room temperature
1 cup Italian peppers, chopped
1 shallot, diced
2 tablespoons fresh parsley, minced
3 teaspoons lemon juice
1/4 cup white wine

Directions

In a non-stick skillet, heat the olive oil over moderately-high heat.

Then, sear the sausage until well browned on all sides; pour in the wine and continue to cook for about 4 minutes. Set aside.

Make the salsa by blending the remaining ingredients.

Enjoy!

Per serving: 156 Calories; 4.2g Fat; 5.1g Carbs; 16.2g Protein; 0.9g Fiber

738. Turkey Sausage in Spicy Sauce

(Ready in about 15 minutes | Servings 4)

Ingredients

1/4 cup white wine
1 shallot, diced
2 teaspoons olive oil, at room temperature
1 cup Italian peppers, chopped
2 tablespoons fresh parsley, minced
2 cloves garlic, smashed
3 teaspoons lemon juice
4 turkey sausages, sliced
1 cup cherry tomatoes, chopped

Directions

In a non-stick skillet, heat the olive oil over moderately-high heat.

Then, sear the sausage until well browned on all sides; pour in the wine and continue to cook for about 4 minutes. Set aside.

Make the salsa by blending the remaining ingredients.

Enjoy!

Per serving: 156 Calories; 4.2g Fat; 5.1g Carbs; 16.2g Protein; 0.9g Fiber

739. Mediterranean Pork with Gorgonzola Cheese Sauce

(Ready in about 30 minutes | Servings 6)

Ingredients

1 tablespoon coconut aminos
6 ounces Gorgonzola cheese
1 tablespoon olive oil
1 teaspoon garlic, chopped
1/3 cup vegetable broth
1 teaspoon cayenne pepper
1 teaspoon Mediterranean spice mix
1/3 cup port wine
1/2 cup leek, chopped
1 ½ pounds Boston butt, boneless and cut into 6 pieces
1/3 cup whipped cream
Salt and pepper, to taste

Directions

Rub the Boston butt with salt, pepper, and Mediterranean spice mix.

Heat the olive oil in a saucepan over a moderately-high heat. Sear the Boston butt on all sides for about 15 minutes and reserve.

In the pan drippings, sauté the leeks and garlic until they are just tender and fragrant. Pour in the wine to deglaze the pan. Now, add in the broth, cayenne pepper, and coconut aminos.

Continue to simmer, partially covered, until the sauce has thickened slightly. Add in the cheese and whipped cream and continue to simmer for a couple of minutes until the cheese melts. Enjoy!

Per serving: 495 Calories; 36.9g Fat; 3.6g Carbs; 33.4g Protein; 0.4g Fiber

740. Tilapia Fillets with Spicy Tomatillo Chutney

(Ready in about 30 minutes | Servings 4)

Ingredients

1 pound cauliflower florets
1 teaspoon red pepper flakes
1 cup Spanish peppers, thinly sliced
2 tablespoons olive oil
1 ½ pounds tilapia fillets
1/2 cup shallots, thinly sliced
Salt and black pepper, to taste
For Tomatillo Chutney:
1 chilli pepper, deseeded and minced
1 teaspoon butter, melted
1 teaspoon garlic, chopped
2 tomatillos, crushed
1 tablespoon mustard seeds
Sea salt and black pepper, to taste

Directions

In a saucepan, heat 1 tablespoon of olive oil over moderately-high flame.

Now, cook the cauliflower florets, peppers, and shallots until they've softened; season with salt, black pepper, and red pepper and reserve.

Heat another tablespoon of the olive oil. Cook the fish fillets for 5 to 6 minutes per side or until thoroughly cooked and opaque. Add the sautéed cauliflower mixture.

Then, melt the butter in a frying pan over a moderately-high heat. Now, sauté the garlic until just tender and fragrant.

Add in the tomatillos, mustard seeds, chili pepper, salt, and black pepper and continue to cook, stirring periodically, for 9 to 10 minutes.

Serve with tomatillo chutney. Enjoy!

Per serving: 291 Calories; 9.5g Fat; 5.6g Carbs; 42.5g Protein; 4.3g Fiber

741. Coffee with Coconut Cream

(Ready in about 10 minutes + chilling time | Servings 6)

Ingredients

5 ounces coconut cream
1/2 teaspoon pure vanilla extract
4 ounces coconut oil
3 tablespoons erythritol
1 teaspoon instant espresso powder
1/2 teaspoon pure coconut extract
A pinch of salt

Directions

Melt the coconut oil in a double boiler; add in the remaining ingredients. Remove from the heat and stir to combine well.

Pour into a silicone mold and place in your freezer.

Per serving: 218 Calories; 24.7g Fat; 1.1g Carbs; 0.4g Protein; 0g Fiber

742. Za'atar Pork Tenderloin and Brussels Sprouts

(Ready in about 20 minutes + marinating time | Servings 4)

Ingredients

1 teaspoon Za'atar
1 onion, chopped
1 tablespoon lime juice
1 cup Brussels sprouts, halved
1 Italian pepper, chopped
2 tablespoons olive oil
1 teaspoon garlic, finely chopped
Sea salt and black pepper, to taste
1 pound pork tenderloin, cut into small pieces
1 chili pepper, deseeded and chopped
1 tablespoon coconut aminos

Directions

Place the tenderloin, coconut aminos, lime juice, salt, salt, black pepper and Za'atar seasoning in a ceramic bowl. Let it marinate in your refrigerator a couple of hours.

Heat the oil in a frying pan over a medium-high heat. Sear the steaks for about 5 minutes on each side.

Add in the onions, garlic, Brussels sprouts, and peppers; turn the heat to a simmer. Continue to cook for about 15 minutes until thoroughly cooked.

Bon appétit!

Per serving: 321 Calories; 14g Fat; 7.3g Carbs; 36.7g Protein; 2g Fiber

743. Fish Salad with Grilled Halloumi Cheese

(Ready in about 15 minutes | Servings 4)

Ingredients

1 ½ tablespoons extra-virgin olive oil
2 tablespoons hem hearts
6 ounces canned salmon, drained
8 ounces halloumi cheese
1/2 head lettuce
1 tablespoon lemon juice
1 Lebanese cucumber, sliced
1/2 cup Italian peppers, thinly sliced
1 cup cherry tomatoes, halved
1 onion, thinly sliced
Sea salt and pepper, to taste

Directions

Cook the halloumi cheese in a grill pan over a moderate heat for about 3 minute; cut into cubes.

In a bowl, toss the remaining ingredients until well combined. Place the grilled cheese on top.

Bon appétit!

Per serving: 199 Calories; 10.6g Fat; 3.1g Carbs; 14.2g Protein; 1.4g Fiber

744. Belgian Gofres with Limburger Cheese

(Ready in about 30 minutes | Servings 6)

Ingredients

3 smoked Belgian sausages, crumbled
1 cup Limburger cheese, shredded
1/2 teaspoon ground cloves
6 eggs
6 tablespoons milk
Sea salt and pepper, to taste

Directions

Whisk the eggs with the milk and spices until pale and frothy.

Add in the crumbled Belgian sausage and Limburger cheese. Mix until everything is well combined.

Brush a waffle iron with a non-stick cooking spray.

Pour the batter into waffle iron and cook until golden and cooked through. Repeat until all the batter is used.

Enjoy!

Per serving: 316 Calories; 25g Fat; 1.5g Carbs; 20.2g Protein; 0.1g Fiber

745. Easy Seafood Bowl

(Ready in about 10 minutes | Servings 4)

Ingredients

1/2 pound sea scallops, halved horizontally
1/2 cup black olives, pitted
1 head of Romaine lettuce, torn into bite-sized pieces
2 tablespoons lime juice
1 cup cherry tomatoes, halved
1 teaspoon Creole spice mix
1/4 cup olive oil
1 bell pepper, sliced
1/2 pound shrimp, deveined
2 cloves garlic, minced
1/2 tablespoon Dijon mustard
Sea salt and black pepper, to taste

Directions

Parboil the seafood in a pot of a lightly salted water for about 2 minutes; rinse and place in a bowl.

Add in the remaining ingredients. Toss to combine well.

Per serving: 260 Calories; 13.6g Fat; 5.9g Carbs; 28.1g Protein; 4g Fiber

746. Provençal-Style Vegetables with Cheese

(Ready in about 15 minutes | Servings 4)

Ingredients

1 onion, chopped
1/2 cup tomato puree
1/4 cup Provençal wine
1/2 pound white mushrooms, chopped
1 cup cauliflower, cut into small florets
8 ounces goat cheese, cubed
1 teaspoon garlic, pressed
2 tablespoons olive oil
1 zucchini, chopped
1 teaspoon Herbes de Provence

Directions

In a Dutch oven, heat the olive oil over a moderately-high heat. Sauté the garlic until just tender but not browned for about one minute.

Add in the onion, mushrooms, cauliflower, and zucchini; cook for a further 5 minutes, stirring occasionally to ensure even cooking.

Add in the seasonings, tomato puree, and Provençal wine; partially cover and continue to cook for 4 to 5 minutes.

Serve topped with goat cheese and enjoy!

Per serving: 318 Calories; 24.3g Fat; 5.1g Carbs; 15.4g Protein; 2.9g Fiber

747. Nutty and Spicy Keto Salad

(Ready in about 5 minutes | Servings 4)

Ingredients

3 tablespoons olive oil
1 teaspoon chili sauce, sugar-free
Salt and pepper, to taste
1 cup grape tomatoes
1 white onion, sliced
1 ounce macadamia nuts, chopped
1 parsnip, grated
2 tablespoons sesame seeds, toasted
1 cup butterhead lettuce, torn into small pieces
1 tablespoon lemon juice
1 cucumber, thinly sliced

Directions

Combine all ingredients, except for the sesame seeds, in a bowl. Toss until everything is well combined.

Top with the sesame seeds and serve immediately.

Per serving: 184 Calories; 16.8g Fat; 5g Carbs; 2.1g Protein; 2g Fiber

748. Colby Cheese Broccoli Casserole

(Ready in about 25 minutes | Servings 3)

Ingredients

1/2 pound broccoli florets
2 cloves garlic, finely chopped
3 eggs, well-beaten
2 ounces Colby cheese, shredded
1 onion, minced
3 tablespoons olive oil
1/2 teaspoon mustard powder
1/2 cup whipped cream
1/2 teaspoon curry paste
Sea salt and black pepper, to season

Directions

Start by preheating your oven to 320 degrees F.

Melt the olive oil in a sauté pan over a moderately-high heat. Once hot, sauté the onion and garlic until they are tender and fragrant.

Add in the broccoli florets and continue to cook until they've softened. Spoon the mixture into a lightly buttered baking dish.

In another bowl, whisk the eggs, cream, curry paste, mustard powder, salt, and black pepper.

Pour the cream/egg mixture over the broccoli mixture. Bake for 20 to minutes or until thoroughly cooked.

Top with the cheese and place under the preheated broiler for about 5 minutes or until hot and bubbly. Enjoy!

Per serving: 195 Calories; 12.7g Fat; 6.7g Carbs; 11.6g Protein; 7.1g Fiber

749. Vegetarian Cremini Mushroom Burger

(Ready in about 20 minutes | Servings 4)

Ingredients

2 eggs, whisked
6 tablespoons ground flax seeds
1/2 cup Romano cheese, grated
6 tablespoons blanched almond flour
1 tablespoon Italian seasoning mix
1 teaspoon Dijon mustard
1/2 stick butter, softened
2 cups Cremini mushrooms, chopped
1 teaspoon garlic, minced

Directions

In a frying pan, melt 1 tablespoon of butter over medium-high heat. Sauté the garlic and mushrooms until just tender and fragrant; drain excess water.

Add in the remaining ingredients and mix to combine well.

Shape the mixture into 4 patties.

In the same frying pan, melt the remaining butter; once hot, fry the patties for 6 to 7 minutes per side.

Bon appétit!

Per serving: 370 Calories; 30g Fat; 4.7g Carbs; 16.8g Protein; 2.2g Fiber

750. Greek Pork Souvlaki

(Ready in about 20 minutes + marinating time | Servings 6)

Ingredients

1/3 cup apple cider vinegar
1/2 teaspoon dried oregano
1/2 teaspoon dried basil
2 tablespoons parsley, chopped
Salt and black pepper, to taste
2 pounds pork shoulder, cut into 1-inch cubes
3 cloves garlic, smashed
For Tzatziki Sauce:
1 Lebanese cucumber, shredded and drained
1 cup Greek yogurt
2 tablespoons extra-virgin olive oil
1 tablespoon dill weed, finely minced
2 cloves garlic, smashed
Sea salt, to taste

Directions

Place the pork shoulder along with vinegar, parsley, garlic, salt, pepper, basil, and oregano in a ceramic dish; let it marinate for 2 to 3 hours in your refrigerator.

Thread the pork cubes onto bamboo skewers. Cook the skewers on the preheated grill for about 10 minutes.

Thoroughly combine all ingredients for the Greek tzatziki sauce. Bon appétit!

Per serving: 147 Calories; 4.8g Fat; 5.8g Carbs; 17.3g Protein; 0.6g Fiber

751. Chicken Breasts with Deli Mustard Sauce

(Ready in about 25 minutes | Servings 4)

Ingredients

1 tablespoon olive oil
1/2 cup low-sodium chicken broth
2 tablespoons deli mustard
1/2 cup fresh chives, chopped
1/2 cup onions, chopped
2 garlic cloves, minced
1/2 cup whipped cream
1 pound chicken breasts
Salt and red pepper, to season

Directions

Rub the chicken with salt and pepper.

Heat the oil in a frying pan over a moderately-high heat. Sear the chicken for about 8 minutes and set aside.

Then, sauté the onion and garlic for about 3 minutes until aromatic.

Pour in the broth and cook until the liquid has reduced by half. Stir in the whipped cream and mustard.

Add the sauce and chives to the reserved chicken. Bon appétit!

Per serving: 311 Calories; 16.9g Fat; 2.1g Carbs; 33.6g Protein; 0.9g Fiber

752. Mexican-Style Roast Beef

(Ready in about 20 minutes + marinating time | Servings 4)

Ingredients

1/2 cup leeks, chopped
1 teaspoon deli mustard
2 teaspoons garlic, minced
1 tablespoon fresh cilantro, chopped
2 tablespoons coconut aminos
1 teaspoon hot sauce
1/2 tablespoon butter
1 teaspoon Taco seasoning blend
1 ½ pounds bottom eye roast, cubed
1/4 teaspoon fennel seeds
Salt and pepper, to taste

Directions

Whisk the coconut aminos, hot sauce and garlic in a mixing dish. Add in the salt, pepper, mustard, Taco seasoning blend, and leeks.

Add the bottom eye roast and let it marinate for 1 hour in your refrigerator.

Melt the butter in a saucepan over a moderately-high heat. Cook the marinated bottom eye roast for about 16 minutes, stirring periodically to ensure even cooking.

Season with fennel seeds and cilantro.

Bon appétit!

Per serving: 292 Calories; 14.3g Fat; 3.9g Carbs; 36.9g Protein; 0.8g Fiber

753. Homemade Rum Pralines

(Ready in about 25 minutes + chilling time | Servings 10)

Ingredients

1 ½ cups whipped cream
1 tablespoon rum
A pinch of grated nutmeg
8 ounces chocolate chips, unsweetened
1/4 teaspoon cinnamon
1 teaspoon pure vanilla extract
1 cup coconut flour
1/2 stick cold butter
1/2 cup almond meal
2 packets stevia

Directions

Begin by preheating your oven to 340 degrees F.

Mix the coconut flour, almond meal, nutmeg, stevia, cinnamon, vanilla, and rum in your blender or food processor.

Cut in the cold butter and mix again.

Press the mixture into molds. Bake for about 10 minutes and place on a wire rack.

Heat the double cream over medium-low flame; once it is warmed, fold in the chocolate and stir to combine well. Spread the filling over the base and place in your refrigerator. Bon appétit!

Per serving: 119 Calories; 11.7g Fat; 5.2g Carbs; 1.1g Protein; 4g Fiber

754. Easy Bavarian Sauerkraut with Beef

(Ready in about 20 minutes | Servings 4)

Ingredients

1 ¼ pounds ground beef
1 bell pepper, sliced
1 large-sized leek, chopped
1 teaspoon fennel seeds
1 tablespoon lard, melted
1 teaspoon paprika
1 teaspoon garlic, minced
18 ounces sauerkraut, rinsed and well drained
Sea salt and black peppercorns, to taste
1 bay leaf

Directions

In a Dutch oven, melt the lard over medium-high heat. Once hot, cook the leeks until tender and fragrant.

Add in the ground beef and continue to cook for 3 to 4 minutes or until no longer pink.

Stir in the remaining ingredients and continue to cook for 6 to 7 minutes or until everything is cooked through. Bon appétit!

Per serving: 330 Calories; 12.2g Fat; 6.7g Carbs; 44.4g Protein; 4.1g Fiber

755. Thai Beef Sausage Bowl

(Ready in about 40 minutes | Servings 4)

Ingredients

2 tablespoons sesame oil
1 medium onion, chopped
1 teaspoon garlic, minced
1 parsnip, chopped
1 Bird's eye chili, deveined and chopped
1 green bell pepper, deveined and chopped
1/4 cup Marsala wine
1 teaspoon fresh turmeric
1 tablespoon lemongrass, sliced
2 rosemary sprigs
4 beef sausages, sliced
1 cup tomato Nam Prik, no sugar added
1 ½ cups chicken broth
Salt and pepper, to taste

Directions

Ina wok, heat the sesame oil over a moderately-high heat. Sear the sausage for about 3 minutes or until no longer pink.

Add in the onion, garlic, peppers, parsnip, lemongrass, salt, and pepper. Cook an additional 6 to 7 minutes.

Add in the remaining ingredients and bring it to a rapid boil. Reduce the heat to a simmer. Continue to simmer for 20 to 25 minutes.

Bon appétit!

Per serving: 250 Calories; 17.5g Fat; 5.4g Carbs; 6.8g Protein; 2.1g Fiber

756. Vanilla Chocolate Candy

(Ready in about 10 minutes + chilling time | Servings 6)

Ingredients

1 teaspoon vanilla extract
2 tablespoons coconut flakes
10 drops liquid Monk fruit
1/4 cup coconut oil, melted
2 tablespoons cocoa powder

Directions

Melt the coconut oil, vanilla, and liquid Monk fruit in a pan over a moderately-high heat.

Add in the cocoa powder and stir to combine.

Spoon the mixture into a silicone candy mold tray. Top with coconut flakes and place in your freezer until set.

Bon appétit!

Per serving: 84 Calories; 8.9g Fat; 1.5g Carbs; 0.8g Protein; 1g Fiber

757. Cheesy Cauliflower Cakes

(Ready in about 35 minutes | Servings 6)

Ingredients

4 tablespoons almond meal
1 cup Romano cheese
2 eggs, beaten
1 garlic clove, minced
1 pound cauliflower, grated
2 tablespoons ground flaxseed
1 ½ tablespoons butter, room temperature
1 small onion, chopped
1/2 cup Colby cheese, shredded
Sea salt and pepper, to taste

Directions

Begin by preheating your oven to 390 degrees F.

Melt the butter in a non-stick skillet over medium heat. Cook the onion and garlic until they are tender and fragrant.

Add in the remaining ingredients and stir until well combined. Form the mixture into patties.

Bake in the preheated for about 30 minutes, flipping them halfway through the cook time.

Bon appétit!

Per serving: 199 Calories; 13.8g Fat; 6.8g Carbs; 13g Protein; 2.8g Fiber

758. Meatloaf Muffins with Vegetables

(Ready in about 35 minutes | Servings 6)

Ingredients

1 tablespoon stone-ground mustard
1 cup soft cheese, shredded
1 cup tomato puree
1 teaspoon garlic, smashed
1 cup parsnip, shredded
1 tablespoon soy sauce
1 ounce envelope onion soup mix
1/2 pound chuck, ground
1 egg, beaten
1 pound pork, ground
Salt and pepper, to taste

Directions

In a mixing bowl, thoroughly combine all ingredients until well combined.

Press the mixture into lightly greased muffin cups. Bake in the preheated oven at 356 degrees F for about 35 minutes.

Bon appétit!

Per serving: 220 Calories; 6.3g Fat; 5.4g Carbs; 33.8g Protein; 2.2g Fiber

759. Thai Cod Fish Chowder

(Ready in about 30 minutes | Servings 6)

Ingredients

1 ¼ pounds cod fish fillets, cut into small chunks
3/4 cup full-fat milk
1 chili pepper, deveined and sliced
1/2 teaspoon cayenne pepper
1 tablespoon oyster sauce
2 ½ cups fish stock
1 bell pepper, deveined and sliced
1 teaspoon Five-spice powder
1 tablespoon galangal, chopped
1 garlic clove, smashed
1/2 cup Thai shallots, sliced
2 tablespoons sesame oil
1 celery rib, diced

Directions

In a heavy-bottomed pot, heat the oil over a moderately-high flame. Sauté the shallots until they are just tender and fragrant.

Add in the remaining ingredients, except fish and milk. Continue to cook, covered, for about 15 minutes.

Add in the fish and continue to cook, partially covered, an additional 13 minutes or until the fish is opaque. Add in the milk, stir, and remove from heat. Bon appétit!

Per serving: 165 Calories; 5.5g Fat; 4g Carbs; 25.4g Protein; 0.6g Fiber

760. Mediterranean Eggplant Casserole with Romano Cheese

(Ready in about 1 hour | Servings 4)

Ingredients

1 onion, sliced
1 cup tomatoes, sliced
1/3 cup Romano cheese, shredded
2 tablespoons olive oil
1 celery stalk, peeled and sliced
4 garlic cloves, crushed
3/4 pound eggplant, cut into slices
1 teaspoon Italian seasoning mix
1 chili pepper, minced

Directions

Place the eggplant with 1 teaspoon of coarse salt in a bowl; let it stand for about 30 minutes; drain and rinse the eggplant.

Preheat your oven to 340 degrees F. Brush the bottom and sides of a casserole dish with a cooking spray.

Place the vegetables along with the spices and olive oil in the prepared casserole dish. Roast the vegetables for 18 to 20 minutes.

Place the cheese on the top and continue to bake for a further 10 minutes.

Bon appétit!

Per serving: 159 Calories; 10.4g Fat; 7.7g Carbs; 6.4g Protein; 3g Fiber

761. Baked Eggs with Steak and Spanish Peppers

(Ready in about 30 minutes | Servings 6)

Ingredients

2 Spanish peppers, chopped
2 garlic cloves, minced
1 ½ pounds flank steak, cut into strips
1/2 cup onions, finely chopped
6 eggs
2 tablespoons lard, melted
1/2 teaspoon cayenne pepper
Salt and black pepper, to taste

Directions

In a non-stick skillet, melt the lard over a moderately-high heat. Sear the steak for 10 minutes, stirring frequently to ensure even cooking.

Season with salt, black pepper, and cayenne pepper and set aside.

In the same skillet, sauté the onion, garlic, and peppers for about 4 minutes or until they are tender and fragrant. Add the meat back to the skillet.

Create six indentions in the sautéed mixture. Crack an egg into each indention. Cover and continue to cook for about 5 minutes or until the eggs are set. Enjoy!

Per serving: 429 Calories; 27.8g Fat; 3.2g Carbs; 39.1g Protein; 0.6g Fiber

762. Easy Bok Choy with Bacon

(Ready in about 20 minutes | Servings 6)

Ingredients

1 pound Bok choy, shredded
1/2 pound bacon, chopped
1 celery stalk, finely chopped
1 cup chicken bone broth
1/2 teaspoon red pepper flakes
1 garlic clove, minced
1 tablespoon butter, at room temperature

Directions

Melt the butter in a wok over a moderately-high heat. Now, cook the Bok choy, celery, and garlic until they've softened.

Add in the remaining ingredients and turn the heat to a simmer. Let it simmer, covered, for 10 to 12 minutes longer.

Bon appétit!

Per serving: 259 Calories; 18.1g Fat; 6.6g Carbs; 15.5g Protein; 1g Fiber

763. Mediterranean Eggs with Herring and Capers

(Ready in about 20 minutes | Servings 6)

Ingredients

1/3 cup aioli
1 tablespoon small capers, drained
12 eggs
1/4 cup tarragon
2 pickled jalapenos, minced
Salt and pepper, to taste
1 (6.7-ounce) can smoked herring, drained
1 teaspoon paprika

Directions

Place the eggs in a saucepan and cover them with water by 1 inch. Cover and bring the water to a boil over high heat. Boil for 6 to 7 minutes over medium-high heat.

Peel the eggs and slice them in half lengthwise; mix the yolks with the aioli, herring, paprika, capers, tarragon, jalapenos, salt, and pepper.

Divide the mixture between the egg whites and arrange the deviled eggs on a nice serving platter.

Enjoy!

Per serving: 203 Calories; 13.3g Fat; 3.8g Carbs; 17.2g Protein; 0.3g Fiber

764. Colorful Vegetable Croquettes

(Ready in about 15 minutes | Servings 6)

Ingredients

2 cups zucchini, shredded
1 cup shallots, chopped
2 tablespoons cilantro, chopped
2 tablespoons butter, melted
1 egg yolk
1 large parsnip, shredded
1 large celery stalk, shredded
1 garlic clove, crushed
1 cup Colby cheese, grated
Salt and pepper, to taste

Directions

Place the shredded vegetables in a colander to drain away the excess liquid. Mix in the other ingredients until everything is well combined.

Divide the mixture into 12 patties. Place them in a parchment-lined baking pan.

Bake in the preheated oven at 365 degrees F for about 10 minutes.

Bon appétit!

Per serving: 153 Calories; 11.8g Fat; 6.6g Carbs; 6.4g Protein; 0.3g Fiber

765. Stuffed Tomatoes in Marinara Sauce

(Ready in about 25 minutes | Servings 4)

Ingredients

1/2 pound ground chicken
1 tablespoon fresh cilantro, chopped
1/2 cup onion, chopped
1 tablespoon avocado oil
4 medium-sized tomatoes
2 cups mozzarella cheese, freshly grated
1/2 cup marinara sauce
1/2 teaspoon garlic, minced
Salt and black pepper, to taste

Directions

Slice the tomatoes in half horizontally and scoop out the pulp and seeds using a spoon.

Heat the oil in a frying pan over a moderately-high heat. Once hot, sear the ground chicken for about 4 minutes and reserve.

In the same frying pan, cook the onion and garlic until they've softened or about 5 minutes. Add in the reserved meat, tomato pulp, cilantro, salt, and black pepper.

Place the tomatoes in a baking dish. Spoon the stuffing into your tomatoes and pour the marinara sauce around them.

Now, bake in the middle of the preheated oven at 365 degrees F for about 20 minutes.

Bon appétit!

Per serving: 413 Calories; 28.2g Fat; 7.8g Carbs; 35.2g Protein; 3.2g Fiber

766. Fish Cakes with Mustard and Cheese

(Ready in about 30 minutes | Servings 6)

Ingredients

1 ½ pounds tilapia, boned and flaked
1/3 cup almond meal
2 tablespoons flaxseed meal
2 teaspoons deli mustard
1/2 cup soft cheese, at room temperature
2 eggs, whisked
2 tablespoons fresh chives, chopped
2 tablespoons olive oil
Salt and pepper, to season

Directions

Begin by preheating your oven to 395 degrees F. Line a baking pan with parchment paper.

In a mixing bowl, combine all ingredients until everything is well incorporated.

Form the mixture into 12 patties using your hands. Arrange them on the baking pan and bake for about 15 minutes; turn them over and cook for another 10 minutes.

Bon appétit!

Per serving: 234 Calories; 10.6g Fat; 2.5g Carbs; 31.2g Protein; 1.2g Fiber

767. Double Cheese and Cauliflower Fritters

(Ready in about 35 minutes | Servings 6)

Ingredients

1 cup Romano cheese
1 pound cauliflower, grated
1/2 cup cheddar cheese, shredded
1/2 teaspoon dried basil
1/2 teaspoon garlic, minced
2 eggs, beaten
5 tablespoons almond meal
1 ½ tablespoons sesame oil
1 onion, chopped
Salt and pepper, to taste

Directions

In a frying pan, heat the sesame oil over a moderate flame. Then, sauté the onions and garlic until they've softened.

Add in the grated cauliflower along with the remaining ingredients. Shape the mixture into patties and arrange them on a parchment-lined baking sheet.

Bake in the preheated oven at 395 degrees F for 20 to 22 minutes. Turn them over and cook on the other side for 8 to 10 minutes more. Bon appétit!

Per serving: 199 Calories; 13.8g Fat; 6.8g Carbs; 13g Protein; 2.1g Fiber

768. Porterhouse Steaks in Red Wine

(Ready in about 2 hours 15 minutes | Servings 4)

Ingredients

1 pound Porterhouse steaks, thinly sliced
1 parsnip, chopped
1 teaspoon lemon zest
1 red onion, sliced
1 teaspoon garlic, minced
1/2 teaspoon cayenne pepper
2 tablespoons coconut aminos
1 ½ cups vegetable broth
1 tablespoon olive oil
1/3 cup red wine

Directions

In a frying pan, heat the olive oil in over a moderate heat. Sear the Porterhouse steaks for about 12 minutes and reserve.

In the same skillet, cook the onion, parsnip and garlic for about 3 minutes, stirring frequently to ensure even cooking.

Add in the remaining ingredients and bring to a boil. Turn the heat to a simmer and continue to cook for about 2 hours.

Bon appétit!

Per serving: 238 Calories; 9.2g Fat; 6.3g Carbs; 27.4g Protein; 1.4g Fiber

769. Salmon with Cauliflower and Cheddar Cheese

(Ready in about 25 minutes | Servings 4)

Ingredients

4 salmon steaks
1 pound cauliflower florets
1 cup Cheddar cheese, shredded
1 teaspoon Creole seasoning mix
2 tablespoons butter, melted
Salt and red pepper flakes, to season

Directions

Preheat your oven to 395 degrees F. Brush the sides and bottom of a baking dish with 1 tablespoon of butter.

Parboil the cauliflower in a pot of a lightly-salted water until crisp-tender.

Transfer the cauliflower florets to the buttered baking dish. Season with salt and red pepper and bake for 15 to 17 minutes.

Meanwhile, heat the remaining tablespoon of butter over a moderately-high heat. Cook the salmon until golden and crisp on all sides. Season with Creole seasoning mix.

Place the shredded cheese on top and place under the preheated broiler for 5 to 6 minutes. Bon appétit!

Per serving: 508 Calories; 22.9g Fat; 4.7g Carbs; 68.6g Protein; 2.6g Fiber

770. Mexican Sausage with Cabbage

(Ready in about 50 minutes | Servings 4)

Ingredients

6 ounces Cotija cheese, grated
1 onion, chopped
1 tablespoon lard, at room temperature
1 cup vegetable broth
1/2 cup whipped cream
4 chicken sausages, sliced
1 pound cabbage
Salt and pepper, to season

Directions

Begin by preheating your oven to 365 degrees F. Melt the lard in a saucepan; once hot, cook the sausage until no longer pink and reserve.

Then, in the pan drippings, sauté the onion and cabbage until they've softened. Add in the salt, pepper, and vegetable broth and continue to cook for about 3 minutes or until cooked through.

Place the sautéed cabbage in a lightly buttered casserole dish. Top with the reserved sausage.

Cover with foil and bake in the preheated oven for 40 to 45 minutes.

In a bowl, mix the whipped cream with the Cotija cheese. Pour this mixture over the sausage and bake an additional 5 minutes or until hot and bubbly. Enjoy!

Per serving: 189 Calories; 12g Fat; 6.6g Carbs; 9.4g Protein; 3.1g Fiber

771. Curried Greens with Ricotta Cheese

(Ready in about 10 minutes | Servings 4)

Ingredients

1/2 teaspoon curry powder
1 teaspoon garlic, minced
1 cup Ricotta cheese
1/4 cup butter
2 pounds mixed greens, torn into pieces
Sea salt and pepper, to taste

Directions

Melt the butter in a large saucepan over a moderately-high heat. Once hot, cook the garlic until just tender and aromatic.

Add in the mixed greens, salt, pepper, and curry powder; cook for a further 3 minutes, stirring frequently.

Turn the heat on high and continue to cook for about 2 minutes more.

Top with the cheese and reheat in the saucepan until the cheese melts completely. Enjoy!

Per serving: 208 Calories; 13.5g Fat; 6g Carbs; 14.5g Protein; 4.4g Fiber

772. Cheesy Mushrooms with Salami

(Ready in about 25 minutes | Servings 6)

Ingredients

2 ounces Swiss cheese, shredded
1 tablespoon soy sauce
3 slices of salami, chopped
2 tablespoons fresh parsley, minced
6 Chanterelle mushrooms, stems removed
3 teaspoons olive oil
1 teaspoon fresh basil, minced
Salt and pepper, to taste

Directions

Toss the Chanterelle mushrooms with olive oil, soy sauce, salt, and pepper.

Thoroughly combine the salami, parsley, basil, and Swiss cheese; mix well and stuff the mushroom caps.

Bake in the preheated oven at 360 degrees F for about 20 minutes.

Per serving: 98 Calories; 5.8g Fat; 3.9g Carbs; 8.4g Protein; 0.7g Fiber

773. Meatloaf Cups with Swiss Cheese

(Ready in about 10 minutes | Servings 2)

Ingredients

1/2 cup Swiss cheese, shredded
1/2 pound ground pork
2 garlic cloves, minced
1 teaspoon shallot powder
1/2 cup marinara sauce
1/2 teaspoon mustard powder
1/2 teaspoon red pepper flakes
Salt and pepper, to season

Directions

In a mixing bowl, combine all ingredients until everything is well combined.

Spoon the mixture into two microwave-safe mugs.

Microwave at 70 percent power for about 6 minutes until no longer pink in the center.

Per serving: 327 Calories; 16.6g Fat; 5.8g Carbs; 40g Protein; 1.8g Fiber

774. Spicy Vegetable and Mushroom Stew

(Ready in about 30 minutes | Servings 4)

Ingredients

1 teaspoon jalapeno pepper, finely minced
1 tablespoon lard, melted
2 garlic cloves, minced
1/2 pound button mushrooms, chopped
1 cup tomato puree
1/2 teaspoon ground allspice
3 cups vegetable broth
1 teaspoon ground bay leaves
1/3 cup fresh parsley, chopped
2 celery stalks, chopped
1 cup onion, chopped
Salt and pepper, to taste

Directions

In a heavy-bottomed pot, melt the lard over medium-high heat. Cook the onion, jalapeno pepper, garlic, celery, and mushrooms for 7 to 8 minutes.

Add in the vegetable broth, tomato puree, and spices, and bring to a boil. Turn the heat to a simmer; cover and let it cook for about 20 minutes.

Bon appétit!

Per serving: 133 Calories; 3.7g Fat; 6.7g Carbs; 14g Protein; 1g Fiber

775. Creamed Egg Salad with Cheese and Anchovies

(Ready in about 20 minutes | Servings 8)

Ingredients

For the Salad:
8 eggs
1 cup butterhead lettuce, torn into pieces
1/2 cup onions, chopped
1/3 cup sour cream
1 teaspoon deli mustard
1/2 cup Gruyère cheese, crumbled
1 (14-ounce) can anchovy fillets, deboned, drained and flaked
For Aioli:
1/2 cup extra-virgin olive oil
1 tablespoon lime juice
1 egg
1 teaspoon garlic, minced
Salt and pepper, to taste

Directions

Place the eggs in a saucepan and cover them with water by 1 inch. Cover and bring the water to a boil over high heat. Boil for 6 to 7 minutes over medium-high heat.

Peel the eggs and coarsely chop them. Add in the remaining ingredients for the salad and toss to combine well.

To make the aioli, beat the egg, garlic, and lime juice with an immersion blender. Add the extra-virgin oil, salt and pepper, and blend until everything is well mixed.

Add the prepared aioli to the salad and gently stir to combine well. It should be consumed within two days. Bon appétit!

Per serving: 285 Calories; 22.5g Fat; 1.8g Carbs; 19.5g Protein; 0.3g Fiber

776. Chicken Drumettes with Mediterranean Herbs

(Ready in about 30 minutes | Servings 4)

Ingredients

4 chicken drumettes
1 teaspoon Mediterranean herb mix
1/2 cup onions, chopped
1 cup chicken broth
1 teaspoon garlic, minced
1 tablespoon coconut aminos
1 parsnip, sliced
2 tablespoons butter, room temperature
2 tomatoes, pureed
1 teaspoon paprika
Salt and black pepper, to taste

Directions

In a frying pan, melt the butter over medium-high heat. Season the chicken drumettes with the salt and black pepper.

Sear the chicken drumettes until they are no longer pink; reserve. Cook the vegetables until they've softened for about 5 minutes.

Turn the heat to a simmer and add in the remaining ingredients along with the reserved chicken drumettes. Leave the lid slightly ajar and let it simmer, partially covered, for about 20 minutes.

Enjoy!

Per serving: 165 Calories; 9.8g Fat; 7.7g Carbs; 12.4g Protein; 3g Fiber

777. Sea Bass with Mustard and Paprika

(Ready in about 30 minutes | Servings 4)

Ingredients

1/2 tablespoon deli mustard
1 tablespoon lime juice
1 teaspoon lime zest
1 teaspoon onion powder
1 teaspoon paprika
2 garlic cloves, minced
1/4 cup fresh parsley, chopped
4 sea bass fillets
2 tablespoons butter, at room temperature
Salt and pepper, to season

Directions

Begin by preheating your oven to 410 degrees F. Then, grease a baking dish with a cooking spray.

In a mixing bowl, combine the butter, mustard, garlic, lime juice and zest, and spices. Rub the mixture on all sides of the fish fillets.

Bake for about 20 minutes or until opaque.

Bon appétit!

Per serving: 195 Calories; 8.2g Fat; 0.5g Carbs; 28.7g Protein; 0.8g Fiber

778. Cabbage and Ground Beef Soup

(Ready in about 35 minutes | Servings 4)

Ingredients

2 tablespoons oil
1 celery stalk, diced
1 cup tomato, puree
4 cups vegetable broth
1 cup full-fat sour cream
1/2 cup onions, chopped
1 teaspoon garlic, chopped
1 parsnip, diced
1 cup green cabbage, shredded
1 bay leaf
3/4 pound ground beef
Salt and black pepper, to taste

Directions

In a stockpot, heat the olive oil over medium-high heat. Cook the ground beef for about 5 minutes and reserve.

Now, cook the onions, garlic, parsnip, cabbage, and celery in the pan drippings, stirring constantly, until they've softened.

Stir in the remaining ingredients along with the reserved ground beef and bring to a boil. Immediately, turn the heat to a simmer and continue to cook for another 25 minutes.

Serve dolloped with sour cream. Bon appétit!

Per serving: 307 Calories; 23.6g Fat; 6.4g Carbs; 14.8g Protein; 2.7g Fiber

779. Keto Mac and Cheese

(Ready in about 15 minutes | Servings 4)

Ingredients

1/2 cup double cream
1 large-sized head cauliflower, broken into florets
1/2 teaspoon shallot powder
1 teaspoon dried parsley flakes
2 tablespoons olive oil
1 cup Cottage cheese
1/2 cup milk
1 teaspoon garlic powder
Salt and pepper, to taste

Directions

Start by preheating your oven to 420 degrees F.

In a lightly oiled baking dish, toss the cauliflower florets with the olive oil, salt, and pepper. Bake in the preheated oven for about 15 minutes.

In a mixing dish, whisk the milk, cream, cheese, and spices. Pour the mixture over the cauliflower layer in the baking dish.

Bake for another 10 minutes, until the top is hot and bubbly. Bon appétit!

Per serving: 357 Calories; 32.5g Fat; 6.9g Carbs; 8.4g Protein; 1.3g Fiber

780. Chunky Pork and Vegetable Soup

(Ready in about 20 minutes | Servings 6)

Ingredients

1 medium-sized leek, chopped
1 celery stalk, chopped
1/4 cup fresh cilantro, roughly chopped
1 avocado, pitted and sliced
1 cup tomato puree
1 teaspoon garlic, minced
3 cups vegetable broth
1 ¼ pounds pork butt, cut into chunks
2 tablespoons olive oil
Salt and pepper, to taste

Directions

In a stock pot, heat the olive oil over a moderately-high flame. Sauté the leek, garlic, and celery for about 3 minutes or until the vegetable are tender and fragrant.

Add in the pork and continue to cook for 4 to 5 minutes more, stirring frequently to ensure even cooking. Add in the remaining ingredients.

Leave the lid slightly ajar. Turn the heat to a simmer for 10 to 12 minutes.

Serve topped with fresh cilantro and sliced avocado. Bon appétit!

Per serving: 423 Calories; 31.8g Fat; 6.5g Carbs; 25.9g Protein; 3.5g Fiber

781. Steak a La Moutarde

(Ready in about 20 minutes | Servings 4)

Ingredients

1 tablespoon olive oil
4 1 ½-inch thick steaks
1 tablespoon Dijon mustard
2 sprigs thyme, chopped
1 ½ tablespoons coriander, chopped
1/3 cup sour cream
Salt and pepper, to taste

Directions

In a bowl, combine the sour cream, Dijon mustard, and coriander; reserve in your refrigerator.

Sprinkle the steaks with salt, pepper, and thyme.

Heat the olive oil in a pan over moderately-high heat; once hot, cook the steak for 4 to 5 minutes per side.

Bon appétit!

Per serving: 321 Calories; 13.7g Fat; 1g Carbs; 45g Protein; 0.4g Fiber

782. Turkey and Mediterranean Vegetable Skewers

(Ready in about 30 minutes | Servings 6)

Ingredients

1 ½ pounds turkey breast, cubed
1 tablespoon fresh cilantro, chopped
1 cup zucchini, cut into thick slices
2 tablespoons olive oil
1 tablespoon Italian seasoning mix
1 cup bell peppers, sliced
1 cup red onion, cut into wedges
1 ½ cups grape tomatoes, sliced

Directions

Toss the turkey breast with the olive oil and Italian seasoning mix. Thread the turkey onto skewers, alternating them with the vegetables.

Continue until all the ingredients are used up.

Grill the kebabs for about 10 minutes, turning them occasionally to ensure even cooking. Toss the kebabs with the cilantro.

Bon appétit!

Per serving: 293 Calories; 13.8g Fat; 5.7g Carbs; 34.5g Protein; 1g Fiber

783. Creole Tilapia Soup

(Ready in about 30 minutes | Servings 4)

Ingredients

1 parsnip, chopped
3 ½ cups fish stock
1 teaspoon Creole seasonings mix
2 bell pepper, chopped
1 cup onion, chopped
1 celery stalk, chopped
1/2 cup coconut milk
3 teaspoons olive oil
1 ¼ pounds tilapia, chopped
1/4 cup Marsala wine
Sea salt and black pepper, to taste

Directions

Heat the oil in a heavy-bottomed pan over medium-high flame. Once hot, sauté all vegetables until they are just tender or about 5 minutes. Add in the seasonings.

Add in the tilapia along with the fish stock; partially cover and continue to cook for about 13 minutes or until cooked through.

Pour in the wine and coconut milk and bring to a rapid boil. Let it simmer for about 13 minutes.

Bon appétit!

Per serving: 170 Calories; 5.8g Fat; 6.2g Carbs; 20g Protein; 2.8g Fiber

784. Marinated Spare Ribs with Veggies

(Ready in about 25 minutes + marinating time | Servings 6)

Ingredients

2 teaspoons olive oil
1 celery stalk, sliced
2 tablespoons coconut aminos
1/4 cup red wine
2 garlic cloves, minced
1 bell pepper, chopped
2 cups kale
2 tablespoons red wine vinegar
1 ½ pounds spare ribs
1 medium leek, sliced
Salt and pepper, to season

Directions

Season the pork ribs with salt and pepper. In a bowl, make the marinade by whisking the coconut aminos, vinegar, red wine, and garlic.

Allow the spare ribs to marinate for at least 3 hours in your refrigerator.

Heat 1 teaspoon of the oil in a frying pan over a moderately-high heat; cook the leeks, celery and bell pepper for 4 to 5 minutes until they are crisp tender.

Heat the remaining teaspoon of the olive oil and sear the pork, adding the marinade as needed; cook for about 12 minutes.

Add in the kale and continue to simmer until the leaves are wilted, about 5 minutes. Bon appétit!

Per serving: 234 Calories; 11g Fat; 2g Carbs; 29.8g Protein; 1g Fiber

785. Pork with Chevre Goat Cheese

(Ready in about 30 minutes | Servings 6)

Ingredients

6 ounces Chevre goat cheese
1/3 cup port wine
1/3 cup roasted vegetable broth
1/2 teaspoon hot chili flakes
1 teaspoon Mediterranean spice mix
1 tablespoon olive oil
1/2 cup scallions, chopped
1 tablespoon coconut aminos
1/3 cup whipped cream
1 ½ pounds boneless Boston butt, and cut into 6 pieces
1 teaspoon fresh garlic, minced
Salt and black pepper, to taste

Directions

Rub each piece of the pork with salt, black pepper, and Mediterranean spice mix.

Heat the oil in a saucepan over moderately-high heat. Sear the pork for about 20 minutes (an internal temperature of 145 degrees F); reserve.

In the same saucepan, sauté the scallions and garlic until they are soft and aromatic. Add in the port wine and broth and stir to deglaze the pan.

Turn the heat to a simmer and stir in the remaining ingredients; let it simmer until the liquid has thickened and reduced. Add the pork back to the saucepan. Enjoy!

Per serving: 495 Calories; 36.9g Fat; 3.6g Carbs; 33.4g Protein; 0.3g Fiber

786. Baked Spicy Chicken in Marinara Sauce

(Ready in about 30 minutes + marinating time | Servings 6)

Ingredients

2 eggs
1/2 teaspoon Sriracha sauce
2 tablespoons marinara sauce
3 teaspoons red wine vinegar
1/4 cup flax seeds, ground
2 tablespoons coconut aminos
1 pound chicken, cut into strips
1/2 stick butter, melted
2 cloves garlic, minced
Salt and black pepper, to taste

Directions

Start by preheating your oven to 400 degrees F. Brush the bottom and sides of a casserole dish with a cooking spray.

Toss the chicken with the butter, salt, pepper, coconut aminos, vinegar, Sriracha sauce, marinara sauce and garlic. Let it marinate in your refrigerator at least 1 hour.

In a mixing bowl, whisk the eggs with the ground flax seeds. Dip each chicken strip in the egg mixture. Transfer the chicken strips to the casserole dish.

Bake for about 25 minutes, turning once or twice. Place under the preheated broiler until the top is crispy. Enjoy!

Per serving: 420 Calories; 28.2g Fat; 5g Carbs; 35.3g Protein; 0.8g Fiber

787. Swiss Cheese and Tomato-Glazed Meatloaf

(Ready in about 1 hour 10 minutes | Servings 8)

Ingredients

1 pound ground pork
8 ounces Swiss cheese, shredded
1 pound ground beef
1/2 cup salsa, no sugar added
1/2 cup tomato paste, no sugar added
1/2 teaspoon garlic, minced
1 tablespoon Swerve
1/2 cup green onions, chopped
1 teaspoon cayenne pepper
1 tablespoon balsamic vinegar
2 eggs, beaten
1 tablespoon deli mustard
Salt and black pepper, to season

Directions

Begin by preheating your oven to 365 degrees F.

Thoroughly combine the ground meat, eggs, green onions, salsa, Swiss cheese, garlic, cayenne pepper, salt, and black pepper.

Press the mixture into a lightly oiled loaf pan.

Whisk the balsamic vinegar, deli mustard, tomato paste, and Swerve until well combined; pour the mixture over the top of your meatloaf.

Bake for about 1 hour, rotating the pan once to ensure even cooking. Lastly, place under the preheated broiler for about 5 minutes or until the top has caramelized.

Bon appétit!

Per serving: 318 Calories; 14.7g Fat; 6.2g Carbs; 39.3g Protein; 1.3g Fiber

788. Garlicky Portobello Mushrooms

(Ready in about 10 minutes | Servings 4)

Ingredients

2 cloves garlic, minced
1 pound Portobello mushrooms, sliced
2 tablespoons butter
1 tablespoon white wine
Salt and black pepper, to taste

Directions

In a wok or large saucepan, melt the butter over a moderately-high flame. Sauté the garlic for a minute or so until aromatic.

Add in the mushrooms and continue to sauté them for 3 to 4 minutes until they are caramelized.

Add in the wine, salt, and pepper and continue to cook for 3 to 4 minutes more until heated through. Bon appétit!

Per serving: 75 Calories; 5.2g Fat; 3.3g Carbs; 2.9g Protein; 1.1g Fiber

789. Greek Beef and Cheese Casserole

(Ready in about 25 minutes | Servings 4)

Ingredients

1 cup Swiss cheese
1 pound ground chuck
2 garlic cloves, minced
1/2 cup onion, finely chopped
1 tablespoon tallow, melted
1 teaspoon Italian seasoning mix
3/4 cup Greek-style yogurt
1 ¼ cups marinara sauce
Sea salt and ground black pepper, to taste

Directions

Begin by preheating your oven to 395 degrees F.

In a frying pan, melt the tallow over a moderately-high flame. Once hot, cook the ground chuck, breaking apart with a spatula. Then, sauté the onion and garlic until just tender and fragrant.

Add in the marinara sauce, salt, pepper, Italian seasoning mix,

Spoon the sautéed mixture into a casserole dish. Bake in the preheated oven for about 20 minutes.

Mix the swiss cheese and yogurt in a bowl. Spoon the mixture over your casserole and place under the preheated broiler for about 5 minutes until hot and bubbly.

Per serving: 509 Calories; 29.6g Fat; 6.1g Carbs; 45.2g Protein; 2g Fiber

790. Easy Cheesy Meatloaf Cups

(Ready in about 35 minutes | Servings 6)

Ingredients

1/2 pound chuck, ground
1 tablespoon deli mustard
1 cup parsnip, shredded
1 ounce envelope onion soup mix
1 pound pork, ground
1 tablespoon coconut aminos
1 teaspoon garlic, smashed
1 egg, beaten
1 cup Colby cheese, shredded
1 cup tomato puree
Sea salt and black pepper, to season
1 teaspoon Mediterranean herb mix

Directions

Begin by preheating your oven to 360 degrees F.

Thoroughly combine all ingredients for the mini meatloaves.

Scrape the mixture into a lightly buttered muffin tin. Bake in the preheated oven for 30 to 35 minutes.

Bon appétit!

Per serving: 321 Calories; 16.3g Fat; 8.8g Carbs; 32.8g Protein; 2.1g Fiber

791. Taco Turkey Wings

(Ready in about 1 hour + marinating time | Servings 2)

Ingredients

1 tablespoon Taco seasoning mix
2 turkey wings
2 tablespoons olive oil
2 tablespoons red wine vinegar
Salt and red pepper, to taste

Directions

In a mixing bowl, combine the red wine vinegar, Taco seasoning mix, olive oil and turkey wings. Let the turkey wings marinate at least 2 hours in the refrigerator.

Grill the turkey wings on a lightly greased grill pan until a meat thermometer has reached the temperature of 180 degrees F. Sprinkle with salt and red pepper on all sides. Bon appétit!

Per serving: 488 Calories; 24.5g Fat; 2.1g Carbs; 33.6g Protein; 1g Fiber

792. Stuffed Tomatoes with Tuna

(Ready in about 30 minutes | Servings 6)

Ingredients

6 tomatoes
1 onion, finely chopped
2 tablespoons parsley, chopped
1 teaspoon deli mustard
10 ounces tuna, flaked
1 teaspoon garlic, smashed
1 ½ cups Chèvre cheese, crumbled
1/2 cup mayonnaise
Sea salt and black pepper, to season

Directions

Begin by preheating your oven to 395 degrees F. Slice your tomatoes in half horizontally and scoop out the pulp, set them aside.

Thoroughly combine the tuna, onion, garlic, parsley, mayonnaise, deli mustard, salt, and black pepper.

Divide the filling between the tomatoes and bake for about 23 minutes until they are thoroughly cooked.

Top each tomato with the cheese. Bake in the preheated oven at 200 degrees F until they are completely warm. Bon appétit!

Per serving: 303 Calories; 22.9g Fat; 5.8g Carbs; 17g Protein; 2.1g Fiber

793. Nona's Stuffed Peppers

(Ready in about 45 minutes | Servings 4)

Ingredients

12 ounces Cottage cheese, room temperature
1 ½ cups pureed tomatoes
1 teaspoon garlic, smashed
1 teaspoon Italian herb mix
1/2 cup pork rinds, crushed
4 bell peppers

Directions

Parboil the peppers in salted water for about 5 minutes.

In a mixing bowl, combine the cheese, pork rinds, and garlic until everything is well incorporated. Divide the filling among bell peppers.

Whisk the pureed tomatoes with the Italian herb mix until well combined. Pour the tomato mixture over the stuffed pepper.

Bake in the preheated oven at 350 degrees F for 35 to 40 minutes. Enjoy!

Per serving: 359 Calories; 29.7g Fat; 6.7g Carbs; 17.7g Protein; 2.5g Fiber

794. Pizzelle della Nonna

(Ready in about 20 minutes | Servings 2)

Ingredients

- 1/2 cup goat cheese, crumbled
- 4 eggs
- 4 slices Genoa salami, chopped
- 1/2 teaspoon chili pepper flakes
- 2 tablespoons olive oil
- Salt and black pepper, to your liking

Directions

Strat by preheating your waffle iron and brush it with a non-stick cooking oil.

Mix all ingredients until everything is well combined.

Pour the batter into waffle iron and cook until golden and cooked through. Repeat until all the batter is used.

Enjoy!

Per serving: 470 Calories; 40.3g Fat; 2.9g Carbs; 24.4g Protein; 0.6g Fiber

795. Mediterranean Stuffed Peppers with Salmon

(Ready in about 25 minutes | Servings 4)

Ingredients

- 10 ounces canned salmon, drained
- 4 bell peppers
- 1/3 cup black olives, pitted and chopped
- 1 red onion, finely chopped
- 1/2 teaspoon garlic, minced
- 1/3 cup mayonnaise
- 1 cup soft cheese
- 1 teaspoon Mediterranean spice mix
- Salt and red pepper flakes, to taste

Directions

Broil the bell peppers for 5 to 6 minutes, turning them halfway through the cook time.

Cut the peppers into halves and remove the seeds and skin.

In a mixing bowl, combine the salmon, onion, garlic, mayonnaise, olives, salt, red pepper, Mediterranean spice mix, and soft cheese.

Divide the mixture between the peppers and bake them in the preheated oven at 390 degrees F for 10 to 12 minutes or until cooked through.

Per serving: 273 Calories; 13.9g Fat; 5.1g Carbs; 28.9g Protein; 1.7g Fiber

796. Traditional Hungarian Pörkölt

(Ready in about 1 hour 25 minutes | Servings 4)

Ingredients

- 1 ¼ pounds stewing beef, cut into 1/2-inch pieces
- 1 celery stalk, chopped
- 1 tablespoon Hungarian paprika
- 1/2 teaspoon caraway seeds, coarsely crushed
- 2 bell pepper, chopped
- 1 tablespoon flaxseed meal
- 4 cups beef broth
- 1 cup onion, chopped
- 2 tablespoons lard, at room temperature
- 1 bay leaf
- Sea salt and pepper, to taste

Directions

In a heavy-bottomed pot, sear the meat until no longer pink, for about 4 minutes; reserve. Season with salt, pepper, Hungarian paprika, and caraway seeds.

Pour in a splash of broth to scrape up any browned bits from the bottom of the pot.

Add in the remaining beef broth, bay leaf, onion, celery and bell pepper and continue to cook, covered, for 1 hour 10 minutes over a moderate heat.

Add in the flaxseed meal to thicken the cooking liquid; whisk for 2 to 3 minutes.

Bon appétit!

Per serving: 357 Calories; 15.8g Fat; 7g Carbs; 40.2g Protein; 2.5g Fiber

797. Rustic Slow Cooker Pork Shoulder

(Ready in about 1 hour 15 minutes | Servings 8)

Ingredients

- 1 bell pepper, deveined and chopped
- 1 ½ cups chicken broth
- 1 tablespoon sesame oil
- 1 chili pepper, deveined and chopped
- 1/2 teaspoon celery seeds
- 1 cup coconut milk, unsweetened
- 1/2 tablespoon turmeric powder
- 1 cup tomato puree
- 1/2 teaspoon mustard powder
- 1/2 cup onion, chopped
- 1 teaspoon garlic, minced
- 2 pounds pork shoulder, cut into strips
- Salt and Sichuan pepper, to taste

Directions

Heat the sesame oil in a wok over a moderately-high heat. Toss the pork with salt, pepper and mustard powder.

Sear the pork for 8 to 10 minutes, stirring continuously to ensure even cooking.

Now, sauté the onion, garlic, and turmeric powder in the pan drippings. Place the mixture into the slow cooker.

Add in the remaining ingredients and continue to cook, covered, for 1 hour 30 minutes on Low setting. Enjoy!

Per serving: 369 Calories; 20.2g Fat; 2.9g Carbs; 41.3g Protein; 1.2g Fiber

798. Rum Chocolate Truffles

(Ready in about 15 minutes + chilling time | Servings 16)

Ingredients

1/4 cup coconut oil
1 ½ cups dark chocolate, sugar-free, broken into chunks
4 tablespoons coconut, shredded
1/2 teaspoon almond extract
1 tablespoon rum
1 cup whipped cream
3 tablespoons granulated Swerve
1/4 cup cocoa powder unsweetened
1 teaspoon vanilla
1/4 teaspoon grated nutmeg

Directions

In a mixing bowl, combine the chocolate, coconut, coconut oil, whipped cream, Swerve, almond extract, nutmeg, and vanilla.

Microwave the mixture for 1 minute on medium-high and then, let it cool down for a few minutes. Add in the rum and stir again.

Place in your refrigerator for 2 to 3 hours until firm. Roll the mixture into balls; roll each ball in the cocoa powder.

Bon appétit!

Per serving: 90 Calories; 6.3g Fat; 4.9g Carbs; 3.7g Protein; 0.5g Fiber

799. Roasted Asparagus with Goat Cheese

(Ready in about 15 minutes | Servings 6)

Ingredients

2 tablespoons olive oil
1 ½ pounds asparagus spears
1/2 cup fresh cilantro, roughly chopped
1 teaspoon fresh garlic, minced
1/2 cup shallots, chopped
1 cup goat cheese, crumbled
Salt and red pepper, to season

Directions

Begin by preheating your oven to 410 degrees F. Brush the bottom of a rimmed pan with non-stick spray.

Brush the asparagus with the olive oil. Toss the asparagus spears with the shallots, garlic, salt, and red pepper.

Place the asparagus on the rimmed pan in a single layer. Roast for about 15 minutes.

Scatter the crumbled cheese and cilantro over the asparagus spears. Enjoy!

Per serving: 128 Calories; 9.4g Fat; 2.9g Carbs; 6.4g Protein; 2.6g Fiber

800. Paprikás with Beef and Wine

(Ready in about 1 hour 25 minutes | Servings 4)

Ingredients

2 tablespoons lard, room temperature
1 celery with leaves, chopped
1 tablespoon flaxseed meal
2 bell pepper, deveined and chopped
4 cups beef broth
1 cup leeks, peeled and chopped
1 ¼ pounds beef roast, diced
1 tablespoon Hungarian paprika
1/2 cup dry white wine
Salt and pepper, to taste

Directions

In a heavy-bottomed pot, melt the lard over moderate heat. Cook the beef and leeks for about 5 minutes. Sprinkle with salt, pepper, and Hungarian paprika.

Add in the wine to deglaze the bottom of your pot. Add in the beef broth, celery, and peppers. Turn the heat to a simmer and continue to cook for a further 1 hour 10 minutes.

Stir in the flaxseed meal; continue stirring for about 4 minutes to thicken the liquid. Bon appétit!

Per serving: 357 Calories; 15.8g Fat; 5g Carbs; 40.2g Protein; 2.2g Fiber

Printed in Great Britain
by Amazon